Statistics and Reality

IMISCOE

International Migration, Integration and Social Cohesion in Europe

The IMISCOE Network of Excellence unites over 500 researchers from European institutes specialising in studies of international migration, integration and social cohesion. The Network is funded by the Sixth Framework Programme of the European Commission on Research, Citizens and Governance in a Knowledge-Based Society. Since its foundation in 2004, IMISCOE has developed an integrated, multidisciplinary and globally comparative research project led by scholars from all branches of the economic and social sciences, the humanities and law. The Network both furthers existing studies and pioneers new research in migration as a discipline. Priority is also given to promoting innovative lines of inquiry key to European policymaking and governance.

The IMISCOE-Amsterdam University Press Series was created to make the Network's findings and results available to researchers, policymakers and practitioners, the media and other interested stakeholders. High-quality manuscripts authored by IMISCOE members and cooperating partners are published in one of four distinct series.

IMISCOE Research advances sound empirical and theoretical scholarship addressing themes within IMISCOE's mandated fields of study.

IMISCOE Reports disseminates Network papers and presentations of a time-sensitive nature in book form.

IMISCOE Dissertations presents select PhD monographs written by IMISCOE doctoral candidates.

IMISCOE Textbooks produces manuals, handbooks and other didactic tools for instructors and students of migration studies.

IMISCOE Policy Briefs and more information on the Network can be found at www.imiscoe.org.

Statistics and Reality

Concepts and Measurements of Migration in Europe

edited by Heinz Fassmann, Ursula Reeger & Wiebke Sievers

IMISCOE Reports

AMSTERDAM UNIVERSITY PRESS

Cover design: Studio Jan de Boer BNO, Amsterdam
Layout: The DocWorkers, Almere

ISBN 978 90 8964 052 9
e-ISBN 978 90 4850 637 8
NUR 741 / 763

Table of contents

List of figures

List of tables

Preface

Statistics are not synonymous with reality but are, rather, a way of representing the complexity of the world in categories and figures attached to such categories. This becomes immediately obvious when we compare the ways in which comparable phenomena – such as international migration – are statistically represented in different national contexts. The national statistics used to describe international migration are based on different conceptualisations that are closely related to the history of the respective country as well as to the particular history of migration from and to this country. Moreover, countries have various ways of counting their foreign citizens, foreign-born populations, immigrants and ethnic minorities in censuses, population registers, aliens registers and permit databases.

That such differences, in both the concepts and techniques used to measure migration, make any international comparison of the existing data impossible was first pointed out more than 150 years ago. As early as 1891, the congress of the International Statistical Institute drafted a first uniform definition of an international migrant. Since then, several international institutions, most prominently the International Labour Organisation and the United Nations, have heavily invested in harmonising data on international migration by organising conferences and issuing recommendations on concepts, definitions and measurements of this phenomenon (see Kraly & Gnanasekaran 1987; Herm 2006). More recently, such organisations were joined in their efforts by the European Commission. Utilising newly acquired competences, the European Commission proposed a regulation on migration statistics in 2005, which was adopted in a slightly adapted form in 2007, and also invested in a European project investigating the feasibility of its implementation (see Poulain, Perrin & Singleton 2006). Yet, despite all these efforts, the concepts and techniques used to measure migration in the individual countries still differ massively.

As many of the above-described initiatives, the present publication departs from these differences in the measurement of migration. Yet, unlike these ameliorative initiatives, it does not aim to issue a further set of recommendations for the standardisation of data on international migration in Europe. Nor does it try to harmonise existing data on this topic, as does Eurostat or the so-called SOPEMI (Système d'observation permanente des migrations), a continuous reporting system on international migration established by the OECD (for more information on international data collection see Herm 2006: 90-105). This volume intends to look at the existing national data from a critical perspective with a view to answering the following questions: How do the approaches to counting international migrants vary between countries? How far are these different approaches related to the histories of migration in these countries? How far do the existing statistics mirror the reality of migration in each of these countries? And what historical, political and legal knowledge is necessary in order to correctly interpret the existing data in the different European countries?

The researchers who joined forces in producing this book first realised that there were no answers to these questions in the existing literature on international migration statistics when they put together a state-of-the-art report on this topic for the EU-funded Network of Excellence IMISCOE (International Migration, Integration and Social Cohesion in Europe) or, to be more precise, for the thematic cluster dealing with migration and its regulation, which is coordinated by Heinz Fassmann (see Fassmann, Kohlbacher, Reeger & Sievers 2005). In order to fill this gap, several experts involved in this cluster wrote reports on the statistics in their country and met to present and discuss these in three workshops. These took place in Vienna in April 2005, Osnabrück in September 2005 and Istanbul in March 2006. These workshops resulted in common guidelines for the structure of the chapters collected in this volume.

This background explains the higher level of coherence across contributions than is often the case in comparative studies based on individual country chapters. Each chapter starts with a short overview of the history of migration to the respective country since the Second World War and explains the importance of migration both in real terms and in terms of public and political opinion. This is followed by an overview of stock and flow statistics, including a consideration of their implementation and of the concepts and instruments used to measure migration. In the third part, the authors provide a critical insight into the stocks of immigrants living in their countries and the numbers of people entering and leaving per year. In addition, they comment on trends observed in recent literature, such as the feminisation of migration or the diversification of migrants' origins if the statistics collated in their countries allow this (which was not the case in Poland and Romania, where the data are highly unreliable). The final section is devoted to a critical outlook that emphasises the problems of existing statistical instruments and explores possible future developments. Each chapter is supplemented by an appendix, which, apart from the most important publications, contains links to available datasets and addresses of statistical offices.

The selection of countries described in this volume includes examples from Western, Central, Southern and Eastern Europe and of both post-colonial and labour migration. It contains reports on the three European countries that have received the largest numbers of immigrants since the Second World War – namely France, Germany and the United Kingdom – but also on smaller countries such as Austria and Belgium, where the share of resident immigrants is similarly high. On the other hand, the book examines several different sending countries, including Turkey – one of the most important countries of origin for migration to the European Union and an accession candidate – and Portugal. Both countries have more recently also begun to receive immigrants. Finally, through Switzerland, the book also looks at the concepts of measuring migration in a non-EU country in the centre of Europe.

We divided the twelve countries described in this book into four groups based on their histories and migration regimes:

1. post-colonial countries: Belgium, France and the UK, which received immigrants from their (former) colonies;
2. guestworker receiving countries: Austria, Germany and Switzerland, which actively recruited workers in Southern and South-Eastern Europe;
3. post-communist countries: Poland, Hungary and Romania, where emigration and more recently immigration have (re-)gained importance after the fall of the Iron Curtain; and
4. new immigrant receiving countries: Greece, Portugal and Turkey, which used to be major sending countries of labour migrants but have recently also become receiving countries of migration.

These groups should, however, not be understood as strict categorisations. Thus, both Belgium and France received immigrants from their (former) colonies but also actively recruited workers in Eastern Europe in the interwar period and in Southern Europe after the Second World War. In fact, in Belgium this form of migration is numerically more important, which partly explains why Belgium also shares some statistical traditions with the Central European countries. On the other hand, a large majority of the immigrants in Portugal originate from former Portuguese colonies. As a consequence, some traits of the Portuguese statistics bear close resemblances to those in the post-colonial countries. Notwithstanding these overlaps, the four groups of countries described above share some basic characteristics in conceptualising and measuring international migration, which we will further discuss in the concluding chapter of this volume.

This book is the joint effort of many researchers who came together through the European Network of Excellence IMISCOE. The editors would like to thank the contributors for their willingness to cooperate, for all the work they invested, not only in their texts but also in discussing their co-contributors' work, and for their patience during the publication process. Without them this book would not exist. Thanks are also due to the European Commission for funding our meetings, which were of great importance in making this joint venture a success. We are very grateful to the anonymous reviewers for their comments and remarks on an earlier version of this book. Walter Lang from the University of Vienna was kind enough to produce the maps that precede the chapters. And, last but not least, we would like to express thanks to our proofreader Keri Jones for his meticulous work on all the texts collected in this volume.

Heinz Fassmann, Ursula Reeger and Wiebke Sievers
Vienna, June 2008

Bibliography

Fassmann, H., J. Kohlbacher, U. Reeger & W. Sievers (eds.) (2005), *Cluster A1: International Migration and its Regulation: State of the Art Report*. IMISCOE Working Paper 2. www.imiscoe.org.

Herm, A. (2006), 'Recommendations on International Migration Statistics and Development of Data Collection at an International Level', in M. Poulain, N. Perrin & A. Singleton (eds.), *THESIM: Towards Harmonised European Statistics on International Migration*, 77-106. Louvain-la-Neuve: Presses universitaires de Louvain.

Kraly, E.P. & K.S. Gnanasekaran (1987), 'Efforts to Improve International Migration Statistics', *International Migration Review* 21 (4): 967-995.

Poulain, M., N. Perrin & A. Singleton (eds.) (2006), *THESIM: Towards Harmonised European Statistics on International Migration*. Louvain-la-Neuve: Presses universitaires de Louvain.

European migration: Historical overview and statistical problems

Heinz Fassmann

1 Preliminary remarks

Public perception always lags behind actual migration development, and statistical surveys react even more slowly. On the one hand, this has to do not only with the institutional sluggishness of the statistics bureaus, but also with the persistence of their conceptual frameworks and counting methods. What migration constitutes and how it is measured is anything but a matter of consensus, which implies that the resulting data are not comparable, either across national borders or over time. On the other hand, statistics influence the public's perception of the issue. The concepts and techniques used to measure migration structure the understanding of this phenomenon and thus also influence social discourse. The perception, the measurement and the actual phenomenon thus interact in an interesting dialectical relationship.

The following article deals with this dialectic and demonstrates how the actual development of migration has influenced statistical surveys and public perception. The article argues historically and tries to show that the states' perceptions and controls have led to divergent systems of migration surveys, which even today characterise the situation in Europe. Indeed, even now, the concepts and measurements of migration used in the European countries still differ massively. The European Union is trying to develop a common migration and integration policy but is still far from having a standardised definition, either of who is a migrant or of how migrants are to be counted.

2 Historical migration patterns

Migration out of, to and within Europe is nothing new. Political and religiously motivated displacement, the migration of the elite, the seasonal migration of farm labourers or the migration of trades people or students, had already existed before the nineteenth century in various forms. A regionally oriented migration history would be full of pertinent examples of such events. What changed with the industrialisation of the eighteenth and nineteenth centuries was the quantitative degree of intra-European and intercontinental migration, as well as the average distance of migration. Geographical mobility 'exploded' in the nineteenth century and the amount of long distance migration reached previously unseen values. The German demographer Gunther Ipsen has correctly termed this phase the 'century of the great drift' (Ipsen 1961).

2.1 *The nineteenth and early twentieth centuries*

Geographical mobility in the Europe of the nineteenth century meant, in most cases, rural to city migration and, at the same time, internal migration. All European metropolises experienced an exorbitantly fast growth, almost exclusively through immigration from the rural regions, both in the immediate vicinity of these cities and further afield. However, emigration overseas remained much stronger in the collective memory than this internal migration. In the Austro-Hungarian Empire towards the end of the nineteenth century, for example, the portion of overseas migration represented only between 15 and 20 per cent (see Fassmann 1985). Nevertheless, the authorities compiled detailed data on overseas migration and the topic was publicly discussed, while interior migration, as an expected result of the liberation of the serfs, and urban industrialisation were accepted without further ado.

That overseas migration was more strongly thematised was to some extent due to the more comprehensive state statistics on this phenomenon. One could speak about emigration to the United States because there were figures on these movements. In the harbours of emigration (Hamburg, Rotterdam, Bremerhaven, Amsterdam, Trieste or Liverpool) and in the admission points of the destination countries (for example, Ellis Island in New York), immigration and emigration officers meticulously logged all travellers in long lists. They included the names of those immigrating or emigrating, as well as age, gender, occupation, geographic and ethnic origins, in addition to distinctive features, such as personal disabilities. However, the data were not always correct, although they were based on personal interviews; for example, Polish-speaking citizens of Austria-Hungary were frequently allocated to Poland, as a result of the fact that the information provided by the interviewee was unclear and/or that the immigration officer did not know the states and boundaries in Europe at the time.

Unlike overseas migration, national and intra-European migration data were only indirectly collated. No one recorded the internal migrant when he or she left his or her hometown and moved to the next city. In fact, such a registration was technically impossible. Internal migration could only be reconstructed indirectly from the census, meaning the information on the place of birth. The Austrian and Hungarian censuses additionally gathered information on the place of domicile.

Every citizen of the empire had the 'right of domicile' (*Heimatberechtigung*) in one municipality. This form of local citizenship implied that the municipality would have to take over the social care of the person in question if necessary. The citizen could move this right to another municipality by an application process if he or she had been living in this municipality for a long time. Nevertheless, a comparison of the total population living in a municipality with the number of those having right of domicile in the same municipality provided some, if not very precise, information on the extent and the geographic dispersion of national and European internal migration (see Ladstätter 1973).

Some censuses would also collate information on emigration by asking in households if a family member was abroad and for what period of time. However, not all censuses in Europe included this question, for the simple reason that it did not yield any precise or verifiable results, since the census takers had no possibility of double-checking or amending the information about the 'missing' persons.

Apart from the collection of data on emigration in the country of origin, the country of destination also attempted to provide data on these emigrants. The statistical offices in Europe registered all resident foreign citizens and sent these registration cards back to their countries of origin. Based on these cards, the statistical authorities calculated the sum of their citizens living abroad. Once again, it must be stressed that these statistics on citizens living abroad were not very precise, because only a few countries agreed to swap registration cards; furthermore, there were no precise data on the length of the stay abroad. Whether a person remained abroad for a month or a year was irrelevant; this distinction was and is, however, integral to the definition of migration.

In sum, there were relatively precise data on emigration flows from Europe at the end of the nineteenth century, whereas the extent of internal migration within the European nation states and migration across European borders could only be gathered from the stocks of the foreign-born residing in the municipalities and countries at the times of the censuses. The same has been true for the censuses held regularly since 1790 in the US. While they count the immigrant stocks in this destination country, by definition, they do not include any data on return migrants or deceased immigrants. In other words, the census data do not yield any information on the migration flows between Europe and the US. Moreover, even the rough figures from the available flow statistics of European overseas migration show considerable discrepancies. Ferenczi and Wilcox claim that roughly 50 to 55 million people emigrated from Europe to the US and approximately another ten million Europeans left for Argentina, Canada and Brazil between 1846 and 1924 (1929: 185). The same authors quote a figure of only around 30 million immigrants who arrived in the US and around 13 million who entered Canada, Brazil and Argentina between 1856 and 1924. Chermayeff, Wasserman and Shapiro (1991), in turn, provided the figure of only around 60 million immigrants into the US for the period between 1600 and 1924. It is obvious that, despite the considerably better statistical data on overseas migration, there are still massive discrepancies.

Taken altogether, the data gathered both in the emigration ports and in the countries of destination only provide rough estimates on European overseas migration. While these are enough to ascertain tendencies, they should not be confused with unequivocal and precise statistics (see Chermayeff, Wasserman & Shapiro 1991). Nevertheless, they show an 'old immigration' into the US which lasted until approximately 1880 and which principally originated from Ireland, Britain, Germany and the Scandinavian states, as well as a 'new immigration' from Italy, Austria-Hungary and Eastern Europe. Furthermore, they illustrate a change from the definitive emigration of entire families or even towns aimed at settlement in the country of destination, to individual migrations of men and increasingly also of women with a growing contingent of people returning to their countries of origins. These, however, are trends rather than hard statistical facts.

The end of the nineteenth century also saw the first discussions on how to collate internationally comparable statistics on migration at the congress of the International Statistical Institute (ISI) held in Vienna in 1891. However, the only result of this discussion was the rather vague conclusion that a standardised definition and procedure was necessary. The next congress of the ISI, held in Budapest in 1901, resulted in the recommendation that a distinction ought to be made between permanent and temporary migration. The Institute passed further resolutions concerning internationally comparable migration statistics at its various meetings in Rome (1926), Warsaw (1929) and Madrid (1931) (see Kraly & Gnanasekaran 1987: 969).

2.2 *The inter-war years: 1918-1939*

The factors affecting immigration and emigration changed massively in the inter-war years, resulting in a decrease in international migration. This decrease was caused less by the changed social acceptance or the dismantling of businesses and institutions that facilitated and gained from migration (the so-called 'migration industry'), than by economic crises and the associated changes in the legal system. The US, Europe and, later on, Canada, as well as the South American countries, plunged into a deep economic crisis from the middle of the 1920s, which became even graver in the 1930s. As a consequence, the public increasingly perceived immigration as a threat and as a form of additional competition; this perception facilitated the introduction of a legal framework regulating migration and limiting the number of people allowed to enter the respective country in a given year. Austria and Germany enacted preferential treatment of their citizens in the labour market, while the US limited annual immigration and imposed regional quotas. The First Quota Act of 1921 allowed an annual immigration of 350,000, the second Quota Act of 1924 only 150,000, which was just over a quarter of the overall annual average of the period from 1856 to 1924.

Due to the increasing negative perception of migration, its statistical collation received greater attention. The ISI endorsed a data collection programme in 1924 which would have resulted in an internationally uniform system. 'The "international combined method" adopted national identity documents that would include an information sheet with detachable carbon copies. The copies would then be submitted at each entry point during travel' (Kraly & Gnanasekaran 1987: 969).

At the start of the 1920s, the International Labour Organisation (ILO) recommended that each member of the ILO should make agreements with other members for the adoption of a uniform definition of the term 'emigrant' and the use of a uniform method of gathering statistics on international migration. In 1924, the ILO held the International Conference on Emigration and Immigration in Rome, which, in its closing document, stated the need for a standardised definition of immigration and emigration.

> The Conference recognized the need for internationally comparable migration statistics for statistical and social scientific purposes. It went on further, however, to suggest the need for standard international migration statistics as a '... basis for the regulation of migration by international convention and to facilitate cooperation of the administrative authorities of different countries'. (Kraly & Gnanasekaran 1987: 969)

It is difficult to establish why this and other attempts to standardise a definition of international migration failed. One plausible explanation may be that the individual nation states followed separate routes with respect to the above-mentioned relations between perception, recording and policies of migration. Such national autonomisation began early on and was largely resistant to attempts at standardisation. Just to cite one example of the variety: from 1924, the French Bureau International du Travail (BIT) and the Société Générale d'Immigration (SGI) recruited large groups of workers directly in Poland and Russia. The amount of these inflows was collated in both administrative statistics and the census. There was, however, no noteworthy emigration out of

France in the nineteenth century or in the inter-war years. As a consequence, France has never had, and has still not developed, any instruments for collating data on emigration. Austria is a totally different case; after the First World War, immigration to the new Austria decreased massively while at the same time large numbers of people emigrated to the new independent successor states of Austria-Hungary, but also to the US, Canada and South America. As a consequence of these changes, the 1923 Census in Austria, unlike earlier censuses, did not include a question on birthplace, because counting immigrants made less and less sense. Conversely, the Interior Ministry precisely registered and counted organised overseas emigration. These examples show that statistics are always connected to specific problems in a society, which international recommendations can, at best, only partially address.

In the inter-war years, a significant development was that of forced migrations which had nothing to do with economic disparities, with social acceptance of immigration or with voluntary choice of a better life elsewhere. The majority of the migrations after 1918 resulted from the new order laid down in the Peace Treaties after the First World War. The victorious Entente revised the borders in East Central Europe and in the Balkans, thereby helping the people of this region to achieve national self-determination. However, the formation of these new nation states at the same time created a large number of ethnic minorities, whose emigration was organised or at least facilitated. This affected ethnic Greeks, Turks, Hungarians, Poles and Germans. Moreover, Russians, Ukrainians and Belo-Russians were forced to emigrate as a result of the October Revolution and the subsequent civil war. Later, the National Socialist repressions and threat of genocide forced the European Jewry to leave for Czechoslovakia, France, Britain and, especially, the US. These flights and expulsions also influenced the standardised usage of the term 'migration', which until then had connoted citizens leaving their state of origin in order to settle in a different state. However, these movements were less about citizens leaving their states of origin but about (new) states producing migrants and stateless people who became a particularly disadvantaged group of refugees.

Forced migrations, expulsions and ethnic cleansing also left traces in the statistics because these changes in the populations were registered and collated. Lists were compiled in refugee camps, while countless lists and inventories were made in concentration and work camps. The expelled persons received identity cards or temporary documents or were registered when they claimed financial compensation for losses suffered in the Second World War (*Lastenausgleich*). Since the statistics resulting from these administrative procedures were based on the concepts of individual legal frameworks, the different data sources that describe similar phenomena are neither exact nor comparable. Hence, the frequently quoted numbers of expelled and persecuted persons in the inter-war years are always estimates which are subject to political exploitation and are, therefore, to be treated with scepticism.

2.3 *The post-war years*

The same holds true for the immediate post-war period. Once again, due to the new political order, there was a considerable increase in migration, which was in no way voluntary and which was not considered a normal form of labour migration by either the affected people or the host countries. Flight and expulsion became symbols of the immediate post-war years; the numbers of refugees could only be approximated. In view of the suffering of millions of displaced persons (prisoners of war, forced labourers and surviving concentration camp prisoners), the expelled Germans as well as Poles, Ukrainians, Italians and Hungarians who were forced to leave their homes, exact numbers were probably not decisive. In any case, precise or allegedly exact figures are often exploited by countries comparing and contrasting the suffering they experienced.

European migration becomes more differentiated once again from the 1950s. On the one hand, this is due to the changes in the two colonial empires of France and Great Britain. After the Second World War, France resumed the active recruitment of immigrants that it first started in the inter-war period. For this purpose, it established the Office National d'Immigration (ONI), which signed a first recruitment agreement with Italy in 1947. Apart from the labour migrants entering France under these agreements, there were regular movements between France and the then still-existing colonies. Several million civil servants, soldiers and settlers of European origin had moved to the colonies held by France, the Netherlands, Belgium and Portugal in Africa, the Middle East, South and Southeast Asia and the Caribbean. Following the independence of these colonies, many Europeans moved back permanently to their countries of origin. Thus, the average of 304,000 people per year immigrating into France in the first five years of the 1960s is also a result of the Algerian War and Algeria's subsequent independence. Moreover, a large number of native Algerians, who at the time were French citizens, moved to France after the Second World War to live and work there.

The situation was similar in the UK. However, Britain up to the 1960s not only allowed the subjects of existing colonies but also those of former colonies to enter the country without having to undergo any immigration controls. All of these immigrants were, at best, only selectively counted in the censuses held at the time. They were not considered immigrants or emigrants, but were regarded as internal migrants moving within a colonial empire or the Commonwealth. As a consequence, the extent of these movements can only be gathered from the migration balance, which is obtained by comparing the total population recorded in two consecutive censuses plus the number of births and minus the number of deaths registered between these two census dates.

Conversely, the German-speaking countries of central Europe also changed both their mechanisms of counting migrants and their migration regimes after the Second World War. Austria reintroduced the criterion of 'birthplace' into its census in 1951 in order to be able to assess the degree of flight and expulsion. After that, however, another form of migration began. Germany, and later Austria, started systematically to recruit foreign workers in Southern and South-Eastern Europe in the 1960s, since the Cold War and the Iron Curtain had cut off their traditional reservoirs for labour migrants from Eastern Europe. However, the workers coming from Italy, Greece, Spain, Yugoslavia and Turkey were not necessarily perceived as immigrants. Rather, the Austrian and German policies at the time were guided by the idea that the labour migrants should enter their countries for a limited period of time in order to fill the labour shortages resulting from economic growth. The motto of their policy was 'rotation', which implied short-term help through foreign labour when there was demand, but also a return home when this demand decreased. Foreign workers were supposed to behave like spinning tops on the domestic labour market. They should come and go, if possible alone and without families, and be very flexible both occupationally and geographically. This would bring maximum benefits to German and Austrian businesses while relieving society from fundamental questions of integration, which were inevitable when labour forces began to settle. Neither did countries of origin or destination regard these migrants as permanent emigrants or immigrants, respectively, and therefore did not count them as such.

Additional labour forces from abroad were looked upon favourably, both publicly and politically, as they worked for lower wages and were thus useful to domestic businesses. They could also easily fade from the public conscience. Accommodation in makeshift lodgings, barracks or caravans right on the construction sites made it even easier for the public to ignore the presence of these workers. In addition, the chosen terminology – foreign workers (*Fremdarbeiter*) or guestworkers (*Gastarbeiter*) – signalled that they would only stay temporarily and were therefore not immigrants. These workers were consistently described as temporary resident population in the Austrian census and from 1965 onwards were recorded in separate administrative statistics on 'registered guestworkers' rather than in the normal population registers (see

Lichtenberger 1984). The German government had already established such separate statistics in 1953. However, the Central Aliens Register (Ausländerzentralregister) not only contained information on residence and place of work but also on violations of the law.

The phase of rapid growth in Western Europe in the 1950s and 1960s was followed by an economic slump in the 1970s, which also brought the recruitment of foreign workers to a halt. As a result of the oil price shock and the ensuing economic stagnation, the fight for jobs became harder. Foreign workers came to be seen as a threat and their presence discussed in the public arena. While the British government introduced regulations that tried to stop immigration from their former colonies, the German and Austrian governments introduced political measures that aimed to make the 'guestworkers' leave. However, these measures did not always produce the desired result. Although some guestworkers did indeed return to their countries of origin, others not only stayed, but also brought their families. In fact, the end of active recruitment seems to have been a clear signal that those who wanted to stay would have to attain permanent residence. For this reason, the total foreign population residing in Austria, Germany and Switzerland rose much more significantly than the number of foreign citizens working in these countries. These changes also meant that the counting and collating of data on the foreign population gained increasing importance once again. The Austrian and German governments invested heavily in improving the quality of the census data in Austria and of the microcensus, register and socio-scientific data (e.g. the socio-economic panel) in Germany.

At the same time, the quality of migration statistics in all European states improved significantly thanks to the beginning internationalisation and standardisation of the definitions of migration. Following many years in which the nation states had designed their statistics separately, a new approach became at least conceivable in regulations, such as the 1951 Geneva Convention relating to the Status of Refugees, which agreed not only on the legal position of refugees but also on a precise definition of what constituted a political refugee. This first distinct definition of a form of international migration was soon to be followed by others. In the late 1940s, soon after their creation, the Population Commission and the Statistical Commission of the United Nations addressed the issue of producing recommendations on international migration statistics. The first set of recommendations was adopted in 1953. It centred on the definition of 'permanent immigrants' as non-residents (both nationals and aliens) arriving with the intention to remain for a period exceeding a year and of 'permanent emigrants' as residents (nationals and aliens) intending to remain abroad for a period exceeding one year (see United Nations 1998). The first revision of these recommendations followed in 1976, the second in 1998, which is also the most recent definition of migration recommended by the UN. The recommendations came late, perhaps too late, which might explain why the nation states have been slow in implementing them. In fact, the repeated revisions aimed not only to develop the existing definitions of migration and to adapt them to social discourse, but also to remind the states of the necessity of their observance.

2.4 *The end of European partition*

With the fall of the Iron Curtain there was a significant change in the general framework for European migration. The low and high wage areas that had been divided by a border up to 1989/90 immediately entered into a process of exchange once this border was opened. While capital moved from the high wage area into the low wage area, labour moved in the opposite direction. Germany and Austria experienced a rise in inflow of workers. In addition, the numbers of war refugees and asylum seekers entering these countries rose significantly as a result of the civil war in former Yugoslavia. In these years, the migration balance in Germany reached an all time high of over 560,000 people (see Table 1). At the same time, the economies of the southern European countries caught up with their northern neighbours, also as a result of increasing European integration. While the Portugal, Spain, Italy and Greece of the 1960s were countries of origin of labour migration, they became destination countries at the beginning of the new century. Surprisingly for many, Spain ranked in fourth place of the countries receiving the largest numbers of immigrants in Europe in 2005.

Table 1 *Annual migration balance for the EU-25, 1960-2003*

	EU-25	*Germany*	*France*	*UK*	*Spain*
1960-1964	230	163	304	60	-109.7
1965-1969	-34	221	95	-45	-30.1
1970-1974	82	171	115	-32	-32.1
1975-1979	265	15	34	-11	28.3
1980-1984	15	2	52	-34	0.8
1985-1989	382	332	50	22	-19.7
1990-1994	856	563	23	22	49.4
1995-1999	645	204	8	81	129
2000-2003	1,329	155	118	161	507
Average 1960-2003	377	205	87	18	37

Source: Eurostat; author's calculation

Since the turn of the century, asylum and migration politics has also increasingly come on the European agenda. With the 1997 Treaty of Amsterdam, the agendas referring to migration, previously anchored in the intergovernmental 'third pillar', were transferred to the jurisdiction of the European Union. Articles 61-69 of this contract obliged the Member States to develop joint visa, asylum and immigration policies by May 2004, including regulations on the recognition of refugees, the legal position of third-country nationals and family reunification, as well as minimum standards for asylum procedures (see Perchinig 2007). However, a joint asylum and migration policy is inconceivable without an integrated data collation system that serves as a basis for planning these policies. That is why the European Commission has also increased its efforts to convince the individual states to adopt binding standards for the definition and measurement of migration. It published a set of recommendations in 2005 that aim to harmonise the European statistics on migration. Whether these will be more successful than their predecessors remains to be seen. But, as the present study shows, the shortcomings of international migration data are momentous.

3 Problems of measuring international migration

Migration to, within and out of the EU is diverse and complex. Passenger lists, information provided by port authorities or records gathered at the points of entry no longer do justice to the variety of types of migration. Moreover, the individual nation states use long-established but very different instruments for determining population and migration figures, which are not necessarily easy to harmonise with each other. As long as these national statistics constitute the smallest building blocks of comparability, the enormous efforts of the OECD to collate and present internationally standardised statistics within the framework of their SOPEMI (Système d'observation permanente des migrations) are doomed to failure. Similarly problematic are the efforts of Eurostat, which accesses and aggregates these national statistics. On its website, Eurostat refers quite openly to this problem: 'The completeness of the tables depends largely on the availability of data from the relevant national statistical institutes'.[1]

The aggregation of national statistics will remain deficient unless these are radically reformed or Europe carries out its own surveys (such as the Labour Force Survey). Even when the Member States have tried to implement the definition of an international migrant recommended by the UN, the definitions still 'vary significantly between countries, within countries over time, and between different sources of statistical information', as Nowok, Kupiszewska and Poulain show clearly and impressively (2006: 214). The associated problems of measuring international migration in flow and stock statistics will be illustrated more clearly below.

3.1 *Flow statistics*

Flow statistics measure the degree of migration within a specific time period (usually one year). They are more sensitive than stock statistics and directly show changes in migratory patterns. For this reason, more and more countries have begun to implement flow statistics that are usually compiled in the course of administrative procedures (such as registrations and deregistrations at registry offices or issuance of residence and work permits, etc.). One disadvantage of these instruments is that they depend upon the specific legal requirements of the respective state at a specific point in time. Consequently, the resulting statistics are not comparable across borders or over time. Moreover, as the statistics are by-products of an administrative procedure, they are compiled by administrative staff and not by staff trained in statistics. This can have a negative impact on the quality of the information. Usually, statistics of this type only provide very basic information such as the total number of migrants, sometimes differentiated by sex and age. However, they rarely contain information on the occupational history, the educational background, the place of birth or the last residence of the respective person or whether he or she has left behind a family, a piece of information that would be essential in estimating the potential of family reunification.[2]

When implementing flow statistics, most European states follow, in principle, the definition of international migration recommended by the UN. These recommendations define a long-term migrant as 'a person who moves to a country other than that of his or her usual residence for a period of at least a year (12 months), so that the country of destination effectively becomes his or her new country of usual residence. From the perspective of the country of departure the person will be a long-term emigrant and from that of the country of arrival the person will be a long-term immigrant' (United Nations 1998: 18). A short-term migrant is consequently:

> a person who moves to a country other than that of his or her usual residence for a period of at least 3 months but less than a year (12 months) except in cases where the movement to that country is for purposes of recreation, holiday, visits to friends and relatives, business, medical treatment or religious pilgrimage. For purposes of international migration statistics, the country of usual residence of short-term migrants is considered to be the country of destination during the period they spend in it. (United Nations 1998: 18)

The first problem, which arises when this definition is implemented, is that of defining what 'usual residence' is. Although the UN has clearly defined what this term means ('the geographical place where the person usually resides'), not all European states adhere to this definition or they interpret it differently. Many countries still count their nationals as part of the resident population at least for a few months after they have left. Austrians are categorised as emigrants after they have left Austria for more than three months (see the chapter on Austria in this publication), Belgians after six months (see the chapter on Belgium in this book), the Dutch if they their stay exceeds eight months out of the forthcoming twelve-month period and Poles and Romanians are only counted as emigrants if they declare that they leave for good (see the chapters on Poland and Romania in this book). Residents of Romania are counted towards the Romanian population if they have a permanent registered address in Romania, even if they live and work in another country. *De facto* these people are emigrants: *de jure* they are not categorised as such in Romania (see Romania in this book).

The second practical problem concerns the question of whether all people who change their usual residence should be counted. While the UN recommendations imply that every person settling in the country for a specific period of time should be included in the statistics, many European countries exclude ethnic immigration or immigration from countries to which they have specific historical or political links. Until 1974, Portugal did not register entries from the Portuguese-speaking African countries (Países Africanos de Língua Oficial Portuguesa, PALOP), since these were not regarded as a change of place of residence but as a special form of colonial internal migration (see the chapter on Portugal in this book). However, when these countries became independent, the legislation changed. From 1975, those arriving from the PALOP who were of African origin were regarded and registered as regular immigrants, whereas immigrants of Portuguese origin were not counted as international migrants.

Perhaps the most prominent example of immigrants not being counted as such can be found in Germany. The German *(Spät)-Aussiedler* (ethnic Germans who have the right to resettle to Germany) are not categorised as 'foreigners' but as German citizens despite the fact that they are the quintessential migrants. The sheer number of these shows how significant the varying treatments are. Between 1991 and 2005 more than two million ethnic Germans settled in Germany.

The same holds true for Romanians of Hungarian origin entering Hungary (see the chapter on Hungary in this book), Moldovans of Romanian origin entering Romania (see the chapter on Romania in this book), ethnic Greeks from the area of the former Soviet Union entering Greece (see the chapter on Greece in this book) or Bulgarians of Turkish descent entering Turkey (see the chapter on Turkey in this book). That these groups are not counted as regular immigrants can be traced back to the fact that these states are based on an ethnic concept of the nation that includes all ethnics, irrespective of where they live. As a consequence, these border crossings are not categorised as instances of immigration of foreign nationals but as the return migration of people who have always formed part of the nation.[3]

The third and crucial problem in applying the UN recommendations for flow statistics is the duration of residence in the target country. The UN recommendations define migration as a change of place of residence that involves a crossing of an international border and a stay of at least one year in the new country of destination. Thus, a person has to cover a certain distance and stay for a significant amount of time in order to be called a migrant. Following the UN recommendations, statistical offices should only count a person who has entered their country as an immigrant from the second year of his or her stay. However, if the statistical offices rigorously stick to this suggested time frame, their data are outdated before they are published. Therefore, some countries (for example, the Netherlands) use the intended duration of stay and implicitly assume that this will coincide with the actual duration of stay. However, the arriving immigrants may only have a vague idea of how long they will be staying or they simply cite the period of stay granted by their visas rather than their real intentions. Other countries, such as Austria, try to circumvent the problem of delayed statistics by counting those who have crossed their borders as international migrants after they have stayed for more than three months (see the chapter on Austria in this book). While this might be consistently applied within Austria, the immigration figures resulting from these guidelines will always be higher than in countries that stick to the one-year limit.

Finally, many European countries have as yet not implemented proper statistics on the counterflow to immigration, that is, emigration. Registration of emigration in Europe is poor to non-existent (see the chapters on France and Poland in this book) as has also been observed by Nowok, Kupiszewska and Poulain: 'Most efforts should be focused on the registration of emigration, of both nationals and non-nationals, by facilitating the administrative procedure and by introducing incentives for both the people concerned and the local administration to register the move' (2006: 220). The underestimation of emigration results in an overestimation of the migration balance. Comparisons of emigration statistics to immigration statistics in the respective destination countries of these emigrants in a so-called double entry matrix show how large these numerical gaps can be. In fact, these are particularly high in the post-communist countries (see the chapters on Poland and Romania in this book).[4]

Nowok, Kupiszewska and Poulain come to the conclusion that 'currently available data on international migration flows are still far from being internationally comparable' (2006: 217). Only Cyprus and the UK currently apply the UN recommendations consistently, while Finland and Sweden alone treat emigration in a different way to other countries that have signed the Nordic Agreement. All other EU Member States have their own exceptions, traditions and statistical instruments. The THESIM Report (Poulain, Perrin & Singleton 2006) is a useful source for this Babylonian confusion.

Table 2 *The registration of resident population and the inclusion of immigrants*

	Name of the population registry	*Persons included (apart from nationals and EU citizens)*	*Arrivals are counted as immigrants after a period of*	*Absent persons are counted as emigrants after a period of*
Austria	Zentrales Melderegister (ZMR)	TCN with permanent and temporary permit, asylum seekers	3 months	3 months
Belgium	Registre National des Personnes Physiques (RN)	TCN with permanent permit (with temporary permit after 3 months), asylum seekers	3 months	Permanent/ permit expiry
Cyprus	Archeio Plithismou		1 year	1 year
Czech Republic	Informacni system evidence obyvated (ISEO)	TCN with permanent and temporary permit, no asylum seekers	1 year	Permanent/ permit expiry
Denmark	Det Centrale Person Register (CPR)	TCN with permanent permit (with temporary permit after 3 months), no asylum seekers	3/6 months	6 months
Estonia	Rahvastikuregister	TCN with permanent permit (with temporary permit after 3 months), no asylum seekers	3 months	No time criteria
Finland	Väestötietojärjestelmä	TCN with permanent permit (with temporary permit after 12 months), no asylum seekers	1 year	1 year
France	Repertoire National (RNIAM)		1 year (TCN), no statistics for EU citizens	No statistics
Germany	Melderegister	TCN with permanent and temporary permit, asylum seekers	Depends on the Länder	No time criteria
Greece	Dimotologio		1 year (TCN), no statistics for EU citizens	No statistics
Hungary	A polgarok szemelyi adatainak es lakcimenek nyilvantartasa	TCN with permanent permit (but not with temporary permit), no asylum seekers	3 months (EU)/1 year (TCN)	Permanent/ permit expiry
Ireland	Central Records System (CRS)		No time criteria	No time criteria

	Name of the population registry	*Persons included (apart from nationals and EU citizens)*	*Arrivals are counted as immigrants after a period of*	*Absent persons are counted as emigrants after a period of*
Italy	Anagrafe della popolazione residente	TCN with permanent permit (with temporary permit after 6 months), no asylum seekers	6 months	1 year
Latvia	Latvijas Republikas Iedzivotaju registrs	TCN with permanent permit (with temporary permit after 3 months), no asylum seekers	1 year	6 months/ permit expiry
Lithuania	Gyventoju registras	TCN with permanent permit (with temporary permit after 12 months), no asylum seekers	1 year	6 months/ permit expiry
Luxembourg	Repertoire general des personnes physiques et morales	TCN with permanent and temporary permit, asylum seekers	No time criteria	No time criteria
Malta	Public registry		Permanent	No statistics
The Netherlands	Gemeentelijke Basis Administratie persoonsgegevens (GBA)	TCN with permanent and temporary permit, asylum seekers 6 months after application	4 out of the forthcoming 6 months	8 out of the forthcoming 12 months
Poland	Powszechny Elektroniczny System Ewidencji Ludnosci (PESEL-CBD)	TCN with permanent and temporary permit, no asylum seekers	Permanent	Permanent
Portugal	Registro des Identificacao Civil	TCN with permanent and temporary permit, no asylum seekers	1 year	1 year
Romania	Inspectoratul National pentru evidența persoanelor	TCN with permanent and temporary permit, no asylum seekers	permanent	permanent
Slovakia	Register obyvatel'ov Slovenskej republiky (REGOB)	TCN with permanent and temporary permit, no asylum seekers	Permanent/ 3 month	Permanent/ permit expiry
Slovenia	Centralni register prebivalstva (CRP)	TCN with permanent and temporary permit, no asylum seekers	Permanent/ permit expiry	Permanent/ permit expiry
Spain	Fichero de Coordinacion de los Padrones municipales	TCN with permanent and temporary permit, asylum seekers	No time criteria	No time criteria
Sweden	Folkbokföringen	TCN with permanent permit (with temporary permit after 12 months), no asylum seekers	1 year	1 year
Switzerland	Zentrales Migrations-informationssystem (ZEMIS ou SYMIC)	TCN with permanent and temporary permit, asylum seekers	No time criteria	No time criteria
Turkey	Türkiye İstatistik Kurumu (TUİK)	TCN with permanent and temporary permit, asylum seekers	No time criteria	No time criteria
UK	Registers on births, marriages and deaths		1 year	1 year

Note: 'TCN' refers to third-country nationals.
Source: modified after Poulain, Perrin & Singleton 2006

3.2 *Stock statistics*

In this unsatisfactory situation many researchers turn from flow statistics to stock statistics. Census data provide an excellent basis for scientific analysis and policy development. They are detailed, accurate and provide information on a large number of topics. For all that, censuses have the disadvantage of not being comparable on an international level.

In most EU Member States the census includes all international immigrants, regardless of their legal status (see Table 3). The only precondition for inclusion is that the person has been living or intends to stay in the country for at least one year. However, some Member States differentiate between EU citizens and third-country nationals by shortening the necessary period of stay for the latter to six months (e.g. France) or even three months (e.g. Austria, Belgium, the Czech Republic, Ireland and Hungary) (see Cantisani & Poulain 2006). The treatment of asylum seekers also varies. In ten out of the 25 EU Member States, asylum seekers are excluded from the resident population and therefore not included in the base population of the census. In these countries, asylum seekers are included in the census if and when they are granted refugee status as laid down in the Geneva Convention. Only Finland includes asylum seekers but excludes political refugees if we believe the information gathered in the THESIM project.

All EU Member States gather information on the places of birth of their resident population (see Poulain, Perrin & Singleton 2006). The birthplace is to some extent a valid criterion for defining international migration as it allows for the distinction of those born in the respective country from those born abroad (usually described as the foreign-born population). If a person was born abroad, this automatically implies that he or she migrated at least once during his or her lifetime. However, this does not apply in those countries where the borders changed. Thus, a large majority of the foreign-born population in Poland are Poles born before or during the Second World War in the then Polish territories that are now part of Ukraine, Belarus or Lithuania (see the chapter on Poland in this book). Another disadvantage of using the birthplace to define international migration is that it does not supply any indication of as to when exactly the respective person migrated.

Except for the UK, all EU Member States that regularly carry out censuses also ask their respondents for their citizenship. Citizenship is also a useful criterion for the estimation of international migration, since it seems reasonable to assume that a foreign citizen would have had to cross an international border at some time. Although, like place of birth, citizenship does not supply any information on the exact date of this change of residence, the possible time frame is shorter, since it is reasonable to assume that the longer the person has been living in

Table 3 *Main characteristics of the census in several European countries*

	Date of the last census	*Minimum required stay to be counted as resident (in months)*	*Asylum seekers*	*Country of citizenship*	*Country of birth*
Austria	15.5.2001	3+	Excluded, with refugee status included	Yes	Yes
Belgium	1.10.2001	3+	Excluded, with refugee status included	Yes	Yes
Cyprus	1.10.2001	12+	Included	Yes	Yes
Czech Republic	1.3.2001	12+	Included	Yes	Yes
Denmark	1.1.2001	-	Excluded, with refugee status included	Yes	Yes
Estonia	31.3.2000	12+	Included	Yes	Yes
Finland	31.12.2000	-	Included, with refugee status excluded (!)	Yes	Yes
France	1.1.2004	6+	Included	Sample extrapolation	Sample extrapolation
Germany	25.5.1987	-	Included	Out of date	Out of date
Greece	18.3.2001	12+	Excluded	Yes	Yes
Hungary	1.2.2001	3+	Included	Yes	Yes
Ireland	28.4.2002	3+	Included	Yes	Yes
Italy	21.10.2001	3+	Included	Yes	Yes
Latvia	31.3.2000	12+	Included	Yes	Yes
Lithuania	6.4.2001	12+	Excluded	Yes	Yes
Luxembourg	15.2.2001	12+	Included	Yes	Yes
Malta	26.11.1995	12+	Excluded	Yes	Yes
The Netherlands	1.1.2001	12+	Excluded, with refugee status included	Yes	Yes
Poland	21.5.2002	12+	Excluded, with refugee status included	Yes	Yes
Portugal	12.3.2001	12+	Included	Yes	Yes
Romania	18.3.2002	3+	Excluded, with refugee status included	Yes	No
Slovakia	26.5.2001	-	Excluded	Yes	Yes
Slovenia	31.3.2002	12+	Included	Yes	Yes
Spain	1.11.2001	12+	Included	Yes	Yes
Sweden	1.11.1990	12+	Excluded, with refugee status included	Yes	Yes
Switzerland	5.12.2000	12+	Included	Yes	Yes
Turkey	22.10.2000	-	Included	Yes	Yes
UK	29.4.2001	6+ (12+)	Included	No	Yes

Source: modified after Poulain, Perrin & Singleton 2006

the country, the higher the probability that he or she receives the citizenship of this country. However, as convincing as this proxy variable may appear at first sight, it seems dubious when looked at in detail. The main problem of using citizenship as a proxy variable for migration is the fact that the requirements for receiving citizenship differ massively in the EU Member States. While some countries, such as Belgium, only require three years of residence, others such as Austria demand a minimum stay of ten years. Moreover, many countries facilitate naturalisation, for instance by shortening the required periods of stay for EU citizens or immigrants originating from former colonies or from other countries linked to them by history or international agreements. Moreover, children born of foreign citizens are foreigners in some countries, while they are citizens in others. Hence, the number of foreign citizens residing in a country only partly reflects the extent of international migration, since it is closely linked to the legal practice of granting citizenship in the respective country.

A final disadvantage of census data is the long time lag between the collection and the publication of the data, on the one hand, and between two consecutive censuses, on the other. Over the course of a decade, the structure and dynamics of a population can change significantly. Moreover, certain information can already be out-of-date by the time all the census data are available.

While France has completely redesigned its census to counter these drawbacks, Austria and other countries have introduced sample surveys (the so-called microcensus) that provide some information on the resident population between two complete censuses (see the chapters on France and Austria in this book). Since the microcensus aims to report on how the population structures change over the course of time, it usually contains a section of standard questions, which allow comparisons across time, and specific questions, which vary according to the particular issue addressed. The fixed component is, however, very limited in terms of information detail. The microcensus is nonetheless an important data source in the field of migration research, because it gives some indication of changes in the number of immigrants between census dates. Moreover, it can be planned and organised as an internationally comparable survey (e.g. Labour Force Survey, Eurobarometer). On the downside, the official nature of the microcensus also limits the validity of the data source. The sample only contains officially registered foreign citizens. Moreover, the interviewers have to announce their visit in advance by means of an official letter. As a consequence, the microcensus underestimates the immigrant population, collects insufficient data on illegal immigrants or those who have arrived recently and is thus biased towards the long-established immigrant population. This bias applies in some states also to the census (see the chapters on Portugal and Romania in this book).

3.3 Selected examples: Germany, France and the United Kingdom

Despite the foregoing critical reflections on definitions and statistics, it should have become clear that the importance of migration within and to the EU has increased. In a majority of European countries immigration and emigration have a bigger impact on population size and structure than the balance of births and deaths. Since the beginning of the 1990s the inflow of asylum seekers, labour migrants and family members has been the most important demographic event in Western Europe. Of the approximately 475 million people residing in the EU, around 23 million hold a citizenship of a country different to their country of residence. Approximately one-third of these originate from another EU state, and two-thirds are from outside the EU, i.e. third-country nationals. At 40.5 million, the number of those born abroad is much higher than the number of those holding a foreign citizenship. This is mostly the effect of naturalisation; 5.2 per cent of the total population of the EU are foreign citizens, while 8.8 per cent were not born in the country where they reside (see Table 4). This percentage is highest in the smallest states, i.e. Luxembourg and Lichtenstein, and clearly above average in Austria, Ireland, Sweden, Germany and Spain. Figures from Cyprus and the Baltic States have to be handled with care. Thus, the Baltic States count those who came as internal migrants in the Soviet period as international migrants.

The most important target country in the EU – in terms of absolute volume of immigration – is the Federal Republic of Germany with approximately 10.1 million foreign-born residents and 6.7 million foreign residents. After the US and Russia, it is the third most popular country for immigration worldwide. The first people who immigrated to the then Western Zones and later FRG after the Second World War were ethnic Germans from former German territories in Eastern Europe.

Table 4 *Foreign citizens and foreign-born in the EU-27 and in Germany, France and the UK, 2005*

	EU-27	*Germany*	*France*	*UK*
Resident population (in 1,000)	475,067	82,501	58,521	58,614
Resident foreign citizens (in 1,000)	22,875	6,739	3,263	2,857
In %	5.2	8.9	5.6	2.9
Resident foreign-born (in 1,000)	40,560	10,144	6,471	5,408
In %	8.8	12.3	10.7	9.1

Sources: Eurostat; Münz, Straubhaar, Vadean & Vadean 2007

These were followed by the guestworkers, initially from Italy, Spain and Greece, and later also from Turkey, Yugoslavia and other European and non-European countries. Today, Germany is the most important country of destination for immigrants from Eastern and South-Eastern Europe.

Germany does not use place of birth but citizenship to categorise and count its immigrant population. The figures are usually based on the registrations in the Central Aliens Register. However, those who naturalised or returned are not automatically deleted from the Register, meaning that the statistics based on this data source always overestimate the real number of immigrants. This was clearly seen in 2004 when the number of registered foreigners dropped from 7.3 to 6.7 million after corrections had been carried out on the data collected in the AZR. Conversely, German resettlers (*Aussiedler*) are not registered in the AZR at all because they are not considered foreigners by law. The AZR collects data from different sources on all foreigners who have been residing legally in Germany for a minimum of three months without differentiating between short-term and long-term migrants. A census, which both provides information on the resident foreign-born population and could be used to correct the data gathered in the AZR, was last carried out in 1987. The only additional source of data on the resident foreign population and the naturalised foreign-born population is therefore the microcensus, which is only a sample survey. Hence, the state of statistical information on the immigrant population residing in Germany is anything but satisfactory (see the chapter on Germany in this book).

France is the second most important country of destination for immigrants in Europe. Around 3.3 million people currently residing in France are foreign citizens, while 6.5 million residents were born abroad. This means that almost half of those born abroad hold French citizenship, which can, on the one hand, be explained by the fact that a large number of the immigrants originate from French colonies. On the other hand, it has always been much easier for immigrants to receive citizenship in France than in Germany. While the immigrants residing in West Germany almost exclusively originate from Eastern and South-Eastern Europe, the immigrants residing in France have come from the entire Mediterranean, including Portugal, Spain, Morocco, Algeria, Tunisia and Italy. Only a marginal number of labour migrants in France originate from former Yugoslavia and Turkey.

Unlike in Germany, the census constitutes the main data source for analysis of immigration to France (see the chapter on France in this book). The last traditional and complete census was carried out in 1999. In 2004, France implemented a redesigned annual census, which, however, only samples 14 per cent of the population. The sample is changed every year, so that after a five-year cycle 70 per cent of the population have been interviewed. The census not only contains information on both the country of birth and the citizenship of the resident population, but also gathers information on a vast amount of other features such as language, education and occupation. However, while the French stock statistics are impressive, their flow statistics are rather poor. Since these usually draw on residence permit data administered by the Ministry of the Interior, they only include EU citizens and third-country nationals. France does not gather any data on the immigration of French citizens. Nor does it gather any information on emigration, either of French or of foreign citizens. As mentioned above, this lack of interest in emigration can be traced back to the long tradition of immigration in the country. Nevertheless, France needs figures on emigration and has to estimate these in order to calculate the migration balance and extrapolate figures on the population size.

The third most popular country for immigrants is Britain, with roughly 2.9 million foreign citizens and 5.4 million foreign-born residents. Of the 2.9 million resident foreign citizens, roughly 60 per cent come from African or Asian countries (particularly India, Pakistan and Bangladesh). Immigration from Europe is, by comparison, low; Britain never actively recruited guestworkers from Yugoslavia or Turkey. Almost three-quarters of all European immigrants originate from Ireland, Britain's socio-economic and demographic reservoir.

Britain's system of measuring migration differs vastly from those in Germany and France (see the chapter on the UK in this book). While the census constitutes the main data source, the British definition of immigration relies solely on the place of birth. Citizenship has less meaning as a marker for immigration in the UK due to its colonial past. Instead, the census includes a question on 'ethnicity', which, in turn, would not suffice to define immigration in the central European context. The British flow statistics are considerably poorer than in Germany, where the population register is a reliable source for statistics on geographic mobility. Since Britain does not have a population register, the British flow statistics draw on the International Passenger Survey (IPS). The IPS is based on interviews with 0.2 per cent of all the people entering and leaving Britain. These interviews include a question on the duration of the intended stay (or absence) that serves to identify short-term and long-term immigrants and emigrants as defined by the UN recommendations. Even if the number of interviewed people is comparatively large, the results have to be regarded as rough estimates of the actual immigration and emigration because of the sampling error, which is of relevance for differentiated breakdowns. Asylum seekers are counted in separate statistics.

4 Outlook

In 2005, the European Commission made a proposal for the development of harmonised European statistics on migration. It states that, due to the development of Community policies and legislation on migration and asylum, the need for comprehensive and comparable European statistics on a range of migration-related issues has become a priority. Moreover, '[t]he further development, implementation and monitoring of common immigration and asylum systems implies a need for much better statistical information than is currently available'. The Commission is familiar with the situation and knows that the development of comparable statistics is difficult: 'The introduction of harmonised Community statistics on migration and asylum will be a complex procedure that must take into account the policy needs for statistics, international practices and recommendations and the practicalities of applying the definitions in each of the Member States' (European Commission 2005: 4).

The European Parliament finally adopted the proposal in 2007 (Regulation No. 862/2007 of the European Parliament and of the Council on Community statistics on migration and international protection). This Regulation provides clear definitions for important terms, including usual residence, emigration and immigration. In addition, it describes which data the Member States have to transfer to Eurostat. However, the regulation leaves it to the Member States to decide how they realise the transfer of the required data, which means that the fundamental problem has not been solved.

Nevertheless, there is no way around the harmonisation of migration statistics; if the European Commission wants to realise the objectives stated in the Treaty of Amsterdam in 1997 and detailed more clearly at the Tampere European Council in 1999, then it has to find a unified approach to the gathering of data on immigration. Such data are the necessary basis for both an objective discourse and the development of policies on immigration.

Notes

1 See europa.eu.int.
2 The country chapters demonstrate how important it is to have flow statistics differentiated by demographic and socio-economic variables. There is a clear trend towards feminisation of migration, a growing share of highly qualified migrants and a growing diversity regarding countries of origin.
3 A similar problem relates to how dual citizens are counted. In most cases, albeit not always, nation states treat them as citizens of their country and do not count them as foreign citizens.

4 In 2002, the national statistical institute in Poland (CSO) registered 17,806 Polish citizens leaving for Germany while the German population register counted 100,986 Poles entering Germany the same year (see Bijak & Koryś in this publication).

Bibliography

Cantisani, G. & M. Poulain (2006), 'Statistics on Population with Usual Residence', in M. Poulain, N. Perrin & A. Singleton (eds.), *THESIM: Towards Harmonised European Statistics on International Migration*, 181-202. Louvain-la-Neuve: Presses universitaires de Louvain.

Chermayeff, I., F. Wasserman & M.J. Shapiro (1991), *Ellis Island. An Illustrated History of the Immigrant Experience*. New York: Macmillan.

European Commission (2005), *Proposal for a Regulation of the European Parliament and the Council on Community statistics on migration and international protection*. COM (2005) 375 final. Brussels: European Commission.

Fassmann, Heinz (1985), 'A Survey of Patterns and Structures of Migration in Austria, 1850-1900', in: D. Hoerder (ed.), *Labor Migration in the Atlantic Economics. The European and North American Working Classes During the Period of Industrialization*, 69-95. Westport: Greenwood.

Ferenczi, I. & W. F. Wilcox (1929), *International Migrations, Volume I: Statistics*. New York: National Bureau of Economic Research.

Ipsen, G. (1961), 'Die atlantische und die deutsche Wanderung des 19. Jahrhunderts', *Jahrbuch des Ostdeutschen Kulturrates* 8: 48-62.

Kraly, E.P. & K.S. Gnanasekaran (1987), 'Efforts to Improve International Migration Statistics', *International Migration Review* 21 (4): 967-995.

Ladstätter J. (1973), 'Wandel der Erhebungs- und Aufarbeitungsziele der Volkszählungen seit 1869', in: H. Helczmanovszki (ed), *Beiträge zur Bevölkerungs- und Sozialgeschichte Österreichs*, 267-296. Wien: Verlag für Geschichte und Politik

Lichtenberger, E. (1984), *Gastarbeiter. Leben in zwei Gesellschaften*. Wien: Böhlau.

Münz, R., Th. Straubhaar, F. Vadean & N. Vadean (2007), *The Costs and Benefits of European Immigration*. HWWI Policy Report 3. www.hwwi.org.

Nowok B., D. Kupiszewska & M. Poulain (2006), 'Statistics on International Migration Flows', in M. Poulain, N. Perrin & A. Singleton (eds.), *THESIM: Towards Harmonised European Statistics on International Migration*, 203-232. Louvain-la-Neuve: Presses universitaires de Louvain.

Perchinig B. (2007), 'Die Europäisierung der österreichischen Migrations- und Integrationspolitik', in: H. Fassmann (ed.), *Zweiter Österreichischer Migrations- und Integrationsbericht*, 131-141. Klagenfurt: Drava.

Poulain, M., N. Perrin & A. Singleton (eds.) (2006), *THESIM: Towards Harmonised European Statistics on International Migration*. Louvain-la-Neuve: Presses universitaires de Louvain.

United Nations (1998), *Recommendations on statistics of international migration*. Revision 1. New York: United Nations.

Part 1

Post-colonial countries

1 Belgium

François Gemenne

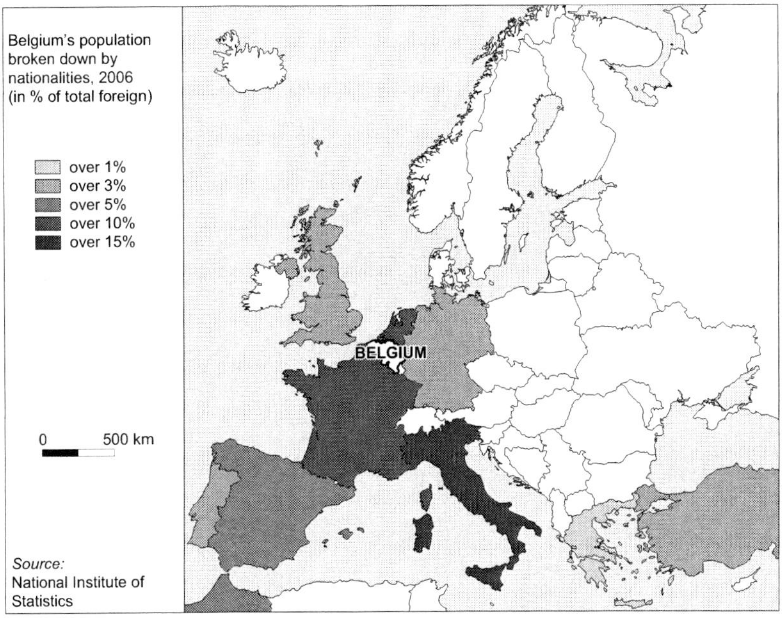

Cartography: Walter Lang, University of Vienna

1.1 Introduction

Belgium first attracted immigrants through its industries in the then prosperous region of Wallonia. In the nineteenth century, workers were recruited in Flanders and neighbouring countries. During that period, Belgium was a colonial empire exporting officers, merchants, priests and workers. The most important among Belgium's colonies, Congo, was acquired by King Leopold II at the Berlin Conference in 1885 and then transferred to the Belgian government in 1908. Between the 1880s and the 1920s, a considerable number of Belgians left to administer, explore and exploit the resources of Congo. Between 1880 and 1960, Belgium's economy was largely dependent upon Congo.

After the Second World War, the Belgian government began to recruit foreign mine workers in Southern Europe and later in Northern Africa, negotiating bilateral agreements with countries such as Italy, Spain or Morocco. When Congo became independent in 1960, about 100,000 Belgian citizens living in Congo returned to Belgium. Unlike in other European countries, these migrants did not really represent a challenge to social cohesion.

In the late 1960s, Belgium moved slowly towards a more restrictive immigration policy and eventually halted labour migration in 1974. Nevertheless, Belgium continued to attract large numbers of migrants, especially through family reunification.

The mid-1980s witnessed a new increase in immigration along with a decrease in emigration, resulting in a higher net migration. In the early 2000s, the migration balance (around 30,000) was comparable to the balance of the 1960s, when migration to Belgium reached its peak. This increase was accompanied by a diversification in the migrants' profiles: their origin, age and sex and the factors driving their migration changed considerably throughout this period (Martiniello & Rea 2001), as will be illustrated in this chapter.

The 1990s witnessed a steep increase in the number of undocumented migrants and asylum seekers. The wars in former Yugoslavia accounted for a large part of these migrants, but a significant part also came from Iran and republics of the former USSR. Between 1990 and 1999, about 180,000 asylum applications were lodged in Belgium.

In 2005, Belgium's total population reached 10,445,000 people. Among them, 1,065,000 were born abroad (10.2 per cent), while 871,000 were of foreign nationality (8.3 per cent). Among the 1,570,000 who were of foreign nationality at their birth almost half (700,000) had become Belgian by 2005. Therefore, the criterion of nationality alone is not sufficient to allow us to analyse Belgium's data on immigration; one must also take into account the previous nationality and the country of birth. Since the early 1980s, the number of foreigners living in Belgium has been stable, while the number of immigrants who have acquired Belgian nationality has sharply increased. Most of Belgium's immigrants are Europeans, although immigration from Southern Europe, which used to be very significant, is now characterised by a negative balance. Moroccans and Turks represent the main communities not originating from Europe. However, migrants from more distant countries such as China or India are also growing in number.

The number of asylum seekers reached a peak in 2000 with 42,691 claims, though the figure has since declined considerably, now around 15,000. The foreign population is heterogeneous and its distribution uneven throughout the country; 30 per cent of foreigners live in Brussels, though the population of Brussels only accounts for 9.5 per cent of the whole population.

Belgium is a country still in search of its national identity, tending to describe itself as multicultural and cosmopolitan. Being made up of two main cultural communities, the country had a bicultural dimension from the beginning. Foreign communities are increasingly seen as adding a new dimension to this biculturalism. In recent years, the input of foreigners has been particularly recognised at the political level; an increasing number of politicians of foreign origin have been given important positions and foreigners have been entitled to vote in local elections.

Despite the fact that Belgium put an official 'stop' to legal immigration in 1974, it has still never ceased to be a country of immigration, although it still seems to be rather reluctant to phrase it that way. Despite the official discourse and the fact that minorities are now represented on the political level, Belgium's policy towards immigration is still harsh, with a significant number of forced repatriations and closed detention centres. Time and time again, undocumented migrants who have been in the country for a while demand to be regularised and have been involved in occupying churches and leading hunger strikes. The population is widely sympathetic to these often dramatic situations. In addition, far-right movements and political parties are increasingly vociferous, especially in Flanders where the political party Vlaams Belang has now become a mainstream political actor.

Belgian policies toward undocumented aliens sparked much controversy, in particular the aspects related to forced repatriation and internment in closed detention camps. Political debate over asylum in Belgium mostly revolves around these two issues. A peak was reached in 1998 when a young Nigerian woman suffocated during her forced expulsion. This raised much public attention and the government pledged to implement a legalisation campaign for undocumented aliens, which took place in 2000. Detention of asylum seekers, and of children especially, in closed detention camps is also a highly controversial issue. In the early 2000s, more initiatives were taken to facilitate the integration of foreigners, such as the granting of the right to vote in local elections or the setting up of a Muslim council. However, some of these measures are still controversial, such as the introduction of compulsory language courses for foreigners in Flanders.

1.2 Belgian statistics on immigration

Most of Belgium's statistics on immigration are easily accessible through many websites and are sometimes published in different languages. However, some statistics are missing, despite their relevance for the study of migration in and out of Belgium; for example, no data related to ethnicity are available, since the law does not permit such data to be collected (see Perrin, Dal & Poulain 2007).

Belgium's official statistics are based on nationality. Neither the place of birth nor the nationality of the parents is taken into account in the official data. Therefore, a significant part (about 45 per cent) of the population of foreign origin is not accounted for, despite the fact that comprehensive data on naturalisation exist. A recent study by a research team from the University of Louvain (Eggerickx, Bahri & Perrin 2006) vigorously pleaded for an adaptation of current data and also for the lift of the ban on statistics related to filiation, which would allow statistics on ethnicity to be produced. While the criterion of nationality used to be considered sufficient to grasp migration patterns in Belgium, reforms of naturalisation procedures since 1984 have led to a situation where the number of immigrants has been increasing, while the number of foreigners has remained steady, as pointed out by Perrin, Dal and Poulain (2007: 1). The use of additional data, including data based on the origins of the migrants, thus became necessary in order to understand migration flows in the country, despite numerous limitations on the use of such data. For instance, municipalities collect statistics on filiation, but have no obligation to communicate them to the National Register, Belgium's main database on population.

The main source for statistical information is the National Institute of Statistics (Institut National de Statistique, INS). The INS produces annual statistics based on the data contained in the National Register as well as decennial tables based on the data provided by the national census.

1.2.1 *National Register*

The main population database is the National Register, placed under the authority of the Ministry of the Interior. Since 1988, all legal residents, apart from asylum seekers waiting for a decision on their case, have been registered in this database, kept by the municipalities and centralised in the National Register. The National Register is made up of two main registers: the population register and the aliens register, also kept by the municipalities. Belgians and aliens with a settlement permit are registered in the population register, while foreigners allowed to stay in the country are registered in the aliens register. Therefore, the term 'aliens register' is misleading, since aliens holding a settlement permit are registered in the population register – not in the aliens register.

All migrants residing legally in the country are supposed to register after one week upon arrival (residences are verified by police controls), but only if they intend to stay for more than three months, a period shorter than the one used by the UN to define international immigration and emigration, as pointed out by Perrin and Poulain (2006: 389). As a consequence of this definition two groups of migrants are automatically excluded from registration: short-term migrants and irregular migrants. Moreover, diplomats and civil servants of the EU and NATO, as well as their families, are not obliged to register but can be registered at their request. Finally, Perrin and Poulain (2006: 382) question the coverage of EU citizens in the register, since they are far less controlled than other foreigners.

Since 1995 and a change in the legislation on asylum, asylum seekers have been registered in a separate register, called the 'waiting register'. This change of legislation might have been prompted by the perceived need to present lower figures of foreigners, since, if the asylum seekers are accounted for separately, the proportion of foreigners among the population declines. When granted refugee status, asylum seekers appear in the population register, but are impossible to identify; nothing distinguishes them from other foreigners holding a settlement permit. In addition, separate registers also exist for EU employees and their families, as well as for employees of other international organisations. Since Belgium hosts the headquarters of both the EU and NATO, this part of the population is not to be neglected. Finally, Belgians living abroad are supposed to register with their local embassy or consulate, which is responsible for managing 'consular population registers' and is also part of the National Register. Many expatriates, however, fail to complete this task, and the reliability of these consular population registers is thus to be treated with scepticism.

The process of deregistration is quite similar to the process of registration, but far less reliable. Any person intending to live abroad for more than three months has to deregister from the register of his or her municipality, and is therefore considered an emigrant. However, many emigrants (both Belgians and aliens) tend not to deregister upon leaving the country. Perrin and Poulain (2006) identify diverse reasons for this under-reporting, including the lack of incentives, the fact that the process seems unnecessary and fastidious, as well as the fear of losing some advantages and/or benefits, with the latter being particularly common amongst foreigners, and especially refugees, who are afraid of being denied entry when they return to the country. Any person –

national or foreigner – who has deregistered from one municipality and has not registered in a new one within six months is automatically withdrawn from the population register. Belgian nationals who have left the country but have not deregistered from their municipalities can be deregistered if they decide to register with the diplomatic post abroad.

The National Register includes the following variables: first name and surname, sex, date and place of birth, address of residence, nationality, refugee or stateless status, filiation,[1] marital status, PIN code, profession, composition of the household, place and date of death, legal incapacity (if the person is a minor), declaration related to the burial type, driver's licence, passport/ID card, social security card, pension regime, declaration regarding the use of organs after death, title or status given after a war, possibility of being designated as the president of a polling station during elections and suspension or exclusion from the voters' roll.

In addition, the aliens register provides the following information: immigration service number, country and place of origin, limitations of the stay, work permit, professional card, return right, information on visa, name, place of birth, address, nationality of the spouse and every child, immigration service number of parents, spouse and children, inclusion in voters' roll (for EU citizens), date of recognition as a refugee, place of registration.

Not all of these variables are used for statistical purposes – this is the case for ethnicity, since the law forbids the establishment of statistics based on filiation. Every week, the data from the National Register are transmitted to the National Institute of Statistics and computed into statistical tables. These tables are the main source of information on migration, but can only include the 'legal variables': date of immigration/emigration, nationality, municipality of residence in Belgium, sex, date of birth, marital status and household composition.

1.2.2 *Census*

A general census is carried out every ten years by the INS. The last census, conducted in October 2001, was a so-called 'General Socio-Economic Survey'. This census relied entirely on the National Register, as far as the counting was concerned, and did not involve a field inquiry, unlike previously held censuses. Instead, a questionnaire collecting data related to education, housing, etc. was mailed to all the people registered in the National Register. The general census allows the INS to publish comprehensive reports on some aspects of immigration, such as housing or work.

1.2.3 *Other registers and databases*

Besides the statistics published by the INS, which are based on the National Register and on the national censuses, other reports and databases exist and complement these data. They are kept by various entities and institutions.

1.2.3.1 *Asylum registers*

Asylum seekers are registered in a special register, called the 'waiting register', which is kept by the Ministry of the Interior through various agencies, including Fedasil, the federal agency for asylum seekers, the Immigration Service (Office des Étrangers) and the General Commissioner for Refugees and Stateless Persons (Commissariat Général aux Réfugiés et aux Apatrides, CGRA). This register contains information related to asylum applications, detailed on a month-by-month basis. Since the register is neither included in the general population register nor in the aliens register, asylum seekers are not taken into account in the statistics on the foreign population residing in Belgium. This is a major bias of immigration data collected in Belgium. The CGRA provides statistics on the progress of claims and the decisions made upon them, based on the waiting register. Once an asylum seeker is granted refugee status, he or she is incorporated into the general population register and is not considered to be an immigrant.

Asylum seekers have to fill in a claim to be lodged at the Aliens Bureau upon their arrival in Belgium. The procedure then comprises two phases: first, the admissibility of the claim will be examined; then a decision on the claim will be made ('merits phase') by the CGRA. The number of claims reaching the second stage of the procedure varies greatly from year to year.

If asylum is granted, the asylum seeker receives refugee status; if it is denied, he or she has to leave the territory. Around 10 per cent of the applicants are granted refugee status, but the figures vary greatly according to the country of origin. If they refuse to leave the territory on a voluntary basis, rejected asylum seekers can be placed in a closed internment centre before being expelled.

1.2.3.2 *Work and residence permits*

Work permits are issued by the federal Ministry of Labour and Employment, but the regional ministries are responsible for the implementation of the legislation and also hold the permit data, using different methodologies. Moreover, the previous distinction between permits that allow migrants to enter Belgium and those allowing them to stay was abandoned in 1988. As a consequence of both this change and the regionalisation of the information, the data cannot really be used for statistical purposes.

The Immigration Service also holds a database recording many aspects of the migrants' files. The database is linked to the National Register, but includes additional information linked to the Immigration Service, such as the residence status of the migrant, regulated by a settlement permit, a residence permit or a residence document, the latter being a temporary document issued for the period of examination of some queries. Any foreigner wishing to stay in Belgium for more than three months has to get authorisation from a Belgian diplomatic post abroad.

1.2.3.3 *Visas and expatriates*

The Ministry of Foreign Affairs issues visas through Belgian diplomatic posts abroad. However, information on the number of visas issued (and refused) is very limited and varies greatly according to the technology available at the different posts. There is no central database on visas.

The Belgian diplomatic posts abroad also manage the information related to expatriates. However, many expatriates choose not to register with the diplomatic post of their country of residence. Hence, the information on expatriates is incomplete. There are some incentives to register though; these include the right to participate in elections (voting is compulsory in Belgium) and the possibility of being assisted by the embassy or the consulate in case of a crisis in the country.

1.2.3.4 *Database on the acquisition of citizenship*

There is no general database dealing with the acquisition of citizenship. Any acquisition of citizenship is recorded in the National Register and there are databases relating to some specific procedures. The acquisition of citizenship, which requires the expression of the will of the person concerned, needs to be distinguished from the attribution of citizenship, which is automatic (e.g. in the case of a child of a naturalised parent).

A common form of acquisition of citizenship is naturalisation, which is granted by the Chamber of Representatives (the lower chamber of the Parliament). Since 1984, this procedure has undergone considerable reform, and access to nationality is now much easier than it used to be, resulting in a sharp increase in the number of naturalisations. The Chamber of Representatives holds a complete database, as well as detailed statistics, on naturalisations, while the Immigration Service holds a database on all types of acquisition of citizenship but does not produce any statistics based on these data. Only successful applications are recorded in the National Register.

1.2.3.5 *Statistics produced by universities and NGOs*

In addition to the official statistics, many research centres and NGOs produce statistics on selected aspects of immigration. Among recent studies, the most significant is undoubtedly the Charles Ullens Initiative, an inter-university survey coordinated by the King Baudouin Foundation. Charles Ullens was a philanthropist who commissioned a large and comprehensive survey on immigration in Belgium, involving all major Belgian universities. The survey is currently under way, including quantitative and qualitative aspects.

Regarding the quantitative cluster of the project, Eggerickx, Bahri and Perrin (2006) have already produced a preliminary report based on the criterion of the nationality at birth rather than on current nationality only. Their study allows us to distinguish between immigrants born abroad and those born in Belgium (second-generation immigrants).

1.2.4 *A critical view of the statistical sources*

As stated above, one of the main shortcomings of Belgian statistics on immigration is the fact that some data exist, but cannot be used for statistical purposes. This is the case for data regarding filiation and ethnicity, since the INS is not allowed to publish statistics that include these variables.

INS statistics are based on nationality, and therefore do not take into account those who have acquired Belgian nationality after their birth (in Belgium or abroad). The recent study by Eggerickx, Bahri and Perrin (2006), based on nationality at birth, makes a step towards a more accurate description of immigration in Belgium.

Some data, usually highly controversial, are not available to the general public; this holds true for information on the number of people held in closed detention camps, for example. This lack of information hinders the democratic debate surrounding these practices.

Furthermore, in a study conducted for the King Baudouin Foundation, Lennert (2001) points out some major flaws in Belgium's management of migration data. Some have been corrected since, but not all of them:

1. missing information:
   Information is missing on some important points such as the number of illegal migrants in the country, and information on visas is still far from complete.
2. incomplete or unreliable information:
   In particular, data on emigration are unreliable, since so many emigrants fail to deregister from their municipality. Though it is possible to erase them from the registers, this is only a partial correction

of the bias. As said above, statistics based on the sole criterion of nationality are also misleading.

3. difficult retrospective analysis:
   Statistical series over longer periods of time are often inconsistent, due to changes of methodology and presentation as well as geographical reconfigurations: some countries no longer exist, while others have been created. Furthermore, some data from the past have not been digitalised and thus cannot be compared with more recent figures.
4. regionalised information:
   Since Belgium is a federal state, some data such as work permit data are directly managed by the regions, which use different methodologies and presentations. As a consequence, these data cannot be compared or aggregated.

Fortunately, statistical tables produced by NGOs and academics make up for some of these shortcomings, but they are unable to correct all of them, especially when the law forbids doing so.

Overall, it is widely recognised that Belgian statistics are insufficient in addressing important social issues such as the fight against discrimination, and many voices are now in favour of new statistical categories, that would go beyond the sole nationality criterion and apprehend the origins of the population on a more 'objective' basis (Perrin, Dal & Poulain 2007).

1.3 Stock of foreign population

1.3.1 Overview of the stock of foreign population

On 1 January 2005, Belgium had 10,445,852 inhabitants, 870,862 (8.3 per cent) of whom held a foreign nationality. The population of foreign descent accounted for 15 per cent of total population (1,570,475 persons). Among them, 699,613 were naturalised, representing 44.5 per cent of the population of foreign origin. Half of these naturalised were born in Belgium (332,474 – 47.5 per cent). Those born abroad represented about two-thirds (1,064,906 – 67.8 per cent) of the population of foreign descent (Eggerickx, Bahri & Poulain 2006). It is to be noted that, among the population of foreign descent, those born in Belgium were about twice more likely to acquire Belgian citizenship than those born abroad (65.8 per cent of those born in Belgium, 34.5 per cent of those born abroad).

1.3.2 Size of main nationalities

Unlike other European countries, most of the foreigners living in Belgium (68 per cent) come from other EU Member States, which is to some extent due to the fact that EU citizens are less likely to naturalise, as will be shown below. Moroccans and Turks are the main groups of non-EU nationals. Moreover, whereas some other countries have observed an increasing dispersion of origins, this does not seem to be the case for Belgium, at least for the most important groups of immigrants. Over the last five years, the top ten nationalities of the foreign population have remained the same. The smaller groups, on the other hand, tend to diversify: recent years have witnessed waves of immigration from more distant countries of origin, such as China, Brazil, India and so on (Table 1.1).

Table 1.1 *Belgium's population broken down by nationality, 2005*

Nationality	*Totals*	*Part of total polulation (%)*	*Share of foreign population (%)*
Italy	179,015	1.7	20.5
France	117,349	1.1	13.5
The Netherlands	104,978	1.0	12.1
Morocco	81,279	0.8	9.3
Spain	43,200	0.4	5.0
Turkey	39,885	0.4	4.6
Germany	36,324	0.4	4.2
Portugal	27,373	0.3	3.1
UK	25,982	0.3	3.0
Greece	16,588	0.2	1.9
DR Congo	13,171	0.1	1.5
US	11,476	0.1	1.3
Total EU-25	591,404	5.7	67.9
Foreign population	870,862	8.3	100.0
Total population	10,445,852	100.0	–

Source: SPF Economie – DG Statistique

1.3.3 Geographical distribution of foreign population

The foreign population is unevenly distributed. Given that Belgium is a federal country, this fact has crucial importance; though immigration policy is decided on the federal level, many integration policies (housing, education, etc.) lie within the competence of the regions.

While Italians settled mainly in the industrial regions of Wallonia (Hainaut and Liège), more recent waves of immigration concentrated in Flanders. Brussels, representing 9.5 per cent of the total population, is home to 30.7 per cent of the foreign population. Finally, EU nationals tend to live in conurbations in Wallonia and Brussels, though in the countryside in Flanders, which explains why non-EU nationals are often more numerous than EU nationals in Flemish conurbations (see Table 1.2).

Table 1.2 *Regional distribution of foreign population in Belgium, 2002*

	Total population		*Belgian population*		*Foreign population*		*EU nationals*		*Non-EU nationals*	
	Abs.	*%*	*Abs.*	*%*	*Abs.*	*%*	*Abs.*	*%*	*Abs.*	*%*
Brussels	978,364	9.5	718,344	7.6	260,040	30.7	142,431	25.2	117,609	41.6
Flanders	5,972,781	57.9	5,697,558	60.2	275,223	32.5	170,965	30.3	194,258	36.9
In conurbations	*1,926,996*		*1,799,263*		*127,733*		*56,900*		*70,833*	
Outside conurbations	*4,045,785*		*3,898,295*		*147,490*		*114,065*		*33,425*	
Wallonia	3,358,580	32.6	3,047,089	32.2	311,471	36.8	250,776	44.5	60,695	21.5
In conurbations	*999,076*		*864,099*		*134,977*		*101,617*		*33,360*	
Outside conurbations	*2,359,504*		*2,182,990*		*176,494*		*149,159*		*27,335*	
Total Belgium	10,309,725	100.0	9,462,991	100.0	846,734	100.0	564,172	100.0	282,562	100.0

Source: Centre for Equal Opportunities and Opposition to Racism

1.3.4 *Age and sex of the foreign population*

Compared to the Belgian population, the population of foreign descent represents an increasingly significant share (Eggerickx, Bahri & Poulain 2006). Perrin and Poulain (2007: 16) estimated that about 2 million people had at least one foreign parent on 1 January 2005, representing around 20 per cent of the total population. This share has steadily been growing faster than the total population; between 1991 and 2005, the population of foreign descent increased by 28 per cent, while the total population only grew by 0.9 per cent.

During the times when migrant workers were recruited, the population of foreign origin used to be predominantly male, but this has changed since. In 1991, there were 100 men to 100 women among the population of foreign descent, while there were only 96 men to 100 women in 2005, a ratio comparable to that of the Belgian population. However, this trend towards the feminisation of the foreign-born population varies according to the country of origin: the share of women is larger among those groups originating from Eastern Europe and the Southern hemisphere than among those originating from other countries. That the sex ratio is balanced also holds true when we consider the foreign nationals rather than the foreign-born, as shown in Table 1.3.

The average age of the foreign population also rose sharply between 1980 and 2004, due to the fact that immigrants tend to stay in Belgium even after their retirement. As a consequence, the age gap be-

Table 1.3 *Foreign population in Belgium by sex, 2000-2005*

	2000	2001	2002	2003	2004	2005
Men	465,903	445,908	438,115	439,652	442,639	445,710
Women	431,207	415,777	408,619	410,425	417,648	425,152
%	48.1	48.3	48.3	48.3	48.5	48.8
Total	897,110	861,685	846,734	850,077	860,287	870,862

Source: SPF Economie – DG Statistique; author's calculation

tween the Belgian and the foreign population has been closing, although the foreign population, as well as the population of foreign origin, still tended to be younger than the Belgian population in 2004 (Table 1.4).

Table 1.4 *Age structure of foreign population in Belgium for four selected nationalities, 2004*

	0-17		18-64		Over 64		Total	
Nationality	*Abs.*	*%*	*Abs.*	*%*	*Abs.*	*%*	*Abs.*	*%*
Italian	13,601	7.1	142,757	74.8	34,434	18.0	190,792	100.0
French	15,233	13.7	82,790	74.5	13,123	11.8	111,146	100.0
Turkish	9,439	20.6	33,392	72.8	3,035	6.6	45,866	100.0
Moroccan	20,786	22.9	64,392	71.0	5,464	6.0	90,642	100.0
Belgian	2,033,773	21.5	5,776,720	61.0	1,652,498	17.5	9,462,991	100.0

Source: SPF Economie – DG Statistique; author's calculation

1.4 Net migration and migration flows

Between 1962, when the first bilateral agreements were signed, and 2004, immigration to Belgium was consistently higher than 35,000 people a year, with peaks in the 1960s, 1990s and 2000s. Over the same period, between 20,000 and 40,000 people left Belgium annually. Tighter immigration policies led to a significant immigration decrease in the early 1980s, averaging around 35,000 people per year. Combined with a relatively stable rate of emigration, this resulted in a low net migration in the early 1980s, with a negative balance for the year 1983. However, these figures do not account for illegal migration, the level of which is impossible to verify. The 1980s also marked the start of the easing of the naturalisation procedures, resulting in a stagnation of the foreign population, despite a consistent increase in net migration from the mid-1980s.

In the 1990s, as in many European countries, immigration increased sharply. Booming globalisation, cheaper transportation and expansion of the EU are undoubtedly external factors that accounted for this increase. As a consequence, net migration was consistently above 10,000 (and for foreigners above 20,000). As stated before, asylum seekers were excluded from the general population register in 1995 and were therefore also not included in the net migration figures after 1995.

Today's immigration to Belgium is mostly European (EU and Eastern Europe). As early as in the 1980s, immigrants from Europe accounted for 60 per cent of the immigration to Belgium. The net migration varies greatly according to the nationality of the migrant: it is far lower for migrants from North America, Southern Europe and Japan than for migrants from Maghreb, Turkey, Africa and Asia.

The net migration of Belgians was consistently negative; during the 1980s, the number of Belgian emigrants exceeded the number of Belgian immigrants by 10,000 every year. Belgian emigration decreased in the 1990s. Nevertheless, the net migration was still negative (over -5,000). Moreover, these figures are underestimated, since many emigrants do not deregister, as was explained above.

Most Belgian emigrants are between twenty and 40 years old, and settle in the neighbouring countries, but many go as far as Canada, the United States, South Africa or Brazil. The exact number of Belgians living abroad is unknown, since many do not register with a diplomatic mission upon arrival. The official number of Belgians registered abroad is around 300,000, though estimates from diplomatic missions suggest that the actual number is higher.

As shown in Table 1.5, flows to and from Belgium were quite stable throughout the 1990s, then soared from 1999 onwards. This trend

Table 1.5 *Belgium's net migration, 1992-2005*

	Immigration	*Emigration*	*Net migration*
1992	66,763	33,707	33,056
1993	63,749	34,202	29,547
1994	66,147	36,572	29,575
1995	62,950	36,044	29,906
1996	61,522	36,674	24,848
1997	58,849	39,320	19,529
1998	61,266	40,236	21,030
1999	68,466	41,307	27,159
2000	68,616	43,487	25,129
2001	77,584	42,221	35,363
2002	82,655	41,349	41,306
2003	81,913	41,897	40,016
2004	85,378	42,046	43,332
2005	90,364	43,719	46,645

Source: SPF Economie – DG Statistique

kept getting stronger in the 2000s, with the number of entries into the country topping 90,000 in 2005. Throughout the period, the net migration of foreigners was consistently positive, ranging from around 20,000 to around 30,000.

1.5 Asylum seekers

The claims for asylum reached a peak in 2000 and have consistently decreased since then, partly due to far more stringent conditions for the granting of asylum (see Figure 1.1). Most of the asylum seekers who lodged claims in 2004 and 2005 originated from the former USSR, the Democratic Republic of Congo, former Yugoslavia and Iraq (Table 1.6).

Figure 1.1 *Number of asylum claims lodged at the Immigration Service in Belgium, 1990-2005*

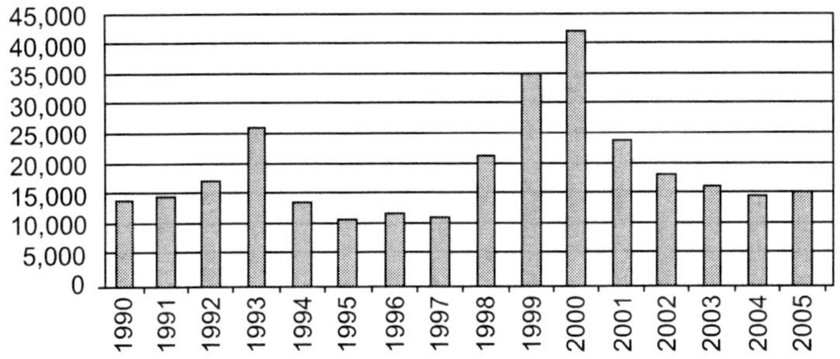

Source: Immigration Service

Table 1.6 *Main countries of origin of asylum claimants in Belgium, 2004-2005*

Country of origin	*2004 (lodged)*	*2005 (lodged)*	*2005 (granted)*
Russia	1,361	1,438	1,259
DR Congo	1,471	1,272	204
Serbia & Montenegro	1,294	1,203	166
Iraq	388	903	63
Slovakia	730	773	NA
Armenia	477	706	NA
Guinea	565	643	48
Rwanda	427	565	445
Nepal	373	557	NA
Cameroon	506	530	NA

Note: NA = not available
Source: Immigration Service

Data on the claims still awaiting a decision are not available to the general public. The Aliens Bureau used to be notorious for its long delays (sometimes of several years) when it came to deciding on asylum claims, but the setbacks have been significantly reduced. Statistics on the numbers of forced repatriations are also not published.

1.6 Naturalisations

Since 1984, naturalisation has been considered one of the main tools for integration in Belgium. Hence, the Code of Belgian Nationality allows for broad access to nationality and has been amended several times since 1984 in order to ease the procedure for migrants willing to acquire Belgian citizenship. These changes are reflected in the numbers of naturalisations (Figure 1.2); every major change in the legislation was followed by a sharp increase in the number of naturalisations. The code is based on *ius sanguinis*, the attribution of nationality by filiation, but also allows for *ius solis*, the attribution of nationality by birth in the country.

Figure 1.2 *Number of naturalisations in Belgium, 1985-2005*

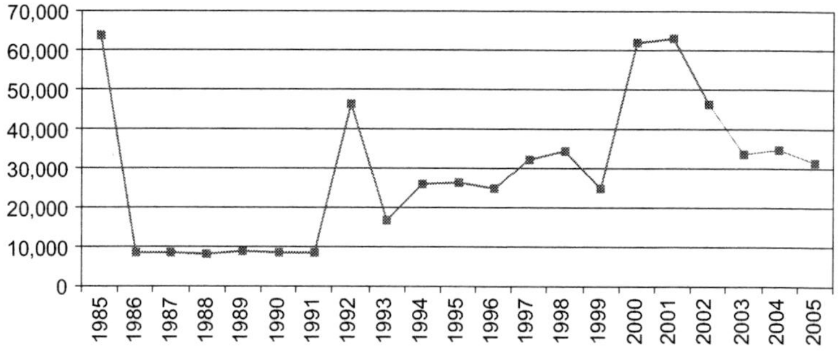

Source: SPF Economie – DG Statistique

The law of 28 June 1984 introduced the Code of Belgian Nationality. The new code abolished the legal distinction between father and mother, as well as between legitimate and illegitimate children by allowing the transmission of nationality through the mother. The following year, the number of naturalisations reached an all-time peak of 63,824. In 1991, access to naturalisation for children of the second and third generations was eased by introducing a *ius soli* regulation. While children of the third generation automatically acquire Belgian citizenship, children of the second generation can acquire citizenship through a simple declaration of their parents before they reach the age of twelve. Once again, this change was followed by a sharp increase in the number of naturalisations. Finally in 1999, the naturalisation procedure was radically simplified by abolishing the controversial 'integration test' and the fees and by reducing the delays before a decision is made. This reform again resulted in a dramatic increase in the number of naturalisations.

Figure 1.3, which shows the countries of origin of the new Belgians, illustrates that the willingness to obtain Belgian citizenship is highly dependent upon the advantages resulting from this new citizenship. It therefore comes as no surprise that fewer EU nationals are interested in obtaining Belgian citizenship.

Figure 1.3 *Countries of origin of people naturalised in Belgium, 1980-2001*

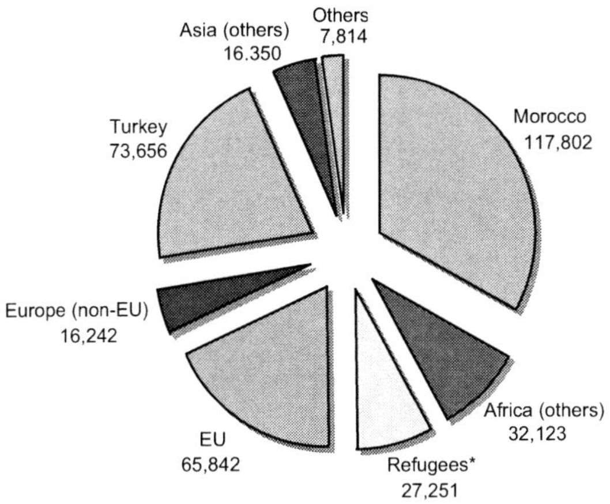

* Mostly originated from Africa

Source: Centre for Equal Opportunities and Opposition to Racism

The number of Belgian citizens abandoning their nationality to acquire another one remains consistently low, at around 100 per year. Belgian legislation does not currently allow dual citizenship. Therefore, in order to acquire a new citizenship, any Belgian national needs to abandon her/his Belgian nationality. This acts as a deterrent for many, who are afraid of losing some advantages and benefits. However, probably the most important reason is that most expatriates settle in a neighbouring European country, which makes the acquisition of a new citizenship quite useless, since they benefit, as EU citizens, from most of the advantages and benefits of the nationals (with the exception of voting rights in national elections). At the time of writing, a change in the legislation that would allow dual citizenship was due to be discussed in parliament.

1.7 Conclusions

Belgian statistics on immigration could be greatly improved if they were adapted to the development of society. Current statistics do not allow for the development of policies addressing discrimination and do not reflect the major changes that have occurred in Belgian society over the last decades. References to ethnicity or ethnic groups are not yet widely accepted and this unease is reflected in the statistics produced.

Most of the statistics are produced by the National Institute of Statistics, which can only produce statistics based on legal variables. These statistics are based on the National Register, which has not been seriously updated since 1988. Some improvements are easily feasible using existing data (including the country of birth as criterion in addition to nationality), while others would require a change in the legislation (e.g. statistics on filiation). For now, the sole use of the nationality criterion for statistical purposes does not take into account 45 per cent of the population of foreign descent. A major improvement would also be the production of more reliable data regarding visas, emigration and Belgians living abroad.

Nevertheless, the actual figures are quite reliable, often easily available and usually match the figures of Eurostat and UNHCR. They are centralised in the National Register and, since other data on migration are frequently checked against the National Register, the risk of discrepancies is rather limited.

However, the difference between the figures and the political and public discourse is striking. As one can see, European nationals constitute around 68 per cent of the foreign population. However, when referring to foreigners, media and political discourses often refer to the non-European nationals, despite the fact that they constitute a small minority of the foreign population. Moroccans and Turks are easy targets of anti-immigration discourse, though they constitute only a small minority of the foreign population. Likewise, the debate on discrimination often implies that discrimination ceases once Belgian nationality is acquired, which is far from being the case. No doubt the democratic debate on these matters would greatly benefit from improved and more publicly available statistics.

Note

1 The municipalities are not obliged to provide this information.

Statistical soures

Organisation	*Content*	*URL*
Aliens Bureau	– asylum claims – geographic distribution of the foreign population – unaccompanied minors	www.dofi.fgov.be
Centre for Equal Opportunities and Opposition to Racism	– immigration – naturalisation	www.diversiteit.be
Federal Agency for Asylum (Fedasil)	– asylum (excluding expulsions and deportations)	www.fedasil.be
King Baudouin Foundation	– asylum – labour market – collection of statistics in Belgium	www.kbs-frb.be
National Institute of Statistics	– national register – census	statbel.fgov.be

Bibliography

Carlier, J.-Y. & A. Rea (2001), 'Les étrangers en Belgique', *Dossiers du CRISP* 54.

Eggerickx, T., A. Bahri & N. Perrin (2006), *Migrations internationales et populations 'd'origine étrangère'. Approches staistiques et démographiques*. www.kbs-frb.be.

Eggerickx, T., N. Perrin & L. Thomsin (2007), 'Les sources statistiques et démographiques sur l'immigration et les populations étrangères en Belgique du 19ème siècle à nos jours', in M. Martiniello, F. Dassetto & A. Rea (eds.), *Immigration en Belgique francophone, l'état des savoirs*: 43-82. Brussels: Academia-Bruylant.

Lennert, M. (2001), *Flux migratoires de et vers la Belgique*. www.kbs-frb.be

Martiniello, M. & A. Rea (2001), *Et si on racontait... une histoire de l'immigration en Belgique*. Brussels: Communauté française.

Perrin, N. & M. Poulain (2006), 'Country Report: Belgium', in M. Poulain, N. Perrin & A. Singleton (eds.), *THESIM: Towards Harmonised European Statistics on International Migration*, 381-390. Louvain-la-Neuve: Presses universitaires de Louvain.

Perrin, N., L. Dal & M. Poulain (2007), 'Appréhender "objectivement" les origines pour lutter contre les discriminations en Belgique: alternatives méthodologiques et implications', paper presented at the Symposium 'Social Statistics and Ethnic Diversity', Montréal, 6-8 December 2007.

2 France

Xavier Thierry

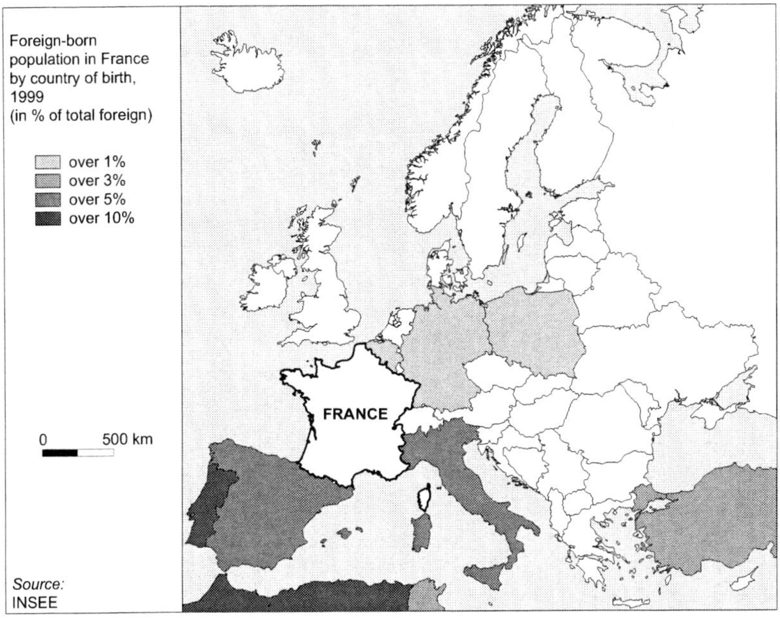

Cartography: Walter Lang, University of Vienna

2.1 Introduction

France has received successive waves of immigrants who arrived in the country from the second half of the nineteenth century in order to offset sluggish population growth. This demographic revolution, in combination with the industrial revolution, created a strong demand for new immigrant workers in France, a country of early fertility decline and early economic prosperity. This labour demand was satisfied by migrants from other European countries that were unable to support a more rapidly growing population, as these sending countries did not have enough jobs to offer their young adults.

Migration from Belgium, Italy, Poland and Spain peaked in the early twentieth century, though it continued after the Second World War.

During this period, migration was also influenced by a key political factor, namely the founding principles of the French nation – from the Universal Declaration of Human Rights in 1789 to the Constitution of 1958 – which guarantee asylum to victims of persecution. France was long perceived as a country of refuge and harboured populations fleeing totalitarian regimes in Russia, Nazi Germany, Italy under Mussolini, Spain under Franco, Portugal under Salazar and Southeast Asia, to name but a few.

The world wars of the twentieth century also created a need for immigrant inflows to make up for the human losses incurred and to contribute to reconstruction or, more generally, to meet the needs of industry. From 1946, after freedom of movement was granted to the Algerian population, a massive wave of 'French Muslim' workers arrived from Algeria. Heading a colonial empire, France was better placed than its neighbours to attract African populations after the Second World War. Hence, French populations of immigrant origin come from a wide range of geographical areas. The decolonisation process initiated in 1956 further increased immigration, with the return of populations of French descent from the lost territories. The most well-known wave of this kind was the repatriation of French settlers from Algeria in 1962-1963, though repatriates also came from Tunisia, Morocco and a part of sub-Saharan Africa.

With the rise in French unemployment after the oil crisis, as elsewhere in Europe, new legislation introduced in 1974 made it more difficult for immigrant workers to enter the country. However, this development coincided with the recognition of the right to family reunion, resulting in large-scale family migration, thanks to which net migration has never fallen to zero or below. The immigrant population has thus continued to grow at least as fast as the native population. However, the specific features of French migration trends mentioned above are tending to disappear since many former European sending countries have now in turn become receiving countries with a positive net balance. The key trend observed over recent years in France is a level of fertility that remains higher than elsewhere, a fact that reduces the importance of migration in population renewal. Only one-quarter of total population increase is due to migration, a very low proportion compared with other European countries, which are generally characterised by declining fertility and major immigration flows.

2.2 Overview of stock and flow data

Statistics on migrants in France are produced on the basis of census data and also as a by-product of various administrative sources. Among these, the census has by far the longest tradition, since questions related to the numbers of foreigners have been included in all censuses since the mid-nineteenth century. Conversely, administrative sources are quite recent: first statistics on annual migration were published in the 1970s but with very few details on demographic characteristics. Statistics on residence permits have been extracted since the mid-1990s, which has led to more reliable and relevant figures on migration. Obviously, as in most European countries, none of these statistical sources take into account foreigners who enter illegally, except if they are regularised after their entry, which implies that they will be counted, albeit after a certain delay. Neither do the sources include short-term migrants staying in France for less than one year (such as seasonal workers or rejected asylum applicants), which is in compliance with the UN recommendations for international migration statistics (Breem & Thierry 2006).

France does not have a population register. As a consequence, not all issues related to international migration are covered. There are no statistics on the inflows or outflows of French citizens. The same is true for the outflows of foreigners. The only flow statistics available are the entries of foreigners into France based on the numbers of first residence permits issued each year. No new data collection and no new registration processes are foreseen to redress this lack of information. Regarding statistics on stocks, the lack of a population register also limits the updating of the statistics for the years between successive censuses (the last ones were in 1990 and 1999). However, in 2009, statistics on stocks will be available on an annual basis. This continuous measurement will significantly improve the estimate of annual net migration compared to the indicator currently disseminated by the National Institute for Statistics and Economic Studies (INSEE).

2.2.1 *Census*

INSEE carries out the census. The last traditional census took place in 1999 and involved universal coverage and a simultaneous count. The achievement of the 1999 Census illustrates the difficulty of ensuring equal coverage from one census to the next. As a matter of fact, the population counted at the beginning of 1999 (58,497,000) was significantly below the expected figure previously published by the INSEE (58,977,000) by a margin of 480,000.

As of 2004, a new method of census has been in use, although the design of the questionnaire regarding migration issues is unchanged. The Redesigned Census of the Population (Recensement Rénové de la Population) is now a continuous annual census, which means that the population is no longer counted every eight or nine years, but by annual rotation over a five-year cycle (2004-2008, 2009-2013 and so on). It is conducted on a sample of dwellings, situated in geographical zones selected at random and enumerated comprehensively.[1] The continuous population census is a sample-based survey. However, the size of the sample is very large compared, for instance, to the German microcensus: it is foreseen that 14 per cent of the population will be interviewed each year so that around 70 per cent of the total population will have been enumerated at the end of the first cycle. Hence, reliable estimates are expected even if these more sophisticated methods are not as transparent as was the traditional census.

The statistics presented below refer to the 1990 and 1999 censuses, since only limited statistics based on the Redesigned Census have been published so far. The INSEE aims to complete a full five-year cycle before disseminating results. However, preliminary results show the opposite of the gap observed in 1999: the new census reported 460,000 people more than the current estimate. All these unexpected discrepancies between successive censuses and the lack of up to date estimates based on a continuous population register complicate the measurement of annual net migration.

Censuses cover all persons who have or wish to have their usual residence in France for a period of at least six months (including the temporarily absent declared by persons present in the household at the moment of the enumeration). In principle, this includes asylum applicants and illegal immigrants. However, as these groups are difficult to identify, they are probably underestimated in the resulting statistics.

The stock of population can be distributed by citizenship, country of birth or by a combination of both in order to identify 'immigrants'. The definition is as follows: an immigrant is a person born as a foreigner abroad and residing in the country. This means that a person who has acquired French nationality since arriving in France is still counted as an immigrant. Conversely, a person born a French national abroad is not an immigrant. That is also the case for those children born in France and defined as foreigners because both of their parents are foreigners. Because no information is gathered on the foreign background of people born in France indirect estimates are needed for this purpose (Tribalat 2004). However, the census includes a question on the country of residence at the time of the previous census. Moreover, since the 1999 Census people born abroad have been asked to indicate the year of their arrival in France.[2] A more extensive overview of characteristics of the foreign population is presented in INSEE 2005.

2.2.2 *Administrative sources*

Statistical monitoring of entries of foreigners into France improved substantially in the 1990s thanks to the use of a new data source. Before 1994 the production of aggregate immigration statistics was based on combining data resulting from the procedures of various administrative bodies. As a consequence, the data were weak in their coverage (for instance, nationals of the EU were not included). Since 1994, the Institut national d'études démographiques(INED) has been producing immigration statistics by extracting appropriate data from a centralised computer file administered by the Ministry of the Interior which lists residence permit issuances. These statistics are more reliable (including the arrivals of EU nationals, who only became exempt from the legal requirement to have a residence permit in 2004), fully disaggregated, as far as possible, and fulfil most of the international recommendations (United Nations 1998).

Indeed, the INED count differs from that provided by other French agencies which apply a restrictive definition of immigration, thus resulting in underestimation. A major example is the case of the student category; students are not taken into account in the latter statistics because they are considered temporary migrants, although many of them receive a residence permit for one year and have the legal right to renew it in order to pursue their studies (Thierry 2001). Moreover, as the official body in charge of this field, the Observatory of Statistics on Immigration and Integration publishes few detailed statistics (OSII 2006).

The figures presented in this report comply with the international recommendations for statistics on international migration, defining a 'long-term immigrant' as a person having his/her usual residence in the receiving country for at least one year. By counting the first permits issued to adult aliens for at least one year's duration as well as adding under-age children – who are exempt from the permit requirement – we can determine the number of aliens authorised to reside in France. Given the fact that first residence permits are automatically issued after the foreigners have entered the country, statistics cover the number of individual migrants rather than the number of cases. Of course, renewed residence permits are not taken into account in the total number of foreigners newly authorised to stay. In fact, this figure includes legal entries and foreigners regularised at the date of their admission. It excludes foreigners who are passing through, seasonal workers, asylum seekers awaiting a decision and illegal aliens.[3]

These annual statistics are broken down according to sex, age, citizenship and motive for granting a residence permit (see INED website). The official ground for admission mentioned on the residence permit is not a totally reliable indicator of the actual intention of the migrant. In particular, in certain restrictive contexts, the use of administrative data has shortcomings; labour migration occurs partly through the procedure for admission on family grounds and so the number of residence permits issued for work purposes represents only a small part of the phenomenon (Thierry 2007).

2.3 Description of the stock of foreign population

2.3.1 *Stock according to the 1999 Census*

At the beginning of 1999, the French census counted a population of 58.5 million people having their usual residence in France (excluding overseas French territories). As Table 2.1 indicates, 3.3 million of these did not hold French citizenship (5.6 per cent) and 5.9 million were born abroad (10 per cent). The number of French citizens (55.3 million) may be divided into those who are French by birth (52.9 million) and those who have acquired French citizenship after birth (2.4 million). This latter category is numerically significant, considering that France applies a double *ius soli,* which means that foreign children born in France of a parent already born in France automatically acquire French citizenship at birth. In France, as said before, the immigrant category is defined as those individuals born abroad having a foreign citizenship at birth, regardless of whether they are still foreigners or not. In 1999, there were 4.3 million immigrants in France: 2.75 million foreign citizens born abroad plus 1.56 million French citizens who acquired French citizenship after moving to France (within the total of 3.12 million French citizens born abroad). This number represents a share of 7.4 per cent of the total population. One immigrant out of three is no

Table 2.1 *Population in France by nationality and place of birth according to the 1999 Census*

	Place of birth in France	*Place of birth abroad*	*Total*
Numbers in 1,000			
Nationality French	52,140	3,120	55,260
Nationality foreign	0,510	2,750	3,260
Total	52,650	5,870	58,520
Of which:			
Immigrant	-	4,310	4,310
Numbers in %			
Nationality French	89.1	5.3	94.4
Nationality foreign	0.9	4.7	5.6
Total	90.0	10.0	100.0
Of which:			
Immigrant	-	7.4	7.4

Source: Census data, INSEE

longer a foreign citizen. No substantial increase has been observed compared to the five previous censuses: 4.2 million in 1990, 4.1 million in 1982, 3.9 million in 1975, 3.3 million in 1968 and 2.9 million in 1962. Due to the growth of the inflows in recent years (see below), preliminary data provided by the first wave of the 2004 Census show a significant increase, equivalent to 14 per cent of the stock (+600.000). Currently, the immigrant population (4.9 million) represents a share of 8.1 per cent of the population (Borrel 2006).

Concerning the countries of origin of the stocks of the foreign-born in France, the situation changed slowly between the early 1990s and 2004. Table 2.2 presents the ten major countries of birth as enumerated in the three last censuses. Most immigrants living in France still originate from Southern Europe and North Africa. In 1999, the five main countries of birth for immigrants were Algeria, Portugal, Morocco, Italy and Spain. More than half a million individuals originated from the first three countries, more than 300,000 from either Italy or Spain. People originating from these five countries constituted 50.4 per cent of all foreign-born in France in 2004. In the years 1999 and 1990, this share was a little higher, at 54.7 and 59.0 per cent, respectively.

Due to the decline of the number of migrants from South European countries of origin and the increase of the new wave from Africa and

Table 2.2 *Country of origin of French immigrant population in 1990, 1999 and 2004-2005*

	Foreign-born population in 1990		*Foreign-born population in 1999*		*Foreign-born population in 2004-2005*	
Country of birth	*Abs.*	%	*Abs.*	%	*Abs.*	%
Portugal	600,000	14.4	572,000	13.2	565,000	11.5
Italy	484,000	11.6	379,000	8.8	342,000	6.9
Spain	397,000	9.5	316,000	7.3	280,000	5.7
Portugal + Italy + Spain	1,481,000	35.5	1,267,000	29.3	1,187,000	24.1
Turkey	168,000	4.0	174,000	4.0	225,000	4.6
Germany	114,000	2.7	123,000	2.8	128,000	2.6
Poland	129,000	3.1	99,000	2.3	90,000	1.8
Belgium	92,000	2.2	93,000	2.2	102,000	2.1
Algeria	558,000	13.4	574,000	13.3	677,000	13.7
Morocco	457,000	11.0	523,000	12.1	619,000	12.6
Tunisia	207,000	5.0	202,000	4.7	220,000	4.5
Algeria + Morocco + Tunisia	1,222,000	29.3	1,299,000	30.1	1,516,000	30.8
Other African country	273,000	6.6	393,000	9.1	570,000	11.6
Other country	687,000	16.5	872,000	20.2	1,106,000	22.5
Total	4,166,000	100.0	4,310,000	100.0	4,924,000	100.0

Source: INSEE

Asia, the foreign population diversified. Indeed, the ranking of the top five was different in 1990 when migrants from Portugal were more numerous than those from Algeria. Between 1990 and 1999 the order was reversed, with the latter being the main immigrant community in France with 574.000 persons in 1999. The same is true for Italy and Morocco: the former was the third biggest group in 1990, immediately followed by migrants from Morocco. In 1999, there were more immigrants of Moroccan than of Italian origin. In 2004, Portugal fell to the third position, immediately preceded by Morocco. In addition, the percentage of North Africans (representing 29.3 per cent of the total foreign-born in 1990, against 30.1 per cent in 1999 and 30.8 per cent in 2004) grew to a lesser extent than the percentage of other Africans (6.6 per cent, 9.1 per cent and 11.6 per cent, respectively).Their number became significant in 2004 (570,000), although these were distributed through a large range of countries (mainly the French-speaking area with Senegal and Mali being the most important).

These changes were due, on the one hand, to the ageing – which would imply an increase in mortality – of the population that settled after the Second World War and, on the other hand, to the new geographical distribution of the recent migration flows (as described below). These two factors explain why the share of the Italian and Spanish stream decreased. As a matter of fact, the populations that arrived in France first showed the highest proportion of people over 60 (almost 60 per cent for Italian and Polish and around 50 per cent for Spanish migrants). Moreover, a significant share of these three immigrant groups were women, since a long time had elapsed since their first arrival and family reunification had largely been completed (females outnumbered males for the three latter countries of origin). People originating from Maghreb countries and Turkey demonstrated a very different demographic profile, characterised by limited proportions of 60+ and females. For instance, only 23.6 per cent of migrants from Algeria were older than 60 and 43.8 per cent of them were female. The low percentage of old migrants from Portugal (14.6 per cent) – although they arrived 30 years ago – can be traced back to their marked tendency to return after having retired. Migrants from Germany and Belgium demonstrated an age structure lying between the two extremes due to the freedom of circulation (Table 2.3).

The census does not include questions on the reasons for migration. However, according to a large survey linked to the 1999 Census, which gathered more detailed information on the life course of immigrants, 61 per cent of the immigrant population arrived after the age of eighteen and were already with a spouse or a partner (living in France or abroad at the time of their entry) (Tavan 2005). The majority of the respondents migrated for family reasons. Even for males, who had tradi-

Table 2.3 *Age, sex and length of stay of foreign-born population in France in 1999*

Country of origin	*% of 60 +*	*% of female*	*Median year of arrival*
Italy	59.6	50.8	1957
Poland	58.6	65.0	1960
Spain	51.8	55.0	1961
Portugal	14.6	48.7	1970
Algeria	23.6	43.8	1972
Tunisia	23.2	42.5	1972
Morocco	11.4	45.6	1978
Germany	36.3	61.3	1979
Turkey	7.6	47.0	1981
Belgium	37.2	58.0	1981
Total	24.1	49.7	1972

Source: INSEE

tionally left their country to find a job, this figure reached 48 per cent (73 per cent for females). The difficulty of identifying the actual motive for migration is further illustrated by the gap between the above survey and a similar survey conducted in one of the sending countries. In Morocco, 70 per cent of the candidates for migration declared that they intended to leave for economic reasons, whereas only 12 per cent put forward family reasons (Hamdouch & Khachani 2007). This discrepancy reveals that a given person may have multiple reasons for migrating; thus, it is difficult to identify the real motive for migration.

The comparison of the foreign-born population from one census to another shows a limited development compared to a larger historical perspective which also includes the descendants of immigrants; this larger perspective illustrates how the migration patterns have changed over several generations. The population with a migratory background is not directly counted in the census. It is estimated through the Study of Family History (EHF) survey, which was conducted in 1999 and gathered information on country of birth of parents and grandparents, combined with information on parental linguistic practices during the early childhood of the respondents (Tribalat 2004). According to this study, 9.2 million persons born in France had at least one immigrant parent (the so-called 'second generation') or grandparent ('third generation'). All in all, nearly 14 million persons (23 per cent of the total population) living in France in 1999 had a migratory background.

Table 2.4 illustrates that more than 40 per cent of the parents and grandparents of the native population with a foreign background originated from Southern Europe, namely Italy (23.7 per cent), Spain (12.5 per cent) and Portugal (6.2 per cent), whereas only 18.5 per cent had parents and grandparents from North Africa. Tribalat pointed out that 'public debate in France in recent years has been prompt to equate the

Table 2.4 *Country of origin of French immigrant population and its offspring in 1999*

	Foreign-born population		*'Second and third generation'*		*Total population of foreign origin*	
Country of birth or parental birth	*Abs.*	*%*	*Abs.*	*%*	*Abs.*	*%*
Portugal	572,000	13.3	572,000	6.2	1,144,000	8.5
Italy	379,000	8.8	2,178,000	23.7	2,557,000	19.0
Spain	316,000	7.3	1,148,000	12.5	1,464,000	10.9
Portugal + Italy + Spain	1,267,000	29.4	3,898,000	42.5	5,165,000	38.3
Other EU	363,000	8.4	1,439,000	15.7	1,802,000	13.4
Turkey	174,000	4.0	148,000	1.6	322,000	2.4
Algeria	574,000	13.3	1,003,000	10.9	1,577,000	11.7
Morocco	523,000	12.1	482,000	5.3	1,005,000	7.5
Tunisia	202,000	4.7	215,000	2.3	417,000	3.1
Algeria + Morocco + Tunisia	1,299,000	30.1	1,700,000	18.5	2,999,000	22.2
Other African country	393,000	9.1	286,000	3.1	679,000	5.0
Other country	812,000	18.8	1,702,000	18.6	2,514,000	18.6
Total	4,310,000	100.0	9,172,000	100.0	13,482,000	100.0

Sources: INSEE; INED

population of foreign origin with its Maghrebin component. Yet individuals of Maghrebin origin belonging to the three generations studied here represent only around three million persons, or just 22 per cent of the total foreign-origin population [...] Among those of Maghrebin origin, slightly more than half are immigrants or descendants of immigrants from Algeria' (Tribalat 2004: 64).

However, the population with an African background is expected to grow in the future due to the increasing inflow of the foreign-born of this origin, combined with their higher fertility rate.

The foreign-born population residing in France was older than the native-born due to the fact that the majority of immigrants were aged eighteen or above when they left their country of origin. The proportion of immigrants that was under eighteen years old amounted to 6 per cent, whereas minors constituted 20 per cent of those born in France (Table 2.5). Conversely, people aged over 60 were over-represented in the immigrant category. On the other hand, the proportion of minors among those born in France with at least a parent or a grandparent born abroad ('second' and 'third' generation) was higher than among natives without migratory background: every third native with foreign origin was under eighteen years old (20 per cent in the case of natives without foreign origin). According to Tribalat's estimate, 60 per cent of

Table 2.5 *Native and foreign-born population in France by sex and age according to the 1999 Census (in per cent)*

	Born in France				Foreign-born			
	Male		Female		Male		Female	
	Total	Of which second + third generation	Total	Of which second + third generation	Total	Of which not born in EU-14	Total	Of which not born in EU-14
Under 18	24.4	33.6	21.8	32.1	6.1	7.6	6.0	8.0
18-39	31.9	37.0	29.6	36.7	31.6	36.2	34.7	42.4
40-59	25.5	22.0	24.7	21.7	38.8	38.6	34.7	33.6
60 or over	18.2	7.5	23.8	9.5	23.5	17.6	24.6	16.0
Total	100.0	100.0	100.0	100.0	100.0	100.0	100.0	100.0

Sources: INSEE; INED

these second- and third-generation minors had African and Turkish backgrounds. By contrast, the parents and grandparents of those aged 60 and above usually originated from European countries; indeed, 'the higher the age, the higher the proportion of persons originating from an EU country outside southern Europe. This attests in particular to the effects of the much older Belgian immigration, of the late nineteenth and early twentieth century' (Tribalat 2004: 68).

There were only minor differences on the basis of sex when considering the age structure of the population with a foreign origin, except for the fact that there were, due to their lower mortality, more old women (9.5 versus 7.5 per cent). However, if we consider the foreign-born population, there was a clear trend towards feminisation in migration flows, especially for those originating from outside the EU. Accordingly, the proportion of women aged eighteen to 39 was higher than those among men (42.4 versus 36.2), whereas the opposite was true for those aged 40-59 (33.6 versus 38.6). As a result of the growth in female migration and their longer life expectancy, the stock of the foreign-born in 2004 was balanced, with an equal number of both sexes after a long period of predominantly male migration.

2.3.2 *Naturalisations, births and deaths*

The number of foreigners acquiring French citizenship per year was frequently under the 100,000 mark until the mid-1990s (Table 2.6). At the turn of the millennium, nearly 150,000 persons per year changed their legal status in France; this increase was confirmed in more recent years with almost 170,000 new citizens in 2004. Foreign immigration flows were more or less offset by the acquisitions of nationality, which explains the relative stability of foreign population stocks over

Table 2.6 *Naturalisations in France according to former citizenship and legal basis*

	Total	Of which				Previous country of citizenship					
		Based on length of residence		Based on marriage		Africa		EU Member States		Asia and Oceania	
		Abs.	%	Abs.	%	Abs.	%	Abs.	%	Abs.	%
1990	64,991	34,889	53.7	15,627	24.0	23,099	35.5	22,543	34.7	11,202	17.2
1991	72,242	39,445	54.6	16,333	22.6	29,184	40.4	11,971	16.6	11,565	16.0
1992	71,601	39,346	55.0	15,601	21.8	32,094	44.8	9,090	12.7	11,273	15.7
1993	98,170	35,988	36.7	15,246	15.5	33,738	34.4	8,292	8.4	11,309	11.5
1994	126,337	44,008	34.8	19,493	15.4	44,761	35.4	9,843	7.8	13,943	11.0
1995	92,410	36,280	39.3	16,659	18.0	49,111	53.1	18,373	19.9	16,344	17.7
1996	109,823	50,730	46.2	19,127	17.4	59,722	54.4	18,063	16.4	21,363	19.5
1997	116,194	53,189	45.8	20,845	17.9	62,470	53.8	19,833	17.1	22,222	19.1
1998	123,761	51,303	41.5	22,113	17.9	59,788	48.3	16,140	13.0	20,220	16.3
1999	145,522	59,836	41.1	24,088	16.6	80,434	55.3	17,547	12.1	25,621	17.6
2000	150,025	68,750	45.8	26,056	17.4	84,179	56.1	14,948	10.0	28,042	18.7
2001	127,548	57,627	45.2	23,994	18.8	74,941	58.8	12,267	9.6	22,536	17.7
2002	128,092	56,942	44.5	26,351	20.6	76,468	59.7	11,642	9.1	22,008	17.2
2003	144,640	69,272	47.9	30,922	21.4	88,817	61.4	12,444	8.6	23,710	16.4
2004	168,826	87,497	51.8	34,440	20.4	106,501	63.1	13,470	8.0	27,500	16.3

Sources: Ministry of Employment, Labour and Social Cohesion; Ministry of Justice

time. In 1999, 5 per cent of the estimated total foreign population in France were naturalised. With its *ius soli* tradition, France grants a significant number of naturalisations on the basis of the period of time spent within the country (legal requirement of at least five years). This holds true for 51.8 per cent of the decisions in 2004 (against 34.8 per cent in 1994). An increasing number of foreigners acquired French citizenship on the grounds of marriage with a French spouse (after two years of marriage); this number increased from around 20,000 in 1994 to 34,000 ten years later (20.4 per cent of all decisions). Not all of those who acquire French citizenship are immigrants. In fact, 41.9 per cent of the people who were granted citizenship in 2003 were born in France. These are mostly children of non-national parents, who can claim French citizenship from the age of thirteen. In 2004, the descendants of migrants born in France who acquired French citizenship before the age of eighteen represented 20 per cent of all decisions. As a consequence, the average age of those acquiring French nationality was comparatively low (25 years), with those born in France being on average fifteen years and the partners in mixed couples being on average 31 years when they acquired French nationality. The sex ratio is balanced, with 49.6 per cent of males being granted French nationality in 2002.

More than 60 per cent of the people who acquired nationality in 2004 were citizens of an African country (among these 50 per cent were from North Africa). This share was equivalent to the proportion of African citizens in inflow statistics. Naturalisations among EU citizens have been declining, as they are no longer convinced of the advantages of this procedure.

In order to get a more complete picture of the demographic significance of the foreign population in France, we also need to consider statistics on births, deaths and marriages (Table 2.7). Between 1999 and 2004, about 52,000 foreign children (i.e. those whose parents were both foreigners at the time of the children's births) were born each year (6.8 per cent of the total number of births), while annually, roughly 23,000 foreigners died over the same period of time (4.3 per cent of all deaths). Thus, the natural balance for foreigners was clearly positive due to the young structure of the foreign population.

While births and deaths of foreigners did not change significantly compared to the figures for the 1990s, an increasing effect of migration is visible in the statistics on marriages, especially for those involving a French person and a foreigner.[4] Between 1999 and 2003, these specific couples accounted for 13.7 per cent of the total number of marriages (16.2 per cent including marriages between two foreigners) against 10 per cent over the previous decade. As a consequence, births from mixed parentage including one French partner rose sharply, accounting for 9.2 per cent of children born at the turn of the millennium against 5.6 per cent previously. These children acquire French citizenship at birth, whereas those born of foreign parents may only acquire it after having turned thirteen. All in all, children born from at

Table 2.7 *Births, marriages and deaths relating to the foreign population in France*

		1990-1998	*1999-2003*
Births of foreign children	Total	500,661	260,359
	Annual average	55,629	52,072
	% (/a)	7.6	6.8
Deaths of foreigners	Total	188,932	114,507
	Annual average	20,992	22,901
	% (/b)	4.0	4.3
Marriages between foreign citizens	Total	59,941	36,185
	Annual average	6,660	7,237
	% (/c)	2.5	2.5
Marriages between French and foreign citizens	Total	243,652	195,710
	Annual average	27,072	39,142
	% (/c)	10.0	13.7
Births of children one of whose parents is French	Total	372,455	351,075
	Annual average	41,384	70,215
	% (/a)	5.6	9.2

Denominator: total of (a) births, (b) deaths, (c) marriages
Source: INSEE, Statistics of civil registration

least one foreign parent now represent 16 per cent of all births in France. In 2005, foreign women had a fertility rate of 3.3 births per women (2.8 in 1999), which is higher than the index for French nationals (1.8). However, foreign women contribute less than 0.1 per cent to the total number of births. With or without immigration, fertility in France is among the highest in Europe (see Heran & Pison 2007).

Between the last two traditional censuses in 1990 and 1999 more than 500,000 foreign children were born and 189,000 foreigners died (natural balance equal to 310,000). As we will see below, one million foreigners entered France, whereas 850,000 persons acquired French citizenship, yielding a net difference of 150,000. This means that the number of foreigners in France should have increased by about 460,000 (excluding outflows as these are not counted). The censuses, on the other hand, counted 3.6 million foreigners in 1990 and only 3.3 million in 1999. This would mean that around 800,000 foreigners left France over this period of nine years if the data from the two censuses are comparable. However, according to the statistical office the population was probably underestimated in 1999 compared to 1990 (fewer double counts and more omissions).

2.4 Description of flows

The only data available on migration among French people are statistics from the Ministry of Foreign Affairs counting those registered in the consulates. This number increased from 821,000 in 1991 to 1,100,000 in 2002, giving an annual growth rate of 2.7 per cent. However, these data indicate a general trend rather than the exact stock of French population living abroad, since the incentives to register are low, especially in developed countries where there are no security considerations. Nevertheless, it is estimated that between 1.5 and 2 million French citizens live abroad (Gentil 2003). Moreover, the geographical distribution of the registered population changed considerably over the 1990s. While the number of French citizens registered in the French-speaking countries in Africa decreased, their registrations in other European and in North American countries increased. This implies that French emigration probably rose considerably more over the 1990s than was indicated by the official figures.

As shown in Table 2.8, immigration to France, measured solely on the basis of the number of foreigners obtaining their first residence permit valid for one year or more, increased almost continuously between 1997 and 2004, after declining between 1994 and 1995 when 120,000 and 106,000 foreigners, respectively, were admitted for legal residence. This number was stabilised until 1996 (106,000). The num-

Table 2.8 *Inflow of foreign nationals to France (legal long-term immigration), 1994-2004*

	Total	Annual growth rate (%)	EEA nationals	Third-country nationals, of which:			
				Total	Africa	Asia*	America
1994	119,563		47,697	71,866	34,748	13,123	9,797
1995	106,180	-11.2	44,423	61,757	28,610	11,177	9,216
1996	105,986	-0.2	43,258	62,728	29,343	11,447	9,352
1997	127,431	+20.2	41,306	86,125	46,615	14,972	10,256
1998	155,879	+22.3	43,033	112,846	64,884	19,668	11,255
1999	145,120	-6.9	42,791	102,329	54,006	17,759	11,499
2000	160,428	+10.5	43,282	117,146	64,181	21,001	12,776
2001	182,694	+13.9	42,552	140,142	78,753	25,234	14,083
2002	205,707	+12.6	42,744	162,963	94,317	29,027	14,682
2003	215,397	+4.7	42,085	173,312	101,658	30,346	14,958
2004	210,076	-2.5	43,217**	166,859	100,567	21,310	14,917

* Turkey is not counted as part of Asia but as part of Europe (not listed in this table).
** Includes the new ten EU Member States (in third-country category before).
Sources: Ministry of the Interior; OMI (Office des Migrations Internationales, now called Agence Nationale d'Accueil des Étrangers et des Migrations (ANAEM)); data processed by INED (see Thierry 2004)

ber admitted rose in 1997 (127,000) and especially so in 1998 (156,000). However, the end of the special regularisation programme in 1998 was not followed by a large reduction in the number of foreigners entering France in 1999 (145,000 against 156,000 in 1998). The upward trend continued in 2000 (160,000), accelerated in 2001 (183,000) and was confirmed in 2002 (206,000) and 2003 (215,000). The peak reached as a consequence of the regularisation in 1998 was thus exceeded as of 2000, and the number registered in 2003 was the highest since immigration of foreign workers was officially suspended in 1974. Immigration flows, all ages and nationalities combined, grew at a rate of 10.5 per cent in 2000, 13.9 per cent in 2001, 12.6 per cent in 2002 and 4.7 per cent in 2003.

Inflows of nationals originating from the European Economic Area varied little between 1994 and 2004, accounting for approximately 43,000 people annually. The general increase in immigration flows to France therefore resulted from that of third-country nationals. With 173,000 entrants in 2003, they represented the largest share of the total inflow (80 per cent). Their proportion of total admissions for residence grew continuously over the period under discussion, but their number was subject to sharp variations. Between 1996 and 1997, it rose by over 37 per cent thanks to the programme that regularised the status of several tens of thousands of foreigners, then it fell by 9 per cent between 1998 and 1999 when this programme ended; it rose by over 20 per cent between 2000 and 2001 helped by favourable economic conditions, and rose again by nearly 6 per cent in 2003.

Nationals of African countries reinforced their position at the top of the classification of immigration flows by geographical origin, accounting for 47.9 per cent of total admissions for residence in 2004 (27.7 per cent in 1996, Table 2.9). As illustrated in Table 2.9, nationals of the North African (*Maghreb*) countries still accounted for two-thirds of African immigration (66.9 per cent in 2003), far ahead of migrants from the countries of sub-Saharan Africa formerly under French rule (25.7 per cent). Asian (12.2 per cent in 1999, 14.1 per cent in 2003) and American (7.9 per cent and 6.9 per cent, respectively) immigrants were far behind. The eight main countries of origin for foreigners admitted for residence in 2003 were Algeria (33,000), Morocco (25,000),

Table 2.9 *Inflow of foreign nationals to France (legal long-term immigration) for selected years and countries of origin*

Citizenship	*1994*	*1996*	*1998*	*2000*	*2002*	*2003*	*2004*
Citizenship eligible for free circulation (EEA)	47,697	43,258	43,033	43,282	42,744	42,085	40,000
UK	9,267	8,021	7,712	7,850	9,444	10,834	-
Portugal	9,124	7,522	5,899	6,530	6,601	7,791	-
Germany	9,531	8,155	8,020	7,464	6,647	5,959	-
Belgium	3,880	4,005	4,267	4,746	4,762	4,200	-
Other European citizenship	13,519	10,954	16,289	18,630	24,278	25,712	-
New EU-10 Member States	2,276	2,251	2,899	3,313	4,242	4,426	3,217
Turkey	4,456	3,165	5,723	5,814	7,706	7,544	7,701
Maghreb	23,029	18,746	36,138	40,953	63,107	68,040	65,695
Morocco	9,267	7,669	16,243	21,507	26,177	24,948	24,014
Algeria	10,911	8,469	14,523	12,760	27,936	32,596	31,846
Tunisia	2,851	2,608	5,372	6,686	8,994	10,496	9,835
Other African countries	11,720	10,597	28,746	23,228	31,210	33,617	34,826
Senegal	1,249	1,257	3,175	3,422	4,163	3,907	3,920
Cameroon	675	768	1,798	2,039	3,190	3,724	4,123
Côte d'Ivoire	812	958	2,020	2,187	3,009	3,594	3,913
Democratic Rep. of Congo	1,293	785	3,620	1,369	2,426	2,650	2,935
Asia	13,123	11,447	19,668	21,001	29,027	30,346	29,310
China	1,358	1,047	5,565	5,036	8,968	8,887	8,329
Japan	2,457	2,562	2,621	3,154	3,118	3,229	3,260
America	9,797	9,352	11,255	12,776	14,682	14,958	14,917
US	4,484	4,645	4,447	4,598	4,632	4,416	4,617
Total	119,563	105,986	155,879	160,428	205,707	215,397	210,076

Sources: Ministry of the Interior; OMI; calculation by INED (for more data see www.ined.fr)

the UK and Tunisia (both 11,000), China (9,000), Turkey and Portugal (both 8,000) and Germany (6,000). Individuals from the eight main emigration countries to France represented 52.1 per cent of the total number admitted for residence in 2002, compared with 44.9 per cent in 1999 and 51.6 per cent in 1994. The diversification in immigrant origins that was observed in earlier years appears to have stopped.

Over the period between 1999 and 2001, the sex ratio of the immigrants from third countries was almost balanced, with 102 females per 100 males entering the country. This stands in stark contrast to the mid-1990s, when the share of women coming to France was far higher. The shift to a more balanced sex ratio in France shows that the feminisation of immigration is not an irreversible trend, as is often postulated. However, the sex ratio differed massively between the types of permits granted. While work permit holders were mainly men (only 45 females per 100 males among the third-country nationals), family members were predominantly women. However, there was a clear difference between family members of foreign nationals (218 females per 100 males) and those of French nationals for whom the sex ratio was more balanced (117 females per 100 males). This latter difference illustrates the new strategies to enter France developed by males in the context of restricted labour immigration. Moreover, male students outnumber female (90 females per 100 males).

The only French information available on the motives for migration to France is the official grounds for admission for residence indicated on the permit (Figure 2.1). The official number of labour migrants who

Figure 2.1 *Grounds for issuance of first residence permits in France*

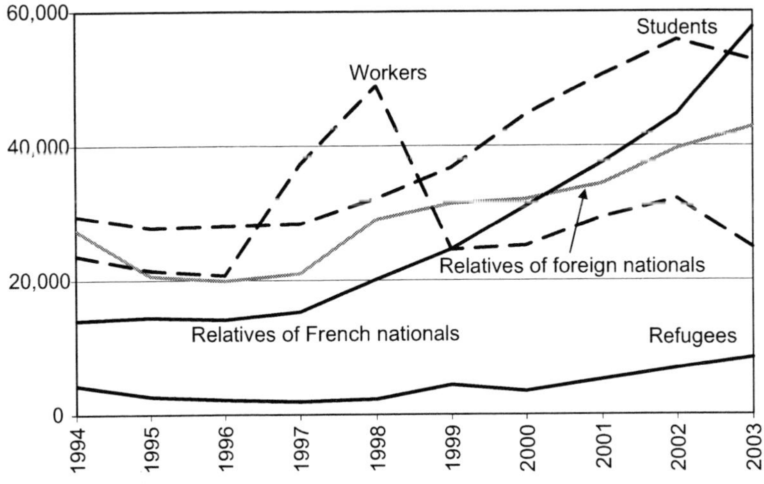

Sources: Ministry of the Interior; OMI; calculation by INED

entered the country in 2003 was similar to 1994, whereas the numbers of foreigners who were granted permits to join their family or to pursue studies soared. After 2000, the traditional family reunification mode involving two foreign partners was superseded by a new type of family migration where a foreigner joined a French partner. This rise may, on the one hand, be related to the restrictive labour immigration policy, which encouraged candidates to find new entry channels. On the other hand, it may be linked to a growing 'second generation' in France now at the age to get married, possibly to a partner of the same origin.

However, the official reason for the stay does not always describe the actual intentions of the immigrants. In particular, labour migration (officially controlled) occurs partly through the procedures for admission on family grounds, since holders of a residence permit granted for family reasons are allowed to work without having to undergo any further administrative procedures. The difficulties of getting a work permit which arose when politicians tried to limit such flows due to the high level of unemployment encouraged people to seek other grounds for admission. Moreover, the administrative procedure for granting the residence permit may introduce some bias into the classification. An example is the regularisation programme of 1997 and 1998, where the residence permits issued were work permits, although the family links were considered an important pre-condition for admission. This is why the relative shares of the official grounds for immigration had to be corrected to get a more realistic statistical estimation (see Thierry 2007). According to these corrected figures, employment was still the main reason for entering France in the period between 1999 and 2001 (38 per cent rather than 16 per cent according to the number of work permits issued), followed by studies (27 per cent) and family reunification (20 per cent instead of 39 per cent when all residence permits mentioning a family reason are counted).

Despite the lack of information on several types of international migration (especially outflows of foreigners and inflows of French citizens), INSEE estimates annual net migration based on some assumptions and information provided by the census (Table 2.10). However, these figures have to be used with caution since they have not been adjusted to reflect the rise in the population in 2004 and 2005 and have been frequently modified over the last years. INSEE estimates that net migration was roughly 100,000 people at the beginning of this millennium. Compared to the natural balance, which amounted to about 250,000, net migration is thus moderate.

Table 2.10 *Annual demographic estimates for France, 1995-2005*

	Natural balance	Net migration		Adjustment	
		a	b	b	c
1995	198,000	40,000		-55,000	
1996	199,000	35,000		-54,000	
1997	196,000	40,000		-54,000	
1998	204,000	45,000		-51,000	
1999	207,000	45,000	60,000	+33,000	+65,000
2000	244,000	50,000	70,000	+33,000	+63,000
2001	240,000	60,000	85,000	+33,000	+61,000
2002	227,000	65,000	95,000	+33,000	+64,000
2003	211,000	55,000	100,000	+33,000	+62,000
2004	256,000		105,000		
2005			95,000		

Sources: INSEE, (a) 'Bilan démographique 2003'; (b) 'Enquêtes annuelles du recensement'; (c) 'Bilan démographique 2005'

2.5 Conclusion

Between the second half of the 1990s and 2003, migration flows intensified in France, as testified by the doubling of the number of incoming aliens between 1996 and 2003 and the unconfirmed increase in the number of French nationals living abroad. So France is not completely turned in upon itself, as some observers would claim. It is true that the number of foreigners or immigrants rose little during the 1990s. Nonetheless, the latest census results have sparked considerable debate and several specialists outside the statistical office claim that immigrant populations were under-estimated in 1999. Indeed, the many enumerations conducted since 2004 tend to confirm this assumption and the statistical office has made upward adjustments to population stocks in the light of initial results. It is also true that the figure of 215,000 incoming foreigners in 2003 was very modest in comparison with 593,000 in Spain, 602,000 in Germany and 393,000 in Italy recorded for the same year. But in fact, these countries experienced the migration revolution that took place in France some years earlier. The new receiving countries mainly attracted labour immigrants, while the immigration flows to France were made up of persons entering the country to join populations who had arrived in previous waves or even populations who were born in France though preferred to choose a partner from their country of origin.

This difference in position in the migration cycle between France and its neighbours explains the current debate in France over the political will to control not so much immigration volumes but rather the characteristics and the duration of stay of new immigrants. The political authorities have coined the notion of 'actively selected' immigration in preference to 'passively accepted' immigration in order to highlight the fact that labour shortages in certain sectors (hotels and the construction industry) cannot be effectively remedied due to a lack of legal provisions permitting the selection of certain types of economic immigrants, while at the same time, by virtue of respect for family life, the country welcomes large numbers of persons who do not necessarily wish to take up such jobs. Based on this distinction, a new law that came into force in July 2006 aims to control the duration of stay of incoming foreigners by granting shorter residence permits both to workers, in order to encourage seasonal and highly qualified labour migration, and to family members who, with each legislative amendment, are subject to an increasingly lengthy bureaucratic process before finally obtaining a long-term (ten-year) permit. This new migration policy is combined with the creation of an assimilation and integration contract which obliges new immigrants to abide by social rules and to receive linguistic or occupational training. The decision to extend their residence permit may depend upon their compliance with these requirements.

Within a decade, politicians have made a U-turn with regard to immigration. In the early 1990s, when the number of asylum seekers peaked in France, political refugees were commonly suspected of being economic migrants in disguise, so measures were taken to restrict their access to the labour market. Today, though unemployment has not fallen in the meantime, regrets are being expressed regarding France's lack of appeal for foreign workers.

Notes

1 A computerised register of addresses of dwellings existing on the territory of large municipalities is continuously updated and records all demolitions and newly built houses. These files differ from a register based on households in the sense that the former does not include the numbers of people per address. Consequently, such a sample of dwellings is not biased by the underestimation of new inhabitants as could be the case in surveys based on a population register. It is therefore to be expected that, statistically speaking, the migrant populations will be accurately represented.

2 However, a significant share (20 per cent) of potential respondents did not reply. It has been shown that non-response was not correlated with particular characteristics (see Thierry 2003).

3 Statistics on asylum seekers are not included in this report due to the uncertainty of their length of stay in the country, although they are available in specific publications (see OFPRA website).

4 Of course, marriages of two partners with different citizenships are not automatically mixed, nor are marriages between French spouses non-mixed. Indicators for intermarriage should be measured through information on the country of birth of the spouses' parents. However, these data have not been updated since the large survey on integration processes among immigrants and their descendants conducted in 1992 (Tribalat 1995, 1996).

Statistical sources

Organisation	*Content*	*URL*
National Institute for Demographic Studies (INED)	– annual flows of foreign immigration (1994-2003)	www.ined.fr
French Office for the Protection of Refugees and Stateless (OFPRA)	– asylum applications – recognised refugees	www.ofpra.gouv.fr
National Institute for Statistics and Economic Studies (INSEE)	– census	www.recensement.insee.fr

Bibliography

Borrel, C. (2006), 'Enquêtes annuelles de recensement 2004 et 2005. Près de 5 millions d'immigrés à la mi-2004', INSEE-Premières, 1098. www.insee.fr.

Breem, Y. & X. Thierry (2006), 'Country Report: France', in M. Poulain, N. Perrin & A. Singleton (eds.), *THESIM: Towards Harmonised European Statistics on International Migration*, 457-466. Louvain-la-Neuve: Presses universitaires de Louvain.

Gentil, B. (2003), 'La population française immatriculée à l'étranger est en forte hausse', *Insee-Première* 919. www.insee.fr.

Héran, F.& G. Pison (2007), 'Two children per women in France in 2006: are immigrants to blame?', *Population and societies* 432. www.ined.fr.

Hamdouch, B. & M. Khachani (2007), 'Les déterminants de l'émigration internationale au Maghreb', *Les migrations internationales. Observation, analyse et perspective*, 209-222. www.aidelf.org.

INSEE (2005), *Les immigrés en France*. www.insee.fr

OSII (Observatoire des statistiques de l'immigration et de l'intégration) (2006), 'Rapport statistique 2002-2004', in Haut Conseil de la Intégration (ed.), *Le bilan de la politique d'intégration 2002-2005*, 183-284. www.ladocumentationfrancaise.fr

Tavan, C. (2005), 'Les calendriers de constitution de la famille: quelle différences entre les immigrés et l'ensemble de la population', in C. Lefèvre & A. Filhon (eds.), *Histoires de familles, histoire familiales*, 443-460. Paris: INED.

Thierry, X. (2001), 'Fréquences de renouvellement des titres de séjour', *Population* 3: 449-466.

Thierry, X. (2003), 'L'année d'arrivée en France: apport d'une nouvelle question au recensement de 1999', paper presented at the Conference of European Statisticians, ECE-Eurostat, Geneva, 28-30 April 2003.

Thierry, X. (2004), 'Recent immigration trends in France and elements for a comparison with the United Kingdom', *Population* 5: 635-672.

Thierry, X. (2007), 'L'utilisation des micro-données relatives à la délivrance des titres de séjour en France: un changement de cap?', *Les migrations internationales. Observation, analyse et perspective*, 109-120. www.aidelf.org.

Tribalat, M. (1995), *Faire France*. Paris: La découverte.

Tribalat, M. (1996), *De l'immigration à l'assimilation, Enquête sur les populations d'origine étrangère en France*. Paris: La Découverte/INED.

Tribalat, M. (2004), 'An estimation of the foreign-origin population of France in 1999', *Population* 1: 51-82.

United Nations (1998), *Recommendations on statistics of international migration*. Revision 1. New York: United Nations.

3 United Kingdom

François Gemenne

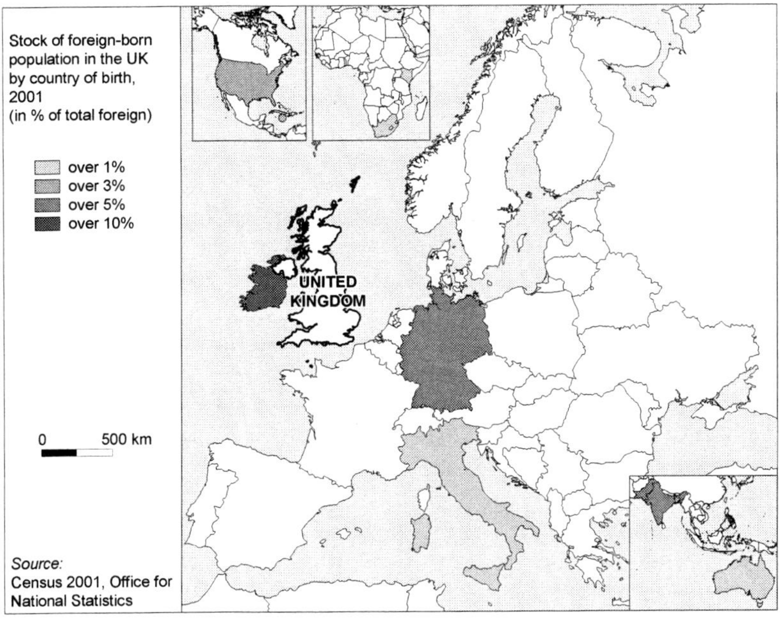

Cartography: Walter Lang, University of Vienna

3.1 Introduction

Britain has never considered itself a country of immigration (Coleman 1994), and this is reflected in the absence of comprehensive data on immigrants (Coleman 1995: 159), even though some improvements have been made in recent years.

One of the reasons for this perception is that Britain has always been a country of emigration: 'Throughout its history it has exported population, particularly to its English-speaking former colonial territories and dominions, both those that broke away – the United States and the Republic of South Africa – and those that remained within the Old Commonwealth – Canada, Australia, and New Zealand' (Coleman 1994: 37). Emigration was seen as an instrument with which to export unemployment and poverty and to strengthen the Commonwealth as a multinational but English-speaking power. In 1922, the Empire Settlement Act was decreed to promote emigration. The Overseas Migration Board, founded in 1953, served a similar purpose.

In addition, Britain is not, and never was, a country actively recruiting immigrants. On the contrary, the British government was always more concerned with limiting the immigration of certain groups. After the Second World War, despite huge labour shortages and the need to rebuild the country, the government, unlike many European counterparts, did not try to attract migrant workers.

> The UK only once recruited workers on an official basis for specific economic purposes. From 1947 to 1950, 75,000 'European Volunteer Workers' were recruited to work in sanatoria, hospitals, and the cotton and other industries. Initially, most were female Balts from displaced persons camps; later, Ukrainian prisoners of war and Germans, Austrians, and Italians of both sexes were recruited. (Coleman 1994: 38)

Whereas Germany, Switzerland and Austria started to encourage foreign workers to migrate to Western Europe, labour migrants from the former overseas colonies arrived without Britain introducing any special policy measures. Under the 1948 British Nationality Act, citizens of the former colonies were British subjects and were therefore allowed to come to Britain. However, 'people of colour' were not very welcome and the government soon started to try to discourage them from coming. Thus, the 1962 Commonwealth Immigrants Act introduced immigration controls for Commonwealth citizens who were not born in the UK or Ireland or did not hold a UK or Irish passport. Since the regulations gave large discretion to Immigration Officers, many African and West-Indian Commonwealth citizens were denied entry, while no barriers were imposed on white applicants. This practice became law when thousands of ethnic Indian British subjects arrived from the newly independent Kenya, where non-citizens had been barred from working. A Bill rushed through Parliament denied entry to this specific group of immigrants, while the 1968 Commonwealth Immigrant Act was designed to prevent further immigration waves of this kind by specifically subjecting those of colonial origin in newly independent countries to entry controls (Dummett 2006: 565-567).

At the same time, like many European countries, the UK was facing a labour force shortage in the 1960s, so it started welcoming guestworkers from, first, Poland and Italy, and then from what remained of the British Empire, notably the West Indies. Thousands of migrants were drawn to Britain, especially to the greater London area. Soon the country had two parallel systems of immigration control: one for foreigners and one for the citizens of the colonies and the Commonwealth. Aiming to merge these two systems, the British government passed the 1971 Immigrant Act, which established a distinction between those who could enter Britain free of control (these were called 'patrial' at the time and included all those who could prove a link to the UK, such as birth, naturalisation, marriage or at least five years ordinary residence in the country) and those who were subject to control, including all aliens, Commonwealth citizens and British subjects whose status derived from the colonies. Ten years later, in 1981, when most of the colonies had become independent, the government enacted the British Nationality Act, which reduced the number of people eligible to pass on British citizenship; this was done in order to further limit immigration (Dummett 2006: 567-570). This relationship between nationality and immigration is peculiar to Britain, a country that has never had a comprehensive immigration policy as such but attempted to limit immigration by differentiating between its subjects.

In contrast to the majority of the EU-15 countries, the UK granted free mobility to the citizens of the states that acceded to the EU on 1 May 2004, a decision clearly linked to the economic boom in Britain and the need for an increased workforce. In fact, Britain follows a liberal tradition, insofar as the government leaves the necessary adjustment to the market. However, Bulgaria and Romania, who acceded on 1 January 2007, do not benefit from the same policy. Meanwhile, Britain also attracted high-skilled migrants from the US, Canada, Australia and South Africa. Moreover, after the collapse of the USSR, the country witnessed a sharp increase in the figures of asylum seekers, contributing to an increase in immigration. Despite stringent policies recently introduced to reduce these figures, such as the 2002 Nationality, Immigration and Asylum Act, the UK keeps attracting large numbers of migrants and asylum seekers.

In 2001, the foreign-born population – enumerated in the census – reached 4,896,600, accounting for 8.3 per cent of the overall population. This number had doubled over the previous 50 years. Among the foreign-born people those born in the EU represented 33.1 per cent. The UK remains a major destination country in Europe, attracting 494,000 foreigners in 2004. Most of the immigrants living in Britain live in London, the South East and major cities such as Birmingham and Manchester. According to projections made by the Office for National Statistics (2005: 14), immigration is expected to contribute 56 per cent to the increase in the UK population by 2029.

Debate over illegal immigration is particularly fierce in the UK and opposition parties, as well as some newspapers, recently accused the government of being unable to provide credible statistics on illegal migration. In 2004, 56,920 aliens were deported from the UK. Though not being part of the Schengen agreement, the UK actively participates in European cooperation projects such as the Dublin Convention and joint repatriation flights. Immigration is one of the main political issues in the country and it was a central axis of the Conservative Party campaign in the 2005 general election. The attacks of July 2005, plotted by UK-born Muslims, have also raised questions about the linkage between immigration and terrorism and Britain's identity, though the terrorists were born and raised in the UK. Reconsiderations of British identity have also led to a questioning of firmly established multicultural policies in the country. Thus, the government introduced measures such as a 'Britishness test' for immigrants seeking naturalisation or indefinite leave in the UK. The concept of the test, officially called the 'Life in the United Kingdom Test', was laid out in the Nationality, Immigration and Asylum Act of 2002, but the test itself was only implemented in late 2005 for naturalisation and in April 2007 for settlement. Those applying for naturalisation or indefinite leave now have to demonstrate 'sufficient knowledge' of life in the UK, as well as sufficient knowledge of English. The test fulfils both requirements, but was highly debated and criticised. It contains questions, not only about everyday life, but also about British history and law.

Notwithstanding these debates on British national identity, the role of immigrants in the economy is widely acknowledged – they are considered one of the main factors for the British economy's dynamism, as well as the continuous growth of its population. Britain continues to actively seek to attract high-skilled migrants to strengthen some sectors of its economy (e.g. IT and the health sector), while fiercely combating illegal migration.

3.2 UK statistics on migration

The main characteristic of UK statistics on migration is the absence of a national register. In addition, UK nationals do not carry ID cards. Therefore, there is no central database of the British population, and one must rely on censuses and surveys. However, other databases do exist and are kept by various agencies. These different sources are detailed below.

The main body responsible for producing data on immigration is the Office for National Statistics (ONS). However, some data produced by the ONS, such as the census, cover only England and Wales and are complemented by censuses produced by the General Register Office for Scotland (GROS) and the Northern Ireland Statistical and Research Agency (NISRA) (Perrin & Poulain 2006: 651). Though these agencies use the same concepts, comparing statistics can be difficult, since data specific to Scotland and Northern Ireland are not always included in national statistics. The ONS includes a Migration Statistics Unit. Statistics are quite transparent and easily accessible. Most statistical reports can be downloaded from the internet free of charge.

3.2.1 *National census*

A national census is conducted every ten years by the Office for National Statistics in England, the General Register Office in Scotland and the Northern Ireland Statistical and Research Agency in Northern Ireland. The last census was conducted in 2001 (Dorling & Thomas 2004). The questionnaire was delivered by a field force to all usual residents (defined as people who spend most of their time residing at the address), who were then asked to return the questionnaire by post. A follow-up was organised for non-respondents. Each household was obliged to complete the census. The next census is planned for 27 March 2011.

Questions in the 2001 Census collected information on accommodation, household, demographic characteristics, internal and international migration, cultural characteristics, health and provision of care, qualifications, employment, workplace and travel to work.

Unlike in many other European countries (see Coleman 1995: 160), British statistics based on the census do not differentiate between citizens and foreigners – the census does not even include a question on citizenship (Perrin & Poulain 2006: 651) – but between those born in British territories and those born abroad. Therefore, these figures also include British people born abroad, as well as naturalised citizens and aliens. The foreign-born population is significantly different from the foreign population, especially in the case of Britain, where many British citizens were born in the UK's overseas territories.

In addition, recent British censuses, like the censuses in other immigration countries such as Canada and the US also contain information on ethnicity, which is used to describe the foreign-born population in more detail, even though it was not collected for this purpose in the first place. Census officials were instructed to collect information on this topic after the introduction of the 1976 Race Relations Act, which aimed to combat discrimination on racial grounds. The census was to provide the necessary information to establish social indicators of discrimination. However, due to objections to the categorisations foreseen for the 1981 Census, the first census that contained a question on ethnicity was the 1991 Census, even though this question had already been asked in the Labour Force Survey since 1981. The 1991 Census differentiated between the following categories that seemed to have been established 'for political rather than statistical reasons' (Coleman

1995: 160): White, black, Indian, Pakistani, Bangladeshi and Chinese. The census thus mixed racial and ethnic categories (Kertzer & Arel 2002: 13-14). The same holds true for the 2001 Census, where respondents were asked to tick one of the following main categories: White, mixed, Asian/Asian British, black/black British or Chinese/other ethnic group. For each category, respondents could either select among various, more specific subcategories (e.g. Indian, Caribbean, etc.) or fill in another category that they themselves would define. In the absence of a centralised registration system, these data create a 'confused picture of populations of immigrant or foreign origin' (Coleman 1995: 160).

During the processing, data are edited to ensure overall consistency, extrapolated in order to compensate for non-responses and statistically adjusted according to surveys done in a follow-up to the census coverage. Throughout the process, data are continuously reviewed and evaluated (Dorling & Thomas 2004).

3.2.2 *The International Passenger Survey (IPS)*

Despite the absence of a national register, all migrants, either arriving in or leaving the country, should be recorded. In practice, however, the main measure of migration to and from the UK is the International Passenger Survey (IPS). This survey is conducted by the Office for National Statistics and consists of a sample survey of all passengers (including transit passengers and UK residents returning home) passing through the UK's main ports and airports. Perrin and Poulain (2006: 653) report that 256,000 travellers were interviewed in 2001, amounting to 0.2 per cent of all travellers. Travellers are first asked how long they intend to stay or be away from the UK. If they answer that they have been away for more than a year (or have never been to the country) and intend to stay for more than a year, they are considered migrants (according to the UN guidelines), and undergo a full interview. Likewise, UK residents who have been in the country for more than a year and intend to leave for more than a year are considered emigrants and also undergo a full interview. Thierry (2004: 749) reports that about 3,000 people, out of 256,000 surveyed in 2001, were considered migrants and therefore underwent a full interview (2,376 immigrants and 689 emigrants). The survey collects information on migration patterns, but also on financial flows and data useful to tourism policy. The data collected are then weighted in order to come to a national estimate. However, the IPS has important flaws:

- Like all surveys, the IPS is subject to a certain level of uncertainty – the standard error was 4.1 per cent in 2001 (Perrin & Poulain 2006: 653).

- Travellers are free to answer the survey or not. Therefore, the non-response rate is quite high (about 20 per cent) and it affects the survey.
- People seeking asylum at the border are not surveyed.
- People entering or leaving the country through non-monitored routes are not surveyed.
- More importantly, travellers who conceal their intentions regarding their stay and declare that they intend to stay less than one year and end up staying more than one year are not taken into account (the same holds true for emigrants). This leads to adjustments operated by the ONS – according to Thierry (2004: 750), the inflows are inflated by about 40 per cent.
- Finally, the ONS also uses other sources to complement the IPS, which makes it far less transparent. Though the IPS is the major source of information for international migration, it is complemented by Home Office asylum seeker data (since asylum seekers are not surveyed in the IPS) and estimates of migration between UK and Ireland provided by the Irish Central Statistics Office. Furthermore, as stated above, the IPS is adjusted to account for those who come as visitors but stay longer than first indicated (so called visitor switchers) as well as those who enter as immigrants but leave before the end of their intended stay (so-called migrant switchers).

3.2.3 *Other databases*

The general database of the Home Office is called the Case Information Database (CID). Subsets of the database include data on the acquisition of UK citizenship, permanent settlement, asylum procedures and other information related to migration; there is no specific database on residence permits. Among these datasets, the two most significant are the databases on asylum seekers and on the acquisition of UK citizenship.

The database on asylum seekers is part of the CID and is operated by the Immigration and Nationality Directorate at the Home Office. Statistics on asylum are widely available and published quarterly. They are frequently audited by the National Audit Office, being found consistent with data from Eurostat and UNHCR. Besides the refugee status that allows them to remain indefinitely in the UK, applicants can benefit from other forms of protection: a temporary Humanitarian Protection status or a temporary Discretionary Leave Status, if it is not possible to return the person in question.

Asylum applicants need to apply at the port of entry or after entry to the Immigration and Nationality Directorate. It should be noted that applicants at the port of entry are not surveyed by the IPS. Decisions on the claims are made on a case-by-case basis by an immigration officer, based on the details given at the interview. If the claim is denied, it is possible to appeal to an Immigration Appeal Adjudicator. However, if the appeal is denied, it is also possible to appeal again to the Immigration Appeals Tribunal, but very few applicants are allowed this last resort of appeal, since the appeal needs to be based on a point of law. The new Asylum and Immigration Act, implemented in April 2005, aims at speeding up the application process and reducing the possibilities of fraud and abuse of the system.

The database on asylum seekers is well maintained and it is regularly updated. An exhaustive report is issued every three months, allowing comparisons between different periods of the year.

The database on the acquisition of citizenship is another subset of the CID, maintained by the Immigration and Nationality Directorate, a division of the Home Office. The British Nationality Act of 1981 recognises six forms of nationality:
- British citizens, who are the majority;
- British overseas territories citizens (BOTCs), who hold citizenship through a connection with a British overseas territory;
- British overseas citizens (BOCs), who hold citizenship through a connection with the former British colonies;
- British Nationals (Overseas), who were residents of Hong Kong before Britain returned the territory to China in 1997;
- British subjects, who are a small group of people born in the Republic of Ireland before 1949 or are connected to a country that became part of the Commonwealth in 1949;
- British protected persons, who are an even smaller group of people. These were citizens of a UK protected state or territory before it attained its independence.

As one can see, British legislation on nationality is rather complex, due to the country's links to its former territories and colonies. In the six categories of citizenship outlined above, the first three categories being the main ones, while the latter are dwindling.

British citizenship can be acquired by birth (for any child born in the UK or a British overseas territory if one parent is a citizen or settled under immigration law), descent, adoption, naturalisation or registration (for some specific categories of citizens). The data on the acquisition of citizenship are published yearly.

Overall, UK statistics suffer from two major shortcomings:
- The absence of a central population register: One needs therefore to rely on the censuses, produced every ten years, to get a comprehensive picture of the stock of foreign-born population.

- The imprecision of the International Passenger Survey (IPS): migration flows are often underestimated, since only travellers declaring that they wish to stay for more than one year undergo a full interview. People who decide to stay longer are not included in the survey; neither are people who enter through unmonitored routes. As early as 1987, Coleman stated that the 'IPS can only provide a crude estimate of the general demographic import of migration flows, incapable for statistical reasons of any refined sub-division or analysis, and prone to both error and bias' (1987: 1162).

Almost twenty years later, a similar statement can once more be made. Although some improvements have been made in recent years, including the computerisation of the databases (Düvell & Jordan 2003: 328), analysis of migration trends in the UK remains greatly hampered by unsatisfactory data (Coleman 1995: 158). Furthermore, these data and the categories they induce often remain politically driven and hardly comparable.

3.3 Stock of foreign-born population

3.3.1 Overview of the stock of foreign-born population

According to the 2001 Census, there were 58,789,194 people living in the UK. Among them, 4,896,600 people were born abroad. Hence, in the 50 years between 1951, when the census counted 2.1 million people born abroad, and 2001, the foreign-born population more than doubled.

The share of the foreign-born population in the UK is now 8.3 per cent, which is slightly higher than the OECD average (7.8 per cent), but significantly below the rate of traditional immigration countries such as the US, Canada or Australia. The diversity of the foreign-born population is also increasing. In 1971, Europe accounted for half of the foreign-born population (50.9 per cent); 30 years later this share had fallen to one-third (33.1 per cent) (see Table 3.1). While North America and Oceania contribute significant numbers to the foreign-born in the UK, the share of Asia in particular rose sharply between 1971 and 2001 (from 600,000 to 1.4 million people, respectively representing 19.8 and 29.2 per cent of the total foreign-born population), with the most important Asian sending countries being Pakistan, Bangladesh and India. Finally, the absolute numbers of people born in the Far East increased four-fold between 1971 and 2001.

The 2001 Census showed that an increasing majority (92.1 per cent) of the British population is 'white' while this is the case for just over half (52.6 per cent) of the foreign-born population (see Table 3.2).

Table 3.1 *UK foreign-born population broken down by country of birth, 2001*

Country of birth	*Numbers*	*Share of the foreign-born population (%)*
Europe	1,620,000	33.1
Republic of Ireland	537,100	11.0
Other Western Europe	834,900	17.1
Eastern Europe	248,000	5.1
North America and Oceania	397,100	8.1
US	158,400	3.2
Canada	72,500	1.5
Australia	107,900	2.2
New Zealand	58,300	1.2
South Asia	1,032,400	21.1
India	467,600	9.6
Pakistan	321,200	6.6
Bangladesh	154,400	3.2
Other South Asia	89,200	1.8
Caribbean	255,000	5.2
Africa	834,100	17.0
South Africa	141,400	2.9
Kenya	129,600	2.6
Other Africa	563,100	11.5
Far East	398,200	8.1
China	52,500	1.1
Hong Kong	96,400	2.0
Other Far East	249,200	5.1
All other countries	359,900	7.3
Total	4,896,600	100.0

Source: Office for National Statistics, 2001 Census

Table 3.2 *UK foreign-born population by ethnic group, 2001*

Ethnic group	*Numbers*	*Part of foreign-born population (%)*	*Part of total population (%)*
White	2,575,100	52.6	92.1
Mixed	140,800	2.9	1.2
Asian or Asian British	1,229,300	25.1	4.0
Black or black British	580,500	11.9	2.0
Chinese	176,200	3.6	0.4
Other	194,700	4.0	0.4
Total	4,896,600	100.0	100.0

Source: Office for National Statistics, 2001 Census

Asian and Asian British people are the second-largest group, followed by the black and black British. Other ethnic groups accounted for around 10 per cent of the foreign-born population. If we rank the main ethnic groups in a decreasing order, we get the same ranking for both the total and the foreign-born populations.

Table 3.3 *Regional distribution of foreign-born population in the UK, 1991 and 2001*

Region	*1991*		*2001*	
	Numbers	%*	*Numbers*	%*
East Midlands	176,488	4.5	224,623	5.4
East of England	255,417	5.0	328,131	6.1
London	1,233,328	18.5	1,779,300	24.8
North-East	47,527	1.9	67,259	2.7
North-West	213,356	3.2	280,055	4.2
Scotland	125,071	2.5	168,142	3.3
South-East	426,314	5.7	580,417	7.2
South-West	162,744	3.5	218,348	4.4
Wales	62,374	2.2	77,312	2.7
West Midlands	270,719	5.3	342,269	6.5
Yorks & Humber	180,037	3.7	235,424	4.7

* part of total population
Source: Office for National Statistics, 2005: 136

Most of the foreign-born population is concentrated in major conurbations and in the South East (see Table 3.3). London, in particular, attracts a large number of migrants; in some boroughs, people born abroad represent roughly half of the borough's population. A large part of the population of Oxford and Cambridge was also born abroad (around 20 per cent) – this is due to the presence of overseas students and faculty in these university towns.

In London, the foreign-born population tends to live north of the Thames, which is partly due to more affordable housing and immigrant networks.

The foreign-born population is significantly younger than the UK-born population: most of the people born abroad are of working age. Females make up a greater proportion of the foreign-born population; this contributes greatly to the feminisation of the workforce in the UK, as illustrated in Table 3.4, which shows the age and sex distribution of

Table 3.4 *Age and sex distribution of the foreign-born and UK-born labour forces, 2001 (in per cent)*

Men	16-24	25-34	35-49	50-64	Total 16-64
Foreign-born	3.8	13.6	20.2	11.8	49.4
UK-born	6.5	12.7	19.2	14.8	53.3
Women	16-24	25-34	35-49	50-59	Total 16-59
Foreign-born	4.9	15.4	20.8	9.5	50.6
UK-born	6.2	12.4	18.0	10.1	46.7

Source: Office for National Statistics, 2001 Census

the labour force (males aged sixteen to 64 and females aged sixteen to 59) in 2001. Female migration is more recent than male migration, which is mirrored in the age patterns: under 34, women are more numerous, but men are more numerous over 50.

While there is obviously a trend of demographic ageing among the migrants who arrived after the Second World War, this trend is compensated by the arrival of younger migrants in recent years.

3.4 Net migration and migration flows

3.4.1 Migration flows according to the International Passenger Survey (IPS)

The information related to migration flows in the UK comes from the International Passenger Survey (IPS), a survey permanently conducted by the National Institute for Statistics at Britain's main ports and airports. However, as stated above, this survey does not take into account every point of entry into the country. Neither does it cover asylum seekers or migrants who declare that they intend to stay for less than a year and later extend their stay. Since 1991, adjustments and corrections have been made in order to take these migrants into account and to thus produce estimates of the Total International Migration (TIM). Therefore, any comparison with data prior to 1991 is biased, since the methodology has changed in the meantime. Thierry (2004: 750) states that these adjustments can account for up to 40 per cent of the TIM inflow figures. They can certainly account for the rise in immigration numbers after 1991, with visitor switchers (or overstayers) outnumbering the migrant switchers (those who left before their intended date of departure).

The corrected figures from the International Passenger Survey translate into an estimate of the total migration flow. However, these figures must be regarded with caution, since they are derived from a survey and not an actual registration process. The extrapolation also takes into account other sources such as figures on asylum seekers from the Home Office. Furthermore, the margin of error is significant, which affects the results of the extrapolation.

Over the last decades, migration both into and out of the UK has increased. The number of people leaving the country increased from 240,000 in 1975 to 350,000 in 2004. Over the same period, the number of people entering the country increased threefold from 200,000 in 1975 to about 600,000 in 2004. In the late 1970s and early 1980s, more people left than entered the country, but this trend was reversed in 1983 and has not changed since. However, between 1994 and 2004, the gap between the inflow and the outflow widened considerably.

Table 3.5 *United Kingdom's net migration, 1994-2004*

	Total	*British*	*Foreigners*
1994	77,000	-17,000	94,000
1995	75,000	-52,000	127,000
1996	54,000	-62,000	116,000
1997	47,000	-60,000	107,000
1998	139,000	-23,000	162,000
1999	163,000	-23,000	186,000
2000	163,000	-57,000	220,000
2001	172,000	-53,000	225,000
2002	153,000	-91,000	245,000
2003	151,000	-85,000	236,000
2004	223,000	-120,000	342,000

Source: Office for National Statistics 2005: 120

In the decade between 1994 and 2004, the UK witnessed a net inflow of around 1.4 million people, a sharp increase from previous decades. As shown in Table 3.5, the number of foreigners entering the country doubled every five years between 1994 and 2004. Net migration of British citizens was consistently negative over the decade and increased six-fold between 1994 and 2004. Overall, net migration was consistently positive over this period, but did not rise continuously; indeed, the years 1996 and 1997, as well as 2002 and 2003, witnessed a decline.

Table 3.6 details the inflow and outflow between 1994 and 2004. The inflow of British citizens was quite stable over the decade, while the inflow of foreigners more than doubled. Both the outflows of British citizens and foreigners rose slightly.

The countries of origin and destination of people emigrating from and immigrating to the UK do not yield many surprises. Among the British citizens leaving the country, 42 per cent moved to an EU coun-

Table 3.6 *Inflows and outflows across UK borders, 1994-2004*

	Total inflow	*British*	*Foreigners*	*Total outflow*	*British*	*Foreigners*
1994	314,000	108,000	206,000	238,000	125,000	113,000
1995	312,000	84,000	228,000	237,000	136,000	101,000
1996	318,000	94,000	224,000	264,000	156,000	108,000
1997	326,000	89,000	237,000	279,000	149,000	131,000
1998	390,000	103,000	287,000	252,000	126,000	126,000
1999	454,000	116,000	337,000	291,000	139,000	152,000
2000	483,000	104,000	379,000	321,000	161,000	160,000
2001	480,000	106,000	373,000	308,000	159,000	149,000
2002	513,000	95,000	418,000	359,000	186,000	174,000
2003	513,000	106,000	407,000	362,000	191,000	171,000
2004	582,000	88,000	494,000	360,000	208,000	152,000

Source: Office for National Statistics 2005: 120

try, while 38 per cent migrating to the UK had been previously living in an EU country. After Europe, Australia is the most common country of origin of those coming to Britain (15 per cent), but is far less popular as a country of destination. It is interesting to note that 38 per cent of British citizens migrating to the UK had been living in a Commonwealth country, and that about the same proportion of those emigrating left for a Commonwealth country (37 per cent).

The countries of origin and destination of foreign migrants are far less well documented. Both in-migration and out-migration of foreign migrants rose throughout the decade, though out-migration increased at a significantly lower pace than in-migration. It is estimated that much of the increase can be linked to people from countries outside the EU and the Commonwealth, especially non-EU European countries and the US.

The 2001 Census provides some data on the factors driving the inflows and outflows. It appears that economic factors are predominant; about 20 per cent of the immigrants to the UK come to take up a specific job, while between 25 and 36 per cent of those emigrating do so for the same reason. The number of immigrants coming to study increased sharply in recent years; in 2003, annual migration data from the ONS showed that students accounted for 25 per cent of the inflows, while they had accounted for 16 per cent only ten years earlier. However, students represent less than 5 per cent of the inflow. Finally, those accompanying a partner or another person account for about 15 per cent of both the inflows and outflows. Other reasons driving migration include job or asylum-seeking (Office for National Statistics 2005: 126).

These reasons might explain why younger age groups are predominant among migrants. In 2003, 84 per cent of the immigrants and 75 per cent of the emigrants were below 44. However, immigrants tend to be younger than emigrants, as well as younger than in previous years. Male migrants slightly outnumber female migrants among both immigrants and emigrants, but female migrants tend to be younger than their male counterparts. Female migrants outnumber male migrants in the age group 15-24 (both for inflows and outflows), but the trend is reversed in the older age group. However, in terms of net migration, female immigrants outnumber male immigrants in all age groups.

3.4.2 *Asylum seekers*

Applications for asylum reached a peak in 2002 and then fell considerably in 2003 and 2004 (see Figure 3.1), more so than in the rest of Europe. This is partly due to some measures taken between 2002 and

Figure 3.1 *Number of asylum claims lodged in the UK (excluding dependants), 1996-2004*

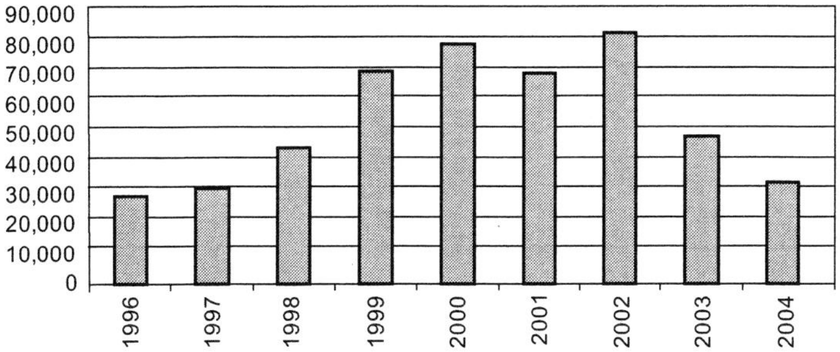

Source: Office for National Statistics

2004 in order to reduce the number of asylum applications: non-suspensive appeals for nationals of 24 selected countries, new detection technology for search of freight bound to the UK from France, Belgium and the Netherlands, restricted access to support and so on.

Only 3 per cent of claimants were granted refugee status in 2004, which was the lowest level since 1995. Most of the claims (88 per cent) were dismissed, while 9 per cent were granted temporary Humanitarian Protection or Discretionary Leave status. Asylum removals also fell to 14,905 (including dependants). Most of the applicants in 2004 were Iranian, Somali, Chinese, Zimbabwean and Pakistani (see Table 3.7).

The data on applications awaiting decisions are also made public; 9,700 claims were awaiting an initial decision in 2004, which is also the lowest figure since 1995.

Table 3.7 *Main countries of origin of the asylum claims lodged in the UK, 1996-2004*

Country of origin	*1996*	*2000*	*2004*
Iran	585	5,610	3,455
Somalia	1,780	5,020	2,585
China	820	4,000	2,365
Zimbabwe	130	1,010	2,065
Pakistan	1,915	3,165	1,710
Iraq	965	7,475	1,695
DR Congo	680	1,030	1,475
India	2,220	2,120	1,405
Afghanistan	675	5,555	1,395
Sudan	280	415	1,305

Source: Office for National Statistics

3.5 Naturalisations

Statistics on naturalisation are produced by the Home Office and are published in a yearly statistical bulletin. Data are broken down into mode of acquisition, age, previous nationality and region of birth.[1] The number of people granted British citizenship has grown continuously and regularly since the late 1990s, to reach 161,780 in 2005 (an increase of 15 per cent over 2004). However, the number of applications reached a peak of 217,475 in 2005, an increase of 64 per cent compared to the previous year (see Figure 3.2). The main reason that can explain this increase is the introduction on 1 November 2005 of a new requirement to demonstrate knowledge of life in the UK in order to be entitled to claim citizenship. This requirement is evaluated by the 'Life in the UK test'. The highly controversial test is administered, as well as based on a brochure edited by, the Home Office. It lasts 45 minutes and contains questions on the history of the UK, everyday life and so on. In October 2005, the month prior to the implementation of the test, the number of applications for naturalisation soared, which suggests that many submitted their application early in order to avoid the requirement. In 2004, a test of English language had already been introduced as a requirement, which led to a decrease in the number of applications that year, but also to an increase in the previous year (2003). The new 'Life in the UK test' incorporates the language test.

On the other hand, the refusal rate is quite stable, around 10 per cent (11 per cent in 2005, 9 per cent in 2004). The decision rate rose by 18 per cent in 2005, thanks to procedural and organisational changes, as well as improved staff productivity – this also accounts for the rise in the number of people granted citizenship in 2005. Residence in the country is the most frequent basis for the granting of citi-

Figure 3.2 *Number of naturalisations in the UK, 1995-2005*

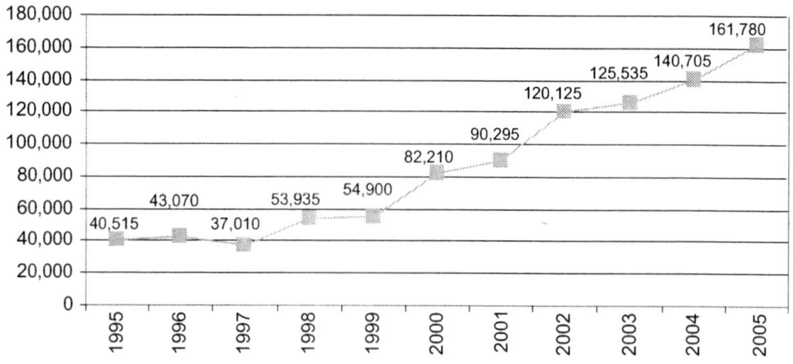

Source: Home Office

zenship (48 per cent of the total in 2005), while marriage to a British citizen accounted for 21 per cent of the total and minor children for 25 per cent of the total.

As shown in Figure 3.3, the largest percentage of people granted citizenship originated from Asia, with 19 per cent coming from the Indian subcontinent. Grants to people from non-EU Europe increased significantly. In 2005, the nationalities with the largest number of citizenships granted were India (9 per cent), Pakistan (8 per cent) and Serbia and Montenegro (6 per cent). The majority of the people granted citizenship were aged between 25 and 44 (51 per cent of the total), while children under sixteen accounted for 23 per cent.

In addition to the data presented above, the Research Development and Statistics Directorate conducts an annual study on the 'tendency of overseas nationals to take up British citizenship' using information from the UK Labour Force Surveys. The study shows that 61 per cent of foreign-born people having stayed in the UK for six years or more were British citizens in 2005. It also shows that nationals from Africa and Asia were much more likely to take up British citizenship after six years than nationals from developed countries such as Australia, the US or the EU Member States. It does not seem too speculative to assume that the incentives to become British are higher for citizens from developing countries. Interestingly, people born in Ireland were very unlikely to become British citizens – only 22 per cent of those who had lived in the UK for over twenty years were actually British.

Figure 3.3 *Country of origin of foreign-born British citizens resident in the UK, 2005 (in per cent)*

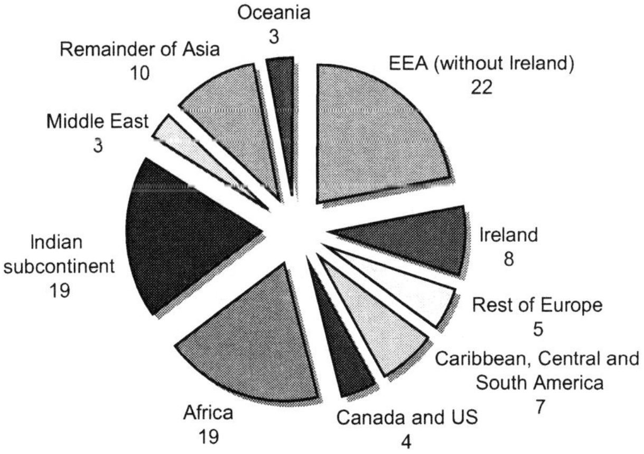

Source: Home Office

3.6 Conclusions

UK statistics on immigration are characterised by the absence of a national register. Therefore, the majority of the available data is based on censuses and surveys. This implies some flaws and biases in the reliability of the data:

- Data on the population stock are only available every ten years, which is the time period of the national census.
- Data on migration flows are produced from a survey covering about 0.2 per cent of all travellers to the UK. The extrapolation makes the figure quite imprecise, even when corrected and adjusted.
- The stocks and flows of illegal migrants are totally unknown.

However, UK statistics respect the relevant UN guidelines and definitions and comprise data on less-documented topics such as ethnicity or the tendency to take up British citizenship. They are also easily available, but remain driven by political rather than statistical reasons, which include the need to control non-European immigration.

Foreign-born residents constitute 8.1 per cent of the total population. This population is increasingly diversified, with Europe representing a declining share of it, and also more female in recent years. Net migration has been positive throughout the last decade, with Britain attracting about half a million foreigners in 2004, a number that has more than doubled in the last decade. Among these foreigners, more than 100,000 are now granted British citizenship every year.

The UK has therefore experienced a major shift in its migration patterns over the last decade: from a country of emigration, it became a country of massive immigration. This tendency is likely to continue, but statistics on migration flows have so far been unable to catch up with this shift and adapt to the changing migration landscape.

Note

1 Data broken down by country of birth should therefore be available, but are not published.

Statistical sources

Organisation	*Content*	*URL*
Office for National Statistics (ONS)	– census – IPS	www.statistics.gov.uk
Border and Immigration Agency, Home Office	– asylum seekers – control of immigration – international migration and the foreign-born population compiled from ONS data	www.ind.homeoffice.gov.uk

Bibliography

Coleman, D. (1987), 'UK Statistics on Immigration: Development and Limitations', *International Migration Review* 21 (4): 1138-1169.

Coleman, D. (1994), 'The United Kingdom and International Migration: A Changing Balance', in H. Fassmann & R. Münz (eds.), *European Migration in the Late Twentieth Century. Historical Patterns, Actual Trends, and Social Implications*, 37-66. Aldershot: Edward Elgar.

Coleman, D. (1995), 'International Migration: Demographic and Socioeconomic Consequences in the United Kingdom and Europe', *International Migration Review* 29 (1): 155-206.

Dorling, D. & B. Thomas (2004), *People and Places: A 2001 Census Atlas of the UK*. Bristol: Policy Press.

Dummett, A. & A. Nicol (1990), *Subjects, Citizens, Aliens and Others*. London: Weidenfeld & Nicolson.

Dummett, A. (2006), 'United Kingdom', in R. Bauböck, E. Ersbøll, K. Groenendijk & H. Waldrauch (eds.), *Acquisition and Loss of Nationality. Policies and Trends in 15 European States. Volume 2: Country Analyses*, 551-585. Amsterdam: Amsterdam University Press.

Düvell, F. & B. Jordan (2003), 'Immigration control and the management of economic migration in the United Kingdom: Organisational culture, implementation, enforcement and identity processes in public services', *Journal of Ethnic and Migration Studies* 29 (2): 299-336.

Kertzer, D.I. & D. Arel (2002), 'Census and identity formation, and the struggle for political power', in D.I. Kertzer & D. Arel (eds.), *Census and Identity: The Politics of Race, Ethnicity and Language in National Censuses*, 1-42. Cambridge: Cambridge University Press.

Office for National Statistics (ONS) (2005), *Focus on People and Migration: 2005*. Report. London: Office for National Statistics. www.statistics.gov.uk.

Perrin, N. & M. Poulain (2006), 'Country Report: United Kingdom', in M. Poulain, N. Perrin & A. Singleton (eds.), *THESIM: Towards Harmonised European Statistics on International Migration*, 645-655. Louvain-la-Neuve: Presses universitaires de Louvain.

Thierry, X. (2004), 'Evolution récente de l'immigration en France et éléments de comparaison avec le Royaume-Uni', *Population* 59 (5): 725-764.

Part 2

Guestworker receiving countries

4 Austria

Ursula Reeger

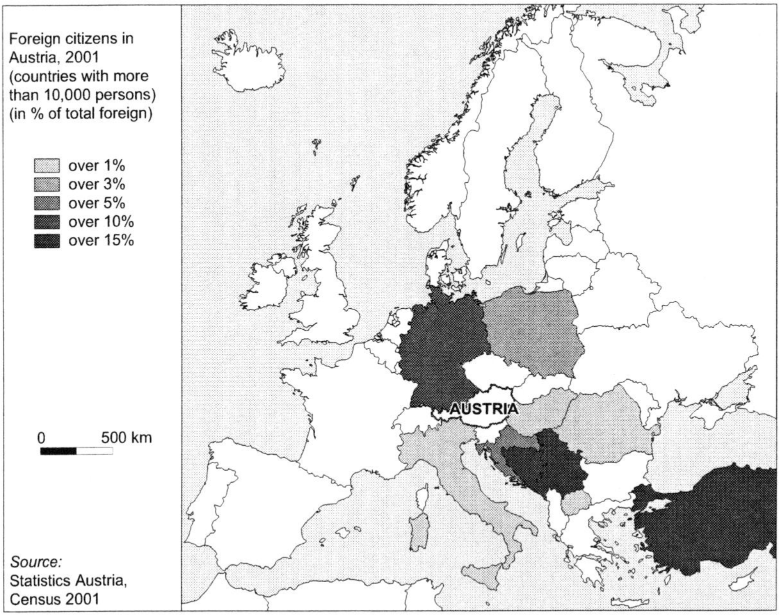

Cartography: Walter Lang, University of Vienna

4.1 Prerequisites

In its eventful history, Austria has been both a sending and receiving country of migration. In the past, these movements were often linked to the changing borders of the country. This no longer holds true for the more recent history of Austrian migration. Since the 1950s, two groups of migrants have been of particular importance: 1) refugees from the communist countries and 2) labour migrants and their families. Due to its neutrality during the Cold War, Austria received three major waves of refugees, namely from Hungary in 1956, from Czechoslovakia in 1968 and from Poland in 1981. However, for most of these, Austria was only a transit country on their way to other – usually overseas – destinations.

At the beginning of the 1960s, Austria was confronted with an urgent need for additional labour and started to recruit workers in Spain (1962; this contract remained unimportant in quantitative terms), Turkey (1964) and the Socialist Federal Republic of Yugoslavia (1966). This so-called 'guestworker immigration' to Austria can be divided into four phases; the first phase was the recruitment phase that lasted up to 1973. While Austria only attracted a few hundred labour migrants in the first years after the recruitment agreements had been signed, the numbers of entries went up to around 35,000 per year at the peak of the recruitment phase. After the collapse of growth following the first oil crisis in 1973, the immigration of guestworkers declined sharply. This was exacerbated by the Austrian government decreeing a moratorium on recruitment. Moreover, the government tried to encourage foreign workers to return home by offering them financial incentives. Both of these policies were rather 'successful' in the sense that Austria was able to keep unemployment from rising or at least to delay its rise. Labour migration from Turkey and Yugoslavia began to increase again with a renewed phase of economic growth in the mid-1980s. At the same time, the political changes in the communist countries led to a growing number of people from Eastern and South-Eastern Europe seeking political asylum in Austria, since they could not know at the time that these changes would be lasting and irreversible. For the same reason, the countries receiving these asylum seekers continued to grant them refugee status. Finally, an economic slump in the early 1990s led the Austrian government to markedly restrict immigration to Austria by introducing stricter requirements for asylum and by setting upper limits (quotas) for the recruitment of new workers and the number of dependants allowed to join them. This resulted in a stabilisation of the proportion of foreign nationals in the population as a whole (Fassmann & Reeger 2001).

The term 'guestworker' demonstrates perfectly how labour immigration was perceived and treated by politicians and the wider society. Initially, nobody considered either the social consequences of recruitment or the possibility that these immigrants might stay longer or even for good. This attitude also left its mark on the 1971 Census, which counted guestworkers, whose spouses and children were still abroad, as commuters on a non-daily basis rather than as resident population. This distinction between 'us' and 'them' still prevails in the minds of both policymakers and the public.

Although the successor states of former Yugoslavia and Turkey are still important countries of origin of new immigration, two other flows have been growing significantly in recent years: on the one hand, Austria has become a turntable of East-West-migration since the fall of the Iron Curtain; on the other hand, the number of people coming from other EU countries has been growing at a steady rate since Austria's accession to the EU in 1995. Altogether, the share of foreign citizens amounted to almost 9 per cent in 2001 when the last census was held. If we also consider naturalised foreign-born people, every seventh person residing in Austria had a migratory background in 2001.

4.2 Overview of the most important stock and flow data sources

In the case of Austria, three main data sources concerning population – and, as a subgroup, international migrants – are going to be discussed in depth, namely:
- the census, which covers the stock of population,
- the population register recently introduced on the municipal level, which is kept up to date continuously and can be used to describe both stocks and flows, and,
- statistics on naturalisations, births and deaths since these have an impact on the stock of the (migrant) population.

Other statistical sources, such as the register of asylum seekers or the registers kept at different ministries that do not cover the whole group of international migrants, will be mentioned when relevant.

4.2.1 *Census*

The history of the census in Austria goes back to 1869 when the Habsburg monarchy carried out the first 'modern' census, using a common basic principle for the whole of their empire, which, of course, covered a much larger area than Austria today. Further censuses followed in 1890, 1900, 1910, 1923, 1934 and 1939. Since 1951, the census has been conducted regularly in the first year of each decade. Hence, the last census was carried out in May 2001 (see also for the following Statistics Austria 2005). This was also the last census based on interviews.

The authorities responsible for the data collection in 2001 were the municipalities. Depending on their size, they could chose between two possible procedures to fulfil this duty; while the larger municipalities usually set up a field force that delivered and collected the forms and provided help and information if necessary, the smaller ones preferred to install counting bureaus and to ask their inhabitants to fill in the forms there. Every household was obliged to fill in forms for every household member and the municipalities had to check whether all the forms were returned. They also had to make sure that all the questions had been answered and had to contact the households for further information if necessary. Once these controls were completed, the forms were sent to the central statistical office, Statistics Austria (Statistik Austria).

The census is not a mere counting exercise. The results also influence important administrative and political issues. These include the distribution of the collected taxes to the provinces and municipalities (based on the numbers of both Austrian and foreign inhabitants) and the allocation of parliamentary seats to electoral districts (based on the numbers of Austrian inhabitants entitled to vote). Hence, the census has a strong political component. As the number of main residents determines the share of state budget to be given to the respective province or municipality, there are manifold examples of communes with a large number of secondary homes that appeal to their inhabitants to fill in the form for them and thereby to declare that the respective commune is their main place of residence.

The Austrian census covers all persons who on the day of counting had their main residence in Austria, with main residence being defined as the centre of life and relationships. This implies that migration-related phenomena that do not aim at settlement in Austria, such as transnational mobility or seasonal migration, are by definition not covered by the census.

While earlier censuses solely drew on the housing register, the 2001 Census combined this data source with the population register so that the interviewers worked from a list of inhabitants per building or flat. Deviations from this list were only accepted in extraordinary cases. Or, to put it differently, the 2001 Census only contains those who were included in the adjusted population register. Hence, the data source does not cover foreigners not registered and thus present in Austria on an undocumented basis.

Nor does the census provide any information on the length of stay in Austria or the date of naturalisation, two variables that would be very helpful in measuring the progress or failure of social integration in different fields. Nevertheless, the 2001 Census provides more information with regard to this particular field of research than earlier censuses since it reintroduced the question regarding the place of birth that was last posed in 1961. This allows migration researchers to include naturalised immigrants in their studies on the performance of immigrants in different social fields.

Besides basic demographic features (sex, age, marital status, place of birth, citizenship), the census includes a large variety of information on the individual level, such as colloquial language, denomination, education and occupational status, which can hardly be found in any other data source. It is an excellent source for various kinds of users, but it has two main, time-dependent, disadvantages: the long time span between the censuses and the long 'waiting period' until the data are processed and available for the public, researchers and politicians.

As mentioned above, the 2001 Census marks the end of classic population counting in Austria via direct interrogation. The new law regulating the census procedure that entered into force in 2006 created the legal basis for using exclusively register-based censuses in the future. The reasons for abandoning the old model are manifold: censuses were very expensive; there was growing resistance to them among the population; the intervals between censuses were too long; and the delay between the inquiry and the publication of the results was enormous. The first register-based census will be carried out in 2011 (Kytir 2006). This change from the traditional to a register-based census will make comparisons between censuses more or less impossible or at least difficult.

4.2.2 *Population register*

The size of the Austrian population had been estimated annually between one census and the next up to 1996, when Austria introduced migration statistics based on the Registration Act of 1991. These statistics draw on a system of continuously reporting on the changes of main residences at the level of the communes (about 2,359 municipalities); that is, they cover both internal and international migration. Up to 2001, each municipality held a population register and directly forwarded the data to Statistics Austria. However, the municipality calculations for the federal states and Austria differed considerably from the results of the population projection based on the census (Lebhart 2005: 2). As a consequence, the data collection procedure was modified. Based on the data of the 2001 Census, a Central Registration System (ZMR) was established within the Ministry of the Interior. Since then, the ZMR has been responsible for sending the registration data to the Central Statistical Office. At the same time, Statistics Austria introduced a new system for population statistics, including migration statistics (POPREG), which ensures uniform data processing (Lebhart & Marik 2005: 396). Moreover, it allows for the checking of the numbers for the stock of population at any time and for all spatial levels for Austria. Unfortunately, there is still a long delay between the gathering and the publication of the data; the results for the year 2002 were published in July 2005.

Every person who changes his or her main residence within Austria or who enters or leaves Austria is obliged to register within three days.[1] The authority responsible for (de)registration is the 'registration service' at the municipality; in Vienna, changes of main residence are registered on the city district level by the registration service at the local authority

(Magistratisches Bezirksamt). New inhabitants can register in person or by post (email or fax are not accepted). They can also be registered by a trusted third person. Documents required are the completed registration form, an identity card stating nationality (passport [obligatory for foreign nationals] or driving licence) and birth certificate. Homeless persons can register by stating that they have no official dwelling or by providing the registration service with a contact address. The registration form contains, *inter alia*, the following information: name, academic degree, sex, citizenship, date and place of birth, current and previous (or future) address of main residence (Gisser 2000: 3).

Before March 2002, the police was in charge of registration. That this was a barrier and in some cases a good reason for avoiding registration if possible, can be deduced from a marked increase in registrations, especially by foreign nationals, in 2002. Some of these were most probably not new immigrants but people who had been residing in Austria for a longer period of time without registering.

The population register has not yet been linked to other registers, as there are no common codes in use. But there are concrete plans to link the ZMR to the Social Security database and other non-administrative registers in order to prepare and carry out the register-based census in 2011 (Bilger & Kraler 2006).

If we use the population register as a source of information on international migration, we have to take into account that the register per se excludes the following groups of persons: diplomats, tourists, seasonal workers and commuters. Asylum seekers in federal care have been registered since the end of 2004.

Generally speaking, the Austrian population register follows the UN definitions for short-term (91 to 365 days) and long-term (over 365 days) migrants. Foreign nationals who stay less than 90 days are not counted as migrants (Kytir, Lebhart & Neustädter 2005: 207). People leaving the country for a longer period of time are advised to deregister. However, many persons leaving Austria do not deregister as it is not obligatory, there are no incentives and they do not want to lose their official status in the country. As a consequence, the number of registered emigrants is usually lower than the number of actual emigrants, which implies that the statistical migration balance is usually higher than the real migration balance.

4.2.3 Statistics on naturalisations, births and deaths

The statistical coverage of naturalisations, births and deaths is rather straightforward, as every case is reported in the same way. These events are continuously collated and influence the calculated stock of (foreign) population.

Austrian naturalisation statistics include data on acquisitions of nationality by 1) grant or extension of grant (the usual, and numerically by far the most important, mode of acquiring nationality, after birth, in Austria), 2) declaration (a special procedure for family members of university professors) and 3) notification (a special procedure for Holocaust survivors). In other words, the statistics exclude all automatic acquisitions of Austrian nationality after birth and thus the following groups of persons: 1) foundlings and stateless children, 2) children born out of wedlock to a foreign mother and an Austrian father who can acquire Austrian nationality by legitimisation and 3) university professors who automatically acquire Austrian nationality upon taking office in Austria (Çınar & Waldrauch 2006: 42). While the Minister of the Interior is in charge of nationality law, the provincial governments implement the law and therefore also gather the data on naturalisations. The data are processed at the Central Statistical Office. The list of variables includes date of birth, date of naturalisation, sex, place of birth, former citizenship, marital status and the reason for naturalisation (see Section 4.3.2).

Statistics on natural population change, i.e. births and deaths, are held by the registrar of civil status. These statistics are a complete inventory count and are highly reliable and exact. However, the data do not cover marriages, births or deaths of Austrian residents outside Austria and per se exclude irregular migrants. Furthermore, death statistics do not provide any information on the place of birth or a possible change of citizenship. Hence, computed mortality rates and life expectancy figures for the immigrant population are biased, as they only ever cover legally resident foreign citizens.

4.3 Description of the stock of foreign population

4.3.1 Stock according to the 2001 Census

In 2001, the Austrian census counted 8,032,926 people resident in Austria. Those holding double citizenship (55,066) were counted as Austrian nationals. As Table 4.1 indicates, 710,926 people resident in Austria did not hold Austrian citizenship (8.9 per cent) and more than one million people living in Austria were born abroad (12.5 per cent). All in all, the number of persons with a direct migratory background amounts to 1,119,414, or 14 per cent of total population, which means that every seventh person recorded in the census either immigrated to Austria or is the child of an immigrant (this excludes children of naturalised immigrants). The combination of the variables nationality and place of birth allows for the identification of four different population groups (see Table 4.1):[2]

1. both variables 'Austria': 86 per cent of total population,
2. both variables 'foreign': 7.4 per cent of total population, foreign citizens who where born abroad,
3. Austrian nationals with a place of birth abroad: 5 per cent of total population, mostly naturalised immigrants but also ethnic Austrians born abroad,
4. foreign nationals born in Austria: 1.4 per cent, usually children or grandchildren of immigrants.

Table 4.1 *Population in Austria by nationality and place of birth according to the 2001 Census*

	Place of birth in Austria	*Place of birth abroad*	*Total*
Nationality Austria	6,913,512	408,488	7,322,000
Nationality foreign	116,015	594,911	710,926
Total	7,029,527	1,003,399	8,032,926
As % of total			
Nationality Austria	86.1	5.1	91.1
Nationality foreign	1.4	7.4	8.9
Total	87.5	12.5	100.0

Source: Statistics Austria, 2001 Census; author's compilation

As in the early 1990s, the majority of the foreigners living in Austria in 2001 originated from former Yugoslavia and Turkey, the two main guestworker sending countries. They represented 61.1 per cent of all foreign nationals in Austria in 1991 and 63.2 per cent in 2001; thus, their share rose slightly. The fastest-growing group(s) of foreign nationals in Austria were those coming from former Yugoslavia (+63 per cent), largely due to the war in this region at the time and the resulting arrival of refugees in Austria. The size of the Turkish national group, by contrast, remained relatively stable between the two Censuses (+7.3 per cent).

Although the share of EU nationals among all foreign residents remained stable in the decade under consideration (14.8 and 14.9 per cent), this group also grew remarkably (+38.8 per cent). This marked rise can most probably be explained by Austria's accession to the EU in 1995, which opened the Austrian labour market to other EU nationals.

If we go by the two fastest-growing groups of immigrants between 1991 and 2001, i.e. nationals from former Yugoslavia and from the other EU Member States (see Table 4.2), Austria seems to counter the hypothesis of a growing diversification of origins that has recently been observed in other European countries. However, the number of immigrants from other or unknown countries also increased markedly in this period. A more detailed analysis of this group reveals that Asian and African immigration gained in importance, albeit not significantly.

Table 4.2 *Population in Austria by citizenship according to the 1991 and 2001 Censuses and by place of birth according to the 2001 Census*

	Citizenship 1991			*Citizenship 2001*				*Place of birth 2001*		
	Abs.	*% tot. population*	*% foreign population*	*Abs.*	*% tot. population*	*% foreign population*	*Change 1991/2001*	*Abs.*	*% tot. population*	*% foreign-born*
Total	7,795,786	100.0		8,032,926	100.0		3.0	8,032,926	100.0	
Austrian	7,278,096	93.4		7,322,000	91.1		0.6	7,029,527	87.5	
Foreign total	517,690	6.6	100.0	710,926	8.9	100.0	37.3	1,003,399	12.5	100.0
Former Yugoslavia	197,886	2.5	38.2	322,261	4.0	45.3	62.9	351,256	4.4	35.0
Turkey	118,579	1.5	22.9	127,226	1.6	17.9	7.3	125,026	1.6	12.5
EU	76,490	1.0	14.8	106,173	1.3	14.9	38.8	198,404	2.5	19.8
Other country, unknown	55,333	0.7	10.7	76,104	0.9	10.7	37.5	127,353	1.6	12.7
Poland	18,321	0.2	3.5	21,841	0.3	3.1	19.2	41,671	0.5	4.2
Romania	18,536	0.2	3.6	17,470	0.2	2.5	-5.8	39,044	0.5	3.9
Hungary	10,556	0.1	2.0	12,729	0.2	1.8	20.6	30,953	0.4	3.1
Slovakia*	-	-		7,739	0.1	1.1		15,981	0.2	1.6
Czech Rep.	11,318	0.1	2.2	7,313	0.1	1.0	-35.4	54,627	0.7	5.4
US	5,770	0.1	1.1	6,108	0.1	0.9	5.9	7,371	0.1	0.7
Switzerland	4,901	0.1	0.9	5,962	0.1	0.8	21.6	11,713	0.1	1.2

* In 1991 there was no distinction between Slovakia and the Czech Republic.

Source: Statistics Austria, 1991 and 2001 Censuses; author's compilation

Apart from a diversification of origins, recent studies also observed a feminisation of international migration. Austria confirms this trend. Between the Censuses of 1991 and 2001, the share of women in the total foreign population increased from 43 to 47 per cent. Moreover, the share of women rose for almost all major sending countries (see Table 4.3). Initially dominated by males, the stock of immigrants from the most important labour-sending countries (former Yugoslavia and Turkey) was made up of equal numbers of men and women at the beginning of the new millennium. These figures imply that family reunification was almost completed for these countries. In comparison, the share of women was still much lower for African countries but nevertheless grew significantly between 1991 and 2001 (the share of Egyptian women, for example, rose from 14.5 to 36 per cent). On the other hand, more than half of the Germans, Romanians, Americans, Indians and Filipinos living in Austria in 2001 were female. The most striking of these are certainly the Filipinos, where the share of women still lay at 60 per cent in 2001, despite the fact that it had fallen by 6 percentage points since 1991. This can be explained by the fact that immigration from the Philippines was initially predominantly female, with most of these women being recruited as nurses in the 1970s.

Finally, the census reveals that foreign nationals (except from the EU-14) residing in Austria are much younger than the Austrian nationals: whereas every fifth immigrant is under fifteen years old, the re-

Table 4.3 *Foreign nationals from selected countries by sex in Austria, 1991 and 2001*

	1991			*2001*		
	Total	*Women*	*% women*	*Total*	*Women*	*% women*
Europe	466,885	203,301	43.5	642,676	305,460	47.5
Former Yugoslavia	197,886	85,333	43.1	322,261	151,589	47.0
Turkey	118,579	47,789	40.3	127,226	55,998	44.0
Germany	57,310	30,062	52.5	72,218	37,483	51.9
Romania	18,536	7,093	38.3	17,470	9,031	51.7
Poland	18,321	7,343	40.1	21,841	9,872	45.2
Africa	8,515	1,787	21.0	14,223	4,856	34.1
Egypt	4,509	652	14.5	4,721	1,698	36.0
Asia	25,805	11,567	44.8	35,271	16,637	47.2
Iran	5,687	2,347	41.3	5,926	2,509	42.3
The Philippines	2,883	1,924	66.7	3,368	2,045	60.7
India	3,043	1,152	37.9	4,879	1,681	34.5
China	3,357	1,560	46.5	4,567	2,235	48.9
America	9,516	5,301	55.7	12,313	7,074	57.5
US	5,770	3,038	52.7	6,108	3,168	51.9
Australia	738	369	50.0	1,026	505	49.2
Stateless, unknown	6,231	2,204	35.4	5,417	2,005	37.0
Total	517,690	224,529	43.4	710,926	336,537	47.3

Source: Statistics Austria; author's compilation

spective share amounts to about 15 per cent among Austrians. On the other hand, every tenth Austrian woman is older than 75 years, while this age group is almost non-existent among immigrants, since many of those, who came to Austria in the 1960s and 1970s either tend to return to the country of origin after having reached retirement age or have naturalised by then. Moreover, recent inflows do not include large numbers of elderly people.

As already mentioned, the new population register allows us to analyse both stocks and flows of immigrants in Austria. As for the stocks, Table 4.4 compares the results of the 2001 Census to the stocks as registered in the population register in 2005.

Table 4.4 *Austrian and foreign nationals by sex in 2001 (census) and 2005 (population register)*

		2001 census		*2005 register*		*2001 = 100*
		Total	*%*	*Total*	*%*	
Austrian nationals	Male	3,514,800	48.0	3,577,095	48.2	101.6
	Female	3,807,200	52.0	3,840,820	51.8	100.8
	Total	7,322,000	100.0	7,417,915	100.0	101.2
EU-14	Male	52,506	49.5	69,257	50.3	126.0
	Female	53,667	50.5	68,406	49.7	122.6
	Total	106,173	100.0	137,663	100.0	124.3
Other foreigners	Male	321,883	53.2	339,944	52.2	103.0
	Female	282,870	46.8	311,002	47.8	106.9
	Total	604,753	100.0	650,946	100.0	104.8
Total		8,032,926		8,206,524		

Source: Statistics Austria; author's compilation

The Table illustrates that the population of Austria grew by about 175,000 people between the last census and 2005, mostly due to immigration. It was mainly migrants from the EU-14 and their descendants who contributed to this development. The number of Austrian nationals, by contrast, remained relatively stable, albeit less due to natural population change than to the high number of naturalisations (around 30,000 per year).

4.3.2 *Births, deaths and naturalisations*

Births and deaths form part of natural population change. Concerning foreign nationals, the number of deaths has been astonishingly constant over the last 35 years, with the annual number remaining consistently below 2,000. There are two reasons for this stability: 1) the majority of the labour migrants still return to their country of origin after having reached retirement age and 2) the longer a migrant has stayed in Austria, the higher the probability that he or she has acquired Austrian citizenship and will not die as a foreign national in Austria.[3] For these reasons, there seems to be much more variation in the number of births than in the number of deaths (see Figure 4.1).

Figure 4.1 *Births and deaths of foreign nationals in Austria, 1970-2006*

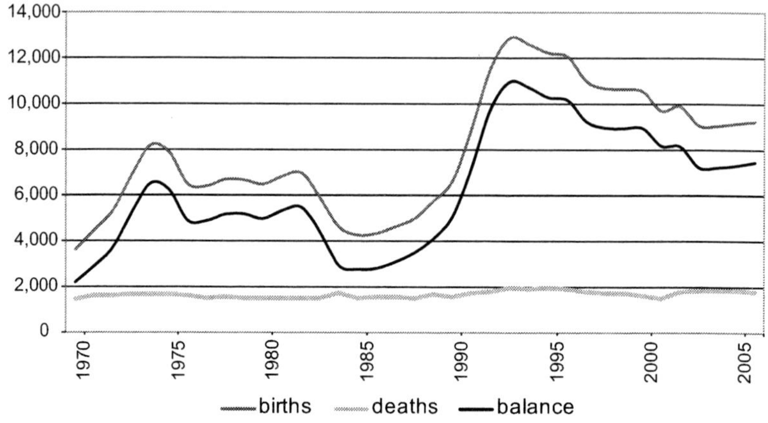

Source: Statistics Austria; author's compilation

After a first peak at the beginning of the 1970s, the number of births declined due to remigration initiated by the economic crisis in the wake of the first oil price crisis and settled at slightly more than 6,000 births per year between 1976 and 1982. Only in the second half of the 1980s did the number of births rise again, reaching a peak with almost 13,000 births in 1992. Since then, the number of births has decreased and is currently stagnating, mostly due to a slight adjustment of the reproductive behaviour of foreign women to that of Austrians.[4]

According to the data provided by Statistics Austria, the number of naturalisations surged steeply in 1999, when it first passed 20,000. This trend continued over the following years, with 44,694 foreigners receiving Austrian citizenship in 2003, when 5.8 per cent of all foreign citizens officially residing in Austria at the time were naturalised. About one-third of the new Austrian nationals were granted citizenship on the basis of ten years residence in Austria, and almost 50 per cent were naturalised on the basis of their spouse or parent having received citizenship (Çınar & Waldrauch 2006).

Of the more than 356,000 people who naturalised between 1991 and 2006, 69.1 per cent used to be citizens of Turkey or former Yugoslavia and its successor states. About 30 per cent of the 356,000 new Austrians

Table 4.5 *Naturalisations in Austria by former citizenship, 1993-2006*

	Former Yugoslavia and its successor states	*Turkey*	*Romania*	*Total*	*In 100 foreign nationals*	*% males of total*	*Place of birth in Austria*
1993	5,780	2,686	672	14,131	2.2	48.1	28.0
1994	5,621	3,377	904	15,275	2.3	47.8	27.0
1995	4,529	3,201	872	14,366	2.1	47.4	27.2
1996	3,118	7,492	691	15,627	2.3	46.7	32.7
1997	3,659	5,064	1,096	15,792	2.3	47.0	29.0
1998	4,142	5,664	1,500	17,786	2.6	48.0	28.7
1999	6,728	10,324	1,635	24,678	3.6	49.4	33.2
2000	7,557	6,720	2,682	24,320	3.5	49.6	30.1
2001	10,737	10,046	2,813	31,731	4.4	50.5	30.4
2002	13,990	12,623	1,774	36,011	4.7	50.8	30.9
2003	21,574	13,665	2,096	44,694	5.8	50.0	30.6
2004	19,045	13,004	1,373	41,645	5.4	50.2	28.0
2005	17,037	9,545	1,128	34,876	4.4	50.3	28.7
2006	12,133	7,549	981	25,746	3.1	48.9	29.9

Note: The table does not include naturalisations of people residing abroad (200 to 700 cases per year).
Source: Statistics Austria; author's compilation

were born in Austria. This might explain why the large majority of those naturalising is comparatively young: almost 60 per cent are under 30, with one-third being younger than fifteen, while only 1 per cent is older than 60. In 2003, just as many men as women acquired Austrian citizenship. Before that, the share of men was slightly lower than that of women.

4.4 Description of flows

The migration flows between the early 1990s and 2006 can be divided into three distinct phases that have different characteristics and (statistical) backgrounds. After immigration had boomed in the wake of the fall of the Iron Curtain and due to the war in Yugoslavia, it stagnated in the second half of this decade, as a result of Austria introducing annual quota for new immigration in 1993. During this period, net immigration was very low, with stable inflows and outflows of both Austrians and foreign nationals. This stagnation phase ended just before the beginning of the new millennium, due to a pronounced inflow from the EU and some preferred third countries. While net immigration remained just below 20,000 between 1999 and 2001, with around 70,000 foreigners entering and 48,000 leaving the country every year, the migration balance rose considerably between 2002 and 2004, when it amounted to 50,582. Since then immigration has been declin-

Figure 4.2 *Migration flows from and to Austria, 1996-2006*

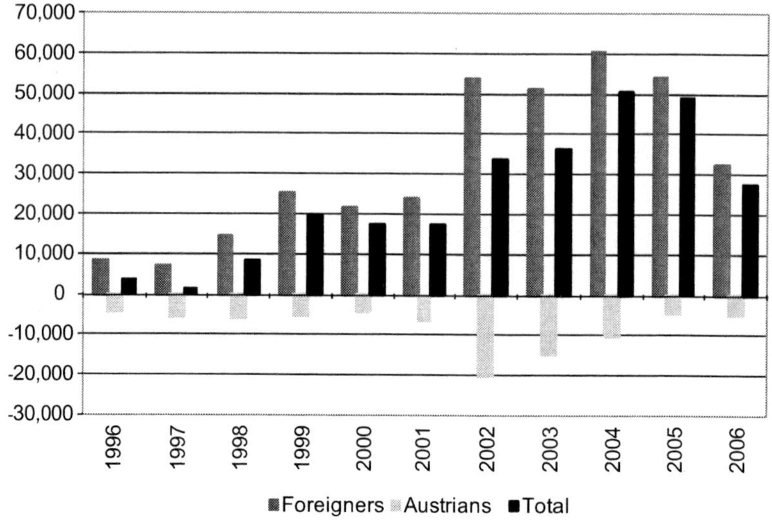

Source: Statistics Austria; author's compilation

ing again mostly due to new political restrictions that came into force at the beginning of 2006.

However, a critical look at the numbers reveals that this increasing total between 2002 and 2004 was not necessarily simply due to rising immigration but also to changes in the registration system. Firstly, as mentioned above, the police was in charge of registrations before 2002, when the municipalities took over this responsibility. So the growing inflows at the time might to some extent be explained by the fact that people who had avoided registration with the police felt more comfortable registering with the municipality. Unfortunately, it is impossible to estimate the amount of these belated registrations. Secondly, asylum seekers have been included in the population register since spring 2004, which increases the numbers of entries by about 10,000 to 15,000 (Kytir 2005: 788).

If we analyse the countries of origin of the inflows in 2006, we might be surprised to find that a large share of the immigrants (15.4 per cent) were Austrian nationals, and 16.1 per cent were Germans, with the rest of the 'old' EU-15 Member States accounting for only 7.1 per cent and thus playing a rather marginal role. Immigration from the so-called guestworker countries still amounted to almost one fifth of the total inflows, with former Yugoslavia accounting for 14 per cent and Turkey for 5 per cent. If we compare these numbers to the outflows in the same year, the share of Austrians leaving Austria seems to

Table 4.6 *International inflows and outflows in Austria in 2006 by nationalities with a balance of more than 1,000*

	Inflow	*Outflow*	*Balance*	*% of balance*
Foreigners total	85,384	52,904	32,480	100.0
Germany	16,223	7,147	9,076	27.9
Poland	6,035	2,899	3,136	9.7
Serbia & Montenegro	7,423	5,162	2,261	7.0
Turkey	4,897	2,948	1,949	6.0
Russian Federation	2,438	871	1,567	4.8
Slovakia	3,669	2,285	1,384	4.3
Hungary	3,734	2,401	1,333	4.1
Bosnia & Herzegovina	3,235	2,080	1,155	3.6
Romania	4,757	3,656	1,101	3.4
Rest	32,973	23,455	9,518	29.3

Source: Statistics Austria, Migration Statistics 2006; author's compilation

be disproportionately high (28 per cent), while 14 per cent of the people leaving Austria were nationals of countries that used be part of Yugoslavia, 4 per cent were Turks.

Table 4.6 offers a different perspective on official Austrian migration statistics. Of more than 100 countries under consideration, only nine made up for almost 70 per cent of the total migration balance in 2006. The clear majority of these were from Germany, the only country in the list representing the 'old' EU-15, immediately followed by Poland that has always had strong migratory ties with Austria. However, the list of the top nine sending countries also includes one country of origin that seems to have gained in importance more recently, the Russian Federation. So, the data based on the population register seem to point towards two parallel trends: a continuation of immigration from traditional sending countries, on the one hand, and a slight tendency towards a diversification of origins, on the other.

Neither the population register nor the census provides any information on the reasons for immigration to Austria, the purpose or legal basis of the intended stay or its probable length. While this information can be found in the Asylum and Foreigners Statistics held by the Ministry of the Interior (see Table 4.7), this source only includes foreign nationals who are subject to permit requirements under the Aliens Law; that is, it excludes citizens of the European Economic Area, Swiss citizens and recognised refugees (Bilger & Kraler 2006: 567-569).

The BMI data on inflows provide some additional information on recent international migration to Austria. In almost all the years between 1999 and 2004, short-term permits accounted for more than half of all the permits issued. Their number almost doubled in this period, with the majority of these being granted to seasonal workers. This can

Table 4.7 *Residence permits issued and asylum applications in Austria, 1999-2004*

	Residence permits			*Short-term permits*		*Asylum applications*	*Total without asylum*
	Quota	*Exempt from quota*	*Familiy reunification*	*Total*	*Seasonal workers*		
1999	5,278	13,383	-	15,268	-	20,129	33,949
2000	5,275	10,938	9,361	19,610	9,071	18,284	35,823
2001	7,776	15,699	13,637	33,602	17,269	30,127	57,077
2002	6,596	20,570	18,054	38,801	19,767	39,354	65,967
2003	8,027	26,537	22,701	35,045	17,384	32,359	69,969
2004	5,138	26,697	23,308	32,209	15,718	24,634	64,044

Source: Statistics Austria 2006 on the basis of POPREG (total inflow); Ministry of the Interior (BMI), Asylum and Foreigners Statistics

be explained by the fact that for many people short-term stays have become the only legal way to enter Austria for work purposes since the government severely restricted labour migration in the mid-1990s. The other category of permits that gained in importance between 1999 and 2004 were those residence permits that cannot be subjected to a quota, with a large majority of these being permits granted on the grounds of family migration. More than 20,000 residence permits were issued for this reason, both in 2003 and 2004. Finally, the number of asylum applications also increased markedly, but only up to 2002, when more than 39,000 asylum applications were filed in Austria. In the two following years the number of asylum applications fell significantly. This corresponds to an international decrease in numbers of asylum seekers due to both an amelioration of the situation in some countries of origin and the new restrictions introduced in many industrial countries that kept migrants from applying for asylum.

The inflows as registered in the population register are considerably higher than the numbers of permits issued to, and asylum applications filed by, third-country nationals. This is mainly due to the fact that the population register also includes those entries that are exempt from permits. Moreover, the different ways of acquiring and counting the data make any comparison between the two datasets difficult.

Table 4.8 provides a synopsis of all the factors influencing the development of the foreign population in Austria: births and deaths (birth balance), immigration and emigration (migration balance) and naturalisations between 1994 and 2004.

In the mid-1990s, the migration balance of foreigners was relatively low (around 10,000 per year). This changed markedly after the turn of the millennium. The birth balance fell steadily from 10,744 in 1994 to 7,247 in 2004, while the number of naturalisations increased considerably from around 15,000 to 44,694 in 2003. In spite of these high

Table 4.8 *Changes in the foreign population in Austria, 1994-2004*

	Foreign population		Change				
	Annual average	*End of the year*	*Total*	*Birth balance*	*Migration balance*	*Naturalisation*	*Statistical adjustment*
1994	669,453	673,792	8,678	10,744	19,107	-15,275	
1995	677,061	680,330	6,538	10,321	9,439	-14,366	
1996	681,709	683,089	2,759	10,200	9,991	-15,627	
1997	683,394	683,700	611	9,263	10,000	-15,792	
1998	686,481	689,261	5,561	8,983	14,300	-17,786	
1999	693,955	698,649	9,388	8,966	29,403	-24,678	
2000	701,768	704,887	6,238	8,971	23,248	-24,320	
2001	718,259	731,631	26,744	8,196	45,372	-31,731	4,907
2002	743,255	755,124	23,493	8,179	53,790	-36,011	-2,465
2003	759,576	765,303	10,179	7,256	51,099	-44,694	-3,482
2004	776,147	788,609	23,306	7,247	60,621	-41,645	-2,917

Sources: Kytir 2005: 778; 1994-2001: population extrapolation; 2002-2004: POPREG; statistical adjustments: 2001: differences between the census and POPREG that cannot be explained demographically, 2002-2004: difference between birth balance from the birth register and POPREG and inconsistencies in the register

numbers of naturalisations and the diminishing birth balance, the number of foreign citizens resident in Austria grew steadily between 1994 and 2004. This was due to new immigration, a fact that is highly surprising if we consider how succeeding governments since the early 1990s have tried to restrict new immigration.

4.5 Conclusion: Statistics and reality in the Austrian context

Austrian migration policy aims at integrating immigrants already present in the country, on the one hand, and at strictly limiting new immigration from third countries, on the other. *De jure* Austria does still not define itself as a country of immigration; *de facto* it has been a country of immigration for decades. This paradoxical situation is also reflected in the statistics. New immigration has constantly increased, despite the restrictions introduced since the 1990s. Moreover, the number of temporary residents not counted as immigrants, such as visitors, tourists, foreign students, and in particular seasonal workers, also increased considerably. In keeping with its self-perception, Austria still applies *ius sanguinis*, which means that children of foreign citizens born in Austria are automatically foreign citizens.[5] While this is irrelevant for migration flows, it influences the stock of foreign population and its reflection in statistics that count persons who have spent their whole life in Austria as foreigners.

For 40 years up until the 2001 Census, Austrian migration-related statistics only used citizenship to describe the resident immigrant population. As a consequence, there was no information on naturalised immigrants, since they could not be identified in any statistical source. This is more than a subtle hint that policymakers were not really interested in these new Austrian citizens, their social situation and housing or their performance on the labour market. Though naturalisations numerically play an important role in Austria, only little could be found out about the sometimes rather successful stories of 'new Austrians' from other statistical sources like the microcensus. The main focus of policymakers' considerations and intentions were foreign citizens, who are – at least at the beginning of their stay – often marginalised and not well integrated. As soon as these foreigners acquired Austrian citizenship, nobody seemed to be interested in them anymore.

As in most other European countries, the main data sources for international migration to Austria fail to capture the wide variety of movements. This is mainly due to the fact that migration is still perceived as a one-time irreversible event with a clear point of departure and destination. However, as mentioned above, temporary migration has been gaining in importance, as people do not always want to, or are not always allowed to, settle down in the country of destination. These forms of migration are *a priori* excluded, as statistical tools are not flexible enough to cover them. Moreover, there are no statistics on transnational mobility, as statistics per se concentrate on national contexts. As to data on the integration of migrants, the situation has slightly improved, as the 2001 Census contained a question on the place of birth. This means that naturalised immigrants can now be included in studies discussing basic factors of integration, such as housing and the socio-economic situation of the person in question.

Although the new population register is a valuable source for inflows and outflows, it lacks important information on the professional background, education or legal status of the migrants. Quantitative studies on migration are therefore more or less limited to the place of origin and basic demographic features. A more detailed insight into international migration might be possible when the population register is linked to other sources. However, this will probably not happen before 2011, the year of the next census and the first one that is not based on interviews. Whether the register-based census will be as reliable a source remains to be seen.

Notes

1 This also concerns tourists who have to fill in a form in their hotel. However, this information is not included in the population register. A change of a secondary residence to a main residence has to be registered within one month.
2 A group of people that cannot be identified by this method are children born in Austria of naturalised immigrants.
3 An analysis of the number of deaths by religion shows that the number of Muslims who died in Austria increased almost fivefold between 1977 (121) and 2004 (545).
4 For Austrian women, the fertility rate dropped from 1.45 in 1985 to 1.31 in 2005. While the decline was similar for all foreign women (2.14 in 1985 and 2.00 in 2005), it was more marked for Turkish women (3.61 in 1985 and 2.86 in 2005).
5 The most recent changes in the Austrian Citizenship Law that came into force in 2006 could be interpreted as a move towards *ius soli,* as they entitle foreign citizens born in Austria to citizenship after six years. However, the children still have to fulfil the general naturalisation requirements that were increased by the same law (see Çınar & Waldrauch 2006: 53).

Statistical sources

Organisation	*Content*	*URL*
Central Statistical Office	– census – population register – naturalisations	www.statistik.at
International Organisation for Migration – National Contact Point Austria	– basic information on population – residence titles – naturalisations	www.emn.at
Labour Market Service Austria (AMS)	– employed and unemployed third-country nationals	www.ams.at
Ministry of the Interior	– foreigners – asylum	www.bmi.gv.at
UNHCR Austria	– refugees	www.unhcr.org

Bibliography

Bilger, V. & A. Kraler (2006), 'Country Report: Austria', in M. Poulain, N. Perrin & A. Singleton (eds.), *THESIM: Towards Harmonised European Statistics on International Migration*, 565-575. Louvain-la-Neuve: Presses universitaires de Louvain.

Çınar, D. & H. Waldrauch (2006), 'Austria', in R. Bauböck, E. Ersbøll, K. Groenendijk & H. Waldrauch (eds.), *Acquisition and Loss of Nationality. Policies and Trends in 15 European Countries. Vol. 2: Country Analyses*, 19-61. Amsterdam: Amsterdam University Press.

Fassmann, H. & U. Reeger (2001), 'Immigration to Vienna and Munich: Similarities and differences', in: H. T. Andersen & R. van Kempen (eds.), *Governing European Cities.*

Social fragmentation, social exclusion and urban governance, 273-295. Aldershot: Ashgate.

Gisser, R. (2000), 'New migration flow statistics in Austria. Methods, problems and outcomes', paper prepared for the Joint ECE-Eurostat-ESCWA Work Session on Migration Statistics, Geneva, 8 May 2000.

Kytir, J., G. Lebhart & C. Neustädter (2005), 'Von der Bevölkerungsfortschreibung zum Bevölkerungsregister', *Statistische Nachrichten* 3: 203-210.

Kytir, J. (2005), 'Demographische Strukturen und Trends 2001-2004', *Statistische Nachrichten* 8: 776-789.

Kytir, J. (2006), 'Registerzählung 2010. Gesetzliche Grundlagen, Konzepte und Probleme der praktischen Umsetzung', paper presented at the Institute of Geography, University of Vienna, 29 November 2006.

Lebhart, G. (2005), 'Austria's migration statistics in the new population register', paper presented at the 28th CEIES Seminar 'Migration Statistics', Riga, 9 June 2005.

Lebhart, G. & S. Marik (2005), 'Internationale und interregionale Migration in Österreich 2002 und 2003', *Statistische Nachrichten* 5: 396-414.

Statistics Austria (Statistik Austria) (ed.) (2005), *Standard-Dokumentation: Metainformationen (Definitionen, Erläuterungen, Methoden, Qualität) zur Volkszählung 2001*. Wien: Statistik Austria. www.statistik.at.

Statistics Austria (Statistik Austria) (ed.) (2006), *Wanderungsstatistik 2005*. Wien: Statistik Austria.

5 Germany

Stefan Rühl

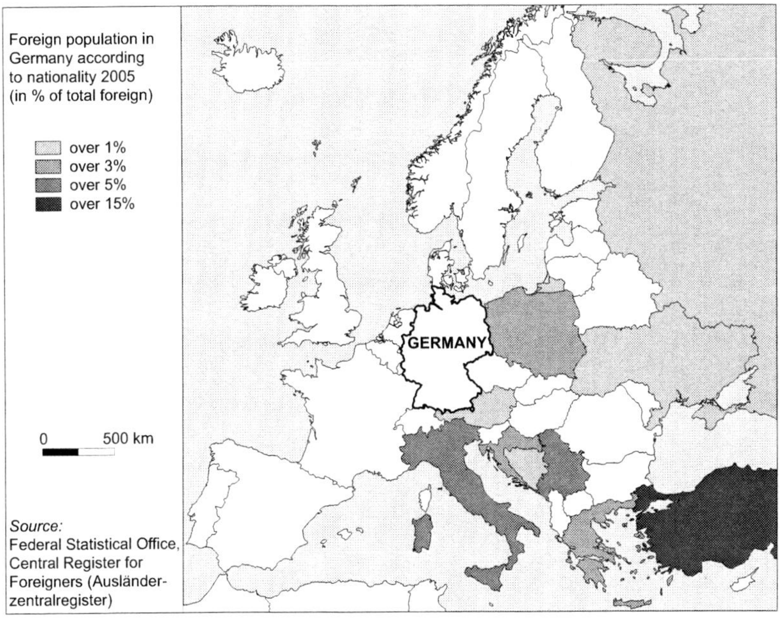

Cartography: Walter Lang, University of Vienna

5.1 Introduction

The first years after the Second World War were characterised by large-scale immigration to Germany. These immigrants were, in the main, German refugees (*Vertriebene*) from the eastern parts of the former 'German Reich', from Eastern European countries and from the Soviet Union. According to the 1950 Census, when the forced resettlements came to an end, 7.9 million refugees and expellees were resident in the Federal Republic of Germany and 3.6 million in the German Democratic Republic. In the same period (1945-1950), about ten million people (forced labourers, prisoners of war and concentration camp prisoners) left Germany and returned to their countries of origin. Between 1950 and 1961, the year of the construction of the Berlin Wall, about 2.6 million Germans moved from East to West Germany (see Bauer, Dietz, Zimmermann & Zwintz 2005: 204-205; Herbert 2001: 192ff.; Bade & Oltmer 2004: 52ff.).

In 1955, a period of labour migration began. Between 1955 and 1968, the German government signed recruitment agreements with Italy (1955), Spain and Greece (both 1960), Turkey (1961), Morocco (1963), Portugal (1964), Tunisia (1965) and Yugoslavia (1968). However, between 1955 and 1961, the number of foreigners living in Germany rose by only about 200,000. After 1961, steady economic growth and the GDR's decision to close its borders to the West, which cut off the flow of workers from East Germany, led to increasing labour shortages.

In total, about 14 million workers ('guestworkers') from the recruitment countries entered Germany between 1955 and 1973 in order to take up temporary employment there. The majority of these recruited workers returned to their countries of origin before 1973 when the German government declared a halt to recruitment in response to the oil shortage and subsequent economic slowdown. In this year about 2.7 million workers were in Germany. For many of these, the ban may have been an incentive to settle in Germany, as the new legal regulations prevented them from re-entering Germany after a temporary return to their country of origin (see Cyrus 2005: 9; Bauer, Dietz, Zimmermann & Zwintz 2005: 206-207).

In the recruitment period from 1955 to 1973, the foreign population in Germany increased from half a million (0.9 per cent of total population) to almost four million (6.4 per cent of total population). Net migration rose almost annually and reached its peak in 1970 at +542,000. Only in the recession year of 1967, was a negative net migration (of about 200,000) registered.

Until the late 1960s, most foreign workers were nationals from Italy, Spain or Greece. Later, workers from Yugoslavia and, particularly, Turkey predominated. In 1968, Turkish nationals made up 10.7 per cent of the foreign population in Germany, with Yugoslavians constituting 8.8 per cent; by 1973, Turkish citizens accounted for 23 per cent of foreigners living in Germany, while Yugoslavians made up 17.7 per cent.[1]

The period between the cessation of recruitment and the end of the 1980s was primarily characterised by migration through family reunification. From 1973 to 1979 the number of foreigners residing in Germany remained stable. Overall, until 1988, the number of foreigners rose quite slowly, from 4 million to 4.6 million.

The political changes in Central and East Europe (i.e. the fall of the Iron Curtain) at the end of the 1980s triggered a new period of migration to Germany. The number of foreigners moving to Germany increased significantly, exceeding the number of those leaving. A large proportion of these incoming migrants were asylum seekers and ethnic Germans (*Aussiedler*).

In spite of rising and diversifying migration inflows, it was not before 1998, when the new government coalition of the Social Democrats and the Green Party took office, that the country's traditional defensive self-definition, according to which Germany was not a country of immigration, was abandoned. The following years saw numerous amendments and reforms in migration and foreign resident policy and legislation. This paradigmatic shift was initiated by the 1999 reform of the German Nationality Law, followed by the appointment of an Independent Commission on Migration in summer 2000, and the passing of the so-called Green Card Regulations in August 2000, which broadened access of non-German specialists to the labour market in Germany. Finally, in 2004, the German parliament passed the new Immigration Act, based on a compromise between the government and the opposition. The new law, which came into force on 1 January 2005, contains, amongst other provisions, regulations on the entry and residence of foreigners (and ethnic German migrants) and aims at simplifying the existing set of migration regulations. Thus, the new law reduces the types of residence permits from five to two: the (temporary) residence permit and the (permanent) settlement permit. Moreover, a much-discussed element of the law enables highly skilled third-country nationals to immigrate to and settle in Germany. This amendment has been interpreted as an important shift in German migration policy since it loosens the restriction on recruitment. Furthermore, the Immigration Act contains, for the first time, regulations on the integration of migrants at a national level. For example, under the new law new residents are generally obliged to participate in integration courses.

5.2 Overview of stock and flow data

Official German statistics differentiate between Germans and foreigners rather than between those born in Germany and those born abroad. As a consequence, these statistics underestimate the proportion of people who have a migratory background, as they do not include naturalised citizens or ethnic German migrants (*Spätaussiedler*), both of whom are incorporated into the statistics as Germans. Addressing this problem, the government passed a new law on the microcensus (Mikrozensusgesetz 2005), which came into force on 1 January 2005. This new regulation facilitates the identification of citizens who have a migratory background (naturalised Germans and ethnic German migrants) in the microcensus and thus improves the measurement of migrants' integration. The first results of the new microcensus were published in June 2006.

In recent years, not only social scientists but also politicians have come to realise that the sole registration of the nationality in the official statistics is insufficient for measuring integration. This holds particularly true for the field of education, where the discussion on how to adequately measure the educational attainment of students with different migratory backgrounds was further intensified by the results of the PISA study (see Herwatz-Emden 2005: 9; Konsortium Bildungsberichterstattung 2006: 139). In 2007, the Conference of the Ministers of Education and Cultural Affairs of the *Länder* in the Federal Republic of Germany (Kultusministerkonferenz – KMK) decided to introduce the criterion of 'migratory background' into the official statistics on students/pupils by way of the 'language spoken at home'.[2] First results should be available for the school year 2008/2009.

The statistics on child and youth welfare (*Kinder- und Jugendhilfestatistik*) have registered the migratory background of children in child care facilities (kindergartens) since 2006. They use the criteria 'country of origin of at least one parent' and 'prevalent language spoken in the family'.

5.2.1 *Data on the stocks of foreigners*

5.2.1.1 *Central Register of Foreigners (AZR)*

The most relevant source concerning data on the foreign population in Germany is the Central Register of Foreigners (*Ausländerzentralregister*). The AZR, as it is known, collects data on all foreigners who legally reside in Germany for a minimum of three months.[3] These data stem from public authorities, mainly from the more than 600 local foreigners authorities (*Ausländerbehörden*),[4] but also from German embassies, the Federal Office for Migration and Refugees (*Bundesamt für Migration und Flüchtlinge*; responsible for the asylum procedures) or the Federal Border Guard (*Bundesgrenzschutz*), amongst others. The Register provides information on foreigners broken down by sex, age, citizenship, residence status and duration of stay. It includes asylum seekers and refugees.

One problem of the AZR is that foreigners who have left the country or have naturalised may still be included in the files because they forgot to deregister or have not yet been deregistered by the foreigners authorities. At the beginning of 2005, the Central Register on Foreigners completed a process of revision and correction. As a consequence of this process, the number of foreigners residing in Germany decreased from 7.3 million at the end of 2003 to 6.7 million at the end of 2004.

Since 2006, the AZR has been recording new characteristics, including the purpose of the stay (according to the regulations of the new Immigration Act). First results will be published in 2007.

The AZR data on foreigners are lower than the ones reported in population updates (*Bevölkerungsfortschreibung*), which registered 7.3 million foreign nationals in 2005. One reason for this difference is that the AZR includes only those foreigners who take up 'non-transitory' residence in Germany (see Federal Statistical Office 2006a: 6; Bilger & Kraler 2006: 421).

5.2.1.2 *Census*

Another reason for the above-mentioned difference is that the population updates are estimates based on the results of the 1987 Census. Due to strong, principled opposition to the last census as well as the high costs involved, there has been no full census since. However, the Federal Statistical Office has announced that it will carry out a register-based census in 2010/11.[5] The necessary data will be drawn from different registers, such as the municipal population register or the registers of the labour and tax offices (see Bilger & Kraler 2006: 420).

5.2.1.3 *Microcensus*

In June 2006, the Federal Statistical Office (2006b) published the first results of the new microcensus. This is the first statistical source that allows for the identification of citizens with a migrant background. The 2005 microcensus differentiated between the following groups:

1. **Foreign nationals**
   - 1.1 Immigrated foreign nationals (first generation)
   - 1.2 Foreign nationals born in Germany (second and third generation)
2. **German nationals with migrant background**
   - 2.1 Immigrated German nationals of migrant background (ethnic German migrants, immigrated foreigners naturalised in Germany)
   - 2.2 German nationals of migrant background born in Germany (naturalised persons, children of ethnic German migrants, children of naturalised persons, children of parents with foreign nationality who receive German nationality by birth (*ius soli*), children with one parent of migrant background)

The results show that about 19 per cent of the population in Germany, or 15.3 million people, are of a migrant background. 7.3 million of these hold a foreign nationality, 8.0 million the German nationality.

5.2.2 *Flow data*

One of the main sources concerning migration flows is the Federal Statistical Office's data on arrivals and departures, which have been published since the 1950s and are based on the records of local registration authorities. Under German law, residents are required to fill in an official registration form at their local registration office every time they change residence, both nationally and across German borders.[6] These registration forms are processed by the Statistical Offices of the federal states (*Länder*) and subsequently compiled into national statistics by the Federal Statistical Office.

The Federal Registration Framework Act allows the federal states to exempt foreigners from the obligation to register if their stay is only temporary. In Brandenburg, Lower Saxony, Saxony-Anhalt, Schleswig-Holstein and Northrhine-Westfalia foreigners are exempted from the obligation to register if their stay does not exceed two months. In Baden-Württemberg and Saxony the period is one month. The different provisions of the federal states lead to a non-uniform registration of migrants. However, the federalism reform involves a transfer of the legislative authority for the registration of the population to the federal government with a view to guaranteeing a standardised registration procedure. Moreover, there are long-term plans to introduce a central population register.

The above regulations imply that the official statistics on arrivals and departures are not based on migrants as such (persons), but on the number of relocations across Germany's national borders (cases). This detracts from the quality of these statistics, as every person relocating across German borders more than once within a twelve month period will be registered repeatedly in these statistics (once per relocation). Thus, the number of recorded migrations will always be somewhat higher than the number of actual migrants for that year. Moreover, the official statistics do not provide any information on the duration of migrants' residence in Germany. This sets German statistics apart from other countries' migration statistics, where migrants' (intended) duration of stay is an essential criterion for defining migration. Thus, besides permanent immigration, the migration statistics in Germany also include, for example, temporary (short-term) stays of seasonal workers, exchange students and guest scientists.

The official statistics tend to underestimate the migration outflows, as not all foreign nationals notify local authorities when leaving Germany. Some of the departing migrants simply forget to deregister; others intentionally neglect to do so in order to secure their legal residence status in Germany. Consequently, the official arrival and departure statistics tend to underestimate the scope of migration outflows and return migration.

Another shortcoming of the official arrivals and departures statistics is the fact that they do not differentiate between different types of migration. On account of that, it is impossible to determine, for example, whether Polish nationals enter Germany as ethnic German immigrants (*Spätaussiedler*), or seasonal and contract workers. Chances are that ethnic German immigrants will settle down in Germany permanently, whereas seasonal workers will have to return to their home countries after three months at the latest. If information on the type of migration were available, it would be easier to provide the necessary facilities and specific integration programmes for the respective groups of migrants.

As the official arrivals and departures statistics only cover those who register or deregister with local authorities, they usually exclude people entering or leaving the country illegally, as these try to avoid any contact with the authorities. Hence the migration statistics underestimate the inflow of migrants.

Since 2006, the AZR can be used as an additional source of information on inflows and outflows of foreign nationals. In July 2006, for the first time, the Federal Statistical Office published information on immigration and emigration on the basis of the AZR (see Section 5.4.1).

In addition to the general data available from the Federal Statistical Office, the following federal offices collect information on individual groups of migrants:

- Federal Office for Migration and Refugees (Bundesamt für Migration und Flüchtlinge): statistics on asylum seekers, refugees and Jewish migrants from the former Soviet Union;
- Federal Employment Office (Bundesagentur für Arbeit): data on labour migration (work permits for contract workers, seasonal workers, IT experts);
- Federal Administration Office (Bundesverwaltungsamt): statistics on ethnic German migrants/ repatriates (*Spätaussiedler*).

5.3 Description of the stock of foreign population

At the end of 2005 about 6.8 million people living in Germany held a foreign nationality. This amounts to a share of 8.2 per cent of the total population (c.f. Table 5.1).

The majority of the foreigners in Germany are nationals of the former recruitment states, most of them of Turkey (26.1 per cent of all foreign nationals), Italy (8.0 per cent), the successor states of former Yugoslavia (14.3 per cent), especially Serbia and Montenegro (7.3 per cent) and Greece (4.6 per cent). In addition, a significant number of nationals of Middle and East European countries live in Germany,

Table 5.1 *Total population and foreign population in Germany, 1991-2005*

Year	*Total population**	*Foreign population**	*% of foreign nationals*
1991	80,274,600	5,882,267	7.3
1992	80,974,600	6,495,792	8.0
1993	81,338,100	6,878,117	8.5
1994	81,538,600	6,990,510	8.6
1995	81,817,500	7,173,866	8.8
1996	82,012,200	7,314,046	8.9
1997	82,057,400	7,365,833	9.0
1998	82,037,000	7,319,593	8.9
1999	82,163,500	7,343,591	8.9
2000	82,259,500	7,296,817	8.9
2001	82,440,400	7,318,628	8.9
2002	82,536,700	7,335,592	8.9
2003	82,531,700	7,334,765	8.9
2004**	82,501,000	6,717,115	8.1
2005**	82,438,000	6,755,811	8.2

* as of 31 December
** The figures for the years 2004 and 2005 are not comparable to previous years. The reduction in the number of foreigners results mainly from a revision of the AZR.
Source: Federal Statistical Office

especially from Poland (4.8 per cent), Russia (2.8 per cent) and the Ukraine (1.9 per cent; for more information, see Table 5.2).

About a quarter of the foreigners (i.e. 1.654 million people) originate from one of the old Member States of the European Union; about a third of these are Italians. 7.1 per cent are nationals of the new Member States (482,864), and about two-thirds of these are Polish. The number of nationals from the new EU Member States increased by 9.8 per cent between 2004 and 2005.

62 per cent of all non-Germans have been living in Germany for more than ten years, 33.9 per cent even for more than twenty years. With regard to non-German employees and their families from former recruiting states this rate is even higher: 77.4 per cent of the Turks, 81.9 per cent of the Greeks, 82.3 per cent of the Italians and 78.3 per cent of the Spanish people have been living in Germany for ten years or longer. The average duration of stay is 16.8 years.

Among the 6.756 million non-Germans, 1.385 million (about 21 per cent) were born in Germany; among the non-German minors the proportion of people who were born in Germany is more than two-thirds (70 per cent).

The age structure of the foreign population differs significantly from that of the German population (cf. Table 5.3). Foreign nationals are characterised by a high percentage of younger and middle-aged people (between six and 39 years). In 2005, 39.0 per cent of the Germans be-

Table 5.2 *Foreign population in Germany by nationality, 31 December 2005*

Country of nationality	*Total*	*Male*	*Female*	*Female in %*
Turkey	1,764,041	937,581	826,460	46.9
Italy	540,810	319,136	221,674	41.0
Serbia & Montenegro*	493,915	262,163	231,752	46.9
Poland	326,596	152,653	173,943	53.3
Greece	309,794	168,705	141,089	45.5
Croatia	228,926	112,616	116,310	50.8
Russia	185,931	75,744	110,187	59.3
Austria	174,812	92,877	81,935	46.9
Bosnia-Herzegovina	156,872	81,098	75,774	48.3
Ukraine	130,674	51,919	78,755	60.3
The Netherlands	118,556	64,691	53,865	45.4
Portugal	115,606	62,955	52,651	45.5
Spain	107,778	54,116	53,662	49.8
France	102,244	47,016	55,228	54.0
US	97,864	56,031	41,833	42.7
UK	96,245	58,140	38,105	39.6
Vietnam	83,446	41,740	41,706	50.0
Iraq	75,927	48,605	27,322	36.0
China	73,767	39,157	34,610	46.9
Romania	73,043	30,210	42,833	58.6
Morocco	71,639	41,974	29,665	41.4
Macedonia	62,093	33,509	28,584	46.0
Iran	61,792	34,894	26,898	43.5
Kazakhstan	59,370	27,270	32,100	54.1
Afghanistan	55,111	29,353	25,758	46.7
Thailand	51,108	7,245	43,863	85.8
Hungary	49,472	28,276	21,196	42.8
India	40,099	26,506	13,593	33.9
Lebanon	40,060	23,215	16,845	42.0
Bulgaria	39,153	16,986	22,167	56.6
Sri Lanka	33,219	16,728	16,491	49.6
Pakistan	30,034	18,099	11,935	39.7
Syria	28,154	16,097	12,057	42.8
Slovenia	21,195	10,588	10,607	50.0
Total	6,755,811	3,493,799	3,262,012	48.3

* The figures for Serbia and Montenegro include persons holding the nationality of former Yugoslavia who cannot be assigned to one of the successor states.
Source: Federal Statistical Office, Central Register for Foreigners (Ausländerzentralregister)

longed to this age group, compared to 58.6 per cent of the foreign nationals. However, 5.5 per cent of the Germans were younger than six years, whereas this is true for only 3.3 per cent of the foreigners; this can to some extent be explained by the fact that nearly half of the children born of foreign parents after the change of the nationality code in 2000 acquired German citizenship by birth. As for the age group '65 and older', 20.4 per cent of the Germans are older than 64, compared to 6.7 per cent of the foreign population.

Table 5.3 *German and foreign population by age groups, 31 December 2005*

Age groups	*Germans*		*Foreigners*	
	Total	%	*Total*	%
Under 6	4,103,769	5.5	205,885	3.0
6-17	9,178,660	12.2	955,634	14.1
18-24	5,988,321	8.0	717,197	10.5
25-39	14,141,080	18.8	2,299,515	34.0
40-59	22,039,962	29.3	1,826,156	27.0
60-64	4,360,961	5.8	299,154	4.4
65 and older	15,336,093	20.4	452,270	6.7
Total	75,148,846	100.0	6,755,811	100.0

Source: Federal Statistical Office; author's calculations

As mentioned above, the statistics on foreigners residing in Germany only capture part of the picture of immigration to Germany as they exclude, amongst others, naturalised Germans who constitute a considerable share of those having a migrant background in Germany. The naturalisation figures presented in Table 5.4 show that the number of migrants who naturalised increased steadily between 1995 and 2000. A major share of these new Germans was of Turkish origin, which can partly be explained by the fact that the Turkish government introduced a privileged non-citizen status, the so-called pink card, which grants Turkish emigrants, who have to renounce their Turkish nationality in order to acquire the nationality of their country of residence, a number of special rights, such as the right to acquire property in Turkey (Kadirbeyoglu 2007: 297-299). A new nationality law, which came into force in 2000, facilitated the access to German citizenship. As a consequence, naturalisation figures reached an all-time high the same year. This was, on the one hand, due to the fact that a large number of cases, which had accumulated over the years, could be decided more quickly than was the case under the previous law (Hailbronner 2006: 232). On the other hand, an interim regulation, which only came into force in 2000, allowed children up to the age of ten to acquire German citizenship based on the new *ius soli* regulation if they fulfilled the requirements of the new law at the time of their birth. These cases were counted as naturalisations (about 20,000 in 2000). Between 2000 and 2005, the number of naturalisations fell continuously (see Table 5.4). In 2005, 117,241 foreigners obtained German citizenship.

Since the introduction of *ius soli* elements in 2000, about 40,000 children born in Germany of foreign nationals have annually acquired German nationality by birth in addition to the nationality of their parents.[7] Between 2000 and 2005, 231,263 *ius-soli* children were born in Germany.

Table 5.4 *Naturalisations in Germany according to former citizenship, 1995-2005*

	1995	*1996*	*1997*	*1998*	*1999*	*2000*	*2001*	*2002*	*2003*	*2004*	*2005*
Turkey	31,578	46,294	39,111	53,696	103,900	82,861	75,573	64,631	56,244	44,465	32,661
Iran	874	649	919	1,131	1,863	14,410	12,020	13,026	9,440	6,362	4,482
Serbia & Montenegro*	3,623	2,967	1,989	2,404	3,608	9,776	12,000	8,375	5,104	3,539	8,824
Afghanistan	1,666	1,819	1,454	1,118	-	4,773	5,111	4,750	4,948	4,077	3,133
Morocco	3,397	3,149	4,010	4,971	4,980	5,008	4,425	3,800	4,118	3,820	3,684
Lebanon	-	784	1,134	1,692	2,515	5,673	4,486	3,300	2,651	2,265	1,969
Croatia	2,637	2,391	1,789	2,198	1,648	3,316	3,931	2,974	2,048	1,689	1,287
Bosnia-Herzegovina	2,010	1,926	995	3,469	4,238	4,002	3,791	2,357	1,770	2,103	1,907
Vietnam	3,430	3,553	3,119	3,452	2,597	4,489	3,014	1,482	1,423	1,371	1,278
Poland						1,604	1,774	2,646	2,990	7,499	6,896
Russia						4,583	4,972	3,734	2,764	4,381	5,055
Ukraine						2,978	3,295	3,656	3,889	3,844	3,363
Iraq						984	1,264	1,721	2,999	3,564	4,136
Israel						1,101	1,364	1,739	2,844	3,164	2,871
Total	71,981	86,356	82,913	106,790	143,267	186,688	178,098	154,547	140,731	127,153	117,241

* until 3 February 2003, the Federa Republic of Yugoslavia

Source: Federal Statistical Office

5.4 Description of flows

5.4.1 *Migration to and from Germany*

Over the last decade of the twentieth century, migration flows to and from Germany were influenced by several factors. One important factor was the fall of the Iron Curtain, which allowed migration outflows from the former eastern European bloc. As for Germany, this has led to an increase in the migration inflows of ethnic German immigrants (*Aussiedler*) and asylum applicants from Eastern Europe, particularly in the first half of the 1990s. Secondly, the civil wars in former Yugoslavia resulted in considerable migration of war and civil-war refugees throughout the 1990s. Thirdly, labour migration from neighbouring states, particularly Poland and the Czech Republic, increased. With Poland, a kind of 'commuter migration' has developed, i.e. Polish nationals enter Germany for a limited period of time in order to seek temporary work (mainly as seasonal and contract workers).

In the period between 1991 and 2004, nearly 13.8 million people were registered as having entered Germany. However, a large number of arrivals often coincides with an increased number of departures. During the same period, almost 9.8 million residents deregistered in Germany in order to settle down in another country. In 2004, nearly 780,000 arrivals and about 698,000 departures were registered, resulting in a net migration figure for all German and non-German residents of +82,543 (net migration for foreigners: +55,217). This was the lowest net migration since 1998 (see Table 5.5). In 2005, about 707,000 people were registered as having come to Germany, the lowest figure since 1987. Moreover, for the first time, the net migration of Germans was negative (-16,764).

Inflows and outflows on the basis of the AZR were published for the first time in June 2006. Because the AZR registers 1) persons rather than cases and 2) only those foreigners who stay in Germany for more than three months, the inflows and outflows are significantly lower than the figures based on the registered arrivals and departures. In 2005, according to the AZR, 401,000 foreigners immigrated to Germany, 323,000 of these for the first time, while 290,000 people left Germany.[8]

If we look at the nationality of those entering and leaving the country, it becomes obvious that the majority of the migrants are European (see Table 5.6; these figures are based on the Federal Statistical Office's statistics on arrivals and departures). In 2005, Polish nationals formed the largest group of immigrants (21 per cent). 18 per cent of all immigrants were Germans, who constituted the largest group until 2004. This group comprises ethnic German immigrants (*Spätaussiedler*) as well as a considerable number of other German nationals returning

Table 5.5 *Migration inflows and outflows across German national borders, 1991-2005*

Year	*Inflows*			*Outflows*			*Net migration*	
	Total	*Of which foreigners*	*%*	*Total*	*Of which foreigners*	*%*	*Total*	*Of which foreigners*
1991	1,198,978	925,345	77.2	596,455	497,540	83.4	+602,523	+427,805
1992	1,502,198	1,211,348	80.6	720,127	614,956	85.4	+782,071	+596,392
1993	1,277,408	989,847	77.5	815,312	710,659	87.2	+462,096	+279,188
1994	1,082,553	777,516	71.8	767,555	629,275	82.0	+314,998	+148,241
1995	1,096,048	792,701	72.3	698,113	567,441	81.3	+397,935	+225,260
1996	959,691	707,954	73.8	677,494	559,064	82.5	+282,197	+148,890
1997	840,633	615,298	73.2	746,969	637,066	85.3	+93,664	-21,768
1998	802,456	605,500	75.5	755,358	638,955	84.6	+47,098	-33,455
1999	874,023	673,873	77.1	672,048	555,638	82.7	+201,975	+118,235
2000	841,158	649,249	77.2	674,038	562,794	83.5	+167,120	+86,455
2001	879,217	685,259	77.9	606,494	496,987	81.9	+272,723	+188,272
2002	842,543	658,341	78.1	623,255	505,572	81.1	+219,288	+152,769
2003	768,975	601,759	78.3	626,330	499,063	79.7	+142,645	+102,696
2004	780,175	602,182	77.2	697,632	546,965	78.4	+82,543	+55,217
2005	707,352	579,301	81.9	628,399	483,584	77.0	+78,953	+95,717

Source: Federal Statistical Office

Table 5.6 *Migration inflows and outflows across German national borders by nationality, 2004-2005*

Country of nationality	*Inflows*		*Outflows*		*Net migration*	
	2004	*2005*	*2004*	*2005*	*2004*	*2005*
Poland	125,042	147,716	96,345	98,190	+28,697	+49,526
Germany	177,993	128,051	150,667	144,815	+27,326	-16,764
Turkey	42,644	36,019	38,005	34,466	+4,639	+1,553
Romania	23,545	23,274	20,275	20,606	+3,270	+2,668
Russia	28,464	23,078	14,078	12,899	+14,386	+10,179
Hungary	17,411	18,574	16,490	15,669	+921	+2,905
Italy	19,550	18,349	35,056	27,118	-15,506	-8,769
Serbia & Montenegro	21,691	17,514	28,345	20,461	-6,654	-2,947
US	15,292	15,228	14,926	14,409	+366	+819
France	12,488	12,260	13,646	10,354	-1,158	+1,906
China	13,067	12,034	12,793	10,468	+274	+1,566
Slovak Republic	11,633	11,806	10,284	9,088	+1,349	+2,718
Ukraine	15,000	10,881	6,357	5,656	+8,643	+5,225
The Netherlands	9,140	10,088	6,230	5,479	+2,910	+4,609
Croatia	10,513	9,260	12,379	11,294	-1,866	-2,034
Bulgaria	11,586	9,057	10,299	9,129	+1,287	-72
Greece	10,205	8,975	20,340	16,391	-10,135	-7,416
Austria	8,998	8,647	9,458	7,639	-460	+1,008
Czech Republic	8,947	8,459	8,302	6,254	+645	+2,205
India	9,125	8,364	7,302	7,095	+1,823	+1,269

Source: Federal Statistical Office

from abroad. More than 5 per cent were Turks, while Romanians and Russians each comprised about 3 per cent. Germans constituted the largest group of nationals leaving Germany in 2005, followed by nationals of Poland, Turkey, Italy and Romania.

Women have a smaller share – compared to men – in both migration inflows and outflows. The percentage of females has remained fairly stable over the last two decades, continuing to be slightly higher for migration inflows (approximately 40 per cent) than for migration outflows (approximately 37 per cent) (see Table 5.7).

Persons migrating to Germany are, on average, younger than the resident population, but this is also true for those leaving Germany (see Figure 5.1). Thus, the effect immigration has on rejuvenating the age structure of German society is partly diminished by migration outflows.

Table 5.7 *Migration inflows and outflows in Germany by sex, 1990-2005*

Year	*Inflows*				*Outflows*			
	Male	*Female*	*% of females*	*Total*	*Male*	*Female*	*% of females*	*Total*
1990	695,231	561,019	44.7	1,256,250	327,796	246,582	42.9	574,378
1991	696,279	486,648	41.1	1,182,927	364,116	218,124	37.5	582,240
1992	911,771	577,678	38.8	1,489,449	450,544	250,880	35.8	701,424
1993	771,018	496,986	39.2	1,268,004	543,675	253,184	31.8	796,859
1994	631,596	438,441	41.0	1,070,037	483,819	256,707	34.7	740,526
1995	651,809	444,239	40.5	1,096,048	454,260	243,853	34.9	698,113
1996	571,876	387,815	40.4	959,691	442,324	235,170	34.7	677,494
1997	496,540	344,093	40.9	840,633	477,595	269,374	36.1	746,969
1998	473,145	329,311	41.0	802,456	470,639	284,719	37.7	755,358
1999	504,974	369,049	42.2	874,023	423,940	248,108	36.9	672,048
2000	487,839	353,319	42.0	841,158	426,798	247,240	36.7	674,038
2001	507,483	371,734	42.3	879,217	383,889	222,605	36.7	606,494
2002	481,085	361,458	42.9	842,543	390,764	232,491	37.3	623,255
2003	439,988	328,987	42.8	768,975	392,541	233,789	37.3	626,330
2004	455,601	324,574	41.6	780,175	436,362	261,270	37.5	697,632
2005	411,024	296,917	42.0	707,352	390,266	238,133	37.9	628,399

Source: Federal Statistical Office

5.4.2 *Types of migration*

The almost 700,000 migrants who enter Germany each year fall into certain classifiable groups (Federal Office for Migration and Refugees 2006; Table 5.8).

The most important group is that of labour migrants, who account for more than half of the annual inflow. Labour migrants from Middle and Eastern European countries have been given an opportunity to take

Figure 5.1 *Migration inflows and outflows and total population by age groups in Germany, 2005*

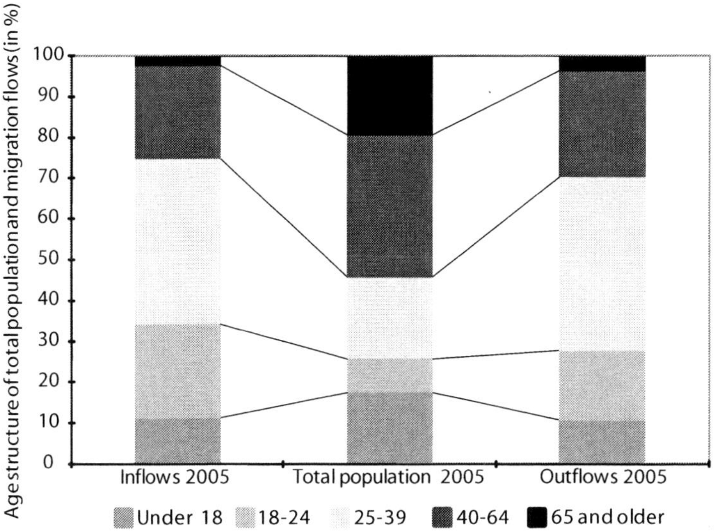

Source: Federal Statistical Office

up (temporary) employment in Germany. The majority of these labour migrants work as seasonal or contract workers. In 2005, the official number of non-German seasonal workers amounted to 330,000 and of non-German contract workers to 22,000. The main country of origin is Poland. About 80 per cent of all work permits were granted to Polish nationals. In addition, the introduction of the so-called Green-Card regulations has opened up a new channel for migration inflows of IT experts. Up to the end of December 2004, a total of 17,931 work and residence permits (so-called 'Green Cards') were granted to non-German IT specialists, most of them being nationals of India, Romania and Russia.

The second largest inflow is EU internal migration, which can include labour migration but also all other types of migration (retirement migration, family reunification, etc.). The number of EU nationals originating from the old Member States fell steadily from 176,000 in 1995 to 89,000 in 2005. In 2005, net migration between Germany and the old EU Member States was negative (-10,000). Conversely, net migration between Germany and the ten new EU Member States was positive (+61,000).

The third most important reason for migration is family reunification. The visa statistics of the Foreign Ministry record all the cases where German embassies abroad have granted permission for a spouse

Table 5.8 *Types of migration in Germany, 1991-2005*

	EU internal migration (EU-14)	*Family reunification*	*Ethnic German migrants*	*Jewish migrants*	*Asylum seekers*	*Contract workers*	*Seasonal workers*	*IT experts*	*Foreign students* (Bildungsausländer)
1991	128,142		221,995		256,112	51,771	128,688		
1992	120,445		230,565		438,191	94,902	212,442		
1993	117,115		218,888	16,597	322,599	70,137	181,037		26,149
1994	139,382		222,591	8,811	127,210	41,216	137,819		27,922
1995	175,977		217,898	15,184	127,937	49,412	176,590		28,223
1996	171,804	55,886	177,751	15,959	116,367	45,753	197,924		29,391
1997	150,583	61,740	134,419	19,437	104,353	38,548	205,866		31,123
1998	135,908	62,992	103,080	17,788	98,644	32,989	207,927		34,760
1999	135,268	70,750	104,916	18,205	95,113	40,035	230,347		39,905
2000	130,683	75,888	95,615	16,538	78,564	43,682	263,805	4,341	45,652
2001	120,590	82,838	98,484	16,711	88,278	46,902	286,940	6,409	53,183
2002	110,610	85,305	91,416	19,262	71,124	45,446	307,182	2,623	58,480
2003	98,709	76,077	72,885	15,442	50,563	43,874	318,549	2,285	60,113
2004	92,931	65,935	59,093	11,208	35,607	34,211	333,690	2,273	58,247
2005	89,235	53,213	35,522	5,968	28,914	21,916	329,789		

Source: Federal Statistical Office

or a child to migrate to Germany. These statistics recorded an increase in migration inflows of family members, from approximately 55,000 in 1996 to approximately 85,000 in 2002, and a decline in the following years. In 2005, the number of successful applications submitted to German embassies was 53,000. Turkey is the main country of origin; 27 per cent of all visas for the purpose of family reunification were granted at a German embassy in Turkey.

The next most important group are ethnic German immigrants/repatriates (*Spätaussiedler*). The inflows of ethnic Germans reached their peak in 1990 (379,073). Subsequently, they steadily decreased, with just 35,522 persons immigrating in 2005, the lowest figure since 1984. Since 1990, people from territories within the former Soviet Union have constituted the largest group. About 99 per cent of all *Spätaussiedler* originated from these territories in 2004. The main countries of origin were the Russian Federation (21,113 people in 2005) and Kazakhstan (11,206 people in 2005).

In the public domain the quantitative importance of the asylum seekers is often overestimated. The number of asylum seekers and refugees entering Germany annually is significantly lower than that of ethnic German immigrants/repatriates (*Spätaussiedler*) or family members. Between 1990 and the end of 2004, more than 2.2 million people applied for political asylum in Germany. After the peak in 1992, application figures decreased almost continuously. In 2005, a total of 28,914 people submitted a petition for political asylum (2004: 35,607), the lowest level since 1983. In 2005, the main country of origin of asylum seekers was Serbia and Montenegro, followed by Turkey, Iraq and Russia. However, between 2000 and 2005, the majority of applicants originated from Asian countries (Vietnam, Iran, Iraq, China and some of the successor states of the former Soviet Union).

A group that gained increasing importance was that of foreign students: from the winter semester 1993/94 to the winter semester 2003/04, the number of first-semester students that entered Germany for the purpose of studying at a German university or college (*Bildungsausländer*[9]) more than doubled, from slightly less than 20,000 to about 42,000. The largest group of '*Bildungsausländer*' starting a university course at a German university or college in 2003 was Chinese (6,676 students), followed by students from Poland (4,028), France (3,427), Russia (2,650) and Spain (2,698). Since the end of the 1990s, the number of foreign students, especially from China, the middle and eastern European countries (Bulgaria, Russia, Ukraine, Romania, Poland and the Czech Republic) and India has risen significantly.

Finally Jewish migrants from the former Soviet Union have to be mentioned. All in all, a total of about 200,000 Jewish emigrants from the successor states of the former Soviet Union[10] entered Germany between 1990 and 2005. In 2005, 5,968 Jewish migrants came to Germany.

5.5 Critical outlook

The main sources for data on migration are the statistics on arrivals and departures based on registration and deregistration of cross-border movement. However, due to some deficiencies, these statistics do not adequately reflect ongoing migration: 1) they do not report the sustainability and the purpose of immigration; 2) they record cases rather than the number of migrating persons; and 3) the obligation to register differs between the individual federal states.

Nevertheless, there have been some improvements in stock and flow statistics. Since 2006 the Central Register of Foreigners (AZR) can additionally be used to get information on inflows and outflows of foreign nationals. The AZR collects data on all foreign nationals that legally reside in Germany for a minimum of three months. With the coming into force of the new migration law, new characteristics have been introduced into the AZR, especially the purpose of the stay (according to the regulations of the new Immigration Act). The remaining gaps have to be filled by new procedures of statistical registration and the harmonisation of migration data on an international level.

Notes

1 Also during the 1970s the GDR began to recruit foreign workers on the basis of bilateral agreements with other socialist countries (Vietnam, Mozambique and Cuba). In 1989, about 93,000 contract workers were living in the GDR (see Bade & Oltmer 2004: 92ff.).

2 See Sekretariat der ständigen Konferenz der Kultusminister der Länder in der Bundesrepublik Deutschland, 'Workshop zur "Datengewinnungsstrategie für die Bildungsstatistik" am 13.02.07 in Berlin'. www.kmk.org.

3 This excludes persons entering Germany for a short visit, such as tourists, business travellers or seasonal workers. According to German law, foreigners are persons who do not hold German nationality (including those who are stateless) or who are not Germans according to Article 116 (1) of the Basic Law. Persons with multiple citizenship, who are nationals both of Germany and an additional country, are registered statistically as German citizens.

4 The foreigners authorities are mainly responsible for the discharging of tasks concerning the residence of third-country nationals (issuing, termination and renewal of residence permits).

5 Federal Statistical Office (Statistisches Bundesamt), 'Intensive preparation of the register-based census starting', press release, 29 August 2006. www.destatis.de.

6 Under federal and state registration law, all inhabitants of Germany are required to notify local authorities if they change residence. However, foreign military personnel

stationed in Germany and diplomatic and consular staff, and their families, are not required to register and therefore form no part of official arrivals and departures statistics. Authorities record the following data when a person is registered or deregistered: last and future place of residence, sex, marital status, participation in gainful employment, date of birth and nationality. Those holding another citizenship apart from the German one are registered as German citizens.

7 These children have to opt for one nationality after coming of age.

8 Inflows include foreigners immigrating to Germany and foreign children born in Germany during the reference year. In 2005, about 30,000 children with foreign nationality were born in Germany. Outflows include cases of unknown destination, and persons registered as dead or 'no longer resident'.

9 It is important to distinguish between two groups of non-German students: one group comprises so-called *Bildungsinländer*, i.e. foreign nationals who have graduated from German schools; most of these were born in Germany and should therefore not be categorised as migrants. The other group consists of so-called *Bildungsausländer*, i.e. foreign nationals with non-German university entry qualifications who enter Germany for the purpose of studying at a German university or college.

10 Based on a decision of the German Chancellor and the sixteen state governors on 9 January 1991, Jewish migrants are allowed to enter Germany under certain conditions.

Statistical sources

Organisation	*Content*	*URL*
Federal Statistical Office	– population register – register of foreigners (AZR)	www.destatis.de
Federal Office for Migration and Refugees	– asylum seekers – refugees – Jewish migrants from the former Soviet Union	www.bamf.de
Federal Employment Office	– contract workers – seasonal workers – IT experts	www.arbeitsagentur.de
Federal Administration Office	– ethnic German migrants/ repatriates (*Spätaussiedler*)	www.bva.bund.de

Bibliography

Bade, K. & J. Oltmer (2004), *Normalfall Migration*. Bonn: Bundeszentrale für politische Bildung.

Bauer, T., B. Dietz, K.F. Zimmermann & E. Zwintz (2005), 'German migration: Development, assimilation, and labour market effects', in K.F. Zimmermann (ed.), *European Migration. What do we know?*, 197-261. Oxford: Oxford University Press.

Bilger, V & A. Kraler (2006), 'Country Report: Germany', in M. Poulain, N. Perrin & A. Singleton (eds.), *THESIM: Towards Harmonised European Statistics on International Migration*, 413-425. Louvain-la-Neuve: Presses universitaires de Louvain.

Cyrus, N. (2005), *Active civic participation of immigrants in Germany*. www.uni-oldenburg.de/politis-europe.

Federal Office for Migration and Refugees (Bundesamt für Migration und Flüchtlinge) (2006), *Migrationsbericht 2005*. Berlin: Bundesamt für Migration und Flüchtlinge.

Federal Statistical Office (Statistisches Bundesamt) (2006a), *Population and employment: Foreign population 2005*. Wiesbaden: Statistisches Bundesamt.

Federal Statistical Office (Statistisches Bundesamt) (2006b), *Leben in Deutschland. Haushalte, Familien und Gesundheit – Ergebnisse des Mikrozensus 2005*. Wiesbaden: Statistisches Bundesamt.

Hailbronner, K. (2006), 'Germany', in R. Bauböck, E. Ersbøll, K. Groenendijk & H. Waldrauch (eds.), *Acquisition and Loss of Nationality, Volume 2: Country Analyses*, 213-251. Amsterdam: Amsterdam University Press.

Herbert, U. (2001), *Geschichte der Ausländerpolitik in Deutschland. Saisonarbeiter, Zwangsarbeiter, Gastarbeiter, Flüchtlinge*. München: C.H. Beck.

Herwartz-Emden, L. (2005), 'Migrant/-innen im deutschen Bildungssystem', in Arbeitsstelle Interkulturelle Konflikte und gesellschaftliche Integration (AKI) (ed.), *Migrationshintergrund von Kindern und Jugendlichen: Wege zur Weiterentwicklung der amtlichen Statistik*, 7-24. Bonn/Berlin: Bundesministerium für Bildung und Forschung.

Kadirbeyoglu, Z. (2007), 'Changing conceptions of citizenship in Turkey', in R. Bauböck, B. Perchinig & W. Sievers (eds.), *Citizenship Policies in the New Europe*, 293-311. Amsterdam: Amsterdam University Press.

Konsortium Bildungsberichterstattung (2006), *Bildung in Deutschland: Ein indikatorengestützter Bericht mit einer Analyse zu Bildung und Migration*. Im Auftrag der Ständigen Konferenz der Kultusminister der Länder in der Bundesrepublik Deutschland und des Bundesministeriums für Bildung und Forschung. Bielefeld: W. Bertelsmann Verlag.

6 Switzerland

Philippe Wanner, Denise Efionayi and Rosita Fibbi

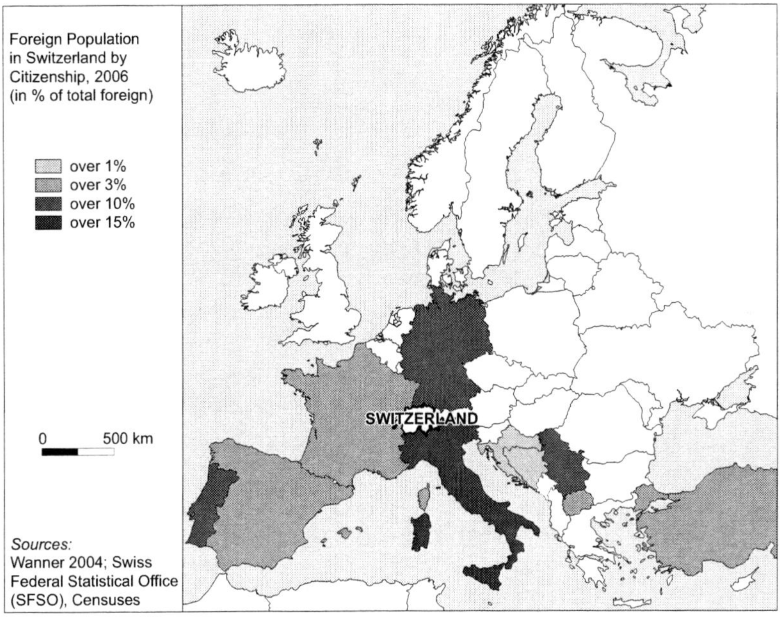

Cartography: Walter Lang, University of Vienna

6.1 Introduction

In the nineteenth century, Switzerland was a poor, rural country. Emigration was common and some examples of this are well known. The so-called Swabian children (*Schwabenkinder*) – the children of poor mountain farmers – were sent to rich farmers and households in Bavaria or Württemberg in spring and returned with presents and money in autumn. Young Swiss men earned their livelihood by serving as soldiers in the armies of various countries. The 'Swiss Guard' protecting the Pope in Rome stands as a reminder of the poverty prevailing at that time.

With the late industrialisation at the end of the nineteenth century and the rise of the tourism industry in the period between the wars,

Switzerland became one of the first European countries to experience immigration in sizeable numbers. Even though a high proportion of foreigners resided in the country at the beginning of the twentieth century, it was not until the 1930s that migration became a major social issue.

After the Second World War, migration flows increased and soon stirred public and political debate. Rotation of the labour force ('guestworker system') ensured that immigration was temporary and prevented immigrant groups from settling permanently in the country. However, this rotation policy rapidly showed its limits, especially with regard to the subsequent integration of the migrant population. As a result, the limitation of migration has been the object of a succession of referenda since the 1960s. The place occupied by these topics in public and political opinion may be measured by the high percentage of the population taking part in these referenda on migration and asylum laws.

Swiss data use the criterion of citizenship to describe immigration. Although this is only a rough indicator of the size of migrant communities, the share of foreigners confirms that migration is of enormous importance for Switzerland. In 2006, with 1.55 million foreigners – or 20.7 per cent of its resident population – on the national territory, Switzerland has one of the highest proportion of foreigners in Europe (i.e. residents with foreign citizenship), significantly ahead of Germany (8.9 per cent in 2001), Austria (9.4 per cent), France (5.6 per cent) and Italy (2.2 per cent). Within Europe, only Luxembourg (37 per cent) has a higher percentage of foreigners. Switzerland is genuinely a country of immigration, in part because of a significant inflow of migrants, notably in the 1990s, as is shown by the fact that 23 per cent of the population were foreign-born.

However, until quite recently, Switzerland was reluctant to acknowledge the need for an integration policy at all levels of governance. The adoption of an article on integration, added to the federal Foreign Nationals Act in 1998, can be considered the turning point in this respect. According to the new law adopted in September 2006,[1] the federal authorities aim to tie the presence of foreigners to the needs of the labour market, placing it 'in the interest of demographic and social development'[2] rather than fighting against *Ueberfremdung* ('excessive foreign presence') as stated in the 1931 law which was in force until 31 December 2007. The new bill aims at securing financial support for integration efforts made by migrants and local receiving communities. This change was brought about not only by the profound transformation of the international context, Switzerland's rapprochement with the European Union under the freedom of circulation guaranteed by the bilateral agreements, but also by the unprecedented rise in unemployment in Switzerland. Integration policies are new at federal level, having traditionally been carried out mainly at cantonal level, since, in the

Swiss federal system, cantons are in charge of education, health and housing. The new integration policy is primarily aimed at newcomers (Niederberger 2005; Mahnig & Piguet 2003).

There is no automatic access to the polity for foreigners; naturalisation occurs on a voluntary basis and requires explicit political approval, resulting in a quite restrictive practice, on the whole (Achermann & Gass 2003). The mode of integration can therefore be described as welfare state inclusion without the rights of citizenship.

6.2 Institutions, definitions and statistical sources

In 1970, the federal government set up the Central Register of Foreigners as an instrument designed to monitor the influx of foreign workers. This records all resident foreign nationals and delivers the bulk of information on this topic. Moreover, the increase in the number of questions regarding citizenship, origin and/or naturalisation in surveys and censuses clearly indicates the need for more data on this part of the population. Recently, surveys such as the Migrant Health Monitoring Survey have been specifically directed at the foreign population, clearly showing the importance of data collection on this issue.

6.2.1 Institutions

The principal institution involved in data collection is the Swiss Federal Statistical Office (SFSO), which is responsible for the production and dissemination of statistics at the national level. Other federal offices, such as the Swiss Federal Office for Migration (FOM) and the Federal Social Insurance Office provide some additional statistical information.

There is substantial coordination between offices involved in the process of data collection, especially with regard to administrative data. Moreover, the offices collaborate in data publication in order to avoid differences.

SFSO tries to provide harmonised registers if possible (for instance, the Register of Foreigners and the Register of Asylum Seekers are harmonised and the variables included are coded in the same way). However, in most cases, different data sets cannot be directly linked (due to the absence of a Personal Identification Number or PIN). Recently, attempts have been made to link databases by probabilistic linkage methods, but results are not yet available at the time of writing. The overall integration of administrative data on asylum seekers and foreigners – through the Central Migration Information System – had been in preparation for several years before the former Federal Office for Refugees and the Office for Immigration and Integration were merged to form the Federal Office for Migration in January 2005. The information system became operational in 2008.

The Swiss Federal Statistical Office (SFSO) is generally responsible for data collection at a national level (including sampling, collection, validation and diffusion). Some regional offices (at the cantonal level) may provide help in the collection of data, for example with the censuses, but this is not systematic. At the local level, institutions such as hospitals, schools or universities are involved in the production of statistics, under the direction of the SFSO.

There is no centralised Population Register in Switzerland (but hundreds of local registers); however, two central registers of foreigners organised at a national level do exist, since immigration falls under the direct competence of the Confederation. Data are collected by regional offices (for example regional police administrations) and centralised by the Swiss Federal Office for Migration. International inflows and outflows, as well as naturalisations, deaths and births, are declared and recorded in the registers of foreigners. The quality of declaration is high for inflows (as declaration is necessary in order to obtain a permit) as well as for outflows (emigration has to be declared in order to gain access to the benefits of the occupational provident insurance, known as the 'second pillar').

6.2.2 Concepts and definitions

In most cases, the variable 'citizenship' is included in registers and surveys and it comprises an exhaustive list of nationalities. In some cases, the place of birth and the age at arrival (or the date of arrival) are also included. In the case of administrative registers, the status of residence (residence permit) is often included, but not always. The only register including information on ethnicity is the Register of Asylum Seekers. The country of birth is only included in the censuses, which list every authorised foreigner living in Switzerland (asylum seekers and diplomats included). The last census, carried out in 2000, was organised by post and internet, which means that every household had to send back the completed form or fill in a form. For this reason, the non-response rate was higher than in 1990 and before (especially for some questions such as religion).

Information on the naturalisation status is also available in some statistics (Labour Force Survey 1991-1995, Census 2000).

Since these statistics do not contain a PIN, it is difficult to link censuses, registers and surveys. Therefore, statistics are generally computed on the basis of one data file.

The coding of citizenship and place of birth is harmonised according to the SFSO nomenclature.

6.2.3 *Availability of data*

The register of foreigners refers to the period 1974 and thereafter (1981 and thereafter for computerised data). The register of asylum seekers covers the period from 1994 to the present. There is a strong relationship between data availability and the volume of migration flows. In fact, both registers reflect the awareness of migration issues on the part of the federal and cantonal administrations.

The register of foreigners includes the structure of the foreign population (according to citizenship, age, sex, place of birth, etc.) as well as changes of place and status (immigration, emigration and naturalisation). Besides data on asylum requests, the register of asylum seekers includes the same information, apart from naturalisation. Both registers are updated by administrative offices in all Swiss regions and are centralised in the Federal administration. Every foreigner with a resident permit is automatically registered. Vital statistics (births, deaths, marriages, divorces, etc.) also provide data on events occurring in Switzerland. This makes it possible to describe the demographic trends in every migrant group defined by citizenship.

The census is another major basis for statistics on foreigners. Organised once every decade, it provides information on the socio-economic situation of inhabitants according to their citizenship and/or place of birth. Censuses – and the last one especially – carried out in 2000, are based on the principle of 'economic population', which means that people are recorded where they spend most of their time. All foreigners holding a permit are covered in the census, including diplomats. The recent decision to abolish the census and to partially replace it by regular (administrative) register and sample surveys has generated considerable discussion among researchers and within the administration.

Recent debates on migration have also led to a wide range of initiatives from the statistical offices to provide data on the participation of foreigners in the labour force (since 2003) or on the health status of migrants (2005). Other statistical activities are planned in the domains of security, criminality and social insurance.

Data sources on the foreign population in Switzerland are considered particularly rich and informative. From a statistical point of view, and because of the very existence of the Register of Foreigners, this population is more precisely described than the Swiss population. However, especially in the field of integration, some topics are only poorly covered by the statistical system. For instance, little information is available on the family structure of foreigners (except through the censuses), income and housing.

Since Switzerland is not a member of the European Union, the statistical system is rather different from that of other European countries. In particular, European Surveys (Eurobarometers, household panels, etc.) are not systematically carried out in Switzerland. However, with the signing of bilateral agreements between Switzerland and the European Union, Switzerland will progressively adapt its standards to those of Europe.

6.2.4 *Categories of foreigners*

As mentioned above, in Switzerland, as in other German-speaking countries, citizenship is the main criterion used to define foreign populations. Other criteria, such as parental origin or place of birth, are not systematically included in the data sources. For this reason, naturalised foreigners are generally considered together with the Swiss in statistics and cannot be studied as a group.

Available statistics generally distinguish between different categories of foreigners according to the permit they hold. In principle, we can therefore easily distinguish between asylum seekers, long-term migrants, short-term migrants and international officials with their families. Only refugees are difficult to identify, as they enter the category of migrants with annual or permanent permits once they are granted refugee or any other residence status.

It is rather difficult to identify foreign groups according to the reason for migration (family reunification, labour migration, etc.), because the specific immigration data only provide information on the legal flow.

During the 1980s and 1990s, illegal migration developed in Switzerland and became a crucial subject on the political agenda. Rough estimates suggest that between 100,000 to 200,000 undocumented foreigners live – and work – in Switzerland, but up to now no official data are available.

6.2.5 *Quality of data*

Though there may be exceptions, the quality of data in Switzerland is generally considered to be high. This is true, in particular, of data from the civil register, survey data and census data (which display a good level of coverage).

As far as administrative data are concerned, the quality depends on the source, the subject and the quality of the work performed by agencies and boards responsible for data collection and computerisation. Data on the socio-demographic characteristics of the foreign population and on migration may be considered exhaustive and of rather good quality. A survey of the sources (foreigner registers, census, etc.) shows that there is consistency between different sources as regards the data about the number of foreigners due to the fact that, under the federalist system, the administrative procedure is comprehensive and precise in Switzerland. For other areas, statistics do not converge. For instance, data concerning the professional activities of migrants are not always reliable and there are discrepancies between sources for indicators such as activity rates or unemployment rates.

Another problem frequently mentioned by researchers concerns the sample surveys. These are not representative as far as the foreign population is concerned because of the difficulty of reaching foreigners who do not speak one of the country's four official languages or who live in collective accommodation. It is also difficult to break down survey data into individual nationalities, because the numbers are too small to be significant. On the other hand, groups of nationalities (Swiss as against foreigners of different nationalities) are too heterogeneous to be meaningful. However, some improvement has been observed during the last decade regarding surveys: the Labour Force Survey, for instance, oversampled the number of foreigners to be included in the survey and organised interviews in foreign languages.

6.2.6 *Accessibility of micro-data to researchers*

According to the Law on Data Protection, the SFSO has access to all administrative data for statistical purposes. The dissemination of such data among researchers is allowed for statistical use only. In practice, Swiss researchers have access to most databases, made anonymous, after signing a contract of data protection. They have no access to identification variables (such as name, surname and address).

The collection of data from public or administrative sources or the gathering of personal data on a voluntary basis may be carried out by the SFSO according to the Swiss Statistics Act. The law allows the office to use administrative data for statistical purposes, in collaboration with other administrative offices or cantons. However, the harmonisation of administrative data and its integration into the statistical system is rather difficult, not least because of the division of competences between local communities, cantons and the federal government in the Swiss administration system.

6.2.7 *Statistics and reality*

Statistics reflect policy. People are grouped into categories which derive from the way social phenomena are understood, as well as the way these are politically and administratively regulated. So, for instance, early statistical data on immigrants concerned the labour force exclusively, and the permit was one of the crucial variables; this was a consequence of the rotation policy pursued by the authorities. Later, the whole foreign population was taken into account, with the mostly used variable being Swiss – as opposed to foreign – nationality.

Today the criterion of nationality is paramount. Often, statistics present data on the foreign population using special geographical categories, namely macro-regional areas (EU vs. other, non-EU European countries and other continents). This has to be seen in the light of the dual recruitment system introduced in 1998, which differentiates EU nationals, who enjoy free movement, from citizens with other geopolitical origins whose entry is subject to strict high-qualification conditions.

However, the nationality criterion no longer suffices to provide a proper description of the migration phenomenon and, in particular, of the dynamics of integration. That is particularly true for two domains: foreigners born in Switzerland and naturalised foreigners.

The relevance of the first problem becomes obvious when we compare the criteria of nationality and place of birth (not included in standard statistical presentation of immigration) in the 2000 Census, the most up-to-date information on the migrant population available in Switzerland (Table 6.1). This comparison reveals that one Swiss citizen in eight was born and grew up abroad, while 22.6 per cent of the foreigners were born in Switzerland, which means that they are not migrants in the true sense of the word, but belong to the second and third generation, who, because of the restrictive *ius sanguinis*-inspired naturalisation policy, remain foreigners even though they were born in the country (Fibbi & Wanner 2004). If data on birthplace are not included, those born in the country and those who recently arrived are discussed under the same heading on the basis of their common nationality; this methodological deadlock may prompt explanations of social dynamics based on essentialised concepts of (unchanging) culture and identity, overshadowing underlying social and individual dynamics. For this reason, the place of birth should be taken into account when monitoring integration processes.

The criterion of current citizenship is so dominant that naturalised persons cannot easily be singled out for statistical purposes. The 2000 Census revealed that 26 per cent of the people who were foreigners at

Table 6.1 *Resident population in Switzerland by nationality and place of birth, 2000*

Nationality/place of birth	*Born in Switzerland (%)*	*Born abroad (%)*	*N*
Swiss	88.2	11.8	5,792,461
Foreigners	22.6	77.4	1,495,549

Source: Swiss Federal Statistical Office, 2000 Census

birth became Swiss during their lifetime. Some 520,000 Swiss citizens were foreigners at birth; this means that one Swiss in ten was naturalised during his/her lifetime. Since naturalised young people are higher than average performers in school, neglecting this population leads to an over-pessimistic assessment of integration processes and success.

6.3 Dynamics and structures of the foreign population

6.3.1 The dynamics of the foreign population

The proportion of foreigners in the population has risen steadily since 1950, when only 5.9 per cent of the residents did not have Swiss nationality. By 1970, that number was 15.9 per cent and, by the end of 2002, this figure stood at 21.6 per cent. Within Europe, only Luxembourg, at 37 per cent, has a higher percentage of foreigners. As Table 6.2 indicates, the number of foreigners decreased at the end of the 1970s after the oil crisis but increased again without interruption after 1980.

Right after the Second World War, female labour immigration exceeded male immigration in number for both demographic (impact of the war on male population) and economic reasons (e.g. demand for female labour in the textile industry), until the gender balance finally reversed. In 1990, male labour immigrants were roughly twice as numerous as female immigrants. This trend was partially compensated by movements resulting from family reunification, which became more marked after 1980.

As elsewhere, births play a significant role in the foreign population's increase. This is largely due to the long history of migration in Switzerland and the presence of families in the country. As a result, natural increase is positive among foreigners (in contrast to the Swiss),

Table 6.2 *Number of foreigners in Switzerland, 1970-2004*

Year	*Total*	*Men*	*Women*	*Sex ratio (%)*
1970	1,001,887	538,456	463,431	116.2
1975	1,032,610	553,245	479,365	115.4
1980	913,497	496,893	416,604	119.3
1985	960,674	531,471	429,203	123.8
1990	1,127,109	629,980	497,129	126.7
1995	1,363,590	738,228	625,362	118.0
2000	1,424,370	757,119	667,251	113.5
2001	1,447,553	767,988	679,565	113.0
2002	1,476,966	782,085	694,881	112.5
2003	1,500,907	792,954	707,953	112.0
2004	1,524,663	804,753	719,910	111.8

Source: Swiss Federal Statistical Office, resident population, excluding asylum seekers and diplomats but tends to diminish because of parental naturalisation. Acquisition of citizenship clearly slows down the increase of the foreign population (Table 6.3).

Table 6.3 *Components of foreign population development, 1998-2004*

	1998	*1999*	*2000*	*2001*	*2002*	*2003*	*2004*
Population 1 January	1,375,158	1,383,645	1,406,630	1,412,937	1,447,553	1,476,966	1,500,907
Births	21,075	21,679	21,573	18,544	19,158	19,417	19,402
Deaths	4,152	4,261	4,338	4,263	4,250	4,492	4,401
Natural increase	16,923	17,418	17,235	14,281	14,908	14,925	15,001
Immigrations	72,202	83,677	84,200	99,746	105,014	98,812	100,834
Emigrations	64,017	62,780	59,302	56,477	53,517	51,046	52,950
Migratory balance	8,185	20,897	24,898	43,269	51,497	47,766	47,884
Naturalisation	21,277	20,363	28,700	27,583	36,515	35,424	35,685
Population 31 December	1,383,645	1,406,630	1,424,370	1,447,553	1,476,966	1,500,907	1,524,663

Sources: Swiss Federal Statistical Office, civil registration (births and deaths) and foreigners registers (migration flows and naturalisation), resident population, excluding asylum seekers and diplomats

6.3.2 *Socio-economic position*

Few data exist regarding the socio-economic position of migrants and only rough descriptions of trends can be undertaken. Since the end of the Second World War, the Swiss economy and its labour force have clearly depended on foreign labour. By the end of the War, immigration flows increased to meet the labour shortage in the construction industry. After 1960, many of the permanent immigrants and seasonal workers were poorly qualified and/or supplied labour-intensive branches and regions suffering from (seasonal) labour shortage. This was likewise the case of the second wave of immigration (1985-1992).

In 2000, immigrants composed 25 per cent of the total workforce, 50 per cent of hotel and catering industry workers and 33 per cent of those in construction. A feature of migration at the beginning of this century is an increase in the proportion of highly skilled migrants from Germany, France and Italy.

6.3.3 *Geographical origin*

The distribution of the foreign population according to citizenship (see Table 6.4) shows the increase in migrants from former Yugoslavia, Turkey and non-European countries. Between 1970 and 2000, the number

Table 6.4 *Foreign Population in Switzerland by citizenship, 1970-2000*

	1970		*1990*		*2000*	
	Abs.	*%*	*Abs.*	*%*	*Abs.*	*%*
Total number of foreigners	1,080,076	100.0	1,245,432	100.0	1,495,549	100.0
Germany	118,289	11.0	86,197	6.9	112,348	7.5
Austria	44,734	4.1	30,172	2.4	29,849	2.0
France	55,841	5.2	52,715	4.2	62,727	4.2
Italy	583,850	54.1	383,204	30.8	322,203	21.5
Spain	121,239	11.2	124,127	10.0	84,559	5.7
Portugal	3,632	0.3	110,312	8.9	142,415	9.5
Former Yugoslavia	24,971	2.3	172,777	13.9	362,403	24.2
Turkey	12,215	1.1	81,655	6.6	83,312	5.6
Other European countries	56,993	5.3	83,721	6.7	99,279	6.6
Africa	5,121	0.5	24,768	2.0	49,873	3.3
North and South America	18,425	1.7	30,357	2.4	51,124	3.4
Asia	8,327	0.8	62,937	5.1	92,145	6.2
Oceania	1,063	0.1	1,763	0.1	2,994	0.2
Unknown	25,376	2.3	727	0.1	318	0.0

Sources: Wanner 2004; Swiss Federal Statistical Office, 1970, 1990 and 2000 Censuses

of Italian and Spanish migrants decreased as the number of Yugoslavs, Turks and Portuguese increased greatly. Sri Lanka, India and China are the main Asian countries of origin, with most Sri Lankans seeking asylum and Indians and Chinese mostly students. The decrease in the number of Italians can be put down to the Oil Crisis (1975) and explained by the fact that most Italians at that time were holders of annual authorisations. Such authorisations are not renewed when businesses are not able to provide work for foreigners. As far as Spanish migration is concerned, inflows reached a maximum during the 1980s and were followed by an outflow of the first generation of migrants. For both countries, naturalisation did not play a major role in the decrease in the numbers of foreigners. Due to labour shortage and the difficulty of finding workers in traditional immigrant countries (especially Italy), other migration flows (especially from Portugal, Turkey and former Yugoslavia) occurred after the 1980s. In 2000, about 15,500 highly skilled migrants coming from outside the EU/EFTA and North America were living in Switzerland. Of those, 6,700 came from Eastern Europe, 4,000 from Asia, 2,400 from Africa and 2,400 from Latin America. Such trends have led to a rapid diversification of origins.

Other studies describing recent migration trends observed a feminisation of flows to Switzerland (especially among African migrants) – a phenomenon also noted in other countries and related both to the development of migration opportunities for more qualified women and to family reunification – and an increase in the average level of qualification of migrant groups, such as Italians and Spaniards, which traditionally presented a low level of skills (Wanner 2004).

6.3.4 Demographic structure

At the end of 2000, the bulk of the foreign population (men and women) were of working age (see Figure 6.1). The age structure of this

Figure 6.1 *Swiss population by place of birth and age, 2000*

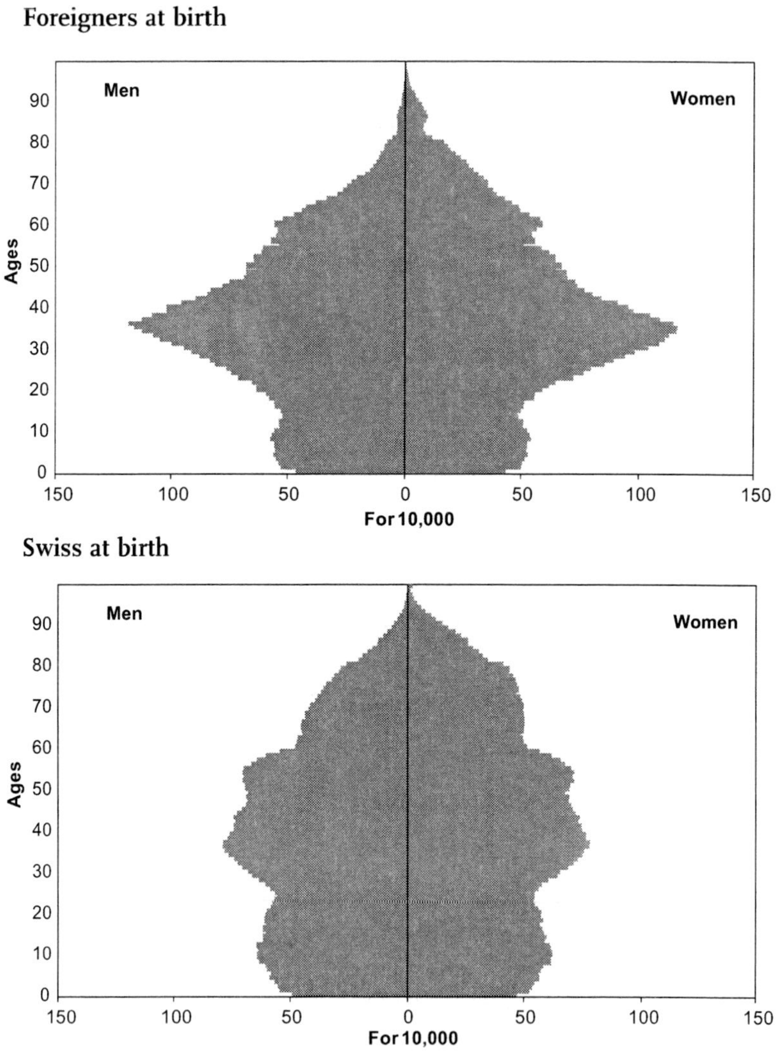

Source: Wanner 2004

Figure 6.2 *Inflows of foreign workers and seasonal workers to Switzerland, 1950-2000*

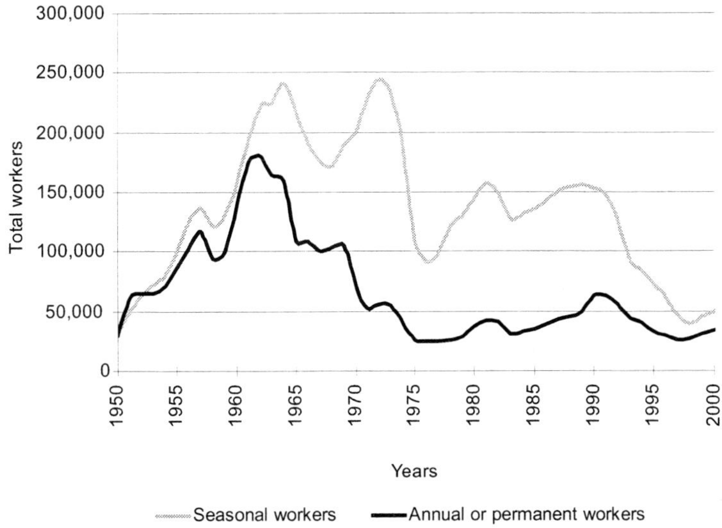

Source: Piguet 2005

population is shaped like a fir tree, with a large number of children and working-age adults. The proportion of migrants over age 50 is clearly smaller than among the Swiss.

Although there are more men in the foreign population, the number of women entering Switzerland has been increasing since 2000, as a consequence of the aforementioned tendency towards feminisation. As a result, the ratio of foreign men to foreign women is levelling out, with men being in the majority, as Table 6.2 indicates.

As Figure 6.2 shows, the amount of new entries for residence (black line) and entries of seasonal workers (grey line) since 1949 has fluctuated strongly over the years.

6.4 Migration policy

Although Switzerland is not a member of the EU, it has partially joined the liberalised European labour market. In June 2002, the Bilateral Agreement on the Free Movement of Persons between Switzerland and the EU Member States came into force.

This agreement means that EU citizens with a work contract, regardless of their skills or qualifications, can live and work in Switzerland under a quota system that provides 15,000 first-time long-term residence permits and 115,500 short-term residence permits per year.

In July 2004, individual admission controls on pay and working conditions for EU nationals were abolished and replaced by measures intended to prevent wage dumping as the latter could damage the interests of workers who live in Switzerland. In return, Swiss citizens will not need special permission to live and work in any of the 27 EU Member States. Between 2008 and 2009, the EU or Switzerland can decide to discontinue this arrangement, but if neither side wants to dissolve the agreement, it will remain in force.

As a result of the agreement, Switzerland has seen the number of immigrants coming from EU countries jump from 34,000 in 1997 to 49,800 in 2003, an increase of 46 per cent (also see Table 6.4 in Section 6.3.3). Most of these EU nationals are from Germany and Portugal, with EU labour migrants most active in finance, trade-related and service industries. In 2005, Switzerland became the first country of destination for German emigrants, with the United States being the second.

The agreement has also helped increase the number of EU nationals who work in Switzerland and live in a neighbouring country, especially in two economic centres, Geneva and Basel. At the same time that Switzerland made it easier for EU nationals to enter the country, the policies pertaining to third-country nationals became more restrictive.

Employers who want to hire a foreign employee have to apply for authorisation at the canton's labour market office, which can issue a work permit if the federal authority considers the economy needs the applicant's qualifications.

A permit may only be issued if the wage and employment conditions meet standards and if no qualified domestic or EU worker willing to work under those conditions can be found. Work permits are granted only to executives, specialists and other highly qualified workers from outside the EU/European Free Trade Association (EFTA). The permit is initially valid for one year and can be renewed every year indefinitely; after ten years the person may receive permanent residence.

The number of first-time year-round renewable residence permits, which includes working rights, is limited to 4,000, while the number of non-renewable one-year residence permits may not exceed 5,000. Any change of job or profession, as well as a move to another canton, requires approval from the cantonal labour market authority.

Under the current law, it is difficult for a foreigner to come to Switzerland and start a business or be self-employed. This situation could change if the federal government passes a new Aliens Law.

6.5 Conclusions

Statistics available in Switzerland provide a fairly good idea of the migrant population in the country and of its main socio-demographic and economic characteristics. It is often said that, statistically speaking, Switzerland's administration is able to provide more information on the foreign than on the native population.

Considering some important recent developments, the type of statistics which are available tend to obscure major structural changes in demographic and social dynamics. Sticking to the sole criterion of nationality implies maintaining the fiction of a monolithic understanding of the nation, while at the same time reinforcing the impression of an unbridgeable dichotomy between 'us' and 'them', the nationals and the foreigners.

However, a large amount of work still needs to be done before these statistics on migrants and foreigners in Switzerland can become a real tool for monitoring the integration of the foreign population, rather than just being a rigid administrative information system focussed on the size and the main characteristics of the 'non-Swiss' population. One of the major challenges for the next decade, in the context of the diversification of migration flows, will be to mount a longitudinal statistical tool which aims to understand integration processes. The setting up of a PIN number for all inhabitants (in the context of the social security system) would probably help in the development of such tools.

Another challenge is linked to undocumented migration and its measurement. Until recently, administrative offices in charge of statistics clearly ignored the fact that illegal migration is a reality in Switzerland as well as in most industrialised countries. As global economic changes and the reinforcement of restrictive migration laws are likely to contribute to perpetuating and most probably increasing irregular migration, this aspect cannot be ignored. An effort is therefore needed to find ways of measuring not only legal migration, but also 'real' migration.

Notes

1 It came into force on 1 January 2008.

2 Federal Law on Foreigners, chapter 2. art. 3, para. 3: 'Bei der Zulassung von Ausländerinnen und Ausländern wird der demografischen, der sozialen und der gesellschaftlichen Entwicklung der Schweiz Rechnung getragen.'

Statistical sources

Organisation	*Content*	*URL*
Swiss Federal Statistical Office	– population register – census	www.bfs.admin.ch
Swiss Federal Office for Migration	– immigration – naturalisations	www.bfm.admin.ch
State Secretariat for Economic Affairs	– unemployment	www.seco.admin.ch

Bibliography

Achermann, C. & S. Gass (2003), *Staatsbürgerschaft und soziale Schliessung. Eine rechtsethnologische Sicht auf die Einbürgerungspraxis der Stadt Basel.* Zurich: Seismo.

Fibbi, R. & P. Wanner (2004), 'La migration entre démographie et démocratie', in C. Suter, I. Renschler & D. Joye (eds.), *Rapport social 2004*, 100-124. Zurich: Seismo.

Mahnig, H. & E. Piguet (2003), 'La politique d'immigration suisse de 1948 à 1998: évolution et effets', in H. R. Wicker, R. Fibbi & W. Haug (eds.), *Les migrations et la Suisse. Résultats du PNR 'Migrations et relations interculturelles'*, 63-103. Zurich: Seismo.

Niederberger, J.M. (2005), 'Le développement d'une politique d'intégration suisse', in H. Mahnig (ed.), *Histoire de la politique de migration, d'asile et d'intégration en Suisse depuis 1948*, 255-287. Zurich: Seismo.

Piguet, E. (2005), *L'immigration en Suisse depuis 1948. Une analyse des flux migratoires.* Zurich: Seismo.

Wanner, P. (2004), *Migration et intégration.* Neuchâtel: Office fédéral de la Statistique.

Part 3

Post-communist countries

7 Hungary

Ágnes Hárs and Endre Sik

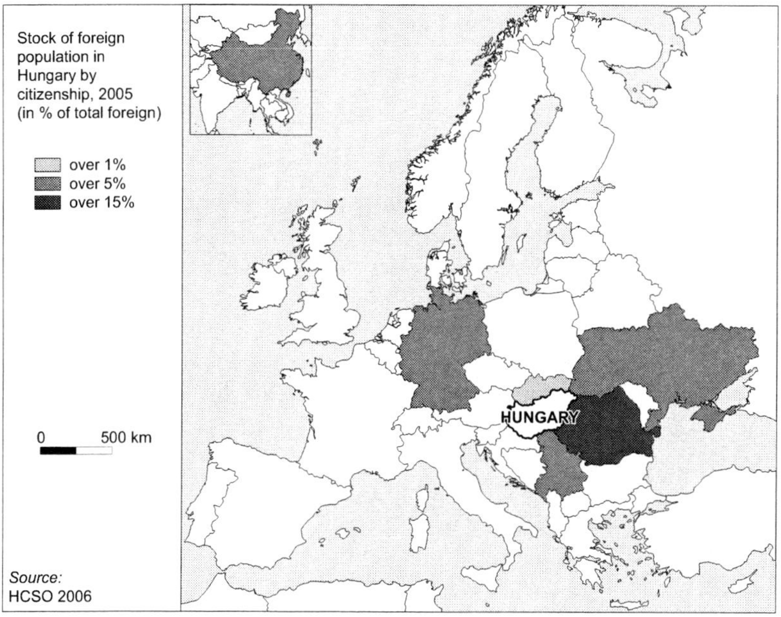

Cartography: Walter Lang, University of Vienna

7.1 Introduction

A general survey of the recent history and current situation of migration in Hungary has to include the country's rapidly changing location in the world system of migration. At the turn of the nineteenth century, Hungary was a country of emigration, sending millions of poor young males (mostly from the fringes of the Monarchy) to the United States.[1] During and after the First and especially the Second World War large-scale forced resettlement movements took place.[2] Moreover, Hungary lost a substantial part of territories with an ethnically mixed population after the First World War. As a result, an ethnically highly homogeneous population was created, very receptive to nationalist or even irredentist ideologies.

Over the following four decades communism turned Hungary into a closed country, with very restricted and state-controlled inward and outward migration. Between 1949 and 1989, there was practically no immigration into Hungary, except for two politically motivated waves, when Greek and Chilean communists were given asylum in the early 1950s and 1970s. However, the Hungarian border was much more permeable with respect to emigration. After the lost revolution in 1956, about 200,000 people left the country. Moreover, there was continuous emigration from Hungary between 1956 and 1989; it is estimated that at least another 200,000 people left the country in this period.

In 1988/89, with the ever-growing number of people arriving from the neighbouring countries, a quasi-refugee regime emerged in Hungary. The term 'quasi' refers to the fact that Hungary signed the 1951 Geneva Convention relating to the Status of Refugees only in late 1989. Hence, no asylum seeker could be formally granted refugee status, although the constitution contained the concept of asylum. However, both the media and politicians called the migrants 'refugees', which can only be explained by the political context; the overwhelming majority of these 'quasi-refugees' in the period were ethnic Hungarians fleeing from the still communist Romania.[3] This sudden and unexpected large inflow of migrants (mostly from Romania) was followed by a considerable outflow of the same people who returned home or left for a third country.

Hungary's accession to the European Union has not brought dramatic changes in the migration trends of the country. Although the number of labour immigrants has been increasing over the past few years, it is still very low compared to the total number of the workforce. On the other hand, the number of asylum seekers decreased from more than 11,000 in 1999 to about 1,600 in 2004 and 2005 and only slightly increased again in 2006 to 2,117 (UNHCR 2007a,b). Thus, the expectations (and in some cases fears) that the numbers of asylum seekers would surge with Hungary's accession to the EU were not confirmed.

7.2 The most important data sources[4]

To explain the merits and limitations of the existing official migration statistics in Hungary, we start by introducing the available statistical sources and publications, the basic definitions used by them and their advantages and shortcomings. This brief and descriptive introduction is followed by a more detailed description of the stock and flow data.

The authority responsible for producing accurate statistical data and publications on international migration, foreign population stocks and asylum seekers in Hungary is the Hungarian Central Statistical Office (Központi Statisztikai Hivatal, HCSO). To fulfil this task the HCSO mainly draws on administrative data sources, such as the population register, aliens police data or work permit data.[5] Among these, the administrative sources held by the Ministry of the Interior, i.e. the Central Aliens Register (Központi Idegenrendészeti Nyilvántartás, CAR) and the Central Population Register (A polgárok személyi adatainak és lakcímének nyilvántartása, CPR), are the most important (for further information, see Sections 7.2.2 and 7.2.3 below). Twice a year the Ministry of the Interior transfers data to the HCSO in electronic form. Based on these data, the HCSO publishes statistics on the immigration and emigration of Hungarian citizens and foreigners, on resident foreigners and on naturalisations.[6] The HCSO also issues separate statistics on asylum procedures; these are produced by the Immigration and Nationality Office of the Ministry of the Interior (BM-BÁH) based on data gathered in the Asylum Information System (Menekültügyi informacios rendszer). Besides these administrative sources, the HCSO uses officially collected survey type statistical data, namely the census (see Section 7.2.1 below) and the Labour Force Survey (LFS), for statistics on international migration, albeit to a lesser extent. For, rich as they are, these data sources either do not cover the foreign population at all or do so only poorly. Thus, the census did not include data on citizenship between 1960 and 1990. Moreover, the LFS, carried out by the HCSO since 1992, only covers a limited share of the immigrants.

Apart from the HCSO, some governmental institutions that collect administrative data on migration produce and publish statistical compilations both in hard copy and online. The Central Office of the Ministry of the Interior uses the population register to publish statistics on emigration, immigration and return migration of Hungarian citizens as well as on naturalisations and Hungarians born abroad. The Department of Aliens Policing of the Immigration and Nationality Office of the Ministry of the Interior (BM-BÁH) publishes, based on the CAR, data on foreign citizens residing in Hungary and the numbers of foreign citizens entering or leaving the country. The Department of Refugee Affairs of the Immigration and Nationality Office of the Ministry of the Interior (BM-BÁH) publishes data on refugees. Finally, the National Employment Service, operating under the auspices of the Ministry of Labour and Social Affairs, collects more detailed data on labour migration when issuing work permits. General data on labour migrants are included in the Aliens Police statistics, as those intending to work in Hungary have to apply for a residence permit.

Hungarian migration statistics are based on the concept of citizenship.[7] The basis of identifying citizenship is registration with the Ministry of the Interior (HCSO 2003). In the case of foreign citizens immigrating or emigrating from countries with changing borders – the Soviet Union, Yugoslavia and Czechoslovakia – the Central Statistical Office decides on the likely citizenship (in the successor states). As such, the classification is made according to the (last) permanent residence or, for lack of that data, according to the place of birth of the people concerned. The basis of the registration at the National Police Headquarters of the Ministry of the Interior is the passport of the foreigner. If this document does not include the latest foreign place of residence, people who were still registered as Soviets, Yugoslavs or Czechoslovaks in the data file were classified as belonging to the new states according to their place of birth. However in the case of foreign citizens residing in Hungary, the citizenship was not changed, if the foreign person arrived in Hungary before the foundation of the successor states and had been staying in the country since then.

International migration means 'leaving the country of the usual residence for a shorter or longer permanent period, the aim of which is to establish residence in another country in order to settle down or to have an income there. In the majority of the cases this also involves acquiring the citizenship of the chosen country sooner or later' (HCSO 2003: 33). Shorter official, business or tourist trips or a longer stay for study purposes cannot be considered as migration. However, if the purpose of staying in Hungary is to earn an income, this is a case of immigration even if the immigrant is likely to return to his or her homeland sooner or later. The distinction made between long-term and short-term migrants regards the period of migration. A long-term migrant is a person who moves to a country other than that of his or her usual residence for a period of at least twelve months so that the country of destination effectively becomes his or her country of residence. A short-term migrant is a person who moves to another country for a period of less than twelve months to earn an income. Since the distinction between temporary and permanent residence permits was abolished on 1 January 2002, the permit data gathered in Hungary no longer allow us to distinguish between these two categories.

In 2001, the understanding of the term 'resident population' as used in Hungarian statistics changed considerably. As will be explained in more detail below, this change meant that more detailed statistics are now available, both on foreign citizens residing in Hungary and on the inflows and outflows of foreign citizens. The 2001 Census was the first to include information on foreign citizens residing in Hungary. Departing from the figures gathered in the 2001 Census, the HCSO provides population updates for the inter-census years based on the CPR for Hungarian citizens and administrative data, i.e. the amount of residence and immigration permits, for foreign citizens.

7.2.1 *Census*

For more than a century, the Hungarian Central Statistical Office has carried out a census every ten years. However, the population included in the census differed markedly. Up to 1960, the census counted those persons who were present in the respective administrative unit on the day of the census, while the censuses carried out between 1970 and 1990 counted registered residents, regardless of whether they were present or absent on the day of the census. Under the communist regime, this system of counting the population was, on the one hand, quite an accurate means of representing the population residing in the Hungarian territory, since both immigration and emigration were strongly controlled. On the other hand, there was no particular political interest in more information about the marginal number of immigrants residing in the country, let alone about the number of Hungarians who left the country without deregistering. However, both the migratory reality and the political interests changed after the fall of the Iron Curtain. In particular, international organisations were interested in comparable data on international migration. In response to this need, the 2001 Census counted the actual resident population, i.e. those who actually lived and could be contacted at a specific address regardless of whether they were registered there or not.[8] As a consequence of this new understanding of the population, the 2001 Census is the first to provide detailed information on foreign citizens residing in Hungary for more than three months. This source includes details such as citizenship, place of birth, sex, age, actual and permanent address, education and occupation (HCSO 2006a: 80-81). Hence, the only disadvantage of this source is that there are no comparable data for earlier years.

7.2.2 *Central Population Register (CPR)*

The Central Population Register holds information on the registered resident population, which is defined as including: Hungarian citizens having permanent residence in Hungary; Hungarian citizens having permanent residence abroad who requested registration; foreigners holding permanent residence permits (including refugees); and EEA citizens holding residence permits (abolished with Hungary's accession to the EU). Data on foreigners are gathered in the Central Aliens Register (CAR), which is linked to the CPR. However, the CAR also contains data on temporary migration, which is not fed into the CPR (Kupiszewska & Nowok 2006: 529-530).

Citizens and holders of a permanent residence permit leaving the country for more than 90 days should inform their municipality of this fact. Those leaving temporarily stay in the register but their place of temporary residence abroad is added to the data; however, there is no information on the place of destination for those leaving for good. Returning residents have to notify their municipality within three days if they have no permanent address in Hungary. However, since there are no incentives for deregistration, emigration is usually underreported. Moreover, immigrations and emigrations of temporary residents are not covered at all (Kupiszewska & Nowok 2006: 530).

7.2.3 *Central Aliens Register (CAR)*

The Central Aliens Register (CAR) includes information on all foreigners who applied for or hold a visa, a temporary residence permit or a permanent residence permit, plus data on the children accompanying these people. The data include the date of application, the date of entry into the country, the type of permit granted or not and the date the respective permit was issued. Due to the administrative character of the data, those whose permits had expired were not necessarily removed from the database. This was corrected in 2001. As a consequence, the number of legally resident foreigners in Hungary dropped by more than 40,000 people between 2000 and 2001 (see Kupiszewska & Nowok 2006: 531, 536).

The HCSO uses the CAR to produce statistics on both the stocks and flows of foreigners. The stock figures include 'foreigners as at 1st January with valid residence permits, permanent residence permits (settlement or immigration permits) and EGT residence permits (for EEA citizens)' (Kupiszewska & Nowok 2006: 536). The flow statistics include the number of temporary and permanent residence permits issued per year.

7.2.4 *Work permit data*

Although labour immigrants are included in the CAR, this source does not provide detailed information on foreigners employed in Hungary. Therefore, the HCSO uses work permit data to give a deeper insight into labour migration to Hungary. Work permit data include information on the sex and citizenship of the employee, industrial branches and region of employment.

In the wake of Hungary's accession to the EU on 1 May 2004, work permit regulations were changed. Labour migrants from the EU Member States no longer need a work permit (except in cases of reciprocity with those countries that still impose work permit requirements on Hungarian citizens). However, those EU citizens who are no longer included in the work permit register still need a green card. Hence, a reliable overview of labour immigration to Hungary will have to summarise work permits, green cards and the obligatory registration of the citizens of the new Member States working in Hungary.

7.3 The stock of foreign citizens in Hungary and the inflows and outflows

In the following section, we will first present the official statistical data on migrants in Hungary and then, in the final section, we will look at non-official sources. The most reliable stock data can be derived from the 2001 Census. The stock and flow data, based on various administrative sources described in Section 7.2, are less reliable and limited in information. However, these are much fresher and provide information on successive years.

Foreign citizens resident in Hungary constituted around 1 per cent of the total population in 2001 (see Table 7.1). Due to the fact that there are more women than men in the total Hungarian population, the share of men holding a foreign citizenship in the total Hungarian male population is slightly higher than that of women, although the number of women holding a foreign citizenship outnumbers that of men. Between 2001 and 2006, the share of those holding a foreign citizenship in the total population slightly increased. The proportion of men and women is still balanced.

The two data sources provide similar information on the geographic origins of the foreigners resident in Hungary (see Table 7.2). The overwhelming majority of foreign citizens originate from Europe, with an increasing proportion coming from Romania and other neighbouring countries. Besides Europeans, immigrants of Asian origin, mostly Chinese and to a lesser extent Vietnamese, constitute considerable immigrant populations.

The 2001 Census provides us with the most comprehensive information on foreign citizens resident in Hungary, including dual nationals, a large majority of whom are returnees who display different characteristics to other migrants.[9] While only 1 per cent of the total population in Hungary are foreign or dual citizens, the proportion of the foreign-born population is considerably higher, at 2.7 per cent of the total population. The share of women is higher among the foreign-born while lower among foreign citizens, perhaps because of the unbalanced marriage market, i.e. females are over-represented both among those coming from the East and moving to the West (see Table 7.3).

Table 7.4 provides a more detailed picture of the population by citizenship and place of birth. While only 2 per cent of the Hungarian citizens were born abroad, 8.8 per cent of the foreign citizens and 39.4

Table 7.1 *Hungarian population by citizenship and sex, 2001 and 2005*

	2001 Census			*Population 2001**			*Population 2005**		
	Total	*Men*	*Women*	*Total*	*Men*	*Women*	*Total*	*Men*	*Women*
Total population (native & foreign)	10,198,000	4,851,000	5,348,000	10,198,000	4,851,000	5,348,000	10,098,000	4,793,000	5,304,000
Foreign citizens (incl. double citizens)	110,839	54,520	56,319	110,028	53,578	56,450	154,430	77,361	77,069
Share of total (male/ female) population (%)	1.09	1.12	1.05	1.08	1.10	1.06	1.53	1.61	1.45

* Data refer to 1 January.

Sources: 2001 Census; HCSO 2006b; authors' calculations

Table 7.2 *Stock of foreign citizens in Hungary by country of citizenship in per cent of total foreigners, 2001 and 2005*

	Census 2001			Foreign population 2001*			Foreign population 2005*		
	Total	Men	Women	Total	Men	Women	Total	Men	Women
Total foreigners	100.0	100.0	100.0	100.0	100.0	100.0	100.0	100.0	100.0
European origin	83.1	79.6	86.4	84.7	81.5	87.8	84.5	82.5	86.6
Of which:									
Romanian	36.3	34.4	38.2	37.8	37.5	38.0	42.9	42.4	43.3
Ukrainian	9.5	7.8	11.2	8.1	7.3	11.7	9.9	9.4	6.2
Yugoslav	9.3	10.3	8.3	11.5	13.0	10.1	7.8	8.6	7.1
Slovak	4.1	2.9	5.2	1.4	1.1	1.7	2.3	2.0	2.7
German	7.1	6.7	7.4	6.8	5.2	8.3	6.8	6.0	7.6
Russian	2.6	1.8	3.3	1.7	1.5	1.9	1.8	1.4	2.2
Polish	2.0	1.5	2.5	2.1	1.6	2.6	1.5	1.1	1.9
Asian origin	10.3	12.2	8.5	11.5	13.5	9.5	12.0	13.2	10.8
Of which:									
Chinese + Vietnamese	5.6	6.2	5.0	7.0	8.0	6.0	7.6	8.3	6.8
African origin	1.5	2.4	0.7	1.1	1.9	0.4	1.2	1.8	0.5
US + Australia	5.1	5.9	4.4	2.7	3.1	2.4	2.3	2.5	2.1

* Data refer to 1 January.
Sources: 2001 Census; HCSO 2006b; authors' calculations

Table 7.3 *Share of foreign and dual citizens and foreign-born population in Hungary, 2001 (in per cent)*

	Total	Men	Women
Share of foreign citizens	0.91	0.94	0.89
Share of dual citizens	0.17	0.19	0.16
Share foreign & dual citizens	1.09	1.12	1.05
Share of foreign-born population	2.7	2.5	2.9
Total population	10,198,300	4,850,600	5,347,600

Source: 2001 Census

Table 7.4 *Breakdown of population in Hungary by place of birth and residency in 2001 (in per cent)*

	Resident in Hungary	Resident in Hungary with permanent residency abroad		Resident in Hungary	
Citizenship	Born abroad		Born in Hungary		
Foreign citizens	74.5	16.3	0.4	8.8	100.0
Dual citizens	54.8	3.0	2.8	39.4	100.0
Foreign & dual citizens	71.4	14.2	0.7	13.7	100.0
Hungarian citizens	2.0	0.0	0.0	97.9	100.0
Total population	2.7	0.2	0.0	97.1	100.0

Source: 2001 Census; authors' calculations

per cent of the dual citizens were born in Hungary. Almost three quarters of the foreign citizens but only about half of the dual citizens were born abroad. Thus, these two groups differ significantly, which is partly a result of the historical border shifts mentioned earlier.

Data from the 2001 Census show that approximately 8 per cent of the national ethnic groups in Hungary are foreign-born, i.e. they are first-generation migrants. The share of the foreign-born was largest among Rusins (54 per cent), Ukrainians (50 per cent), Romanians (49 per cent) and Poles and Bulgarians (both 42 per cent) (Tóth & Vékás 2004).

As Table 7.5 shows, compared to the native population, the foreign and dual citizens are:

- comprised of fewer females;
- more in the range of working age (20-59 years old);
- more highly educated.

Within this group those with dual citizenship are even less frequently female, with more being teenagers or elderly, and being significantly more educated.

Based on the permit data included in the CAR, the HCSO provides statistics on the stocks of foreigners resident in the country (see Figure 7.1). These include all those holding valid residence permits, permanent resident permits and, up to 2004, permits for EEA citizens. As mentioned above, this administrative source is somewhat less reliable than HCSO data. In fact, administrative adjustments carried out in 2001 showed that 40,000 people still included in the CAR no longer held a valid permit. As a consequence, the number of foreigners legally residing in the country fell to a level that was lower than in 1993 but has since increased again to the level reached before the correction.

The HCSO also publishes data on the inflows and outflows of foreign citizens (see Figure 7.2). The inflow of immigrants (calculated on

Table 7.5 *Socio-demographic characteristics of Hungarian citizens compared to those of the foreign and dual citizens residing in Hungary in 2000 (in per cent)*

	Natives	*Foreign and dual citizens*	*Within foreign and dual citizens*	
			Foreign citizens	*Dual citizens*
Gender: female	52.4	50.8	51.3	48.4
Age: under 19	23.2	21.2	20.0	27.6
20-29	15.6	24.0	26.0	13.1
30-59	40.7	43.0	43.6	39.9
Above 60	20.5	11.8	10.4	19.4
Education: secondary	38.0	57.3	56.0	65.1
Higher	12.5	25.3	24.2	31.4

Source: 2001 Census

Figure 7.1 *Number of foreigners residing legally in Hungary, 1 January 1993-2006*

Sources: HCSO 2003, HCSO 2006b (rounded figures)

the number of temporary and permanent residence permits issued per year) increased sharply between 1987 and 1991. Subsequently, the number of foreign citizens entering the country legally remained more or less stable up to the turn of the century, when it grew again. The number of emigrants followed the same trend between 1985 and 1991, albeit on a much lower level, and has since remained stable. This means that most of the immigrants remained in the country, while a smaller number returned home or moved on to a third country. Taken as a whole, Figure 7.2 illustrates that Hungary is an immigration country. At the beginning of the 1990s, the migration surplus was large, de-

Figure 7.2 *Legal inflow and outflow of foreign citizens across Hungarian borders, 1985-2005*

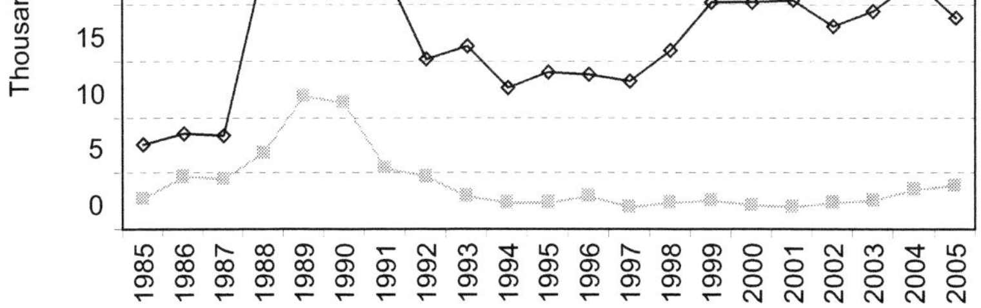

Sources: HCSO 2003: 14, 2006c

spite the fact that a large number of foreigners emigrated. Subsequently, both immigration and emigration of foreigners are stable. Finally, at the turn of the century, Hungary becomes a full-scale immigration country – at least in official statistics, notwithstanding the known shortcomings of emigration data.

Of course, statistics based on permit data exclude, per se, all kinds of illegal migration (for further information on this phenomenon in Hungary, see Section 7.6). Moreover, it does not include the quasi-refugees who arrived in Hungary in the late 1980s and early 1990s. These are included in Figure 7.3. This graph that extends our view beyond permit data and at the same time breaks down immigration into four major types in order to provide a more realistic insight into immigration to Hungary (see Figure 7.3).

The first immigrants coming to Hungary in the transition period were quasi-refugees, here categorised as 'other', who were neither recognised as refugees nor defined as immigrants. Having entered the country in various ways, they either managed to regularise their status and to become legal immigrants or residents in the following years or they left again for a third country. The first wave of quasi-refugees, with a peak of 'other forms' of immigration, was followed by a brief 'immigration permit' period, later overtaken by that of 'residence permits'. The num-

Figure 7.3 *Major inflows of foreign citizens to Hungary by type of permit, 1985-2000*

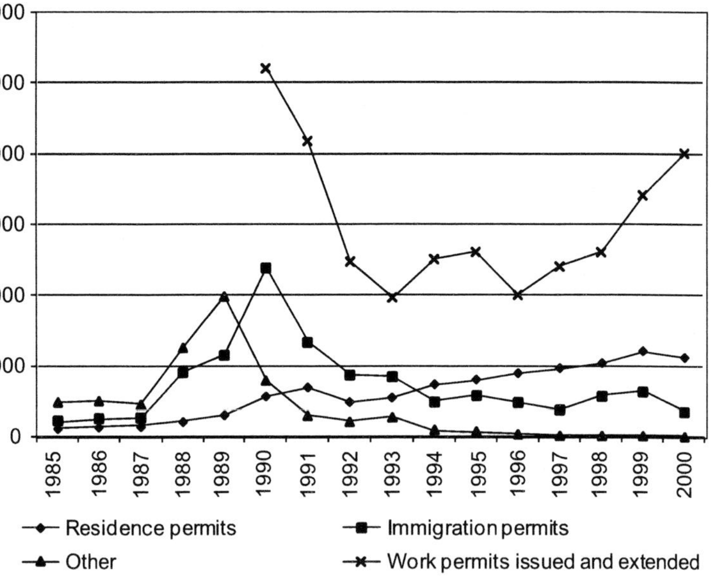

Sources: HCSO 2001: Table 1.8.1 and 1.8.2; HCSO 2003: Table 1.12

ber of work permits issued is closely linked to immigration trends, which is hardly surprising since those intending to work usually need an immigration or residence permit (excluding border commuters; see Section 7.5). Particularly during the transition period, many of the quasi-refugees applied for work permits in order to legalise their status in the country. This high interest in work permits decreased in the mid-1990s when the number of naturalisations surged. More than 20,000 foreign citizens, most of them originating from Romania, were (re-)naturalised in 1992 and more than 11,000, again mostly from Romania, in 1993. With the adoption of stricter naturalisation requirements, this number fell again (see Kovács & Tóth 2007: 150-151).

What this figure tells us, however, is not so much that immigration is changing but that the statistical regimes are changing, following the changes in the legal regulation of migration. For example, both the high number and the disappearance of the 'other' types of immigration were linked to the developing migration regulation and the way statistics caught up with these.

As far as emigration is concerned, foreigners (mostly those coming from Romania and former Yugoslavia) emigrated in large numbers shortly after their arrival between 1988 and 1992, while Hungarian emigration was relatively more pronounced before the change of the system (see Figure 7.4). The annual number of refugees was changing rapidly, which is partly 'normal' (since it reflects the unpredictable changes in the worldwide political landscape and the way these are 'translated' into the mental maps of the refugee population, i.e. their

Figure 7.4 *Emigration of foreign citizens and Hungarians, return migration of Hungarians and inflow of refugees, 1985-2005 (cases)*

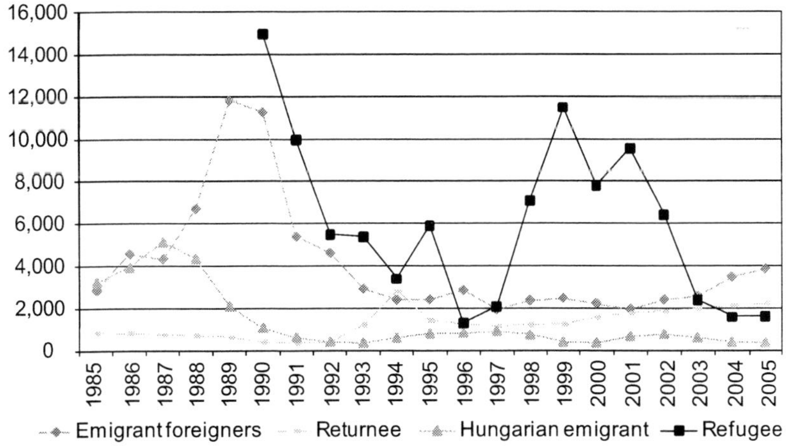

Source: HCSO 2001, 2003, 2006b

views of the world as a space of migration) and partly a by-product of the changes in the Hungarian regulation (Hungary abolished the territorial restriction of the Geneva convention in 1998 and has since also accepted non-European refugees) and how these are reflected in migration statistics. The number of returnees has always been rather low, except for a short period around the mid-1990s.

7.4 Characteristics of recent inflows and outflows

Contrary to what we expected on the basis of standard migration literature, we did not find any sign of a sharply growing feminisation or a geographical dispersion of migration to contemporary Hungary. Figure 7.5 shows the changing proportions of female migrants in various migrant groups in contemporary Hungary.

Figure 7.5 shows that the proportion of females is more or less constant among almost all types of migrants entering or leaving Hungary. Only among Hungarian emigrants did the proportion of women significantly increase, indicating a growing 'export' of Hungarian females, especially between 2001 and 2005.

The average age of male and female immigrants has not changed at all. There was, however some change in some smaller immigrant and emigrant groups (see Figure 7.6).

While both male and female emigrants were, on average, about 30 to 35 years when they left the country, this figure surged to 45 years in

Figure 7.5 *Shares of females among those entering and leaving Hungary, 1990-2006 (in per cent)*

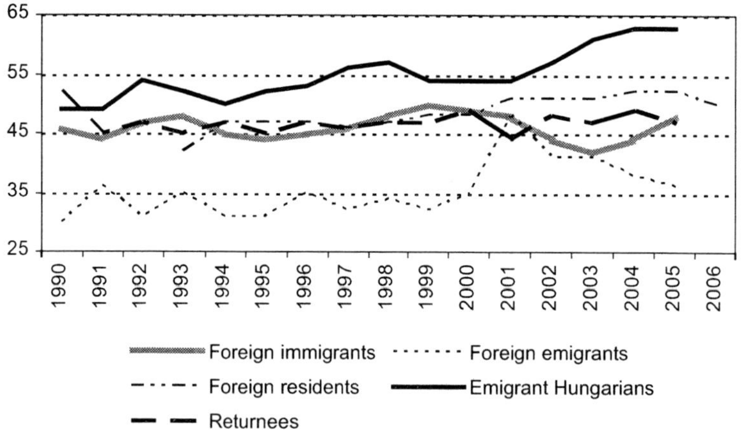

Source: HCSO 2003, 2006b

Figure 7.6 *Average age of emigrants and refugees, Hungary, 1990-2006*

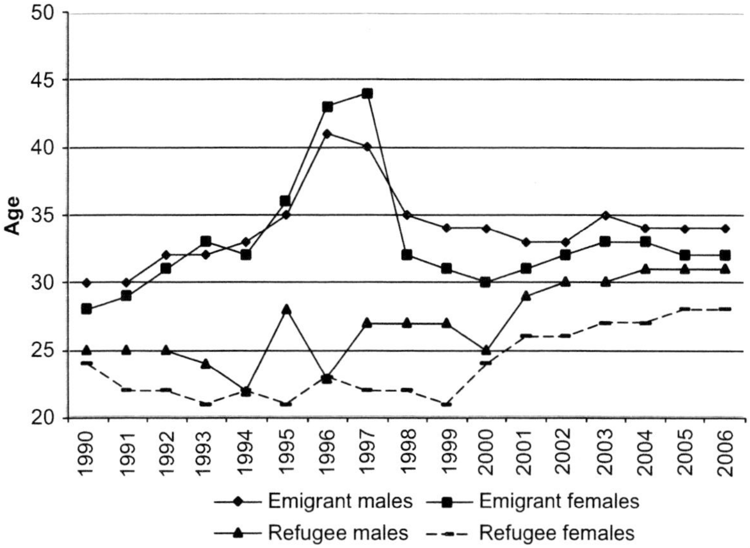

Source: HCSO 2003, 2006b

the mid-1990s. The average age of male and female refugees rapidly oscillates up to 2000 and has constantly risen ever since. In most years, male refugees were older than their female counterparts, which can most likely be explained by the fact that they arrived as families.

As mentioned above, the countries of origin of those entering Hungary have not become more diversified in recent years. On the contrary, in 2003 the overwhelming majority (85 per cent) of the stock of foreigners residing in Hungary for more than a year was of European origin, mostly from neighbouring countries with large Hungarian minorities (see Table 7.6).

While the share of men and women is more or less balanced among the total immigrant population, this proportion differs significantly for the regions of origin. While immigration from Asia (namely China), former Yugoslavia and the miscellaneous countries is predominantly male, more women than men come to Hungary from the EU.

The immigrant stock on the labour market can best be characterised by the number of work permits issued (see Figure 7.7).[10] The overwhelming majority (85 per cent) of the foreign labour is of European origin, mostly from Romania, Ukraine and, increasingly, from Slovakia.

Labour immigrants mainly originate from the countries bordering Hungary. Their proportion steadily increased from 65 per cent of the total in 1996 to 76 per cent in 2000 and finally to 86 per cent in

Table 7.6 *Immigrants in Hungary by sending country/region and sex, 1 January 2004 (in per cent)*

	Share of immigrants by sending region	*Share of immigrants by sending countries and region*	*Percentage of females*
Europe	85		53
Of which:			
EU		23	57
Romania		50	51
Former Yugoslavia		11	47
Ukraine		12	54
Asia	11	100	44
Of which:			
China		46	45
All others	4		38
Total	100		51

Source: HCSO 2004

2004. In fact, the increasing number of work permits (plus green cards and registrations) is due to the growing labour immigration from these countries. The share of Slovak workers increased considerably over the last decade (see Table 7.7). It should be noted that work permit holders who commute on a daily basis are not considered immigrants (see the immigrant population by citizenship in Table 7.2). Nevertheless, they are included in the immigrant labour statistics.

Figure 7.7 *Stock of immigrant labour in Hungary by sending countries, 1990-2004*

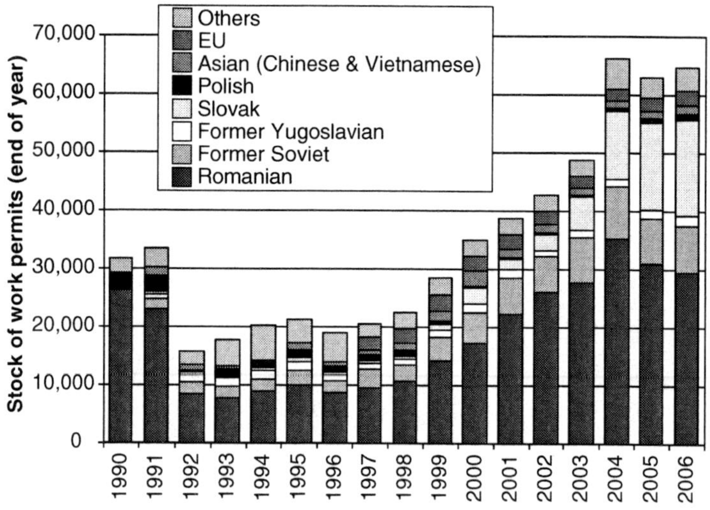

Sources: 1990-2003: work permit statistics; 2004-2006: work permits, green cards and registrations (all data for 31 December)

Table 7.7 *Geographic concentration of immigrant labour stock by sending countries, 1996-2006*

	Immigrant labour							
	Share of total				Share of 4 neighbouring			
	1996	2000	2004	2006	1996	2000	2004	2006
Romania					70	65	62	53
Former Soviet Union					18	19	16	14
Former Yugoslavia					8	5	2	3
Slovakia					4	11	21	30
4 main neighbouring sum	65	76	86	86	100	100	100	100
EU-15*	0	7	3	4				
Asia (China & Vietnam)	4	8	2	2				
Others	32	9	9	8				
Total	100	100	100	100				
	18,763	35,014	66,132	64,626				

* EU-15 data are not necessarily included following the EU enlargement due to the regulation of the registration.
Sources: 1990-2003: work permit statistics; 2004-2006: work permits, green cards and registrations (all data for 31 December)

Table 7.8 shows that the countries of origin of the foreign citizens entering Hungary and of those naturalising in Hungary largely remained the same between 1994 and 2005. In fact, if there is any change in the geographical origin at all, it is the opposite of dispersion, i.e. increasing concentration.
In sum, since the share of females among the migrants increased only slightly, we conclude that the feminisation of migration is not a major

Table 7.8 *Proportion of Romanian, Slovakian, Ukrainian (Russian) and Former Yugoslavian citizens among immigrants, work permit holders and those who naturalised in Hungary, 1994-2005*

	From Romania, Slovakia, Ukraine (Russia) and Former Yugoslavia (%)		
	Immigration	Work permits	Naturalisations
1994	62	68	80
1995	57	73	82
1996	50	65	85
1997	50	71	84
1998	59	65	85
1999	70	74	89
2000	70	76	85
2001	73	82	92
2002	74	70	93
2003	68	71	85
2004	78	72	89
2005	63	76	89

Sources: HCSO 2003, 2006b

trend in contemporary Hungary. Neither is geographical dispersion: the countries of origin of those entering Hungary have largely remained the same since the early 1990s. This is very likely the result of the large quasi-diasporic migration region bordering Hungary and the strong diaspora politics of Hungary (Sik 2000; Sik & Tóth 2003). The only observable change is that migrants tend to be older than ten years ago, which might be interpreted as a sign of the maturation of the migration process.

7.5 A critical but positive outlook

In the previous brief analysis we implied that migration statistics are unavoidably distorted by two opposing influences:
- the historical, political and cultural characteristics of the country where they were produced, and
- the internationalised trends (or fashions) of statistical data production.

This unavoidable double bias can be very lucidly illustrated by analysing Hungarian migration statistics. As to the country-specific bias, we saw characteristics of the Hungarian migration statistics (such as the special returnee statistics or a very detailed analysis of naturalisation), which might be rather unique and are likely to be the result of Hungarian diaspora politics. As to the bias due to internationalisation, we demonstrated that the harmonisation of migration statistics towards the UNHCR and the EU resulted in changes that hardly allow for a reliable time-series analysis.

More importantly, however, there are reasons why we assume that there is an unavoidable and increasing general inability of any official migration statistics to give a comprehensive and reliable picture of the current migration processes.

First of all, some of the newly expanding forms of migration cannot, due to their very nature, be properly covered by standard migration statistics. Examples are the following:
- the increasing spread of transnational commuters (au pairs, seasonal agricultural workers, Hungarian doctors working in UK hospitals over the weekends);
- the spreading of international small entrepreneurs (Portes, Haller & Guarnizo 2001);
- the internationalisation of the informal economy (growing informal remittances, trafficking).

In the case of Hungary the (temporary) spread of certain special forms of migration has further increased the general level of bias between the reality and the statistical depiction of migration processes. This is due partly to Hungary being in the middle of the (former) buffer zone (Wallace 1996), and partly to a long history of 'migrating borders'.

The first of these characteristics implies special migration patterns, such as suitcase trade (Czakó & Sik 1999; Sik & Wallace 1999) and 'Comecon marketplaces' (Sik 1999) and an elaborated system of open-air daily labour markets (Sik 2002).

The second explains Hungary's strong diaspora migration policy, which also influences statistics. This policy addresses the large Hungarian diaspora just on the other side of the Hungarian borders, which has been described as a quasi-diaspora (it was created not by emigration but by the repeated redrawing of the borders). As a consequence, the term 'foreign-born' population has a distorted meaning in Hungary. Among the elderly, a substantial proportion of the 'foreign-born' were born in former Hungarian territory that later became 'foreign' in the statistics (Juhász 1997).

If all the aforementioned claims are correct, the future of official migration statistics is in a perilous state. However, we foresee the supplementation of the existing and unavoidably deteriorating official data by alternative sources registering migration flows. These sources would be a useful addition to the existing statistics and provide us with a better overview of contemporary migration flows. Such alternative sources of information could be very different from border statistics (Futo & Jandl 2005), the analysis of tourist flows and so on.

To illustrate that limited but still useful additional and alternative data sets can contribute to answering relevant questions about migration, the following section will serve to introduce a method we developed at TÁRKI (Social Research Inc.). This method uses municipalities as the unit of analysis of certain (in our view increasingly important) migration processes which are, per se, not included in any standard migration statistics.

7.6 An additional and alternative method of measuring migration: The Local Government Monitoring and Database Project (LGMDP)

TÁRKI started the first phase of Local Government Monitoring and Database Project in 1995. Since then, there have been twelve waves covering the following migration related topics:

1995 informal economy, foreign labour, xenophobia, suitcase trade;

1996 informal economy, foreign labour, xenophobia, suitcase trade;

1997	informal economy, foreign labour, xenophobia, suitcase trade;
1998	local labour market, foreign labour, suitcase trade;
2000/2001	refugee integration;
2002	informal economy, migrants on the local labour market and migration from the municipality, suitcase trade, tourism;
2005	informal economy, foreign labour, suitcase trade.

The LGMDP covers all Hungarian municipalities (No. app. 3100). The basic characteristics of the survey technique are as follows:
- a self-administered questionnaire (max. eight pages, simple structure);
- non-response is corrected by weighting; weights are derived from the Hungarian Central Statistical Office (HCSO) Settlement Database;
- longitudinal panel (all waves are assembled into a cumulative database).

The response rate of the single-phase survey (sending questionnaires to the municipalities only in one wave) is about 25-30 per cent, while it is about 50 per cent of the two-phase survey (two postal questionnaires or a postal wave and a phone wave).[11]

The main advantages of the survey technique are:
- As the database is based on annual surveys that are being built continuously, it will provide longitudinal data, which enable users to make projections for the future.
- It allows a quick and up-to-date analysis (the time required for analysing a survey is about three months).
- LGMDP surveys provide additional information (e.g. ethnic composition, commuting migrant workers, open-air marketplaces) that other existing databases do not contain.
- The data cover parts of the migrant population which cannot be reached by normal statistical methods (illegal migrants, commuting workers, shuttle traders) as well as some aspects of the migration process which are too specific to be properly analysed by macro-statistical methods (such as integration, foreign investors on local level, wages on the local labour market, spread of open-air markets, etc.).

The following two subsections serve to summarise some results of these surveys (for further details, see Sik 1998, 1999).

7.6.1 *Spatial distribution of informal markets and foreign traders*

In 1997, every seventh municipality had at least one informal market. 'Large informal markets' (with at least ten traders regularly present) existed in 12 per cent of the municipalities. On average, these informal markets were open three days a week for six hours throughout the year and were made up of 92 traders. While foreign traders were present in the majority of these informal markets, their number was higher than the national average in Southern Transdanubia, the Great Northern Plain and some towns. Among these foreigners, ethnic Russians and Romanians constituted the largest groups in 1995, followed by Poles, ethnic Hungarians living across Hungary's borders and Chinese. This changed in 1997, when traders of Romanian ethnicity predominated, with the second and third places being taken by Chinese and Russians, while the numbers of Polish traders, Hungarian traders from beyond the country's borders and traders from former Yugoslavia were negligible. The following regional deviations from the national trend were observed:

- For both years, ethnic Chinese traders were to be found mostly in towns. Their proportions decreased along with settlement size;
- For 1997, traders from former Yugoslavia were overrepresented in informal markets in towns, while Romanians and Hungarians from beyond the borders were more likely to be found in informal village markets.

Table 7.9 *Spread and intensity of migrants in Hungary by region and settlement status, 1995, 1997, 1998 (in per cent)*

	1995		*1997*		*1998*	
Region/settlement status	*Settlements with migrants*	*Migrants/ population*	*Settlements with migrants*	*Migrants/ population*	*Settlements with migrants*	*Migrants/ population*
Hungary*	60	0.7	50	0.4	42	0.3
Northwest region	58	0.5	45	0.3	39	0.3
Southwest region	52	0.8	48	0.5	37	0.4
Central Hungarian region	88	1.0	65	0.5	58	0.5
Northern Hungarian region	53	0.4	40	0.2	29	0.1
Northeast region	69	0.6	59	0.4	53	0.4
Southeast region	76	0.8	70	0.5	62	0.5
City	81	0.4	72	0.4	72	0.4
Big village	87	0.7	74	0.4	70	0.4
Mid-size village	73	0.6	66	0.4	52	0.3
Small village	46	0.7	35	0.4	29	0.3

* except Budapest

Source: TÁRKI settlement database 1998

7.6.2 The proportion and spatial distribution of migrants in Hungary

Between 1995 and 1998, the proportion of settlements with migrants[12] (spread) and the proportion of migrants in the population (intensity) decreased in all regions and settlement groups except for the cities, where the share of the migrants remained the same.

The proportion of settlements with migrants and the proportion of migrants in the population were higher in those sub-regions[13] that border on Romania, where a comparatively large number of migrants live in a few big cities. The proportion of migrants in the population is also above average in the Austrian and Ukrainian border sub-regions.

Table 7.10 *The intensity and spread of migrants in the border sub-regions of Hungary in 1998 (in per cent)*

	Border sub-regions					
	Austrian	*Former Yugoslavian*	*Romanian*	*Ukrainian*	*Slovakian*	*Hungary**
Migrants/local active population	1.1	0.7	1.0	1.4	0.5	0.7
Settlements with foreigners	45	41	66	43	31	42

* except Budapest
Source: TÁRKI Settlement database 1998

Notes

1 The two classic books (in Hungarian) that offer a historical and/or anthropological overview are Puskás (1982) and Fejős (1992).
2 This was due to the Holocaust and the expulsion of approximately 200,000 ethnic Germans whose homes were filled with ethnic Hungarians expelled from Czechoslovakia.
3 This remained unchanged for the following seven to eight years. In 1990, 96 per cent of the 'refugees' were from Romania. Subsequently, the number of asylum seekers from former Yugoslavia increased due to the war in this region. Their proportion among all asylum seekers lay between 77 and 91 per cent in the period from 1992 to 1997.
4 The following section draws on Kupiszewska and Nowok (2006).
5 Due to the fact that most of the data are based on administrative sources, the definitions and numbers are somewhat sensitive to the regulations on immigration, residence and naturalisation that were changed in 2002, in 2004 with Hungary joining the EU, and in 2007 in response to the EU directive on free movement of third-country nationals. The present paper avoids discussions of these regulations but refers to them where necessary.
6 Data on the acquisition of Hungarian citizenship are included in both the CPR and the CAR. The HCSO links these sources and harmonises the data.

7 The census and the CAR also contain data on the place of birth of the resident population but these are not of good quality in the CAR (Kupiszewska & Nowok 2006: 536). Moreover, birth in a foreign country does not necessarily mean that the respective person migrated but may instead be traced back to a change of the Hungarian border.

8 In addition, the 2001 Census covered the registered resident population in compliance with the needs of the regular national statistical reporting system (i.e. vital statistics). All published statistics are based on the concept of the actual resident population (HCSO 2006a: 80-81).

9 Hungarian citizens were asked for a possible second citizenship in the 2001 Census, while foreign citizens could only state one citizenship.

10 Following Hungary's accession to the EU on 1 May 2004, EU citizens are no longer included in the work permit register. Consequently, the figure summarises the numbers of work permits, green cards for EU-15 citizens and obligatory registrations of the citizens of the new Member States working in Hungary.

11 Similar surveys were carried out in Romania and Poland in 2000-2001 and in Romania and Slovakia in 2003, using almost identical questionnaires. The response rate was 28 per cent in Poland (fall 2000), and 57 per cent in Romania (spring 2001).

12 The term 'migrants' includes refugees, permanent residents, legal and illegal (i.e. undeclared and/or unregistered) workers and naturalised Hungarians. Naturalised Hungarians were included in this discussion since they show similar characteristics as the other immigrant groups.

13 Regional statistics splits Hungary into about one hundred sub-regions. Sub-regions are cities and their agglomeration within the borders of a county. We defined border sub-regions simply as those of which their border is also the border of Hungary. The naming of the border sub-region refers to the country with which a common border is shared. In some cases a sub-region has common borders with more than one country. In such cases we allocated the sub-region to the country to which the longer border belongs.

Statistical sources

Organisation	*Content*	*URL*
Central Office for Administrative and Electronic Public Services	– central population register	www.registrationshu.org
Hungarian Central Statistical Office	– census – central population register – aliens register	portal.ksh.hu
Ministry of the Interior, Central Office	– emigration – immigration – return migration of Hungarian citizens – naturalisations – Hungarians born abroad	www.bm.hu

Ministry of the Interior	– foreign citizens residing in Hungary – foreign citizens entering or leaving the country – refugees	www.bmbah.hu
Ministry of Labour and Social Affairs, National Employment Service	– work permit data	en.afsz.hu

Bibliography

Czakó Á. & E. Sik (1999), 'Characteristics and Origins of the Comecon Open-air Market in Hungary', *International Journal of Urban and Regional Research* 23 (4): 715-737.

Fejős, Z. (1992), *A chicagói magyarok két nemzedéke, 1890-1940*. Budapest: Közép-Európai Intézet.

Futó, P. & M. Jandl (eds.) (2005), *2004 Yearbook on Illegal Migration, Human Smuggling and Trafficking in Central and Eastern Europe*. Vienna: ICMDP.

HCSO (2001), *Demographic Yearbook, 2000*. Budapest: HCSO.

HCSO (2003), *Time series of the international migration, 1990-2000*. Budapest: HCSO.

HCSO (2004), *Hungarian Statistical Pocket Book, 2003*. Budapest: HCSO.

HCSO (2006a), *Population and Housing Census 2001. 31. Methods of the collection and processing of the data*. www.nepszamlalas.hu.

HCSO (2006b), *International migration, 1995-2005* Budapest: HCSO.

HCSO (2006c), *Demographic Yearbook, 2005*. Budapest: HCSO.

Juhász, J. (1997), 'The statistical characteristics of migration'. in M. Fullerton, E. Sik, & J. Tóth (eds.), *From improvisation toward awareness? Contemporary migration politics in Hungary*, 17-31. Budapest: MTA PTI.

Kovács, M. & J. Tóth (2007), 'Kin-state responsibility and ethnic citizenship: The Hungarian case', in R. Bauböck, B. Perchinig & W. Sievers (eds.), *Citizenship policies in the new Europe*, 135-159. Amsterdam: Amsterdam University Press.

Kupiszewska, D. & B. Nowok (2006), 'Country Report: Hungary', in M. Poulain, N. Perrin & A. Singleton (eds.), *THESIM: Towards Harmonised European Statistics on International Migration*, 529-539. Louvain-la-Neuve: Presses universitaires de Louvain.

Portes, A., W. Haller & L. E. Guarnizo (2001), 'Transnational Entrepreneurs: The Emergence and Determinants of an Alternative Form of Immigrant Economic Adaptation', *Transnational Communities Programme Working Paper* 5. www.transcomm.ox.ac.uk.

Puskás, J. (1982), *Kivándorló magyarok az Egyesült Államokban, 1990-1940*. Budapest: Akadémia.

Sik, E. (1998), *The social, economic and legal aspects of migration in contemporary Hungary in relation with the accession to the European Union*. Paper commissioned by the World Bank, Budapest.

Sik, E. (1999), 'The spatial distribution of informal marketplaces and informal foreign traders in contemporary Hungary', in E. L. Feige & K. Ott (eds.), *Underground economies in transition*, 275-306. Aldershot: Ashgate.

Sik, E. (2000), 'Diaspora: Tentative observations and applicability in Hungary', in I. Kiss & C. McGovern (eds.), *New Diasporas in Hungary, Russia and Ukraine*, 20-41. Budapest: Open Society/COLPI.

Sik, E. (2002), 'Informal labour market-place on the Moscow Square', in R. Neef & M. Stanculescu (eds.), *The social impact of informal economies in Eastern Europe*, 231-247. Aldershot: Ashgate.

Sik, E. & J. Tóth (2003), 'Joining an EU identity: integration of Hungary and the Hungarians', in W. Spohn & A. Triandafyllidou (eds.), *Europeanisation, national identities and migration*, 223-244. London: Routledge.

Sik, E. & C. Wallace (1999), 'The development of open-air markets in East-Central Europe', *International Journal of Urban and Regional Research* 23 (4): 697-714.

Tóth, Á. & J. Vékás (2004), 'Határok és identitás', in: N. Kovács, A. Osvát & L. Szarka (eds.) *Tér és térkép* , 135-190. Budapest: Akadémia.

UNHCR (2007a), *UNHCR Statistical Yearbook 2005: Trends in Displacements, Protections and Solutions*. www.unhcr.org.

UNHCR (2007b), *2006 Global Trends: Refugees, Asylum-Seekers, Returnees, Internally Displaced and Stateless Persons*. www.unhcr.org.

Wallace, C. (1996), 'The Eastern frontier of Western Europe: mobility in the buffer zone', *New Community* 2: 259-286.

8 Poland[1]

Jakub Bijak and Izabela Koryś

8.1 Introduction

Poland is a perfect example of a country whose data on international migration have the typical shortcomings widely discussed in the literature (e.g. Bilsborrow, Hugo, Oberai & Zlotnik 1997; Eurostat 1997; Poulain, Perrin & Singleton 2006). Not only are migration flows severely underreported, but, additionally, the definitions in use do not comply with the international standards determined by the United Nations (1998). Moreover, information on irregular migration to Poland is generally limited to border guard statistics on apprehensions (cf. Futo & Jandl 2005; Kępińska 2005). All of these shortcomings have profound consequences for many areas of socio-economic life since reliable statistics on international migration and the resident population are crucial for many aspects of public policy planning.

8.2 Historical and political background of Polish migration data

8.2.1 Historical background up to 1989

Official Polish data on migration stocks and flows should in general be handled with great care, since their analysis may lead to inaccurate conclusions and spurious findings if the analysts neglect to consider both their implicit shortcomings and the historical and social contexts of current and previous migration flows. It should be noted that the shortcomings and inefficiencies in the current Polish system of collecting and reporting data on international migration can, for the most part, be traced back to the communist political regime (1945-1989).

For centuries, out-migration (both politically and economically motivated) was the major direction of population flows in Poland. The second half of the eighteenth century and the whole nineteenth century were dominated by the emigration of political refugees from the territory then occupied by the three neighbouring empires. At the turn of the twentieth century, the mass economic outflow started. In the years 1871 to 1913 almost 3.5 million people emigrated (which is roughly equivalent to 14 per cent of the average population of Poland at the time). Another 2.1 million emigrants left Poland in the inter-war period (1918-1939; cf. Morawska 1989).

Over a hundred years of substantial outflows firmly established Polish migration networks abroad, which in turn contributed to maintaining the high volume of Polish emigration. As a consequence, the Polish state institutionalised emigration. Largely inspired by the Italian legislation on emigration introduced at the beginning of the twentieth century, Poland developed state agendas dedicated to migration management and the protection of Polish emigrants in their countries of residence. Although regarded as a substantial loss of human capital in the inter-war period, emigration was also seen as an important means of reducing demographic and economic pressure in the overpopulated rural regions of Poland (Jarzyna 1933). If the public and political opinions on international migration issues are to be judged by the richness of data and variables reported in official migration statistics, the policymakers in inter-war Poland seemed to have been much more concerned with international population movements than their contemporary counterparts (CSO 1930-1939; MCL 1938).

Under the communist regime the international migration of Polish citizens became a highly politicised issue. Driven by ideological concerns, the communist government imposed restrictive exit rules, allowing emigration mostly on ethnic grounds or for the purpose of family reunification. However, the political attempts to suppress the outflows proved to be rather futile in the long run. The on-going erosion of communist political power was clearly correlated with the gradual liberalisation of international movement restrictions (Stola 2001). This process was significantly accelerated when the migrants' remittances became an important source of foreign currency for the socialist economy. As a result, the dominant attitude towards international mobility gradually changed, which is reflected in the official statistics of international flows published in the Statistical Yearbooks. Initially sparse and parsimonious, these data were extended and enriched over the years.

Up to the collapse of the communist regime in 1989 and the ensuing socio-economic transformations, the majority of the people leaving and coming to Poland had been Polish citizens. Besides, emigration was usually long-lasting, if not permanent, due to both the difficulties encountered when applying for a permit to leave (especially to the Western countries) and the potential repressions upon return, in the case of overstaying the period spent abroad. Hence, the system of registration and reporting of international migration flows developed after the Second World War might have been relatively accurate in the communist era but became outdated and seriously inefficient, when both the socio-political context and international mobility patterns changed.

8.2.2 *Recent patterns of international migration in Poland*

The political liberalisation and economic transformation that commenced in the 1990s attracted to Poland the first wave of actual (mostly temporary) immigrants, transforming Poland from a typical country of emigration into a sending-receiving country. The incoming immigrants consisted mainly of: (a) small entrepreneurs who filled economic niches on the newly-opened market (for example, Vietnamese traders selling cheap textiles and running oriental fast-food restaurants, cf. Koryś 2004); (b) petty traders from the former Soviet republics who were subsequently absorbed by the emerging secondary labour market in Poland (cf. Stola 1997); as well as (c) highly skilled professionals from Western countries who greatly contributed to the institutional modernisation in Poland and to the transfer of knowledge (Iglicka 2000). An important feature of these movements was their 'provisional' and temporary character. A large majority of these migrants, including the highly skilled, circulated between Poland and their home countries on the basis of tourist visas, doing their business without the required permits. An unprecedented phenomenon was also the first appearance of asylum seekers in Poland in 1992 (Kicinger 2005).

Since the beginning of the twenty-first century, regular migration to Poland has become more significant. Petty traders and small entrepreneurs have gradually been pushed out of the market. Circular migration from the neighbouring post-Soviet countries has been limited by the introduction of visa requirements. At the same time, a certain number of the formerly irregular migrants have been and are being regularised as there has been and still is a continuous demand for migrant labour, especially in the areas of domestic services, agriculture and construction (Koryś 2005).

8.2.3 *Limitations of the Polish statistics on international migration*

Although the patterns of migration in Poland have changed significantly since the end of the communist era, the system of registering international population flows has not. Conceptualised several decades ago under different socio-political circumstances, the system now seems archaic and outdated. For example, due to the prevailing definitions, it still predominantly focuses on capturing return migration instead of the immigration of foreigners to Poland.[2]

This problem is further exacerbated by the legal regulation of immigration in Poland. Some foreigners are not recorded as immigrants in the official Polish statistics, as the Central Statistical Office (CSO) categorises as immigrants only those who hold a so-called *settlement permit*. According to the enacted regulations (Act on Aliens of 2003), settlement permits are granted to those foreign citizens who have lived in Poland for at least three years on the basis of a residence permit, for at least five years as refugees or who hold an appropriate visa. Moreover, the applicants must demonstrate the 'existence of durable family bonds or economic ties with the Republic of Poland' and supply proof of 'accommodation and economic means' (in other words, they must prove that they have a regular income and secured lodging).[3] Rejected applicants who remain in Poland are registered as 'temporary immigrants from abroad staying for a period of more than two months', even if their actual stay lasts for years.[4]

Notwithstanding these problems, there are several sources of accurate data on foreigners coming to and residing in Poland. The Office for Repatriation and Aliens (*Urząd ds. Repatriacji i Cudzoziemców*, URiC) provides registers of the so-called fixed-term and permanent settlement permits. The Central Statistical Office supplies the best available information on temporary migrants and the migrant stock based on the census, while the Ministry of Labour and Social Policy produces statistics based on the numbers of work permits issued (we will further elaborate on these issues in the next section of this chapter).

Of course, statistics are also affected by changes in the legal regulations that apply to foreigners, including the harmonisation of these regulations with EU legislation. As a side-effect of these changes, some migration-related data are not comparable across time. In particular, sudden drops or increases in the figures might exclusively be due to changes in definitions. This holds true for the number of work permits issued to EU citizens, a number which dropped after Poland's accession to the EU in 2004.

Finally, an adequate interpretation of the official statistics requires historical background knowledge on border changes and ethnic movements in the twentieth century. Such information is crucial for a proper understanding of the data on the Polish population broken down by citizenship and by country of birth, as well as of statistics on the stocks of foreigners in some regions. For example, persons with dual Polish-German citizenship happen to be registered as foreigners in the Opolskie voivodship. On the basis of empirical data, we will discuss some of these problems in more detail in the following section.

8.3 Migration artefact: What do the Polish data reveal?

8.3.1 General remarks

Problems with quality, completeness and comparability of international migration data can have various causes, including different definitions used in particular countries, as well as incomplete reporting, especially of emigration, for legal, technical, organisational or other reasons (Bilsborrow et al. 1997). These problems are still very serious in a majority of the post-communist countries in Central and Eastern Europe, despite the visible efforts of the national statistical institutes to improve the quality of the data (Eurostat 1997; Nowok 2005). Poland is by no means an exception to this rule.

The United Nations recommendations propose the definition of a long-term migrant as 'a person who moves to a country other than that of his or her usual residence for a period of at least a year (12 months), so that the country of destination effectively becomes his or her new country of usual residence' (United Nations 1998: 18). Consistently, the UN definition of the 'resident population' includes all those who have actually resided in the respective country for a period of at least twelve months. However, in official Polish statistics the respective definitions are based on the concept of 'permanent residence' instead of 'usual residence' (see Section 8.3.2).

There are typically two major types of bias related to the registration of regular migration. The first concerns the underreporting of migratory events, especially of out-migration, *given the definitions and regulations in use in a particular country*. In practice, this type of bias can be corrected after a population census, by means of the retrospective adjustment of data on population stocks and flows. This is usually done by the national statistical institutes, i.e. in Poland by the Central Statistical Office. The Polish data on stocks are systematically corrected *ex-post* on the basis of census results, but the past net migration figures are not. Instead, a separate category for the statistical adjustment of this error can be created in the population balance equation, in order to account for the census-based corrections.[5]

However, even *if the registration were complete*, the resulting data would still be biased due to differences between the definitions used in a given country and those recommended by the United Nations (1998). The size of this difference can be estimated on the basis of auxiliary data, such as surveys complementing the population census. In practice, this kind of additional information is usually only available for population stocks.

8.3.2 *Migration flows*

The official data of the Central Statistical Office on international migration flows include only those migrants who enter or leave Poland permanently. In practice, this means that only those who declare that they *intend* to come or go for good are counted as international migrants. Hence, the Polish statistics do not define migrants based on their length of stay, which automatically implies that they do not adhere to the one-year threshold used in the 1998 United Nations recommendations. In fact, no data on flows that use a specified time criterion are systematically collected in Poland (Nowok & Kupiszewska 2005: 17). Such information is available only periodically, from surveys and, more recently, from population censuses. The official information on migration flows is collected via statistical forms which have to be filled in upon (de-)registration of residence at the municipal office. Data from the computerised central population register (PESEL) are not used for statistics on population movements (Nowok & Kupiszewska 2005: 7). Therefore, to avoid confusion, we only use the terms 'register', 'registration', etc., to refer to the municipal population registers gathering data through statistical forms – and *not* to the PESEL database.

Apart from data on permanent migration, there is also some information available on 'temporary migrants', i.e. people changing residence for more than two months. The differentiation between permanent and temporary migration in Poland is a legacy of the communist system of population registration. Despite the fact that temporary residence may last for many years, its changes are not reflected in the official migration statistics (Nowok & Kupiszewska 2005: 19). A detailed description of the migration data collection process in Poland can be found in the Polish country report for the project 'THESIM – Towards Harmonised European Statistics on International Migration' (Kupiszewska, Nowok & Kupiszewski 2006).

The Polish 'permanent residence' concept is one of the narrowest possible definitions used in the measurement of international migration. On the other end of the scale, there are countries such as Germany, one of the most important migration countries in Europe, where foreigners have to register with the local authorities and are consequently recorded as migrants within one week.[6] In the case of migration between Germany and Poland, one of the major directions of population flows in Europe in the 1990s, this results in serious discrepancies between the data reported by these countries, which in both cases contain a certain amount of 'demographic fiction' (Kędelski 1990).

With respect to deficient reporting, it has to be noted that the registration of migrants is usually (but not always) more complete in the receiving countries than in the sending countries. Migrants have more incentives to register at their destinations than to deregister in their countries of origin (Kupiszewski 2002: 106). A useful tool for analysing the discrepancies between these data sources is a *double-entry matrix* of migration that juxtaposes the data of sending and receiving countries (cf. Poulain 1999; Kupiszewska & Nowok 2005). Tables 8.1 and 8.2 show the respective *double-entry vectors* for emigration from and immigration to Poland in 2002. The tables include data on eighteen major countries of destination and origin, respectively sorted by their importance for migration exchange with Poland according to the official Polish statistics. It is worth noting that the Polish data on migration only include information on the migrants' countries of origin and destination. The National Statistical Institute does not publish data broken down by citizenship (Nowok 2005).

Based on the observation that migrants are more likely to register at their destination than to deregister at origin, Table 8.1 provides a rough estimate of the overall number of people who left Poland in 2002. This estimate includes only those fourteen countries for which both types of data are available; in other words, it excludes France, the UK, Australia and Greece. There are two reasons for including the German data in the analysis despite the clear conflict of definitions. Firstly, Germany was a key migration partner country of Poland at the turn of the twenty-first century. Secondly, despite the differences in definitions, the discrepancy between the Polish and German statistics with respect to reporting migration from Poland to Germany is very similar to discrepancies observed for the other countries.

Even working under very rough assumptions, a simple statistical analysis shows that the eighteen most significant receiving countries registered about 141,900 emigrants from Poland in 2002, with the 95

Table 8.1 *Data on emigration from Poland by main countries of destination, 2002*

		Sending country data Poland: CSO (1)	*Receiving country data Respective NSIs (2)*	*S/R ratio (1)/(2) in %*	*Source of data for (2)*
1.	Germany	17,806	100,968	17.6	Eurostat: NC
2.	US	2,676	13,304	20.1	NSI website
3.	Canada	1,016	1,076	94.4	NSI website
4.	Austria	525	2,514	20.9	NSI website
5.	France	339	NA	NA	-
6.	Italy	302	3,384	8.9	CoE (2004)
7.	The Netherlands	290	2,275	12.7	CoE (2004)
8.	UK	254	NA	NA	-
9.	Australia	187	NA	NA	-
10.	Sweden	174	1,186	14.7	Eurostat: NC
11.	Spain	166	3,869	4.3	Eurostat: NC
12.	Belgium	119	2,427	4.9	NSI website*
13.	Denmark	95	962	9.9	Eurostat: NC
14.	Switzerland	88	700	12.6	Eurostat: NC*
15.	Greece	75	NA	NA	-
16.	Norway	47	702	6.7	Eurostat: NC
17.	Czech Republic	38	1,679	2.3	Eurostat: NC
18.	Luxembourg	23	97	23.7	Eurostat: NC*
	Total	24,532	141,900	17.3	-

Notes: S/R ratio refers to the number of emigrants registered in Poland as leaving for a specific destination divided by the number of immigrants from Poland recorded in the statistics of that destination country (terminology after Kupiszewska & Nowok 2005: 5); CoE = Council of Europe; NA = not available; NC = NewCronos; NSI = National Statistical Institute; * = flows of Polish citizens.

per cent credible interval ranging from 140,300 to 143,600. Hence, it can be concluded that the registration systems of the destination countries recorded on average almost six times more immigrants from Poland than the Polish statistics.

Such an estimation is not possible for immigration to Poland, as we cannot safely assume that the Polish data cover more immigrants than the statistics of the sending countries, given the permanent residence concept in use in Poland. In fact, the Polish statistics usually capture fewer immigrants than the data of the respective source countries. This holds true for migration not only from Germany, in the case of which the Polish statistics captured barely 3 per cent of the total number of emigrants registered in Germany, but also from other countries of Western and Central Europe (Table 8.2). The only exceptions are the non-EU post-Soviet countries. The Polish statistics record more immigrants from Belarus, the Russian Federation and Ukraine than are registered as emigrants leaving for Poland in these countries.

Nevertheless, it seems that in most cases, apart from population flows to and from Germany, underreporting of emigration is a much more serious problem for Polish statistics than underestimated immi-

Table 8.2 *Data on immigration to Poland by main countries of origin, 2002*

		Receiving country data Poland: CSO (1)	*Sending country data Respective NSIs (2)*	*R/S ratio (1)/(2) in %*	*Source of data for (2)*
1.	Germany	2,335	78,739	3.0	Eurostat: NC
2.	Ukraine	350	137	255.5	CoE (2004)
3.	Italy	251	459	54.7	NSI website
4.	France	247	NA	NA	-
5.	Canada	230	NA	NA	-
6.	Kazakhstan	221	NA	NA	-
7.	UK	208	NA	NA	-
8.	Austria	156	1,538	10.1	NSI website
9.	Belarus	130	81	160.5	CoE (2004)
10.	Russian Federation	86	80	107.5	CoE (2004)
11.	The Netherlands	83	492	16.9	Eurostat: NC
12.	Sweden	70	190	36.8	Eurostat: NC
13.	Spain	63	99	63.6	NSI website
14.	Belgium	61	411	14.8	NSI website*
15.	Greece	60	NA	NA	-
16.	Armenia	50	NA	NA	-
17.	Switzerland	41	277	14.8	Eurostat: NC*
18.	Lithuania	40	89	44.9	CoE (2004)
	Total	6,587	NA	NA	-

R/S ratio = the number of immigrants from a specific country of origin registered in Poland divided by the number of emigrants leaving for Poland recorded in the statistics of the respective sending country (terminology after Kupiszewska & Nowok 2005: 5), CoE = Council of Europe; NA = not available; NC = NewCronos; NSI = National Statistical Institute; * = flows of Polish citizens gration. This has a direct impact on net migration figures and thus also on population estimates made in the periods between the censuses. Both of these usually underestimate population loss due to migration, which also means that all relative figures based on these numbers are incorrect. These problems concern not only demographic rates, as shown in Sakson (2002), but also key economic measures per capita, such as the GDP and so on.

Sakson (2002) made an attempt to assess the size of migration underreporting in Poland in the 1980s, i.e. under the communist regime. Her estimate departed from the official population of Poland as counted in the 1988 Census, which totalled 37,878,600 people. This number was already corrected by the CSO, which means that it excludes about 50,000 permanent emigrants who had left Poland without deregistering since the previous census carried out in 1981. However, this statistical adjustment was most certainly seriously underestimated, mainly for political reasons, since emigration was officially restricted under the communist regime (Okólski 1994; Sakson 2002: 53-54). On the basis of computerised registration of border crossings, previously not used in population statistics, Sakson (2002) estimated that 590,700 'invisible' emigrants (1.6 per cent of the census population) had moved abroad illegally for at least one year between 1981 and 1989.[7] The region with the highest share of 'invisible' emigrants in the 1988 Census population was the former Opolskie voivodship (5.3 per cent, corresponding to 53,900 people).

A similar analysis can also be performed for the period between 6 December 1988 and 21 May 2002, i.e. between the dates of the two most recent population censuses. A first way of correcting the results of the 2002 Census is to compare the register-based and the census-based estimates of the permanent population of Poland on 1 January 2002. This comparison shows that 390,300 people emigrated between 1989 and 2002 'without saying good-bye to the population register'.[8]

In Table 8.3, we distributed this difference of 390,300 people over the years 1988 to 2002 proportionally to the size of net migration from Poland registered in Germany. No correction has been made for 1993, as the responsible German authority adjusted the Polish migrant stock by -23,000 persons for that year. In Table 8.3, the latter adjustment was distributed equally over the period 1988-1992. Figure 8.1 illustrates the difference between the official and the corrected population and net migration numbers as recalculated in Table 8.3. That the official and corrected numbers are the same for 2002 is due to the fact that these figures were already adjusted by the CSO.

The simple analysis presented suggests that the difference between registered and corrected net migration (and thus also population size) was most pronounced in the transition period between 1989 and

Table 8.3 *Official and corrected net migration and population in Poland, 1988-2002*

	1988	*1989*	*1990*	*1991*	*1992*	*1993*	*1994*	*1995*	*1996*	*1997*	*1998*	*1999*	*2000*	*2001*	*2002*
Net migration[a]															
Official	–96.6	–27.6	–12.6	–14.2	–10.0	–14.1	–19.0	–18.2	–12.8	–11.8	–13.3	–14.0	–19.7	–16.7	–17.9
Corrected	–105.2	–210.4	–93.0	–28.0	–26.2	–14.1*	–29.7	–31.8	–20.2	–15.7	–20.1	–26.4	–33.3	–31.4	–23.1
Population[b]															
Official	37.8	38.0	38.1	38.2	38.4	38.5	38.5	38.6	38.6	38.6	38.7	38.7	38.6	38.6	38.2
Corrected	37.8	37.9	37.9	38.0	38.1	38.2	38.2	38.3	38.3	38.3	38.3	38.3	38.3	38.2	38.2
Net migration rate[c]															
Official	–2.6	–0.7	–0.3	–0.4	–0.3	–0.4	–0.5	–0.5	–0.3	–0.3	–0.3	–0.4	–0.5	–0.4	–0.5
Corrected	–2.8	–5.6	–2.5	–0.7	–0.7	–0.4*	–0.8	–0.8	–0.5	–0.4	–0.5	–0.7	–0.9	–0.8	–0.6

[a] thousand persons; [b] mid-year, million persons; [c] per 1,000 mid-year population;
* not corrected (no 1993 German data)
Sources: Eurostat – NewCronos; Council of Europe 2004: Table 8 for Poland; CSO; authors' calculations

Figure 8.1 *Official and corrected net migration and population in Poland, 1988-2002*

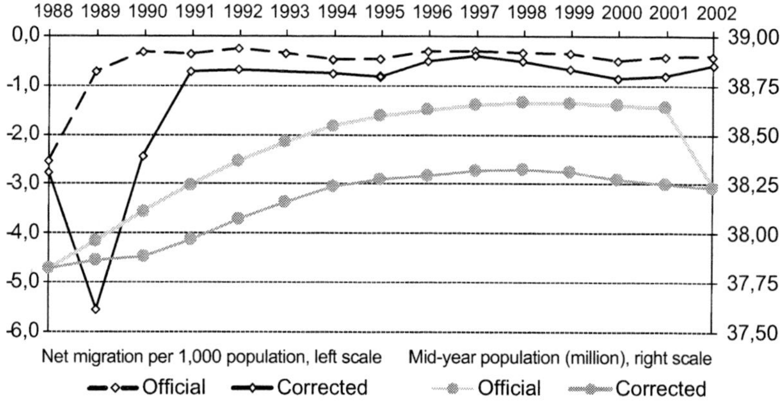

Note: see Table 8.3
Sources: see Table 8.3

1990. According to this simplistic correction, the more realistic net migration rate in 1989 reached about -5.6 per 1,000 inhabitants of Poland, instead of the officially reported -0.7 per 1,000.

8.3.3 *Population stocks*

As has been shown, data on population flows can be corrected on the basis of the census. However, the Polish data on population stocks confront us with a second problem that results from non-compliance with the UN definitions of long-term migrants and thus of usual residents.

The extent of this problem can again be assessed on the basis of the 2002 Census. In 2002, the CSO for the first time decided to count not only the permanent population, as required by law, but also the usual resident population, as recommended by the UN in 1998. For this purpose, the CSO used the following definitions (CSO 2003a: 15-16; authors' translation):

'*Permanent population* (permanent residents): The category includes permanent residents (usually persons registered for permanent residence), who:
- were present in the period of time when the census was carried out;
- were absent during the census, irrespective of the place of stay and the length of absence.'

'*Residents* (resident population) – a new category of population – include:
- permanent residents, except for those who have left their place of residence for at least twelve months, regardless of their place of stay (in Poland or abroad);
- temporary residents from Poland or abroad (foreigners) who have resided in their new place of residence for at least twelve months.'

According to the 2002 Census, Poland had a permanent population of 38,230,100 people, while the resident population lay at 37,620,100, i.e. 610,000 people less. Interestingly, this number has not risen very much since the 1988 Census, when, according to Sakson (2002), it totalled 590,700 people. This may indicate that on balance the stocks of non-deregistered Poles living abroad may to some extent still attest to the legacy of the communist period, especially of the 1980s. Despite the availability of this information, the CSO calculates the majority of its statistics for permanent residents, overestimating the real population size of Poland by more than 600,000 people. A territorial distribution of the net emigration recorded in the 2002 Census is presented in Figure 8.2.

The 2002 Census also contains information on 85,500 people, who arrived or returned from abroad between 1989 and 2002. Out of these, 69,700 were Polish citizens and 15,800 were foreigners, stateless individuals or persons of unknown citizenship (CSO 2003b: 92). The migration survey, conducted at the same time as the census, yielded similar results. The survey found 83,100 immigrants, of whom 67,300 were return migrants, i.e. permanent residents who had left the country for a year or longer; a further 15,700 were newcomers, i.e. permanent residents abroad, staying in Poland for over twelve months (CSO 2003b: 350). Clearly, these figures are strongly interrelated; immigrants

Figure 8.2 *Net long-term emigration (for twelve months or more) from Poland as reported in the 2002 Census*

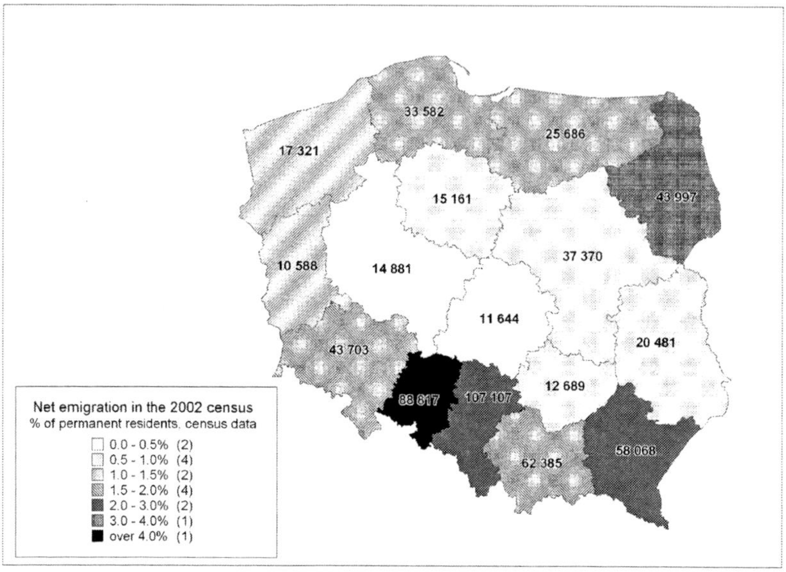

Sources: CSO 2003b: Tables 14 and 38; authors' calculations

with Polish citizenship are most likely return migrants, while foreign citizens are typically newcomers.

All migration-related data published by the CSO (2003b) on the basis of the census are broken down into many categories: by sex, age, voivodship, type of municipality (urban or rural), citizenship, country of previous residence, country of current residence, year of arrival, year of departure, reasons for migration, marital status, level of education, occupation (for survey data), etc. Regrettably, despite the availability of this fairly detailed census-based information, no efforts have as yet been made to recalculate the official data on population flows and stocks from the years preceding the census.

The above-described differences in definitions also impact on the Polish data on population stocks broken down by citizenship and by country of birth (Tables 8.4 and 8.5). On the one hand, the data published by the CSO include only the permanent population. Hence, they do not cover those foreigners who do not hold a permanent residence permit but are *de facto* residents and should therefore be included in the population stocks of Poland. On the other hand, 444,900 (91.6 per cent) out of the 485,600 foreign citizens in Poland have both a foreign,

Table 8.4 *Permanent population in Poland by citizenship and country of birth, 2002*

Citizenship	*Number*	*In %*	*Country of birth*	*Number*	*In %*
Total	38,230,080	100.0	Total	38,230,080	100.0
Only Polish	37,084,821	97.0	Poland	36,871,281	96.4
Foreign (incl. dual)	485,591	1.3	Abroad	775,282	2.0
By number of citizenships:			*Of which:*		
Dual Polish/foreign	444,930	1.2	Ukraine	309,131	0.8
Only foreign/stateless	40,661	0.1	Belarus	104,463	0.3
By citizenship:			Germany	101,633	0.3
German (incl. dual)	287,510	0.8	Lithuania	79,769	0.2
Of which:			Russia	54,226	0.1
Polish and German	279,639	0.7	France	34,634	0.1
Only German	7,871	<0.1	US	9,004	<0.1
US (incl. dual)	31,391	0.1	Czech Republic	6,200	<0.1
Canadian (incl. dual)	14,756	<0.1	Austria	4,312	<0.1
French (incl. dual)	8,070	<0.1	Italy	4,292	<0.1
Ukrainian (incl. dual)	6,361	<0.1	Unknown country	18,390	<0.1
Unknown	659,668	1.7	Unknown	583,517	1.5

Source: CSO 2003a: Tables 26 & 30

Table 8.5 *Permanent population in Poland by citizenship and country of birth, 2002*

Country of Birth	*Citizenship*			
	Polish (incl. dual)	*Foreign (incl. stateless)*	*Unknown*	*Total*
Poland	36,765,038	10,135	96,108	36,871,281
Abroad	741,880	29,748	3,654	775,282
Unknown	22,833	778	559,906	583,517
Total	37,529,751	40,661	659,668	38,230,080

Source: CSO 2003a: Table 32

most frequently German, and Polish citizenship and, in most cases, are not immigrants.

The country of birth does also not yield any information on the number of immigrants residing in Poland, as it refers to present rather than to historical borders (CSO 2003b: 29). This means that a large majority of the foreign-born population in Poland are Poles born before or during the Second World War in the then Polish territories that are now part of Ukraine, Belarus and Lithuania.

8.3.4 Residence permits, asylum, naturalisations and illegal migration

As explained in Section 8.2.3, the migration statistics published by the CSO only include those foreigners who have been granted a settlement permit and are therefore registered as permanent residents in their municipality. The only data that supply information on the actual number of regular foreign newcomers and residents are permits data gathered by the Office for Repatriations and Aliens. Table 8.6 shows the number of permits issued, broken down into main categories, and the number of asylum applications lodged between 1995 and 2004.

Any interpretation of the figures presented in Table 8.6 should take into account the following background information. While temporary residence permits have to be renewed annually, which implies that the numbers reflect the *stock* of temporary residents commencing or prolonging their residence in Poland in a given year, settlement permits are only issued once, thus relating to *flows* of migrants. Upon being granted the settlement permit, the foreigner 'vanishes' from the statistics unless he or she registers in a municipality. Though the stock of newly admitted regular migrants is known from the registers of

Table 8.6 *Foreigners in Poland according to the type of residence permit, 1995-2004*

	Foreigners					
	Studying in Poland	*Granted a work permit*	*Granted a settlement permit*	*Granted a temporary residence permit*	*Granted a period of tolerated stay*	*Who applied for asylum*
Total						
1995	5,202	11,363	3,067	-	-	843
1996	5,313	13,668	2,841	-	-	3,211
1997	5,443	17,498	3,973	-	-	3,531
1998	5,541	20,759	1,657	4,893	-	3,423
1999	6,025	20,618	551	16,810	-	3,061
2000	6,563	19,662	857	15,037	-	4,662
2001	7,380	19,793	690	20,787	-	4,529
2002	7,608	24,643	607	29,636	-	5,170
2003	8,106	19,831	1,735	28,579	72	6,909
2004	8,829	13,179	4,366	25,427	1,097	8,079
Of the 2004 figures, the most significant countries of citizenship:						
Ukraine	1,965	2,743	1,658	8,520	36	72
Belarus	1,211	1,025	389	2,008	18	52
Vietnam	196	1,063	368	1,875	62	16
Armenia	60	268	235	1,793	45	18
Russia	388	584	446	1,605	761	7,183
India	156	430	40	641	7	151
US	623	527	61	898	-	-
Germany	254	982	63 (1,419)*	409 (303)*	-	-
France	53	658	25 (999)*	330 (156)*	-	-
UK	36	319	16 (601)*	212 (135)*	-	-

* The figures in brackets are the numbers of residence permits issued to EU citizens and their families in 2004.

Sources: CSO 2004, 2005; Office for Repatriation and Aliens temporary residence permits, the stock of settled foreigners is unknown, and can be estimated only on the basis of the population census.

The data on work permits, issued originally by the Ministry of Labour and Social Policy, can be problematic due to differences in length of the permits issued. While some of them are valid for two years, others expire after two months. It is unclear whether these discrepancies are taken into account in the data. The data on students, provided by the Ministry of National Education, reflect stocks as of 30 September of a particular year and are thus incomparable with other sources, which reflect either the mid-year or end-year population.

The data on work and temporary residence permits provided by the Office for Repatriation and Aliens seem to imply that the number of immigrants from the EU steadily declined in the period under discussion. However, the opposite is true. EU citizens prolonging their stay in Poland acquired different permits reported in separate statistics (numbers in brackets in Table 8.6). As a consequence, they 'disappeared' from the joint statistics of the Office for Repatriation and Aliens. This is an example of how the adjustments of the legislation to EU regulations led to structural breaks in the series of international migration data.

The official figures on naturalisation are also not comparable over time, albeit for a different reason. While the figures for the years 1992 to 2001 only cover acquisitions of nationality by conferment, the numbers for 2002 to 2004 additionally include acquisitions of nationality through acknowledgment and marriage procedures.[9] This explains why the number of naturalisations increases markedly in 2002 (see Table 8.7). Moreover, many so-called acquisitions of nationality, especially by Israelis or Germans, are actually restorations of the Polish citizenship to those who were illegally deprived of their citizenship by the communist authorities, as well as to their descendants.[10]

An overview of Polish data sources on illegal migration is provided in the ICMPD yearbook, which also supplies selected statistics for 2003 and 2004 (Futo & Jandl 2005). The majority of numbers originate from the database of the Border Guard of the Republic of Poland, including migration-related border apprehensions (5,800 cases in

Table 8.7 *Total number of Polish citizenship acquisitions, 1992-2004*

Year	*1992*	*1993*	*1994*	*1995*	*1996*	*1997*	*1998*	*1999*	*2000*	*2001*	*2002*	*2003*	*2004*
Acquisitions	1,522	834	751	1,036	679	555	871	1,000	975	766	1,186	1,634	1,937

1991-2001: acquisitions of Polish citizenship in the conferment procedure
2002-2004: acquisitions of Polish citizenship in the conferment, acknowledgement and marriage procedures
Source: Office for Repatriation and Aliens (after Kępińska 2005: Tables 35 and 36)

2004), persons rejected at the borders (66,000 in 2004) and deportations (6,200 cases in 2004) (Futo & Jandl 2005: 163-166). Some information on illegal migration can also be drawn from the statistics on border crossings that recorded 98.3 million entries and 97.7 million exits in 2004. The difference, a net total of 600,000 cases, is most likely due to a combination of many factors, including under-recording of outflows at the frontiers, regular long-term immigration and, last but not least, people who entered Poland legally and overstayed their visa.

Though interesting in themselves, the above data sources do not supply any information on either the volume of illegal population flows from and to Poland or the stocks of irregular immigrants residing in the country at a given time. In fact, figures for irregular migration flows and stocks are scarce and usually based on expert judgement rather than on statistical information. For example, Iglicka (2003) estimated that a maximum of half a million irregular migrants (most of them unregistered seasonal workers or petty traders) repeatedly entered Poland each year in the late 1990s. About 100,000 of these were from the countries of the former Soviet Union.

Iglicka's estimate shows that the cases known to the Polish authorities, i.e. the persons apprehended or deported, only represent a small fraction of all irregular migrants in Poland. However, this problem is not specific to Poland. All European countries have difficulties in recording irregular migration due to the very nature of this phenomenon.

8.3.5 *Origins, gender and motives of migration*

Despite their obvious shortcomings, the Polish official statistics are the only source that can be used to describe recent tendencies and changes in immigration patterns and thus to answer the question as to whether Poland confirms the hypotheses of a feminisation and a growing diversification of origins, as observed in recent studies on international migration. Table 8.8 shows selected data on registered immigration to Poland in the years 1997 to 2004 by the main regions of origin. In addition, the Table includes information on the share of women in the migrant population for the period 2002 to 2004.

The figures highlight a clear disproportion between the genders. The majority of migrants from all continents, except for Europe, are men, since men are usually the 'pioneers' of a migration chain. The only exception to this rule is the inflow from the adjacent former Soviet republics, where the large share of women coming to Poland responds to the increasing demand for female migrants in the domestic services such as housekeeping, child-minding and elderly care.

The figures do not allow for the formulation of any clear statements regarding a diversification of origins, mainly due to the shortcomings

Table 8.8 *Inflow of immigrants to Poland by region of origin and by sex, 1997-2004*

	1997	*1998*	*1999*	*2000*	*2001*	*2002*	*2003*	*2004*	*Females as % of the total 2002-2004*
Total	8,426	8,916	7,525	7,331	6,625	6,587	7,048	9,495	47.5
Origin of immigrants, in %									
Europe *	63	63	65	66	69	67	64	69	51.1
EU-24	NA	NA	NA	NA	NA	NA	NA	47	44.0
EU-15	NA	NA	NA	NA	NA	54	50	45	45.2
Former USSR	NA	NA	NA	NA	NA	14	16	24	62.0
Africa	2	2	2	2	1	1	2	2	32.8
America	20	20	25	22	20	21	23	19	46.0
Asia	12	14	6	9	7	8	10	9	41.6
Oceania	2	2	2	2	2	2	2	1	45.7

* including Turkey and Cyprus; NA = not available
Sources: CSO, demography database, demographic yearbooks (various years)

described above. The numbers predominantly include return migrants from Europe and the United States, repatriates and those who hold settlement permits. In other words, the vast majority of actual newcomers to Poland is not included in these figures, as immediately becomes obvious when we compare these with Table 8.6.

As noted in the THESIM country report for Poland (Kupiszewska, Nowok & Kupiszewski 2006: 580, 587), the Office for Repatriation and Aliens (URiC) also gathers data on the reasons for migration (work, family reunification, studying, participation in professional training programmes, etc.). Unfortunately, as the system can register several motives for a single person and does not distinguish between primary and other reasons, the disaggregated data are not made available to the public. For this reason it is not possible to determine on the basis of the official statistics whether migration in Poland is becoming increasingly selective.

8.4 Conclusions and recommendations

The official Polish data on international migration should be handled very carefully. Any analysis of these data should take into account both their evolution and their historical and social contexts. The system of registering international population flows has not yet been adjusted to the changing patterns of migration in Poland. It still predominantly captures return migrants instead of the actual foreign newcomers to Poland. At the same time, changes in the legal regulations, in particular the harmonisation with EU legislation, may render some migration-related figures incomparable across time.

The information about population flows from and to Poland is biased by under-registration and by the fact that the definitions in use differ from the internationally accepted UN standards, as established in 1998. The same applies to the population stocks that, despite the adjustment made after the 2002 Census, are still artificially inflated by over 600,000 people who left Poland without having been deregistered. There are some regions where underreporting of emigration is particularly serious. This holds true for the Opolskie voivodship, for example, where there is a high proportion of ethnic Germans, many of whom hold dual Polish-German citizenship.

As a consequence of underrecorded emigration, the official population of Poland is overestimated by 1.6 per cent, which in turn means that relative demographic and economic measures, such as birth and death rates and GDP per capita, are underestimated on average by the same magnitude. As has been shown by Sakson (2002), estimation errors of age- and region-specific rates can even exceed 20 per cent. In the case of international migration rates, the underestimation of migration and the overestimation of the population lead to seriously underestimated relative indicators of population flows. Hence, the Polish migration statistics seem to construct a social and political reality that does not properly reflect the facts.

In general, the international migration flows in Poland, as seen through the official figures published by the Central Statistical Office, are more a statistical artefact than reality. With respect to irregular migration, the available statistics cover only the cases that are known to the authorities: apprehensions, deportations, refusals of entry, etc. Clearly, this is just the tip of the iceberg. However, this problem is not specific to Poland but is characteristic of all data related to irregular phenomena, including migration.

On the whole, it seems to be of the utmost importance that the tools used to measure migration flows in Poland are adapted to international standards. A more accurate measurement of migration stocks and flows would allow both for the correction of demographic and economic measures and the assessment of the socio-demographic consequences of any migration policy. Hopefully, the rapidly increasing international mobility of Polish citizens as well as the continuous inflow of foreigners will lead to a substantial reform of the Polish system of collecting international migration data.

Notes

1 This chapter partially draws on background information (Kupiszewska & Nowok 2005; Nowok & Kupiszewska 2005; Nowok 2005) gathered during the EU-funded project THESIM – Towards Harmonised European Statistics on International Migration (Poulain, Perrin & Singleton 2006). The authors are obliged to Dorota Kupiszewska, Beata Nowok and Marek Kupiszewski from the Central European Forum for Migration and Population Research, who were responsible for the Polish case study in the THESIM project (Kupiszewska, Nowok & Kupiszewski 2006). In addition, Jakub Bijak gratefully acknowledges the Annual Stipend for Young Scientists of the Foundation for Polish Science (FNP), while Izabela Koryś remains greatly indebted to the Foundation for Population, Migration and Enviroment (BMU-PME) in Zurich. The material presented in this chapter reflects the state of affairs prior to the 2004 enlargement of the European Union. The hardly measurable emigration from Poland following the EU accession only magnified the statistical inadequacies mentioned in the study. However, the size of the problem – though definitely worth a separate investigation – will become fully apparent only after the next population census, scheduled for 2011.

2 The Central Statistical Office does not differentiate between native and foreign immigrants but focuses on the previous country of residence. Furthermore, while natives can immediately register when they enter the country, foreigners have to comply with several regulations before they are allowed to register, which in turn delays their being recorded in the immigration statistics.

3 Art. 65 of the Act on Aliens of 13 June 2003 (*Official Gazette of the Republic of Poland* No. 128, 2003, Item 1175).

4 According to the Office for Repatriation and Aliens, 80 per cent of the 3,589 applications for settlement filed in 2005 were accepted, while 457 applications were rejected and 258 discontinued. Similar proportions can be observed for the previous years.

5 Cf. Council of Europe (2004: Table 8 for Poland). The adjustment can also be calculated directly on the basis of statistical or demographic yearbooks provided by the CSO, by comparing the respective figures including the post-census corrections with those excluding such adjustments.

6 The German Federal Registration Framework Act allows the federal states to exempt foreigners from the obligation to register if their stay is only temporary (see Rühl in this publication).

7 Sakson's estimate conforms to the 1998 UN definition.

8 Sentence attributed to Harri Cruijsen, a Dutch demographer and expert in population projections.

9 'Acknowledgement can be considered as an *entitlement*-based procedure of acquisition, [whereby] *a stateless person* or a person whose nationality is unknown can be granted Polish nationality,' while conferment is 'the most discretionary procedure [which] can be considered as a "fast track" for granting nationality' (Kępińska 2005: 31). The latter can be used for sporting, artistic and scientific purposes or other achievements.

10 Detailed comments on the data on permits, asylum and acquisitions and losses of citizenship can be found in the Polish country report for the THESIM project (Kupiszewska, Nowok & Kupiszewski 2006: 587-588). The SOPEMI report for Poland provides comprehensive statistics on the subject (Kępińska 2005).

Statistical sources

Organisation	*Content*	*URL*
Border Guard of the Republic of Poland	– border crossings – migration-related border apprehensions – rejections and deportations	www.strazgraniczna.pl (site in Polish)
Central Statistical Office (CSO)	– population register – census	www.stat.gov.pl
Ministry of National Education	– foreign students – foreign pupils	www.men.gov.pl
Ministry of Labour and Social Policy	– work permits	www.mps.gov.pl
Office for Foreigners (formerly Office for Repatriation and Aliens)	– settlement permits – asylum applications – citizenship acquisitions	www.udsc.gov.pl

Bibliography

Bilsborrow, R., G. Hugo, A.S. Oberai & H. Zlotnik (1997), *International migration statistics. Guidelines for improving data collection systems.* Geneva: International Labour Organisation.

Council of Europe (2004), *Demographic Yearbook 2004: Recent Demographic Developments in Europe.* Strasbourg: Council of Europe.

CSO (Central Statistical Office) (1930-1939), *Mały Rocznik Statystyczny [The Small Statistical Yearbook].* Warsaw, CSO.

CSO (Central Statistical Office) (2003a), *Raport z wyników Narodowego Spisu Powszechnego Ludności i Mieszkań 2002 [Report on the results of the National Census of Population and Dwellings*]. Warsaw: CSO.

CSO (Central Statistical Office) (2003b), *Migracje Zagraniczne Ludności 2002 [International Migration of the Population*]. Warsaw: CSO.

CSO (Central Statistical Office) (2004-2005), *Rocznik Demograficzny [Demographic Yearbook*]. Warsaw: CSO.

Eurostat (1997), 'Comparing data sources for measuring international migration in Central and Eastern Europe', *Eurostat Working Paper* 1997/1.

Futo, P. & M. Jandl (eds.) (2005), *2004 Yearbook on Illegal Migration, Human Smuggling and Trafficking in Central and Eastern Europe. A Survey and Analysis of Border Management and Border Apprehension Data from 22 States.* Vienna: ICMPD.

Iglicka, K. (2000), 'Ethnic division on emerging foreign labour markets in Poland during the transition period', *Europe-Asia Studies* 52 (7): 1237-1255.

Iglicka, K. (2003), 'The foreign labour market in Poland', in K. Iglicka (ed.), *Migration and labour markets in Poland and Ukraine*, 40-50. Warsaw: Institute of Public Affairs.

Jarzyna, A. (1933), *Polityka emigracyjna [Emigration policy*]. Warsaw: Dom Książki Polskiej.

Kędelski, M. (1990), 'Fikcja demograficzna w Polsce i RFN (Ze studiów nad migracjami zagranicznymi) [Demographic fiction in Poland and in the Federal Republic of Germany (From the studies on international migration)]', *Studia Demograficzne* 99 (1): 21-55.

Kępińska, E. (2005), 'Recent Trends in International Migration. The 2005 SOPEMI Report for Poland', *CMR Working Paper* 2 (60). www.migracje.uw.edu.pl.

Kicinger, A. (2005), 'Between Polish Interests and the EU Influence – Polish Migration Policy Development 1989-2004', *CEFMR Working Paper* 9/2005. www.cefmr.pan.pl.

Koryś, I. (2004), *Migration Trends: Poland – Dilemmas of a sending-receiving country*. Vienna: IOM.

Koryś, I. (2005), 'Country Report of Poland', in International Organization for Migration (ed.), *Dimensions of Integration: Migrant Youth in Central European Countries*, 147-182. Vienna: IOM.

Kupiszewska, D. & B. Nowok (2005), 'Comparability of statistics on international migration flows in the European Union', *CEFMR Working Paper* 7/2005. www.cefmr.pan.pl.

Kupiszewska, D., B. Nowok & M. Kupiszewski (2006), 'Country Report: Poland', in M. Poulain, N. Perrin & A. Singleton (eds.), *THESIM. Towards Harmonised European Statistics on International Migration*, 577-589. Louvain-la-Neuve: Presses universitaires de Louvain.

Kupiszewski, M. (2002), *Modelowanie dynamiki przemian ludności w warunkach wzrostu znaczenia migracji międzynarodowych* [*The role of international migration in the modelling of population dynamics*]. Warsaw: Institute of Geography and Spatial Organisation, Polish Academy of Sciences.

MCL (Maritime and Colonial League) (1938), *Biuletyn Informacyjny Nr 8* [*Information Bulletin No. 8*]. Warsaw: MCL [Liga Morska i Kolonialna].

Morawska, E. (1989), 'Labour Migrations of Poles in the Atlantic World Economy, 1880-1914', *Comparative Studies in Society and History* 31 (2): 237-272.

Nowok, B. (2005), 'Evolution of international migration statistics in selected Central European countries', *CEFMR Working Paper* 8/2005. www.cefmr.pan.pl.

Nowok, B. & D. Kupiszewska (2005), 'Official European statistics on international migration flows: availability, sources and coverage', *CEFMR Working Paper* 5/2005. www.cefmr.pan.pl.

Okólski, M. (1994), 'Migracje zagraniczne w Polsce w latach 1980-1989. Zarys problematyki badawczej [International migration in Poland 1980-1989. A research framework]', *Studia Demograficzne* 117 (3): 3-59.

Poulain, M. (1999), 'International migration within Europe: towards more complete and reliable data?', paper presented at the 'Joint UNECE-Eurostat Work Session on Demographic Projections', Perugia, 3-7 May 1999.

Poulain, M., N. Perrin & A. Singleton (eds.) (2006), *THESIM. Towards Harmonised European Statistics on International Migration*. Louvain-la-Neuve: Presses universitaires de Louvain.

Sakson, B. (2002), *Wpływ 'niewidzialnych' migracji zagranicznych lat osiemdziesiątych na struktury demograficzne Polski* [*The impact of 'invisible' international migration of the 1980s on the demographic structures in Poland*]. Warsaw: Warsaw School of Economics.

Stola, D. (1997), 'Mechanizmy i uwarunkowania migracji zarobkowych do Polski [Mechanisms and determinants of economic migration to Poland]', *ISS Working Papers 'Prace Migracyjne'* 11. www.migracje.uw.edu.pl.

Stola, D. (2001), 'Międzynarodowa mobilność zarobkowa w PRL [International economic mobility in the People's Republic of Poland]', in E. Jaźwińska & M. Okólski (eds.), *Ludzie na huśtawce. Migracje między peryferiami Polski i Zachodu* [*People on the Swing. Migration between the Peripheries of Poland and the West*]. Warsaw: Scholar.

United Nations (1998), *Recommendations on statistics of international migration*. Revision 1. New York: United Nations.

9 Romania

Ancuţa Daniela Tompea and Sebastian Năstuţă

9.1 Introduction

Romania has predominantly been a country of emigration. The first major wave of emigrants left the country at the turn of the twentieth century. Between 1890 and 1924, about 170,000 Romanians left for overseas destinations (predominantly for the United States, Canada and Brazil), mainly for economic reasons. However, a large number of these emigrants returned to Romania (Potot 2003: 89-90). Those who left or were forced to leave the country in the course of the twentieth century were largely members of three ethnic minorities, namely Germans, Jews and, to a lesser extent, Hungarians. Of these, only a small proportion of the Jews immigrated specifically to Romania in order to escape from pogroms in Russia in the late nineteenth century (Magocsi 1993: 107). The large majority of these three minority groups, who together accounted for 18 per cent of the total population in Romania in the interwar period, ended up in this country when the borders were revised during and after the First World War. In this period, Romania (re-)acquired Bessarabia from Russia, Transylvania from Hungary, Bukovina from Austria and South Dobruja from Bulgaria. While the ethnic Hungarians were mainly located in Transylvania, the ethnic Germans, as they came to be known after the First World War, descended from several groups of immigrants who had settled in different parts of these newly acquired Romanian territories between the twelfth and the nineteenth century (for details, see Magocsi 1993: 104-107). Similarly, the ethnic Jews were widely spread in Romania at the time, with significant shares living in the traditional Romanian territory of Moldavia and in Bessarabia, but also in Transylvania and in Bukovina. However, the large proportions of ethnic Jews in these two latter areas can also be traced back to the fact that the 1920 Romanian census was the first to register Jews as a separate nationality. Moreover, nationality was not determined on the grounds of the language used on a daily basis as in earlier Hungarian censuses, which for this reason registered many Germans and Jews as Hungarians; rather, the respondents were asked to indicate their nationality by birth. These changes in counting led, on the one hand, to the intended increase in Romanians in the contested area of Transylvania (Arel 2002: 102, 117; Illyés 1981: 20; Kocsis 2007: 46). On the other hand, both the Jewish and German minorities became much stronger.

Of the ethnic Jews and Germans, who, according to the censuses conducted in 1920 and 1930, constituted about 4 per cent each of the total Romanian population in the interwar period, almost none were left in 2002, albeit for different reasons. Most of the Jews who were not deported or killed due to Romania's alliance with Germany left Romania immediately after the Second World War or, to be more precise, after the foundation of Israel. A substantial share of the Germans, on the other hand, were either relocated to newly acquired German territories when Romania became an ally of Germany, fled or were deported after 1944 when Romania changed sides and joined the Allied Forces (Turliuc 2003: 130; Magocsi 1993: 166-167).[1] The exodus of both groups continued in the communist period, although international migration was strictly controlled in Romania under the communist regime. Those intending to leave, even if only for short periods of time, had to apply for official permission. Yet, despite these strict controls, the numbers of people who emigrated permanently were not insignificant. Of these, relatively high proportions were members of the three largest ethnic minorities in Romania.[2] This can largely be explained by the fact that the emigration of ethnic Germans and Jews was respectively supported by Germany and Israel. Both countries paid the Romanian government lump sums for each individual who was allowed to leave Romania for good.

Probably for this same reason, the Romanian emigration statistics are surprisingly accurate for the communist period. Statistics on immigration, by contrast, have only been available since 1991. However, neither the official flow statistics nor the official stock statistics capture international migration from and to contemporary Romania, mainly due to the fact that migration patterns have changed massively since the fall of the Iron Curtain. In particular, circular migration, especially since the abolition of the Schengen visa requirement, as well as illegal forms of migration, have become far more significant. At the same time, immigration, particularly from Moldova, has continuously grown. Nevertheless, up to 2006 the statistics on migration flows to and from contemporary Romania published by the National Institute of Statistics only captured those who settled permanently in Romania or abroad. Similarly, the stocks of foreign citizens residing in the country were severely underrecorded in the 2002 Census. While statistics from destination countries of Romanian outflows provide more information on emigration from Romania, residence and work permit data give more of an insight into immigration to Romania. Nevertheless, some of the movements from and to this country remain statistically invisible, as they are difficult to capture with the existing statistical instruments; this is due to their frequently temporary and sometimes illegal nature (Baldwin-Edwards 2007: 7-8).

9.2 Overview of the most important stock and flow data sources

The authority responsible for the production of statistics on international migration in Romania is the National Institute of Statistics (Institutul National de Statistica, NIS). Their main data sources are:
- the census which covers the stock of the population and
- the population register.

However, as the following will show, these statistical reports only cover a tiny fraction of the actual immigration to, and emigration from, Romania.

Additional data can be obtained from the Authority for Foreign Persons, which holds a database on registered foreign citizens, the Ministry of Interior and Administration Reform, which publishes statistics based on residence permit data, the General Inspectorate of the Border Police, which holds data on the numbers of people not allowed to enter or leave the country, and the National Office for Refugees, which gathers data on the numbers of asylum claims filed in Romania. Since July 2006, all of these figures have to be reported directly to the NIS. It remains to be seen whether this will improve the availability and the quality of the data on international migration in Romania.

9.2.1 *Census*

The first Romanian census was held in 1859-1860, i.e. in the very year of the union of the Romanian principalitics. Consequently, counting the inhabitants of the new-born nation seems to have been one of the main political priorities at the time. Nine further censuses have followed, with the last two carried out in 1992 and 2002. However, the results of the two most recent censuses are not comparable, as they use different definitions of population. In 2002, the population of Romania was determined according to the 2000 UNO EEC recommendations for Population and Housing that draw on the 1998 UN recommendations for the definition of international migration. This had major implications for who was counted and not counted as part of the population in 2002 as opposed to 1992. While in 1992 Romanian citizens with legal residence in Romania were counted towards the Romanian population irrespective of whether they had lived abroad for years, the 2002 Census excluded those Romanian citizens who had left the country for more than a year on the day of counting, even if they still had legal residence in Romania.[3] At the same time, the 2002 Census for the first time counted foreign citizens and stateless persons who had been living in Romania uninterruptedly for more than a year on the day of the census, while the 1992 Census only included those foreign citizens who had established legal residence in Romania, i.e. who had entered their Romanian address into their identification cards (National Institute of Statistics 2005).

This conceptual change could have provided rich data on the foreign population residing in Romania at the time since the census includes questions on sex, age, marital status, place of residence, place of birth, citizenship, ethnicity (based on the person's declaration), religion, education and occupation. However, as will be explained in detail below, it seems that the foreign population was severely underrecorded in the 2002 Census.

9.2.2 Population register[4]

The data for the Romanian population register are held by the Evidence of Population Department of the Ministry of the Interior and Administrative Reform. Up to July 2006, the data were gathered by the police, who reported every registered change of residence to the county departments of the National Institute of Statistics. These, in turn, transferred the data to their central department, which used these to produce statistics on population flows and stocks.

The main shortcoming of the Romanian statistical registration until 2005 was the lack of a centralised computer system. In 2005, the personnel of the local department of the NIS in Iaşi still used paper registrations. This changed massively in July 2006 when a centralised computer system was introduced. All the information on foreigners can now be reported directly to the Central Office of NIS through this system.

In principle, every movement of a person both within Romania and across borders should be registered by the Evidence of Population Office. A person leaving his or her usual residence temporarily in order to visit another country or to work there should inform the police of this temporary change of address. However, as in many other countries, there are no incentives for deregistration, which implies that emigration is usually underrecorded (see Section 9.3 for more information). Legal temporary and permanent immigrants are registered by the Border Police. Moreover, they should inform the local police of their arrival and obtain the relevant permit. However, there are still no internal guidelines for the registration of foreigners. The only existing guidelines for the registration of the population were published in 1993 and relate to births, deaths and marriages.

9.3 Statistics on emigration flows

Considering that emigration statistics are usually rather unreliable, the statistics on emigration from Romania during the communist period were surprisingly accurate. This becomes obvious if we look at one of the major emigration flows during this period, the emigration of ethnic Germans to Germany. A comparison of the numbers of ethnic Germans deregistered in Romania and of those registered as arriving from Romania in Germany between 1975 and 1988 shows that the Romanian emigration statistics covered more than 80 per cent of this emigrant group (see Table 9.1). As mentioned above, this was mainly due to the strict controls on emigration in Romania. Moreover, since the German government paid a lump sum for each German emigrant allowed to leave, there clearly was an interest in correct emigration figures, at least for this particular group. These preconditions were no longer valid after the fall of the regime. As a consequence, the reliability of the Romanian emigration statistics deteriorated dramatically after 1988 (also see Table 9.2).

Table 9.1 *Ethnic German emigrants registered in Romania and ethnic German immigrants from Romania registered in Germany, 1975-1989*

	Deregistrations of ethnic German emigrants in Romania	*Ethnic German immigrants from Romania registered in Germany*	*% covered in Romanian emigration statistics*
1975	4,292	5,077	84.5
1976	3,200	3,766	85.0
1977	9,809	10,989	89.3
1978	10,993	12,120	90.7
1979	8,617	9,663	89.2
1980	13,608	15,767	86.3
1981	9,948	12,031	82.7
1982	10,954	12,972	84.4
1983	13,441	15,501	86.7
1984	14,425	16,553	87.1
1985	12,809	14,924	85.8
1986	11,034	13,130	84.0
1987	11,369	13,994	81.2
1988	10,738	12,902	83.2
1989	14,598	23,387	62.4
1975-1989	159,835	192,776	82.9

Sources: National Institute of Statistics 2006; Federal Administration Office Germany 2006; authors' calculations

Table 9.2 *Emigration to Germany registered in Romania and immigration from Romania registered in Germany, 1990-2004*

	Emigration to Germany registered in Romania			*Immigration from Romania registered in Germany*			*% covered in Romania*		
	Total	*Of these: ethnic Germans*	*Non-ethnic German*	*Ethnic Germans*	*Romanian national**	*Total*	*Ethnic Germans*	*Other Romanian nationals*	*Total*
1990	66,121	60,072	6,049	111,150	78,068	189,218	54.0	7.7	34.9
1991	20,001	15,567	4,434	32,178	61,670	93,848	48.4	7.2	21.3
1992	13,813	8,852	4,961	16,146	110,096	126,242	54.8	4.5	10.9
1993	6,874	5,945	929	5,811	81,760	87,571	102.3	1.1	7.8
1994	6,880	4,065	2,815	6,615	31,449	38,064	61.5	9.0	18.1
1995	9,010	2,906	6,104	6,519	24,845	31,364	44.6	24.6	28.7
1996	6,467	2,315	4,152	4,284	16,986	21,270	54.0	24.4	30.4
1997	5,807	1,273	4,534	1,777	14,144	15,921	71.6	32.1	36.5
1998	3,899	775	3,124	1,005	16,987	17,992	77.1	18.4	21.7
1999	2,370	390	1,980	855	18,814	19,669	45.6	10.5	12.0
2000	2,216	374	1,842	547	24,202	24,749	68.4	7.6	9.0
2001	854	143	711	380	20,142	20,522	37.6	3.5	4.2
2002	1,305	67	1,238	256	23,953	24,209	26.2	5.2	5.4
2003	1,938	20	1,918	137	23,780	23,917	14.6	8.1	8.1
2004	2,707	36	2,671	76	23,545	23,621	47.4	11.3	11.5
Total	150,262	102,800	47,462	187,736	570,441	758,177	54.8	8.3	19.8

* Ethnic German immigrants are usually counted as Germans in German inflow statistics, so the figures for incoming Romanians should, generally speaking, not include ethnic Germans.
Sources: Romanian National Institute of Statistics 2006; German Federal Administration Office 2006 (ethnic German immigrants); German Federal Statistical Office (Romanian nationals); authors' calculations

Nevertheless, the statistics on the numbers of ethnic Germans leaving the country after 1988 were still comparatively accurate. In the early 1990s, Germany also became a major destination country for other Romanian citizens. Between 1990 and 1993, about 330,000 Romanian citizens registered in Germany (see Table 9.2). Although these figures might include double counts, since the German flow statistics register cases rather than persons, it is nevertheless not an exaggeration to state that far fewer of the non-ethnic German Romanians deregistered upon leaving Romania, most probably since they were not guaranteed residence, let alone citizenship, at their destination. In fact, the large majority of the entrants applied for asylum but were rejected.[5] As a consequence, large numbers of Romanians left Germany again, especially between 1992 and 1994. While the migration balance was positive between 1990 and 1992 (1990: 61,203, 1991: 30,884 and 1992: 57,564), it was negative for the three following years (1993: -20,549, 1994: -13,538 and 1995: -744).[6] Subsequently, both immigration and emigration of Romanian citizens to and from Germany remained stable (between 14,000 and 24,000 immigrants and 13,000 to 20,000 emigrants per year, yielding a migration balance of about 300 to 7,500). These figures confirm that migration from Romania to Germany became a circular movement originating mostly from Southern Transylvania, Banat and Western Oltenia (Sandu 2005: 558, 562). However, circular migration movements were also observed for ethnic Germans who interspersed periods of work in Germany with periods of living back in Romania. Moreover, many ethnic Germans came back as investors or representatives of German companies; permanent relocation to Romania with the family is the exception (Michalon 2004).

That temporary emigration from Romania has become more significant was also confirmed in the 2002 Census. If we go by the figures only, the population of Romania decreased by more than 1 million people between 1992 and 2002 (from 22,810,035 to 21,680,974). Only 330,000 of this population loss can be explained by natural decrease. If we add the recorded inflows of about 70,000, the population loss due to emigration was at least 900,000 or 4.2 per cent of the 2002 population (Baldwin-Edwards 2007: 8). However, since the 1992 Census counted all registered Romanian residents irrespective of whether they were present on the day of the census, we do not know how many of the 900,000 actually left the country between 1992 and 2002. What we do know is that about 310,000 people officially left the country between 1992 and 2001. Another 360,000 were registered as having left the country temporarily (i.e. for more than six months) on the day of the census (Sandu, Radu, Constantinescu & Ciobanu 2004: 1). This leaves us with 230,000 people not accounted for in these statistical sources.

Other important countries of destination for temporary migration from Romania are Italy and, particularly, Spain. As Table 9.3 shows, the Romanian data only capture a fracture of actual emigration to Italy between 1995 and 2003. However, Spain is even more striking a case in point since this country does not feature among the ten most important emigration countries despite the fact that, according to Eurostat figures, more than 370,000 Romanian citizens were registered as having entered Spain between 1992 and 2005. More than 90 per cent of these arrived after 2002 when Romanians no longer required a visa for entering the Schengen area for a period of no more than 90 days. In 2005, Spain recorded about 190,000 legal Romanian residents (Viruela Martínez 2006) and Italy 249,000. Altogether, about 500,000 Romanians were legally resident in Southern Europe in 2005 (Baldwin-Edwards 2007: 9).

Two other important countries of destination for migration from Romania are Hungary and former Yugoslavia. However, as Sandu (2005: 560) points out, the flows to these countries are even more difficult to measure since they include trips for work or trade as well as commuting or small traffic.

Table 9.3 *Emigrants leaving for Italy registered in Romania and immigration of Romanian citizens registered in Italy, selected years between 1995 and 2003*

	Emigration to Italy registered in Romania	*Immigration of Romanian citizens registered in Italy*	*% covered in Romania*
1995	2,195	2,321	94.6
1996	1,640	6,701	24.5
1998	1,877	6,818	27.5
1999	1,415	10,651	13.3
2000	2,142	19,332	11.1
2002	1,317	17,541	7.5
2003	1,993	74,463	2.7
Total	12,579	137,827	9.1

Note: Eurostat does not have figures for Italy before 1995; the figures for 1997 and 2001 are missing in the database.
Sources: Romanian National Institute of Statistics 2006; Eurostat; authors' calculations

Of course, none of these figures cover those Romanians who enter these countries of destination illegally or, more importantly since 2002, those who enter as tourists and work illegally. Viruela Martínez (2006) shows that between 2002 and 2004 only about 27 per cent of the Romanians residing in the country (317,366 on 1 January 2004 according to the National Statistical Institute in Spain) held a residence permit (about 83,000 on 31 December 2003 according to the Spanish Ministry of Labour). However, this percentage probably changed massively in 2005 when the number of residence permits held by Romanians more than doubled due to a legalisation process. Although there are no comparable figures for other Schengen countries, we may assume that working tourists also entered these countries. The Romanian border police registered an increase of border crossings by 1.4 million between 2002 and 2004. Over the same period the number of exit refusals increased by 1.3 million to 1.7 million in 2004. Yet, despite these increased state controls, there were complaints from Schengen and EU states about the high number of Romanians overstaying their tourist visa (Baldwin-Edwards 2007: 10).

All of the above proves that temporary and circular migration have surged while permanent emigration, especially to Hungary and Germany, has become far less significant in recent years. Almost 100,000 people left Romania permanently in 1990. This figure was already halved in 1991 with 45,000 people leaving the country for good. Since then the number of permanent emigrants has fallen almost continuously with minor increases in the mid-1990s. Only the numbers of those leaving for Canada, the US and Italy have remained relatively stable after 1995, albeit on a very low level of about 1,000 to 3,000 for each of these destinations per year (see Table 9.4). Nevertheless, this is the only kind of emigration registered in official Romanian statistics.

Table 9.4 *Permanent emigration from Romania by country of destination, 1990-2005*

	Total	*Austria*	*Canada*	*France*	*Israel*	*Italy*	*Germany*	*US*	*Hungary*	*Others*
1990	96,929	3,459	1,894	1,626	1,227	1,130	66,121	4,924	10,635	3,730
1991	44,160	4,630	1,661	1,512	519	1,396	20,001	5,770	4,427	3,208
1992	31,152	3,282	1,591	1,235	463	528	13,813	2,100	4,726	2,288
1993	18,446	1,296	1,926	937	324	645	6,874	1,245	3,674	1,010
1994	17,146	1,256	1,523	787	417	1,580	6,880	1,078	1,779	1,363
1995	25,675	2,276	2,286	1,438	316	2,195	9,010	2,292	2,509	2,504
1996	21,526	915	2,123	2,181	418	1,640	6,467	3,181	1,485	2,367
1997	19,945	1,551	2,331	1,143	554	1,706	5,807	2,861	1,244	1,841
1998	17,536	941	1,945	846	563	1,877	3,899	2,868	1,306	2,640
1999	12,594	468	1,626	696	326	1,415	2,370	2,386	774	2,097
2000	14,753	270	2,518	809	433	2,142	2,216	2,723	881	2,200
2001	9,921	167	2,483	463	279	1,486	854	1,876	680	1,398
2002	8,154	293	1,437	233	106	1,317	1,305	1,356	903	1,044
2003	10,673	338	1,444	338	164	1,993	1,938	2,012	984	1,315
2004	13,982	491	1,445	436	85	2,603	2,707	2,049	1,553	1,470
2005	10,938	421	1,220	343	64	2,731	2,196	1,679	1,013	1,050
Total	373,530	22,054	29,453	15,023	6,258	26,384	152,458	40,400	38,573	31,525
In %	100	6.2	8.1	4.2	1.8	6.0	42.9	1.3	10.7	8.7

Source: National Institute for Statistics 2006; authors' calculations

9.4 Immigration

The National Institute for Statistics did not publish any data on immigration to Romania before 1991. The 1992 Census recorded about 3,000 foreign citizens permanently residing in the country (as explained in Section 9.2.1, the 1992 Census only counted permanent residents). If we go by figures alone, the number of foreigners increased 9.4 fold between the 1992 Census and the 2002 Census, which recorded 27,910 foreign citizens, with 12.8 per cent of these originating from the Republic of Moldova, 8.5 from Italy, 8.4 from Turkey, 7.0 from China, 6.3 from Germany and 6.0 from Greece (Constantin, Vasile, Preda & Nicolescu 2004: 63). However, as explained above, the 2002 Census was based on a different concept of population. This included foreign citizens and stateless persons who had been living in Romania uninterruptedly for more than a year on the day of the census. Hence, the numbers also increased due to this change in measurement. At the same time, the census most probably vastly underrecorded the foreign citizens residing in the country. This becomes immediately obvious if we compare the census data with permit data and the numbers of foreigners registered by the Authority for Foreign Persons. About 68,000 foreigners held either a permanent (1,400) or a temporary (66,500) permit in Romania in 2002 (OECD 2005). In the same year, 70,857 foreigners (17,336 of whom were EU citizens) were registered by the Authority for Foreign Persons (Baldwin-Edwards 2007: 26).

Table 9.5 *Number of foreigners holding permanent and temporary residence permits in Romania, 1999-2006*

	1999	*2000*	*2001*	*2002*	*2003*	*2004*	*2005*	*2006*
Permanent residence permits	1,300	1,200	1,100	1,400	NA	2,314	3,595	5,429
Temporary residence permits	61,900	69,500	66,500	66,500	NA	44,448	45,890	48,177
Total	63,200	70,700	67,700	67,900	NA	46,762	49,485	53,606

Note: NA = not available
Sources: OECD 2005; Ministry of Interior and Administrative Reform 2006, 2007

However, the number of those holding temporary residence permits has considerably decreased since that date, while the number of those holding permanent residence permits has been increasing steadily, albeit not to such an extent that this could explain the decrease in temporary permits (see Table 9.5).[7] 53,606 foreign citizens held either a temporary or a permanent residence permit in 2006. 21.3 per cent of these originated from Moldova, 11.8 per cent from Turkey, 9.3 per cent from China and 6.7 per cent from Italy. However, while the first three groups had increased since 2005, the number of Italians holding permits had decreased by 11 per cent. 20,4 per cent of the temporary residents are students, with the large majority of these coming from Moldova; 17.7 per cent were granted temporary residence on the grounds of family reunification, again with a majority of these coming from Moldova; and 17.3 per cent of the temporary residents came to Romania to work there, mainly from China, Italy and Turkey. While half of the Chinese and Italian temporary residents are workers, more than 40 per cent of the Moldovans are students (Ministry of Interior and Administration Reform 2007: 37-39).

The number of asylum seekers entering Romania is very low. The number of claims filed reached a peak with about 2,400 in 2004 and has been decreasing ever since, with 594 claims filed in 2005. The most significant countries of origin were Iraq, Bangladesh and China (UNHCR 2007: 473).

Due to its very nature, there is no way of measuring the numbers of immigrants entering or working in Romania illegally. Estimates of the stocks based on the numbers of expulsions and the numbers of persons detected in Romania and at the borders decreased from 20,000 in 2000 to 12,000 in 2002. The number of those caught entering the country illegally is usually much lower than the numbers of those caught leaving the country illegally. Of the 3,600 people arrested in 2002, about 2,540 (both foreign and Romanian) were trying to leave the country (OECD 2005: 260). These numbers of apprehensions at

Figure 9.1 *Number of foreigners who settle in Romania per year according to the NIS, 1991-2005*

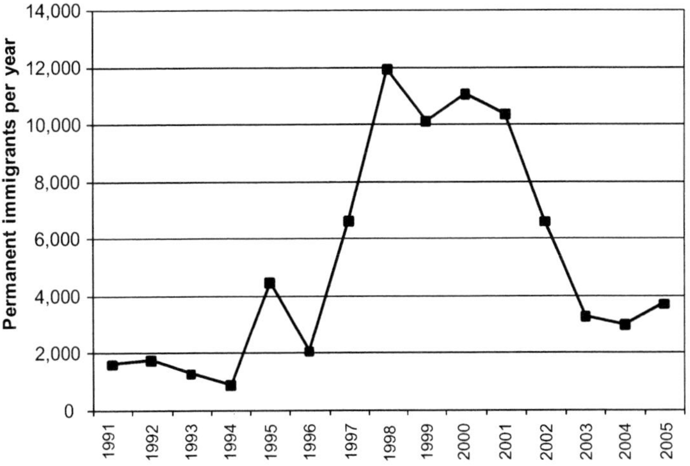

Source: National Institute of Statistics 2006

the borders decreased considerably to about 1,000 in 2006. 380 of these tried to enter the country illegally. The numbers of refusals of entry have also declined, from about 80,000 in 2002 and 2003 to about 50,000 in 2005 and 2006, with more than 50 per cent of those refused entry coming from Moldova. (Ministry of Interior and Administration Reform 2007: 34-35). As Baldwin-Edwards pointed out, these refusals will most probably impact on illegal short-term and circular migration (Baldwin-Edwards 2007: 26).

None of the above immigrants are included in the flow statistics published by the National Institute for Statistics as these only contain data on those immigrants whose address in Romania has been registered in their ID cards and in their evidence files (see Figure 9.1). As pointed out by Constantin et al. (2004), these are mainly repatriates and ethnic Romanians, with a large majority coming from Moldova (66 per cent of the total registered permanent residents between 1994 and 2005).[8] Other important countries of origin are the United States, Ukraine and Germany. More than 80 per cent of these immigrants are under 50 years of age, with the majority being between 26 and 40. 46 per cent of those who have arrived between 1991 and 2005 were female, so the gender ratio is more or less balanced (National Institute for Statistics 2006).

9.5 Conclusions

The statistics on international migration published by the National Institute for Statistics only cover a tiny fraction of the actual movements to and from Romania. This is mainly due to the fact that the system of measuring migration has only changed slightly since the end of the communist period in 1989. The main interest of current statistical reporting seems to be the documentation of the stocks of Romanian citizens, of the permanent emigration of Romanians and of repatriations as well as of the permanent immigration of ethnic Romanians. Temporary movements, which have increased massively since the change of the political system, have generally been ignored. The only exception to this rule was the 2002 Census, which tried to measure the actual population rather than the registered permanent population. Unfortunately, it vastly under-recorded the foreign citizens residing in the country.

Most of the technical shortcomings in Romanian statistics were eliminated in 2006 when the NIS introduced a centralised computer system. However, the central problem remains to be solved and it is necessary to redefine the concept of international migration underlying these statistics if these are to depict a more accurate picture of international migration to and from Romania.

Notes

1 Romania lost Bessarabia, northern Bukovina and southern Dobruja after the Second World War. However, the Germans living in these areas had been resettled to newly acquired German territories during the war, while a majority of the Jews had died in the Holocaust.

2 According to the census conducted in 1977, 88.1 per cent of total population were ethnic Romanians, 7.9 per cent were ethnic Hungarians, 1.7 per cent were ethnic Germans, and 0.1 per cent were ethnic Jews. However, out of the 17,810 people who legally emigrated in 1977, 26.8 per cent were ethnic Romanians, 55.1 per cent were ethnic Germans, 8 per cent were ethnic Hungarians, and 7.9 per cent were ethnic Jews. Of the people who left Romania legally between 1975 and 1989, 44.1 per cent were ethnic Germans, 12.8 per cent were ethnic Hungarians, and 5.4 per cent were ethnic Jews.

3 Legal residence is established on the basis of the address registered in the respective person's identification card. For children under fourteen lacking an identification card, the census registered the address of the parent(s) or the person(s) taking care of them.

4 The following information is based on an interview with an expert from the Iaşi county department of the NIS, 10 July 2007.

5 Between 1992 and 1996, 265,136 Romanian citizens entered Germany. Over the same period, 194,726 people originating from Romania filed an asylum application in Germany (UNHCR 2002: 119). Since then, the numbers of asylum seekers origi-

nating from Romania have decreased massively, not only in Germany. Figures lay at about 10,000 between 1996 and 2000 and decreased to 2,700 in 2005, with the most important countries of destination for these flows being Ireland, Belgium, Italy, Greece and France (UNHCR 2007: 473).

6 A similar pattern can be observed for the migration of Romanians to Hungary; the numbers of immigrants from Romania increased massively in the early 1990s but a majority of these either returned to Romania or moved on to a third destination in the years to follow (see Hárs & Sik in this publication).

7 Foreign citizens residing in Romania can apply for permanent residence after a period of temporary legal residence of at least six years (this requirement is reduced to three years for those married to Romanian citizens).

8 There are no statistics by country of origin for this group before 1994.

Statistical sources

Organisation	*Content*	*URL*
National Institute for Statistics (NIS)	– population register – census	www.insse.ro
Ministry of Interior and Administration Reform	– residence permits	www.mai.gov.ro

Bibliography

Arel, D. (2002), 'Language categories in censuses', in D.I. Kertzer & D. Arel (eds.), *Census and Identity: The Politics of Race, Ethnicity and Language in National Censuses*, 92-120. Cambridge: Cambridge University Press.

Baldwin-Edwards, M. (2007), 'Navigating between Scylla and Charybdis: Migration Policies for a Romania within the European Union', *Southeast European and Black Sea Studies* 7 (1): 5-35.

Constantin, D.-L., V. Vasile, D. Preda & L. Nicolescu (2004), *The Migration Phenomenon from the Perspective of Romania's Accession to the EU*. Bucharest: European Institute of Romania.

Federal Administration Office Germany (Bundesverwaltungsamt) (2006), *Spätaussiedler und deren Angehörige: Verteilverfahren. Jahresstatistik 2006*. Cologne: Bundesverwaltungsamt.

Illyés, E. (1981), *National Minorities in Romania*. www.hungarian-history.hu.

Kocsis, K. (2007), 'Ethnic and Religious Patterns', in K. Kocsis (ed.), *South Eastern Europe in Maps*. 2nd, Revised & Expanded Edition, 37-64. Budapest: Geographical Research Institute, Hungarian Academy of Sciences.

Magocsi, P.R. (1993), *Historical Atlas of East Central Europe*. Seattle, London: University of Washington Press.

Michalon, B. (2004), 'Playing on ethnicity to be there and here: The three paradoxes of "ethnic migrations"', paper presented at the 2nd Conference of the EAPS Working Group on International Migration in Europe entitled 'International migration in Europe: new trends, new methods of analysis', Rome, 25 November 2004.

Ministry of Interior and Administration Reform (2006), *Migraţia şi azilul în România 2005*. www.mai.gov.ro/documente.

Ministry of Interior and Administration Reform (2007), *Imigraţia şi azilul în România 2006*. www.mai.gov.ro/documente.

National Institute of Statistics (2006), *Romanian Demographic Yearbook*. Bucharest: NIS.

National Statistical Institute (2005), *Census of Population and Dwellings, 18 March 2002, Volume V – Population, Households, Dwellings*. Bucharest: NSI. www.insse.ro.

OECD (2005), *Trends in International Migration*. Geneva: OECD.

Potot, S. (2003), *Circulation et réseaux de migrants roumains: une contribution à l'étude des nouvelles mobilités en Europe*. PhD dissertation, Nice Sophia Antipolis University. tel.archives-ouvertes.fr.

Sandu, D. (2005), 'Emerging Transnational Migration from Romanian Villages', *Current Sociology* 53 (4): 555-582.

Sandu, D., C. Radu, M. Constantinescu & O. Ciobanu (2004), *A Country Report on Romanian Migration Abroad: Stocks and Flows after 1989*. www.migrationonline.cz.

Turliuc, C. (2003), *Interwind* [sic] *destinies. Modern Romania and its ethnic groups*. Iaşi: Editura Junimea.

UNHCR (2002), *UNHCR Statistical Yearbook 2001: Refugees, Asylum Seekers and Other Persons of Concern – Trends in Displacements, Protections and Solutions*. www.unhcr.org.

UNHCR (2007), *UNHCR Statistical Yearbook 2005: Trends in Displacements, Protections and Solutions*. www.unhcr.org.

Viruela Martínez, R. (2006), 'Immigrantes rumanos en España: aspectos territoriales y procesos de sustitución laboral', *Scripta Nova* 10 (222). www.ub.es/geocrit.

Part 4

New immigrant receiving countries

10 Greece

Martin Baldwin-Edwards with Katerina Apostolatou

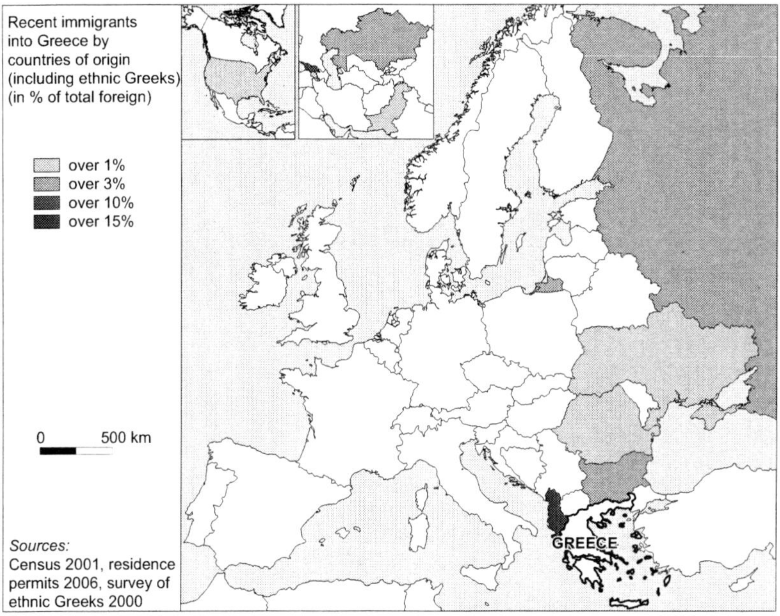

Cartography: Walter Lang, University of Vienna

10.1 Introduction

In all countries, official state data, such as the census, constitute institutions of power, through which the state 'imagines' its dominion – the nature of the human beings it rules, the geography of its domain and the legitimacy of its ancestry (Anderson 1991: 163-164). Since the late nineteenth century, Greece has been preoccupied with homogenising its population with respect to 'ethnicity' (although religion was actually the principal criterion) and with managing extraordinarily large population movements (in excess of two million in the period 1919-1926) with respect to neighbouring countries of the former Ottoman Empire (Pentzopoulos 1962). A popular perception was systematically created that only 'Greeks' lived in, or migrated to, Greece (Clark 2006: 201-

222); the continued exodus of various minorities also served to reinforce that perception.[1] The management of statistical evidence, for the political purpose of showing that the residents of Greece were actually Greeks, was paramount (Michailidis 1998) and had clear parallels in neighbouring Balkan states. Thus, with the same Ottoman population datasets (1900, 1905) for the geographical region of Macedonia (most of which was transferred to Greece in 1913 after the Balkan Wars), Bulgarian, Serb, Greek and Turkish authors were each able to 'prove' statistically that 'the majority of the population was theirs' (Kertzer & Arel 2001: 21). This tendency toward political constructivism with respect to data has not been lost in the region, although arguably it has become more sophisticated.[2]

Emigration of Greeks, which had been significant at around 420,000 in the first quarter of the century, was the dominant form of migration from 1945 to 1974. It began with refugee flight during the 1946-1949 civil war, but no data at all were recorded until 1955 (Fakiolas & King 1996: 172). Greek 'guestworker' (*Gastarbeiter*) migrations to Belgium began in 1953 and led to a recruitment agreement with Belgium in 1957, with Germany in 1960 and subsequently with Switzerland, the Netherlands and Sweden (Vermeulen 2008). Gross emigration is estimated at 1.4 million for the period 1945-1974, with about half going to Germany; some 25 per cent subsequently returned. Official figures on return commence only in 1968, peak in 1975 and the records end – as for emigration data – in 1977 (Fakiolas & King 1996: 172-174). It can be concluded that Greek data on migrations of Greeks were heavily reliant upon estimates, inconclusive concerning return and repeat migrations and, overall, reflected an apparent lack of interest in the matter by the state.

According to Nikolinakos (1973), mass emigration of Greeks in the 1950s and 1960s had left certain sectors of the Greek labour market short of workers, and Africans were employed as private servants, hotel workers and dockyard labourers alongside Turks in industry. By the end of 1972, according to the Labour Secretary of the military government, the number of foreign workers in Greece amounted to 15,000-20,000, mostly Africans (Fakiolas & King 1996: 176). In the 1970s, the first non-European refugees started to arrive – some 3,000 from Lebanon, in 1976 – to be followed later by small numbers of Vietnamese boatpeople, and in the 1980s by asylum seekers and refugees from across the Middle East (Papantoniou, Papantoniou-Frangouli & Kalavanou 1996: 41). After 1985, large numbers of Poles and other Eastern Europeans arrived. Greece at that time refused to allow recognised refugees and asylum seekers the right to work, and they were temporarily housed in refugee camps and rented hotel rooms awaiting relocation to another country; however, the international climate for refugee relocation worsened, and the typical length of stay of the refugees increased from six to nine months to as much as five years (Papantoniou et al. 1996: 42). Most of the asylum seekers and refugees worked in the large Greek informal economy, and played an important role in attracting yet more immigrants from Eastern Europe and the Middle East.

By 1986, the number of legal immigrants was estimated as 92,440, and by 1990 as 173,436 (Fakiolas & King 1996: 176); however, detailed residence permit data suggest a rather lower figure of around 60,000 for 1990 (see Section 10.3.1 below). To these official data should be added the illegal and semi-legal[3] residents, estimated at 100,000 for 1990 (Baldwin-Edwards 2004a). Thus, the immigrant population by 1991 was of the order of 2-3 per cent of total population, although probably constituted a higher proportion of the labour force.

It was not until 1991 that the Greek state or society showed any real interest in immigration policy, with the challenge to Greek border integrity by Albanians who were leaving the collapsed socialist regime of Enver Hoxha. A few tens of thousands crossed the mountainous border with Greece and provoked a near-hysterical reaction in the mass media, with the rapid construction of a 'dangerous Albanian' stereotype (Karydis 1992). Hastily, a new immigration law was approved, to replace the outdated 1929 Law. The 1991 Law makes clear in its Preamble, the underlying rationale: 'Suddenly, Greece started to be flooded with aliens, who, entering, staying and working illegally, create enormous social problems for the state, while they inevitably try to solve their own problems by engaging in criminality (drugs, robberies, thefts, etc.)' (Minutes of the Parliament, Session 10 October 1991; cited in Karydis 1998).

Thus, the main justification for a repressive law was the allegation of criminality, with the mass media playing a central role in the shaping of public opinion, particularly with regard to Albanians. The new law made no practical provision for legal immigration, but instituted several new mechanisms of expulsion and deportation as well as implementing major parts of the Schengen Agreement (Baldwin-Edwards 1997; Baldwin-Edwards & Fakiolas 1998). Over the period, 1991-2001, the Greek police typically expelled without legal process around 150,000-250,000 persons per year, of whom 75-80 per cent were Albanian (Baldwin-Edwards 2004b: 4).

Since the 1970s, small numbers of ethnic Greeks had been arriving from the Soviet Union; however, according to survey data, large inflows began in 1989 and peaked in 1993. Various laws were enacted to facilitate the arrival in Greece of 'repatriates' from the USSR, along with easy naturalisation: yet no reliable records of their arrival in Greece or of their receipt of Greek citizenship have apparently been kept. Ethnic

Greeks from Albania, on the other hand, were not accorded any real privileges over the 1990s, were not described as 'repatriates' and statistically were indistinguishable from illegal migrants (Baldwin-Edwards 2004a: 3). Since 2002, a Special Identity Card for Homogeneis has been issued to Albanian nationals claiming Greek ethnicity: the number of such permits awarded was concealed on the grounds of 'national security' by the Ministry of Public Order until summer 2006, when the Minister confirmed to a Parliamentary Committee that the previously-leaked figure of 200,000[4] was correct (*Athens News*, 4 August 2006).

Public opinion on immigration in Greece has been very much influenced by the mass media, especially in the early 1990s when it was focused on the 'dangerous Albanian' stereotype; the media coverage has improved since about 2000, although the damage has been done (Baldwin-Edwards 2004c: 58-59). Consistently, comparative European opinion polls, such as Eurobarometer, show Greeks as the most xenophobic and intolerant in the EU-15 – at least, when answering theoretical questions on racial attitudes. Greek opinion polls reveal more complex patterns, with Greeks tending to blame immigrants for high(ish) Greek unemployment, but frequently ranking illegal immigration as one of the least pressing socio-political problems in Greece, ranking it in tenth position out of twelve choices (Baldwin-Edwards & Safilios-Rothschild 1999: 214-215). Thus, it is not surprising that Greek citizens make a clear distinction between common xenophobic beliefs and more positive personal experiences, with few real complaints about immigration in everyday life. Immigration has yet to emerge as a significant political issue, despite its salience over the last fifteen years.

10.2 Overview of stock and flow statistics

In the early 1990s, despite the very large number (hundreds of thousands annually) of Albanians involved in illegal migration and subsequent (illegal) expulsions by the Greek state, along with the rapidly-growing xenophobia sponsored by the mass media, there was no shift in state policy on the collection of statistical data. This was primarily, it seems, because both the Greek state and society believed that the immigration of Albanians (and others) was a temporary phenomenon and of little real interest to the country. The official position until the mid-1990s was that 'Greece is not a country of immigration' (Glytsos 1995: 168). After several years of highly restrictive policy and typically circa 30,000 valid work permits and 80,000-90,000 residence permits, by 1994 government estimates of the stock of illegal migrants had reached 500,000-600,000 (Baldwin-Edwards & Fakiolas 1998: 188-191). It was not until Greece's first legalisation programme of

1997, with 372,000 applicants for a six-month 'White Card', that any hard data emerged.[5] A subsequent legalisation programme for one to three year 'Green Cards' yielded only 228,000 applicants and the lack of adequate immigration statistics resulted in increasing criticism from European quarters.

By the time of the decennial population census in 2001 there was some considerable political pressure on Greece to attempt to record its total immigrant population. The 1991 Census, conducted in the normal Greek bureaucratic style, had captured a picture of mainly legal immigrants: the 2001 Census was approached differently. The National Statistical Service of Greece (NSSG) set out to convince immigrant organisations and the illegal immigrant population generally, that its records – although state-owned – were sacrosanct and unavailable to police, immigration or tax authorities. The NSSG mounted sophisticated advertising campaigns to this end and also engaged in direct dialogue with major immigrant groups.[6] The result was that some 762,000 non-Greeks were recorded in the 2001 Census – around 7 per cent of total population – and it was generally considered to be a remarkable success in the recording of illegal immigrants. However, it should be noted that this census, like all Greek censuses since 1951, had no 'sensitive' questions pertaining to mother tongue, religion, ethnicity or multiple nationality.

The latest stage in the evolution of immigration data in Greece has its foundation in the 2001 Immigration Law (2910/2001). This transferred the responsibility for immigration issues away from the Ministry of Public Order (although leaving it with legal competence for border controls, ethnic Greeks, asylum seekers and EU nationals) and to the Ministry of the Interior. In particular, it established a semi-autonomous research body – the Migration Policy Institute – attached to the Ministry, with the mandate to conduct or commission research and to provide policy advice. This institute, under its new political leadership in 2004, awarded a series of research contracts to universities and external authorities. The first was a study of immigration statistical data in Greece in order to advise the Ministry of the current state of affairs, as well as to make recommendations for improvement in the collection and compilation of such data – the latter, particularly, in order to conform to the new EU regulation on migration data. This study was conducted by the current author and is available on the web (Baldwin-Edwards 2004a). Eight of its nine recommendations have now been implemented, and Greek immigration statistics are slowly converging onto a more typical European pattern of data-collection and presentation. The 2005 Immigration Law (3386/2005) continued the modernisation of immigration data collection, although with few specific structural changes.[7]

The principal sources of data on migration are:
- the decennial census (NSSG),
- the quarterly Labour Force Survey (NSSG),
- the register of residence permits for third-country nationals (Interior Ministry),
- the register of asylum applications and decisions (Ministry of Public Order).

The residence permit data allow for the analysis of reasons for the awarding of residence permits – employment, self-employment, family reunification, etc. – and the nationality (but not country of origin) of permit holders. There is no information available on education and skill levels from this dataset, although this information is now beginning to be collected in order to compensate for the lack of data collection by the Labour Ministry. The 2001 Census is the only published source of data on education and skills, although the last few years of the Labour Force Survey are in theory able to provide this.[8] Data on asylum seekers are provided by the Ministry of Public Order and UNHCR, but there are no reliable data on existing stocks of recognised refugees.

In principle, there are also registers for the permits given to Albanian ethnic Greeks (Ministry of Public Order) and for CIS ethnic Greeks not awarded citizenship (Ministry of the Interior); however, neither of these institutions has ever produced relevant data. There are no published data on persons leaving and entering the country – although these are checked and apparently recorded – and there are only poor quality data on the reasons for the granting of Schengen visas, and no information on long-term national visas. There are limited records on the awarding of Greek nationality to foreigners, but no central data collection on the local awards to ethnic Greeks from Pontos (by far the larger): there are, therefore, no proper data on naturalisations. The records of births and deaths of foreigners are kept manually at over 1,000 municipalities and until late 2006 were not collated centrally; these data are reproduced for the first time, below.

The 1991 Law defined foreign nationals as all those without Greek or EU nationality (Art. 1), whilst regulating the residence and employment rights of 'repatriated Greeks' in a separate provision of the Law (Art. 17). The 2005 Immigration Law repeats this definition (Art. 1), but makes no special provision for ethnic Greeks (other than permitting those whose claims of Greek ethnicity had been rejected to apply for legalisation); other legislation exists – see 10.3.2.1 below – which operates apparently independently of immigration law.

10.3 Empirical observations of stocks and flows

10.3.1 *Trends in stocks*

The limited historical evidence strongly suggests that in the post-war period Greece has always had a presence of undocumented immigrants, owing to the inability of the state to enact and enforce coherent legislation in many areas of state activity. Thus, starting from 1990, there was already a large stock of undocumented migrants who do not appear in official data. Table 10.1 uses the latest reliable data to provide a brief summary of information on known immigrants, by geographical origin, 1990-2006.

In terms of *legally present immigrants,* the data are fairly unambiguous; the 1990 data are a reasonable approximation of legal third-country nationals *minus* most EU nationals (who, in Greece, were generally refused permits at that time so they remained as undocumented), privileged aliens of Greek ethnicity (Cypriots, Greek-Americans, Greek Pontians, etc.) and recognised refugees. (Most of these latter three categories appear in the 1991 Census and explain the difference in numbers.) The 2001 Census data capture a substantial number of – although by no means all – undocumented immigrants, totalling 762,000 (including

Table 10.1 *Stock of known foreign population in Greece by region of origin, 1990-2006*

	1990 permits	*1991 Census*	*1997 legalisation*	*2001 Census*	*2006 permits**
Total	57,113	167,276	371,641	762,191	586,474
Eastern Africa	793	1,334	1,575	2,118	1,547
Middle Africa	35	222	142	530	296
Northern Africa	5,393	5,220	7,283	9,026	12,110
Southern Africa	155	564	37	1,085	235
Western Africa	547	503	2,329	2,941	2,391
Americas	6,063	20,872	527	27,347	3,931
Eastern Asia	759	661	363	1,513	2,453
South-Central Asia	3,697	4,481	21,813	28,584	35,091
South-Eastern Asia	4,733	4,002	5,530	7,185	7,257
Western Asia	6,823	33,556	17,228	71,271	29,178
Eastern Europe	12,471	27,968	68,564	108,693	116,588
Northern Europe	5,696	13,803	112	18,151	208
Southern Europe	2,829	27,185	244,403	450,271	374,798
Western Europe	5,487	17,569	30	23,621	22
Oceania	520	6,505	34	9,065	310
Albanian *homogeneis*					200,000
EU-25 estimate					70,000
Total including estimates					856,415

* valid permits as of 15 January 2006

Sources: Permit, legalisation applications and census data; authors' compilation

EU nationals). There is a significant difference in the management of the two censuses, which makes data comparison near impossible. The 1991 Census massively under-recorded illegal immigrants and provides a picture of a small number (60,000-80,000) of legal third-country nationals, along with ethnic Greeks and EU nationals. The 2001 Census, as noted above, adopted a very different strategy. It also appears likely that ethnic Greeks, with or without Greek nationality, were recorded as Greek citizens.

With regard to the 2006 data, the changed stock of third-country nationals with permits since 1990 is of the order of 500,000; to this figure, should be added the number of ethnic Greek Albanian permits (estimated at 200,000). Therefore, the change in stocks of documented third-country nationals over the period 1990-2006 is from circa 60,000 to 780,000. By geographical region, the biggest increases are in immigration from Southern Europe (Albanians), from Eastern Europe (Bulgarians, Ukrainians, Romanians, Russians and Moldovans), from Western Asia (Georgians, Armenians, Syrians and Iraqis) and from South-Central Asia (Pakistanis, Indians and Bangladeshi).

Using various state data sources, along with averaged estimates of illegal stocks, the IMEPO advisory report (Baldwin-Edwards 2004a) constructs a complex synthetic picture of the annual changes in migrant stocks. This is reproduced in Figure 10.1. Several points should be made concerning this diagram. First, official permit data until recently excluded children, who are therefore included as an estimated category in their own right. Secondly, the practice of issuing special permits to ethnic Greeks from Albania was started in 2001/02, and these are of such magnitude (over 200,000) that they are factored in. Thirdly, the practice of issuing very short-term permits has led to rapid movement into and out of legality: this appears quite graphically after the first legalisation in 1997, where the lower application figures for the successor 'Green Card' placed some 150,000 immediately back into illegal status. Awards of 'Green Cards' were very slow and, generally, with a validity of only one or two years (theoretically they could be awarded for one to three years and five years); subsequent renewal application rates were very poor and, of those applying, only 50 per cent were granted. The graph also shows the 2001 legalisation applications and the greater success of the Interior Ministry (which assumed control of permits and legalisations after 2001) in maintaining immigrants in legal statuses.

What Figure 10.1 shows most dramatically however, is the very high inflows of undocumented migrants – including, in reality, ethnic Greeks who later benefited from either the awarding of nationality or *homogeneis* permits. Removal of these from the data is difficult, as these naturalisations have not been properly recorded; equally, re-

Figure 10.1 *Evolution of legal and undocumented non-EU immigrant stock (including* homogeneis*) in Greece, 1988-2004*

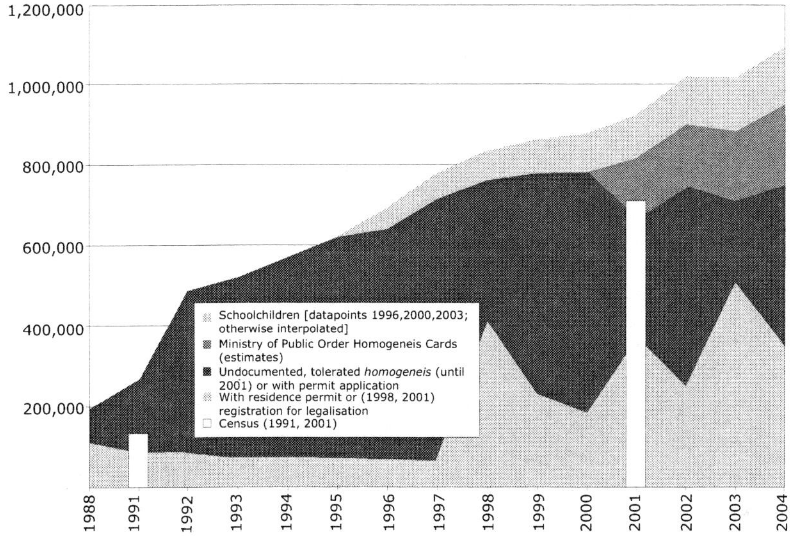

Source: Baldwin-Edwards 2004a

migration of immigrants is not known and, in the case of some nationalities (such as Polish), may be quite high.

Table 10.1 clearly shows the predominance of immigrants from Southern Europe – almost entirely from Albania – along with Albanian *homogeneis* and immigrants from Eastern Europe. No single dataset adequately depicts immigrant stocks, since there are so many different immigration regimes and limited data collection, but it is possible to utilise the 2001 Census and the latest permit data. These are shown, for major nationalities, in Table 10.2.

Although Albanians are the predominant nationality, at 58 per cent in the census and 63 per cent in the permit data, the census data predate the award of 200,000 *homogeneis* permits to Albanians. It is also probable that some Albanians, especially those with three-year *homogeneis* permits, have engaged in 'circular migration', but without data on exit and entry this can only be a matter of speculation. However, the number of valid permits (of both types) awarded to Albanians is probably 500,000-550,000, taking their proportion of total immigrant stocks, including EU nationals and ethnic Greeks, up to around 66 per cent.

Bulgarians have had an increased presence since the 2001 Census, although some of these permits are for seasonal work. Georgians are less visible in the permit data because many will have taken Greek nationality

Table 10.2 *Principal nationalities of foreigners residing in Greece, 2001 and 2006*

	Census 2001			*Residence permits 2006*	
	Abs.	%		*Abs.*	%
Albania	438,036	57.5	Albania	368,625	62.8
Bulgaria	35,104	4.6	Bulgaria	46,114	7.9
Georgia	22,875	3.0	Romania	26,462	4.5
Romania	21,994	2.9	Ukraine	20,283	3.5
US	18,140	2.4	Pakistan	15,478	2.6
Russia	17,535	2.3	Georgia	13,496	2.3
Cyprus	17,426	2.3	India	10,697	1.8
Ukraine	13,616	1.8	Egypt	10,629	1.8
UK	13,196	1.7	Rep. of Moldova	10,561	1.8
Poland	12,831	1.7	Russia	10,084	1.7
Germany	11,806	1.5	Others	54,132	9.2
Pakistan	11,130	1.5			
Others	128,502	16.9			

Sources: 2001 Census; Ministry of the Interior, residence permit data 2006

or *homogeneis* permits; the likelihood is that their actual number will be considerably above the 2001 figure. Romanians show an increase in the permit data, and Ukrainians have shown a large increase since the 2001 Census. Pakistanis also show a significant increase in the 2006 data, while EU-25 and US nationals are almost invisible in all data other than the census, making it difficult to assess changes in stocks.

Only since late 2006 have data been collated for births and deaths of foreign nationals within Greece. Table 10.3 shows the unpublished data for 2005. Immigrant births (as defined by maternal nationality, which might overstate the extent) constituted some 16.5 per cent of all births in 2005. Of these alien births, the majority (60.3 per cent) were to Albanian women and over 70 per cent were to women from four neighbouring countries – Albania, Bulgaria, Romania and Ukraine. Thus, the birth rates are in proportion to immigrant population group sizes. This is slightly surprising, as the more youthful immigrant population has an aggregate birth rate which is apparently similar to the very low birth rate of Greeks. The reason doubtless lies in the very great extent of migrant workers rather than migrant families; there are no calculated data available at this time on the proportion of family units in the total immigrant population.

Data for deaths by nationality also reflect the age structure of immigrant populations and, to a lesser extent, the period when they first migrated to Greece. Total immigrant deaths constituted only 1.5 per cent of deaths in Greece in 2005, with the Albanian proportion at 15 per cent of immigrant deaths – well below their recorded presence. Table 10.4 shows major nationalities; it can be seen that

Table 10.3 *Births of foreign nationals in Greece by nationality, 2005*

Nationality of mother	*Number*
Greek	89,812
Albanian	10,690
Bulgarian	1,025
Romanian	982
Ukrainian	506
Russian	439
Georgian	403
Polish	368
Moldavian	293
Syrian	265
Egyptian	200
Others	2,562
Total aliens	17,733

Source: NSSG private communication

Table 10.4 *Deaths of foreign nationals in Greece by nationality, 2005*

Nationality	*Number*
Albania	241
UK	153
Turkey	153
Germany	123
Cyprus	119
Georgia	64
Poland	60
Italy	56
France	53
Bulgaria	44
Russia	42
US	38
Others	474
Total aliens	1,620
Total for Greece	103,468

Source: NSSG private communication

EU countries are high on the list (reflecting the retirement migration pattern), along with Turkish nationals. These latter are probably people left over from the period of population exchanges between Greece and Turkey (Baldwin-Edwards 2006), who had not changed their citizenship.

There are data on two out of the three methods of naturalisation, but these are highly incomplete and misleading, as well as being very small in number. For a detailed investigation of naturalisation and citizenship data, see the study authored by Harald Waldrauch (2006).

10.3.2 Flow data

Legal immigration flows are very small in the case of Greece, where the typical mode of entry is either illegal border-crossing (from Albania), tourist over-staying and illegal working (Eastern Europeans, amongst others) or student entry and illegal working (Africans). There are no data available at all on the emigration of Greeks or the re-migration of immigrants.

10.3.2.1 Legal inflows

The three principal categories are:
- asylum seekers,
- ethnic Greeks,
- seasonal workers.

Asylum seekers

The trend in inflows is shown in Table 10.5, although it should be noted that the recognition rate is currently around 1 per cent – the lowest in the EU. To some extent, Greece continues its older practice of leaving rejected asylum seekers as illegal immigrants, to work in the large informal economy: rejected asylum seekers and those formerly with refugee status were specifically targeted in the 2005 legalisation, attached to the 2005 Immigration Law.

Table 10.5 *Total number of first asylum applications in Greece, 1997-2005*

	1997	*1998*	*1999*	*2000*	*2001*	*2002*	*2003*	*2004*	*2005*
Number	4,376	2,953	1,528	3,083	5,499	5,664	8,178	4,469	9,050

Source: Kanellopoulos & Gregou 2006: 25

The principal nationalities are Middle Eastern and Asian, as might be expected. Table 10.6 gives the major nationalities for 2005. At this time, Greece seems to suffer to some extent from the 'false asylum seeker' problem, although this had not always been true in the past. However, even the higher number for 2005 is insignificant in comparison.

Table 10.6 *First asylum applications in Greece by principal nationalities, 2005*

Country of origin	*Number*
Georgia	1,897
Pakistan	1,154
Iraq	971
Bangladesh	550
Afghanistan	458
Nigeria	406
Russia	353
Romania	316
Ukraine	268
China	251
Iran	203
India	166
Bulgaria	151
Turkey	126
Sudan	121
Somalia	110
Egypt	104
Ethiopia	100
Myanmar	68
Other countries	1,277
Total	9,050

Source: Ministry of Public Order

Ethnic Greeks

Of much greater significance are the inflows of ethnic Greek immigrants who were rapidly given Greek nationality (as 'repatriated'[9] and 'returning'[10] ethnic Greeks) or other documentation. These inflows were not recorded centrally, nor was the awarding of Greek nationality to them. Furthermore, many ethnic Greeks from Kazhakstan and Ukraine did not wish to acquire Greek nationality, as they would lose their former nationality; the 2000 Law (see Note 10) created a Homogeneis Card, quite different from the Special Homogeneis Card for Albanians, in order to grant some of the privileges of Greek nationality. The number of such cards is not known.

There is only one source of data on inflows of ethnic Greeks from Pontos – a survey carried out in the period 1997-2000.[11] Table 10.7 shows inflows by year in the period 1987-2000, and the proportion that entered in conformity with the 1993 Law. According to the survey, some 155,000 entered Greece over the period 1989-2000, more or less coinciding with the mass immigration of Albanians and others after 1991. Indeed, the peak years of immigration of Pontian Greeks were 1990-1993, over which four-year period some 80,000 arrived. It can be seen that, starting in 1994, some 45 per cent (going up to 95 per cent in 2000) entered with a normal tourist visa; it was this spontaneous 'non-legal' entry which led to the change in the citizenship law in 2000. There is no information on the number of those who may have

Table 10.7 *Immigration of 'repatriated' Greeks, 1987-2000*

Year of entry		*% entered with special visa*
1987	169	99
1988	669	98
1989	5,195	98
1990	16,716	96
1991	17,331	87
1992	19,846	71
1993	25,720	65
1994	14,737	55
1995	14,586	52
1996	14,298	45
1997	12,381	32
1998	5,761	25
1999	4,676	11
2000	1,307	5
Unknown	1,593	63
Total	154,985	63

Source: Emmanouilidi 2003: Table 7

Table 10.8 *Main countries of origin of 'repatriated' Greeks*

Country of origin	*Number*
Georgia	80,644
Kazakhstan	31,271
Russia	20,042
Armenia	8,810
Ukraine	4,660
Uzbekistan	3,442
Others	2,450
Total	155,319

Source: Ministry of Public Order

entered since 2000; any who did so, would have been eligible for rapid granting of Greek nationality or a Homogeneis Card.

Table 10.8 shows the principal countries of origin of 'repatriated' Greeks. The vast majority come from Georgia and have presumably taken Greek nationality. However, of the 31,000 or more from Kazakhstan and the 5,000 from Ukraine (there are probably many more who have arrived since 2000), a large proportion is thought not to have taken Greek nationality but the Homogeneis Card instead.

Ethnic Greeks from Albania were not given such privileged treatment. For political reasons, the Greek state preferred that they remain as Albanian nationals with strong links in Albania; by informal bilateral agreement with Albania,[12] the Greek state until 2007 did not normally award Greek nationality to Albanians. From 2001 they were eligible for a Special Identity Card of three years' duration, of which allegedly some 200,000 were awarded. A government Decision[13] of 2005, with a legal base of Article 17 of the 1991 Immigration Law, grants Albanian *homogeneis* a ten-year standard residence permit along with a Special Homogeneis Identity Card. Curiously, this Decision extends also to Albanian nationals who have resided in Greece before 1990[14] and possess an expired 'foreign identity document'.

Seasonal workers

Greece has few seasonal labour recruitment agreements and uses them very little. The three principal bilateral agreements are with Bulgaria, Albania and Egypt. No data have been published, but residence permit data for the IMEPO study showed that about 1,000 Egyptians, 8,000 Bulgarians and 7,000 Albanians had taken such permits over the period July 2003 to September 2004.

10.3.2.2 Illegal inflows

These are impossible to measure, as in all countries, but interception data can sometimes be used to make extrapolated estimates. Table 10.9 gives unpublished data from the relevant ministry, along with our own interpolated data for actual border apprehensions.

Disregarding the mass illegal expulsions carried out in the 1990s and 2000-2001, there is no clear interpretation possible of what has been going on since 2002. In 2005, some 75 per cent of apprehended illegal aliens and some 85 per cent of removed aliens were Albanian, with Bulgarian and Romanian trailing at about 3 per cent each in both categories (Kanellopoulos & Gregou 2006: 27-28). Thus, it seems that the previous decade's pattern of male Albanian illegal border crossing continues to a great extent; women and children, however, are thought to arrive by more legal means (Baldwin-Edwards 2004b). There is no obvious ratio of interception to successful crossings that can be used,

Table 10.9 *Border apprehensions and expulsions/deportations from Greece, 2000-2006*

	2000	2001	2002	2003	2004	2005
Caught at border[1]	NA	NA	29,019	22,136	15,182	26,919
Caught at sea[1]	NA	NA	3,286	2,636	3,112	3,116
Total border apprehensions[2]	259,403	219,598	32,305	24,772	18,294	30,035
Administrative expulsion decisions	22,227	15,988	25,925	26,259	26,693	36,316
Judicial expulsion decisions	5,715	4,746	3,673	3,283	3,086	4,333
Total expulsion decisions	27,942	20,734	29,598	29,542	29,779	40,649
Of which:						
Male	20,379	16,204	24,802	23,430	25,093	35,369
Female	7,563	4,530	4,796	6,112	4,686	5,280
Expulsions not carried out	3,711	7,492	17,848	14,616	14,059	19,411
Total expulsions carried out	24,231	13,242	11,750	14,926	15,720	21,238

Note: NA = not available

[1] Prior to 2002, undocumented immigrants were removed from Greek territory without legal process. In 2001, the Greek Ombudsman ruled that the Ministry of Public Order had exceeded its authority and such removals were contrary to the Greek Constitution and international law.

[2] Data on border apprehensions are not provided by the Ministry, but are subsumed within other data on apprehensions of illegal immigrants on Greek territory, and those for whom legal process is required. There is some doubt about the validity of the calculated figures given here, which may understate the extent of actual border apprehensions.

Source: Ministry of Public Order, private communication of June 2006

without original research being undertaken. Furthermore, there is real doubt about the accuracy of these data anyway, as the Ministry of Public Order does not supply figures for actual border apprehensions and subsequent response (*refoulement*, asylum procedure, etc.).

10.3.3 *Analysis of trends and patterns*

10.3.3.1 *Skill levels*

The only available information on skill levels of immigrants consists of the data on level of education from the 2001 Census; therefore, no comparison can be made over time. Table 10.10 gives summary data for the nineteen major nationalities, along with a comparison for the Greek adult population. Overall, the data show immigrants as not being significantly different in educational profile from the Greek population, with the exception of a greater number of illiterate[15] persons (9 per cent compared with the Greek 4 per cent) and a much lower proportion of immigrants who failed to complete high school (34 per cent compared with the Greek 44 per cent). By individual nationality, there are striking differences.

The US and the UK have a very high proportion with postgraduate university education, while Ukraine, Cyprus, the UK, Germany, Russia,

Table 10.10 *Educational level among immigrants in Greece by nationality (in per cent)*

	Master's and PhD	*Higher education*	*Higher vocational training*	*Higher secondary (lyceum)*	*Lower secondary (high school)*	*Primary school*	*Incomplete primary school*	*Dropped primary school; literate*	*Illiterate*
Total Greece	0.8	11.3	4.4	27.4	11.8	31.8	0	8.7	3.8
Total immigrants	0.6	9.3	2.7	29.3	16.8	21.9	7.4	2.8	9.2
Albania	0.1	5.0	1.2	25.9	19.8	24.8	9.6	2.6	11.2
Bulgaria	0.3	10.1	2.6	32.0	18.1	23.9	4.2	3.4	5.4
Georgia	0.2	16.9	3.1	28.6	14.5	19.3	7.7	3.2	6.6
Romania	0.3	6.6	2.4	50.5	15.5	15.0	2.5	1.9	5.3
US	5.2	15.9	6.4	26.0	9.3	22.1	6.2	2.9	6.0
Russia	0.5	19.2	4.6	30.3	13.4	16.1	6.8	2.6	6.4
Cyprus	2.9	23.5	4.4	53.3	4.5	7.7	1.5	0.7	1.5
Ukraine	0.4	25.9	7.0	35.9	10.9	11.2	4.5	1.0	3.2
UK	4.9	22.1	10.7	32.8	7.7	10.3	4.9	1.1	5.6
Poland	0.5	9.7	4.9	48.5	13.0	9.6	5.1	0.8	8.0
Germany	2.2	20.6	6.6	33.0	11.0	13.5	5.4	1.8	5.9
Pakistan	0.2	1.8	2.3	21.2	21.6	30.6	0.6	8.0	13.8
Australia	0.9	11.2	5.5	27.3	12.8	27.9	5.3	4.7	4.6
Turkey	0.7	9.4	3.2	32.4	10.6	30.3	1.8	6.0	5.4
Armenia	0.2	17.0	3.2	31.8	13.4	16.3	9.6	2.3	6.1
Egypt	0.6	18.5	4.7	31.2	10.2	15.2	2.7	4.3	12.5
India	0.3	1.6	1.2	22.9	21.1	35.8	0.6	5.7	10.7
Iraq	0.3	5.4	2.2	19.0	14.6	27.9	7.4	7.2	15.9
The Philippines	0.4	10.5	11.7	41.1	13.3	10.9	3.1	1.9	7.2

Source: 2001 Census

Egypt, Armenia, Georgia and the US, with first degrees. These nationalities are significantly more skilled than the Greek population. A similar, but less pronounced, pattern can be observed with higher vocational training.

A second group of nationalities can be identified, which has a high proportion of people who completed lyceum education: these are Romania, Cyprus and Poland (around 50 per cent compared with the Greek 27 per cent).

The third group of nationalities consists of those contributing large proportions of people who failed to progress beyond primary school (including those classed as illiterate). Greece itself is in this class, with 44 per cent of the population falling within the classification. Bangladesh, Pakistan, India and Iraq have just over 50 per cent with this educational level; slightly below Greek levels are Turkey, Syria, Albania and Australia.

Thus, it seems reasonable to talk about a polarisation of economic migration, with the US and the UK providing highly educated workers and the other countries in the first category also providing university educated workers. The medium-skilled category consists of Romanians, Cypriots and Polish – although it is likely that many of the Polish are actually skilled craftsmen. The unskilled category has many similarities with the Greek population and is numerically dominated by Albanians, though it also includes significant numbers of factory workers from Bangladesh, Pakistan and India.

10.3.3.2 Gender dispersion

The IMEPO study compared the major nationalities' gender balance using the 2001 Census and total residence permit data (Baldwin-Edwards 2004a: 10). Whilst noting the gender imbalance of most immigrant groups in the census, it also noted a worsening of the gender imbalance after 2001. Several nationalities showed an increase in males (Syria, Egypt, Romania, Albania) and some nationalities with a female bias showed an increase in females (the Philippines, Ukraine and Russia).

Figure 10.2 shows gender balance by region of origin, according to the 2006 residence permit data. For Southern Europe (Albania) there is a predominance of males; for Eastern Europe (Bulgaria, Ukraine, Moldova) a predominance of females; South-Central Asia (Pakistan, India, Bangladesh) is predominantly male; and Western Asia looks balanced but actually consists of males from Syria and females from Georgia and Armenia.

There is no obvious pattern of feminisation of the immigration; rather, the pattern is one of increasing polarisation by gendered nationality. These trends appear to confirm segmentation of the Greek labour market by both gender and nationality, along with the primacy attached to work in acquiring legal residence.

Figure 10.2 *Gender ratios of immigrants with residence permits in Greece by geographical region of origin, January 2006*

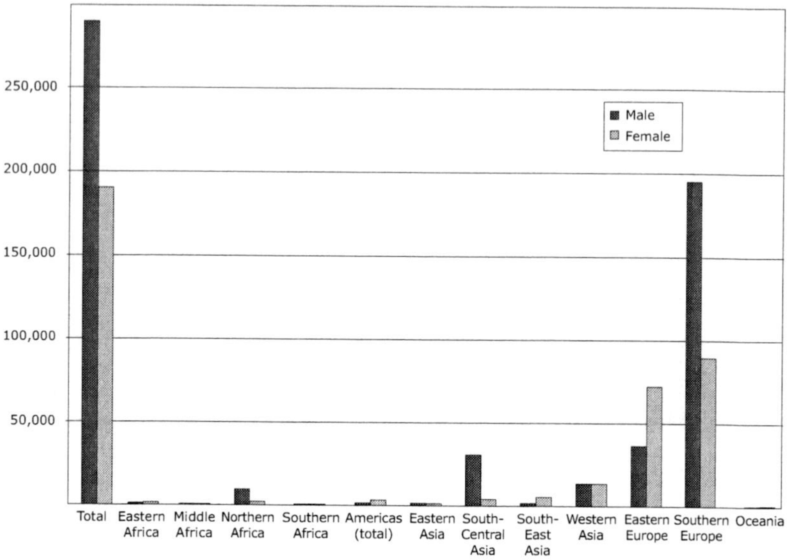

Source: Ministry of the Interior, residence permit database; authors' calculations

10.3.3.3 Migration type

Since there are no data on migration flows, the majority of which are illegal, the only data on migration type are derived from stock data. Figure 10.3 provides summary data from the IMEPO study, which is the only source of information on the type of residence permit; the data are supplemented by UNHCR data on refugee and asylum seeker stocks as well as the large figure for Albanian *homogeneis* permits. There are no other data available, so no comparison can be made concerning trends.

The data given below do not actually constitute stock data, as they are total permits issued over a fifteen-month period. They do give some indication of immigration flows by type, however. They show that the most important category consists of dependent employment, followed by ethnic Greeks from Albania. Two much smaller categories of self-employment and family reunification follow, with the remaining categories more or less negligible. Unlike the case in Northern European countries, refugees and asylum seekers are insignificant in number.

Table 10.11 gives data on permit types for the major nationalities in Greece, by gender, for 2003-2004. These show the importance of dependent employment for legal residence in Greece, with the exception

Figure 10.3 *Immigrants in Greece by permit type, 2003-2004*

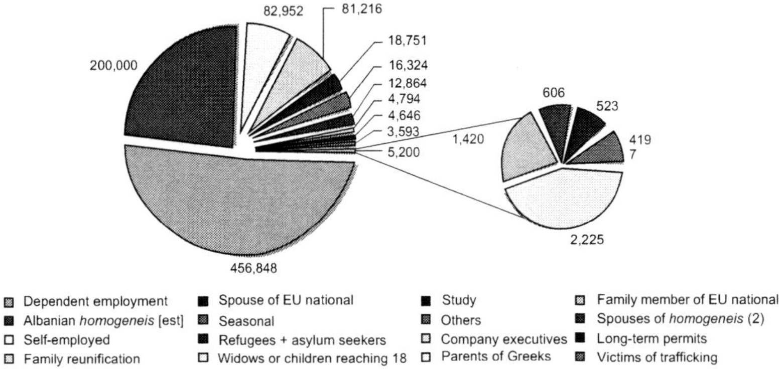

Sources: Baldwin-Edwards 2004a; UNHCR

Table 10.11 *Permit types for major nationalities by gender, 2003-2004*

		Albanian		*Bulgarian*		*Romanian*		*Ukrainian*	
	Totals	*M*	*F*	*M*	*F*	*M*	*F*	*M*	*F*
Dependent employment	465,848	255,442	43,087	18,880	27,584	13,228	7,402	3,054	12,225
Albanian *homogeneis* (estimate)	200,000	NA	NA	0	0	0	0	0	0
Self-employed	82,952	46,212	5,160	1,285	3,398	3,635	1,087	780	3,109
Family reunification	81,216	19,599	46,964	1,487	2,702	450	1,240	361	1,038
Spouses of EU nationals	18,751	633	2,510	117	1,942	101	1,222	102	1,597
Seasonal	16,324	6,180	986	4,101	3,857	9	4	0	1
Refugees + asylum seekers	12,864	NA	NA	NA	NA	NA	NA	NA	NA
Widows or children reaching 18	4,794	2,068	1,677	188	172	33	42	31	56
Study	4,646	336	491	175	298	157	154	60	120
Others (10 minor categories)	3,593	284	184	108	105	87	70	21	34
Company Executives	2,225	5	3	33	32	14	6	84	22
Parents of Greeks	1,420	28	129	7	133	5	114	3	161
Family members of EU nationals	606	42	78	39	87	12	28	22	57
Spouses of *homogeneis*	523	4	16	0	1	3	4	28	40
Long-term permits	419	0	0	23	33	0	1	0	1
Victims of trafficking	7	1	1	0	0	0	0	1	0

Note: NA = not available
Sources: Ministry of the Interior; UNHCR; authors' compilation

of the Albanian *homogeneis* permits. Also apparent is the gender asymmetry, with male Albanians dominating the numbers (except with the Albanian *homogeneis* permits, for which there are no data) and women predominating in the case of Ukraine and Bulgaria.

10.3.3.4 *Trends in dispersion by geographical origin*

The trends by broad geographical region of origin for the period 1990-2006 are shown in Table 10.1, above. In particular, the inflow of Albanians over this period has been massive and they now constitute some 66 per cent of known immigrants in Greece. This unusual predominance of one nationality tends to overshadow some other trends, which are noteworthy. First, there have been smaller but parallel trends in increased immigration from other countries in the region – namely Bulgaria, Ukraine, Romania and the Republic of Moldova – over the period 2002-2006. Secondly, there seem to have been continuous inflows of ethnic Greeks from Georgia, Armenia, Kazakhstan, Uzbekistan and other former Soviet satellite states; these inflows are of unknown magnitude and the awards of Greek nationality and *homogeneis* permits are not collated or published. Thirdly, there have been increased inflows of male guestworkers from Pakistan, India and Bangladesh, along with smaller inflows of other Asian nationalities.

Insofar as dispersion is concerned, this seems to have increased, even though the majority of immigrants are from relatively few countries. Thus, Greece has experienced the simultaneous concentration of regional nationalities alongside the increased presence of previously unknown immigrant groups. By 2001, Greece had an immigrant presence from almost every country in the world, other than some small islands; there is even a small presence from most of the Pacific islands.

Table 10.12 *Number of countries with immigrant presence in Greece, by region of origin, 1990/1991 and 2001*

Continent	*Region*	*1990/1991**	*2001*
Africa	East	12	16
	Middle	6	9
	North	6	9
	South	5	5
	West	13	17
Americas	Caribbean	10	21
	Central	7	8
	North	3	5
	South	10	13
Asia	East	7	14
	South-Central	7	14
	South-East	9	9
	West	14	18
Oceania	Australia and New Zealand	2	3
	Melanesia	0	4
	Micronesia	0	4
	Polynesia	0	8

* 1991 Census data have some omissions and errors, particularly concerning smaller national groups, so these have been supplemented with 1990 residence permit data.
Sources: Ministry of Public Order, 1990 residence permits; 1991 Census; 2001 Census

Table 10.12 shows the changed presence of immigrants from countries by region, 1990/91 to 2001.

10.3.3.5 Age profiles

Information on the age profiles of immigrants are still only available from the 2001 Census; theoretically, these data are recorded for residence permits, but in practice the Ministry is unable to extract them as actual data.

Figure 10.4 shows age distributions for the top five nationalities (according to the census), along with those for Greeks. All nationalities – even the US – have higher proportions of working age people than the native population; in particular, in the age bracket twenty to 34 Romanians are strikingly present, with two-thirds of their number in this range. High proportions also exist in the case of Albanians, especially in the under-30 range, and of Bulgarians and Georgians. The latter two nationalities are also present in high proportions in the older age brackets of 40-55, reflecting the presence in Greece of many older women, often engaged in housekeeping and elderly care, from Bulgaria and Georgia.

The importance of Albanian and, to a lesser extent, Georgian children in Greece can also be seen in this graph. Immigrant children and, to some extent, immigrant births in Greece have substantially

Figure 10.4 *Age profiles of immigrant groups in Greece, 2001*

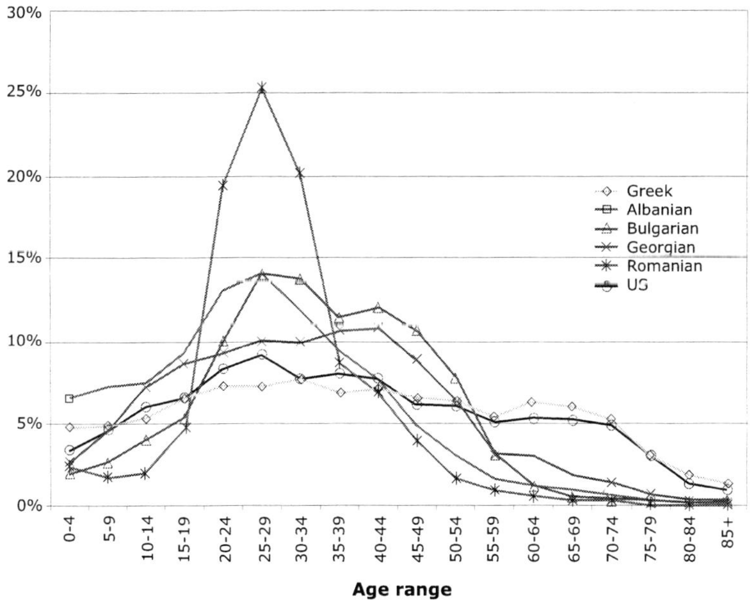

Source: 2001 Census

ameliorated the severe demographic decline of the Greek population (see Section 10.3.1 above). Data on immigrant children in Greek state schools are poor, with the primary distinction being made between children of ethnic Greeks and others *[allogeneis]*, with no record of the children's actual nationalities (Baldwin-Edwards 2004a: 18-19). Recent residence permit data show 108,000 children under fifteen with legal status, as of 15 January 2006; however, it seems probable that there are more without legal residence but who are able to attend state schools.

10.4 Critical outlook

The relationship between Greek immigration statistics and 'reality' cannot be understood in a one-dimensional model of the sort that is implicit in much contemporary western social science; owing to post-Ottoman history and the recent development of the modern Greek nation state, there is not merely one 'reality' which statistical data can be thought to represent. One analytical mechanism that can be used to throw light on the situation is a two-dimensional model of 'alternative realities'. Thus, we can evaluate existing statistical measures according to two distinct questions for criteria:

1. How useful are the statistical instruments in describing an independent, non-politicised 'reality'?
2. How useful are the statistical instruments in permitting (or describing) a politically constructed 'reality'?

The various types of statistical data are evaluated below, using this analytical framework.

10.4.1 Flow data

10.4.1.1 Illegal migration flows

By definition, illegal migration flows cannot be measured. What can be measured with precision are two related categories: border apprehensions and expulsions of detected illegal migrants. The former have consistently been mixed up with the latter, while exaggerated data on border arrests have been provided by ministers in formal EU contexts. The mass expulsions carried out before 2001 (see Table 10.9) did not record the identities, ages, gender or anything other than (alleged) nationalities of people expelled from Greece without legal process. It is thought that many were repeat migrants; thus, the total figures for expulsions were related to cases rather than individuals, as well as exaggerated the apparent extent of illegal immigration.

The lack of adequate data on border apprehensions, as well as the merging of expulsion data with border arrests, have the effect of obscuring the realities of immigration from public scrutiny. In the 1990s, this was used to some effect by linking the illegal expulsions (*skoupa* or 'broom') of, in the main, Albanians, with Greek foreign policy. Thus, when Greek relations with Albania worsened, usually concerning ethnic Greeks in southern Albania, the police would expel all the undocumented Albanians they could find. This was presented as an exercise in enforcing the law (the 'broom'), but it was clear to all that it was used as an expression of Greece's regional hegemony and of the primacy of Greek culture and ethnicity in the Balkan region. In recent years, these low-quality data have permitted Greek politicians to argue for fiscal transfers from Brussels, in order to deal with the 'massive' illegal immigration from which Greece suffers. This is a new political construction, with a different target audience.

10.4.1.2 Legal migration flows

Legal migration flows comprise three types (Section 10.3.2.1): asylum seekers, ethnic Greeks and seasonal workers.

Asylum seekers are subject to much regulation within the EU, so the data should reflect European standards. In practice, there are substantial deviations from lawful procedures, with the result that many asylum seekers are denied the right to apply. It is possible that these data are less accurate than elsewhere in the EU.

Ethnic Greeks' inflows are completely unrecorded; other than in the case of the granting of Special Visas to applicants in Pontos in the 1990s, these visa data were never published or made available. The differing treatment of ethnic Greeks from different countries, the concealment of their mass arrival, the linkage of Albanian ethnic Greeks with foreign policy issues such that they could not until 2006 take Greek nationality, along with the complete lack of transparency and public debate about legislation on ethnic Greeks: all of these are symptoms of extreme political constructivism. Neither the Treaty of Lausanne, nor the Greek Constitution, gives any rights of residence for ethnic Greeks; the legislation conferring these rights was enacted without public debate and its motivation is open to question.

Seasonal workers, although small in number, are recruited from several countries; no data are available on these inflows, although they can be imputed from residence permit data. Given the massive structural need for such workers in agriculture, it is remarkable that so few temporary workers are recruited. Presumably, since these jobs are filled by illegal residents, the state prefers to avoid any public discussion about its lack of immigration policy: the lack of data is of some benefit in this regard.

10.4.2 *Stock data*

10.4.2.1 *Census data*

Despite the presence of a significant immigrant population by 1990 (both legal and illegal), the 1991 Census made no attempt to capture reality. It recorded almost exclusively Europeans, ethnic Greeks and legal residents. By the late 1990s, there existed considerable political pressure – both external and domestic – on the Greek Government to quantify the extent of illegal immigration. Thus, a serious attempt was made to modify the census procedures to this end (see Section 10.2). However, the 2001 Census did not break with a tradition established in the 1961 Census of not recording details relating to religion, ethnicity or mother tongue. There are also many points of confusion in the data as regards who is Greek or not; clear definitions of legal status (Greek national, ethnic Greek of other nationality, etc.) are not used.

Nevertheless, the 2001 Census data constitute the most reliable information set currently available and represent a real challenge to the political constructivist tendencies of the Greek state, despite the absence of any information at all concerning religion, native languages, self-identified ethnicity, etc. Although the 2001 Census was relatively successful in recording a depoliticised reality, access to the raw data is prohibited.[16] The National Statistical Service of Greece has decided that all datasets are subject to the Data Protection Act (which Greece was forced to pass in order to be admitted to Schengen). With this pretext, the Statistical Service is able to control and 'own' the national datasets, since independent analyses of the raw data are prevented. The benefit of this policy is not so clear, but is in line with older approaches to state information, along with a lack of public accountability.

10.4.2.2 *Legalisation data*

There have been five legalisation processes as of early 2008; from 1998, an initial 'White Card' lasting six months was followed by a 'Green Card'. There was another large legalisation in 2001, attached to the Immigration Law; yet another occurred in 2005, followed by one in 2007. From the 1998 procedures, some data were prepared from the first phase; bureaucratic problems with the Green Card meant that the state could not even declare the number of legal immigrants at any given point in time. Although the 1998 data were the first to give any real information about illegal immigrants in Greece, the Green Card data were constructed *post hoc*. They failed to reveal the bureaucratic disasters of the programme, including the cases of hundreds of thousands of people left in limbo for years and others who were unable to renew their one-year or two-year cards. No data (other than total applications and awards) have ever been released of the legalisations in 2001, 2005 and 2007. Most of the data provided reveal little more than the number of applicants and try to give the impression that the Greek state is doing something about the problem of illegal immigration.

10.4.2.3 Residence permit data

This dataset, created by the Ministry of the Interior upon taking over the policy area in 2001 (see Section 10.2), is slowly being improved and proceeding toward a more European approach to data-collection. Nevertheless, there are still many shortcomings, such as the inability to extract age profiles (apparently recently remedied) and duration of residence in Greece. These data, like those contained in the 2001 Census, are part of a modernising trend which continues within the Ministry. At the ministerial level, however, there is some manipulation of data going on, thus exaggerating the Ministry's success in awarding residence permits. Different datasets are handed out to researchers and journalists, when, in fact, they should contain exactly the same data concerning valid permits on a specified date. This problem indicates that political constructivism is alive and well, even when modernisation trends are also flourishing.

10.4.2.4 Homogeneis *permit data*

No data have been published or communicated, except as 'leaked' information in approximate form. The Ministry of Public Order considers these data to be subject to issues of 'national security'; there is a complete lack of accountability or transparency as regards the policy and data on ethnic Greeks, whose total number is thought to be in excess of 400,000 since 1990. The existence and award of the permits for Albanian *homogeneis* is pure political constructivism – an action apparently taken without any political accountability. (There is a smaller dataset on *homogeneis* in the Ministry of the Interior, which is also unpublished.)

The reason given for secrecy – national security – is not entirely baseless. This is because the purported number of permits handed out was 200,000, whereas the total number of ethnic Greeks in southern Albania had previously been estimated at 40,000 by the Albanian state and 200,000-300,000 by the Greek state. Clearly, if all 200,000 reside in Greece, then there should be almost no ethnic Greek population left in Albania! There is no evidence to suggest that that has happened; indeed, something rather more complex has occurred. It has been suggested that Albanians of *Vlach* ethnicity, seeing that their Vlach relatives in Greece had become fully Greek, presented themselves to the

Greek authorities as ethnic Greeks. There is also informal evidence to suggest that the police authorities understood this and were complicit in thus seeking to expand the recognised Greek community. All of this, of course, is quite inconsistent with Greek foreign policy on Albania; hence, we have an issue of national security.

10.4.2.5 Other stock data

These consist primarily of the births and deaths of foreign residents and naturalisations.

Births and deaths data have only just been made available, though this availability has not been made public by the authorities. The presence in Greece of sizeable numbers of Albanian and other non-Greek children is a matter of some contention, especially within the Greek school system, with its declining population of Greek children. It is thought that the appearance of this dataset is because of pressure from the European Commission; the fact that it has not been published on the internet – or even announced – suggests that these data are either of little interest or are not welcomed by the state.

Naturalisation data are not available, since there are three discrete procedures – none of which publish any data at all. The sparse tables which are available from the Ministry of Interior have little connection with reality, and even these do not give former nationality, gender or age of successful applicants. The transformation of large numbers of aliens into Greek nationals is, therefore, unrecorded by statistics. Such data would show how many Pontian Greeks have arrived since 1990 – something toward which the Greek population is fairly hostile. The data for *allogeneis* (non-Greeks) would show how few have been granted Greek nationality, which is something Greece would prefer not to show to the rest of Europe. Thus, all types of naturalisation data are unwelcome for the Greek state.

10.4.2.6 Holistic data compilation

Given the multiplicity of categories of immigrant, along with the involvement of different ministries as well as local authorities in handing out permits, there is a need for central data collation for the publication of a statistical overview. In theory, the National Statistical Service of Greece should be the responsible authority; in practice, it has been provided with very little data. It seems that most official statistics sent to Eurostat were, in effect, constructed from low-quality and incomplete information and are thus of little use for perceiving the realities of immigration into Greece.

10.5 Towards some conclusions

Overall, the balance between the evidence as evaluated with the two criteria is heavily weighted toward the second – that is, the facilitation of a politically-constructed reality. As we have attempted to show in the introduction, this is part of modern Greek history and therefore an integral component of Greek institutional behaviour. Given such a context, the 2001 Census and the Interior Ministry's residence permit database represent a significant shift away from traditional cultural norms; the process is still in its early stages, though.

One might venture to suggest that many countries' politicians would dearly like to be in the Greek situation with respect to immigration data, where they could adopt a certain position one day and the opposite, the next. The downside is that compilation of reliable statistics is seen as an attribute of a developed state, most certainly of one in the European Union. Greek politicians appear not to be very troubled by comments such as 'worse population statistics than almost any African country', and rely upon the phenomenon of illegal immigration as a defence. This is despite the (concealed) fact that Greece has effectively no channels for legal immigration, whilst illegal immigrants seem to find adequate employment quite easily.

Examining actual flows and trends, this last point continues to ring true. Illegal immigration is set to continue, although male Albanians now predominantly have legal status. The new immigrants are arriving from Asia and the Middle East and, to a lesser extent, from Africa. These will not be recorded, except in small numbers as intercepted illegal migrants or asylum seekers; the great majority arrive legally, as in most countries. The lack of data on arrivals and departures means that the Greek state will not even be able to estimate migration flows; instead, as previously, it will simply wait for large stocks of illegal immigrants to appear. The principal positive point is that the residence permit database should improve and the Ministry has adopted many recommendations and made other improvements, such that it will be able to provide limited data on employment and other characteristics of legal immigrants. Slowly and reluctantly, the Greek state is being dragged into the ambit of European practices and standards concerning statistical data on migration.

Notes

1 Notably, the Jewish migration to Palestine after 1920; the Vlach emigration to Romania, from 1926; the Armenian emigration to the USSR, post-1945; the Jewish migration to Israel, from 1948, *inter alii* (Tsitselikis 2005: Fn. 2).

2 See the discussion on the policy towards, and counting of, various nationalities of *homogeneis* (ethnic Greeks), below. Also, the management of Greek censuses since 1951, alongside the inclusion of religion on national identity cards, are clear examples of political constructivism.
3 E.g. 'false tourists' who entered Greece legally, but worked illegally, and either left and returned every three months or paid a small penalty at the border for 'overstaying', when they eventually did leave.
4 First published in Baldwin-Edwards (2004a: 3).
5 This legalisation programme was resisted by certain interests, especially over its inclusion of Albanians, and was reinstated at the last minute by the Prime Minister himself. For a summary of different political positions by various institutional actors, see Baldwin-Edwards and Safilios-Rothschild (1999: 215-217).
6 Personal interviews with Nikos Karavitis, the Secretary-General of the Statistical Service of Greece, February-March 2002.
7 Art. 93 provides for an integrated information system to be established, by future joint decision of the Ministries of the Interior, Foreign Affairs, and Public Order.
8 The NSSG refuses to supply LFS data on immigrant groups on the grounds of 'privacy protection'.
9 On the basis of Law 2130/1993, which required entry by special repatriation visa.
10 Later extended by Law 2790/2000, to grant Greek nationality regardless of the means of entry into Greece.
11 The *Kamenidis 2000 Study*, carried out by the General Secretariat for Repatriated Greeks, in the Ministry of Macedonia-Thrace; cited in Emmanouilidi (2003: 46-50).
12 Such an agreement has been denied by the Albanian government, and in the absence of documentation constitutes a unilateral declaration by Greece.
13 Decision 4000/3/10-d (FEK 646, 13.05.2005): 9187-9189.
14 The reason for the inclusion of this provision is not given, is currently unknown, and it is unclear which category of persons might benefit from it. On the face of it, it would seem not to include the minority group known as Cham or *Tsamides*: these were Greek nationals who were forced to flee across the border into Albania towards the end of the Second World War, as some of them had collaborated with Axis forces. Since 1991, they have made restitution claims for their properties in Greece.
15 Judging by the surprisingly large proportions of 'illiterate' Germans, British and Americans – at approximately 6 per cent – these data seem unreliable. Possibly, the question was misinterpreted by some census takers as meaning literacy in the Greek language.
16 The datasets are handed in their entirety to international agencies such as OECD and Eurostat: it is non-state agencies that are prohibited access.

Statistical sources

Organisation	*Content*	*URL*
Economic University of Athens, Department of Statistics	– immigration (1990-2006)	www.stat-athens.aueb.gr
European Migration Network, Greek contact point	– various unpublished statistics from ministries and other national sources	www.emn.gr
Mediterranean Migration Observatory, UEHR, Panteion University	– summary tables from various statistical datasets – reports on statistical sources	www.mmo.gr
National Statistical Service of Greece	– 2001 Census – Labour Force Survey tables	www.statistics.gr

Bibliography

Anderson, B. (1991), *Imagined Communities.* London and New York: Verso.

Baldwin-Edwards, M. (1997), 'The Emerging European Immigration Regime: Some Reflections on Implications for Southern Europe', *Journal of Common Market Studies* 35 (4): 497-519.

Baldwin-Edwards, M. (2004a), *Statistical Data on Immigrants in Greece: An Analytic Study of Available Data and Recommendations for Conformity with European Union Standards.* A Study conducted for IMEPO, Ministry of Interior, Greece. www.mmo.gr; www.imepo.gr.

Baldwin-Edwards, M. (2004b), 'Immigration into Greece, 1990-2003', paper presented in the panel 'International Migration' at the UNECE Population Forum 2004, Geneva, 12-14 January 2004. www.mmo.gr; www.unece.org.

Baldwin-Edwards, M. (2004c), 'Albanian emigration and the Greek labour market: Economic symbiosis and social ambiguity', *South East Europe Review* 7 (1): 51-65.

Baldwin-Edwards, M. (2006), 'Migration between Greece and Turkey: from the "Exchange of Populations" to the non-recognition of borders', *South East Europe Review* 9 (3): 115-122.

Baldwin-Edwards, M. & R. Fakiolas (1998), 'Greece: The contours of a fragmented policy response', in M. Baldwin-Edwards & J. Arango (eds.), *Immigrants and the Informal Economy in Southern Europe*, 186-204. London: Routledge.

Baldwin-Edwards, M. & C. Safilios-Rothschild (1999), 'Immigration and unemployment in Greece: Perceptions and realities', *South European Society & Politics* 4 (3): 206-221.

Clark, B. (2006), *Twice a Stranger: How mass expulsion forged modern Greece and Turkey.* London: Granta.

Emmanouilidi, E. (2003), *Greek Immigration and Asylum Policy*, Report for the European Migration Network, 11 September 2003. www.emn.gr.

Fakiolas, R. & R. King (1996), 'Emigration, Return, Immigration: A Review and Evaluation of Greece's Postwar Experience of International Migration', *International Journal of Population Geography* 2: 171-190.

Glytsos, N. (1995), 'Problems and policies regarding the socio-economic integration of returnees and foreign workers in Greece', *International Migration* 33 (2): 155-176.

Kanellopoulos, C. & M. Gregou (2006), *Policy Report on Migration, Asylum and Return in Greece*, Athens, March 2006. KEPE, European Migration Network. www.emn.gr.

Karydis, V. (1992), 'The fear of crime in Athens and the construction of the "dangerous albanian stereotype"', *Chronika* 5.

Karydis, V. (1998), 'Social and legal issues concerning migration in Greece', mimeo, University of Thrace, Law Faculty.

Kertzer, D. & D. Arel (2002), 'Censuses, identity formation, and the struggle for political power', in D. Kertzer & D. Arel (eds.), *Census and Identity*, 1-42. Cambridge: Cambridge University Press.

Michailidis, I. (1998), 'The war of statistics: Traditional recipes for the preparation of the Macedonian salad', *East European Quarterly* 32 (1): 9-21.

Nikolinakos, M. (1973), 'The contradictions of capitalist development in Greece: labour shortages and emigration', *Studi Emigrazione* 30: 222-235.

Papantoniou, A., M. Papantoniou-Frangouli & A. Kalavanou (1996), 'Migrants' Insertion in the Informal Economy: Deviant Behaviour and the Impact on Receiving Societies', Athens, December 1996, mimeo.

Pentzopoulos, D. (2002), *The Balkan Exchange of Minorities and its Impact on Greece*. London: Hurst & Co.

Tsitselikis, K. (2005), 'Citizenship in Greece: Present challenges for future changes', mimeo. 6 September 2005, University of Macedonia.

Vermeulen, H. (2008), 'The Greek labour diaspora in Europe, its integration in the receiving societies, especially Germany, and its relation with the home country', *Migrance* 31.

Waldrauch, H. (2006), 'Statistics on Acquisition and Loss of Nationality', in R. Bauböck, E. Ersbøll, K. Groenendijk & H. Waldrauch (eds.), *Acquisition and Loss of Nationality. Policies and Trends in 15 European Countries. Vol. 1: Comparative Analyses*, 269-315. Amsterdam: Amsterdam University Press. An extended version of this chapter is available on: www.imiscoe.org.

11 Portugal

Maria I. Baganha

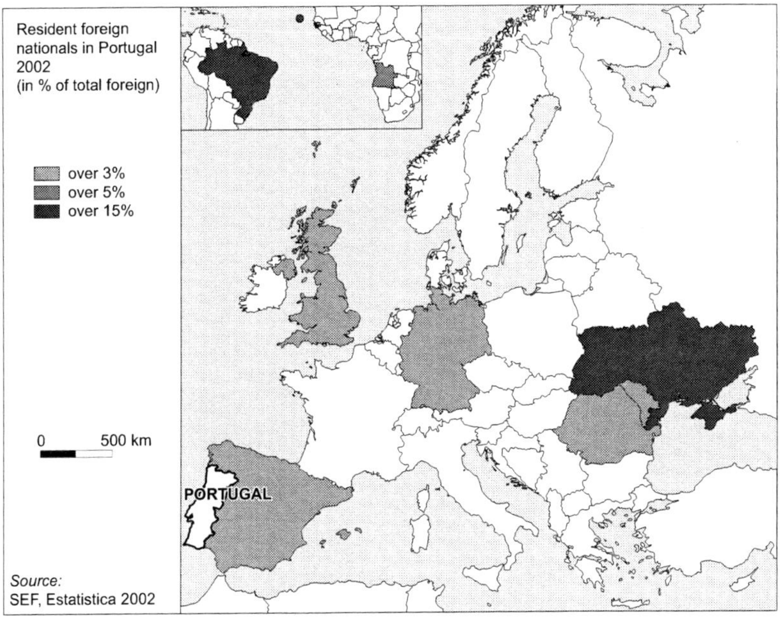

Cartography: Walter Lang, University of Vienna

11.1 Introduction

Migration to Portugal, in sizable numbers, is a very recent phenomenon. In fact, until the mid-1970s only a few thousand foreigners, mostly from neighbouring Spain, were resident in the country.

The migratory situation of the country changed remarkably in the aftermath of the 1974 Revolution and the subsequent independence of the former colonies in Africa.[1] During this period, close to half a million Portuguese nationals returned to Portugal. To clarify their citizenship status, Law 308 – A/75 (24 June 1975) established that only those returnees (*retornados*) who were not of African ancestry were entitled to Portuguese nationality.[2] As a consequence, some of the returnees and some of the African residents from a Portuguese-Speaking African

Country (PALOP) lost their Portuguese nationality. These newly-made foreign citizens constituted the first sizable 'immigrant' communities in Portugal. Through family reunification and family formation, these immigrant communities from the PALOP continued to grow. By 1985, the country had 79,594 foreign legal residents, of whom 44 per cent were from the PALOP (Baganha & Marques 2001: 93).

In 1986, Portugal joined the European Economic Community (EEC), which attracted foreign investment and entailed the transfer of voluminous structural funds. Over the following years, the overwhelming majority of these funds were invested in communication infrastructures (bridges and highways) as well as in public buildings and urban renewal. All these investments in the construction and building sector generated plenty of new jobs at the bottom of the occupational ladder that immigrants from the PALOP, particularly from Cape Verde, were eager to fill.

This boom in construction and building, which essentially attracted unskilled or low-skilled labour, coincided with a boom in tertiary activities, for which the native population was not prepared. These tertiary activities, such as banking, finance, real estate, computer software and marketing, attracted a substantial number of highly skilled immigrants, particularly from Western Europe and Brazil. In fact, the largest rates of change in occupational groups, between 1983 and 1996, occurred in two menial occupational groups: personal and domestic services (428.9 per cent) and construction and industry (288.7 per cent); and in two high-skilled occupational sectors – professionals and technicians (403.9 per cent) and directors and managers (236.5 per cent) (Baganha, Ferrão & Malheiros 1998: 94).

Nevertheless, immigration to Portugal was a relatively minor phenomenon at the end of the millennium. In 1999, 190,896 foreign legal residents were living in the country, which at the time represented less than 2 per cent of the total resident population. More than 90 per cent of these were from the PALOP, Brazil or a Western European country. Furthermore, incoming migration at the time could essentially be attributed to the country's colonial past and economic relations. Without oversimplifying we can say that immigration to Portugal was a bipolar movement, at one extreme constituted by unskilled or low-skilled workers, overwhelmingly from the PALOP, and at the other by highly skilled immigrants, mainly from Brazil and Western Europe. In fact, between 1990 and 1998, the share of active immigrants from the PALOP in unskilled or low-skilled occupations surpassed 90 per cent, while the share of active immigrants from Western Europe and Brazil in professional and managerial occupations represented 55 per cent (Baganha & Marques 2001).

When in 1999 Portugal was selected to organise and host the 2004 European Football Championship, construction and building entered a new phase of growth. Labour shortages in this sector became particularly intense in 2001 and 2002. This time, however, the labour needs of the construction and building sector were not met by the traditional suppliers – immigrants from the PALOP – but by entirely new sources, namely immigrants from Eastern Europe, mainly from Ukraine. This was a very new and puzzling situation since Portugal had no historical, cultural or economic relations with these countries that could justify the massive inflow of their nationals.

Official documents identify three main causes for this sudden and massive inflow from Eastern Europe to Portugal: 1) uncontrolled granting of visas by other EU Member States; 2) the speed and ease of movement within the Schengen area; and 3) the trafficking of human beings, as organised in Eastern Europe under the disguise of 'travel agencies' (High Commissariat for Immigration and Ethnic Minorities, Foreigners and Borders Bureau & General Labour Inspectorate 2002).

These factors are undoubtedly important. A sudden, massive legal migratory flow can only occur if the migrants have easy access to transportation and legal travel documents. However, these factors do not explain why people decide to leave their countries or why they decide to come to Portugal in particular. The answers to these questions are to be found elsewhere (see for the following Baganha, Marques & Góis 2004 and Baganha 2007).

That the people decided to leave can first and foremost be traced back to the fall of the Iron Curtain and the ensuing transition of Eastern European countries to market economies and to democracy. This process considerably increased the propensity for migration because, firstly, the restrictions to moving abroad were progressively dismantled in all these countries so that it became possible for a large number of people to emigrate; secondly, the huge differences in salaries and standards of living between Eastern European and EU countries became publicly known; and, thirdly, these were regions where a strong migratory culture could be reactivated.

Why some of these Eastern European emigrants decided to come to Portugal can be attributed to the following reasons. Firstly, Eastern European travel agencies, particularly in the Ukraine, marketed Portugal by offering very attractive packages, including travel documents, transportation and job opportunities, that were affordable to a large segment of the population. Secondly, salaries in Portugal were several times higher than in the immigrants' home country. For example, the salary for the lowest non-skilled position in the construction sector (Servente da Construção Civil), the main entry gate for newly arrived immigrants, was 458 euros in January 2001 and 474 euros in January 2002 (Ministry of Social Security and Labour 2002). Finally, the regularisation of immigrant workers which was in force from January to November 2001 offered a real alternative to an illegal stay in any other EU country. It is the combination of all these macro- and micro-level factors that explains the sudden and massive inflow from Eastern Europe to Portugal that largely took place during 2001.[3]

The end result of all these movements was that by 2005, 460,000 legal residents plus 23,000 holders of work visas[4] and 11,000 holders of other types of long-term visas were residing in Portugal. These close to half a million legal immigrants represented roughly 5 per cent of the total population in Portugal at the time.

11.2 Stocks

11.2.1 *Sources on stocks*

In Portugal, there are two main sources of information on the foreign population in the country. The first is the census, which registers the resident population in the country on a given day and is carried out every ten years by the National Statistical Bureau (Instituto Nacional de Estatísitca, INE). The second is a continuous reporting system carried out by the Foreigners and Borders Bureau (Serviço de Estrangeiros e Fronteiras, SEF). This Bureau gathers data on all the foreigners who have applied for or hold a residence permit and registers the withdrawal or expiry of such permits, which may occur for three reasons: death, acquisition of nationality or voluntary departure. These data have been published and updated annually since 1980.

Censuses have rarely been used to describe the foreign population for three main reasons. Firstly, when compared to other sources, they have been shown to cover the foreign population very poorly. Secondly, the two most recent censuses, respectively carried out in 1991 and 2001, failed to register a large foreign population that illegally resided in the country and that was brought to light by special regularisations in 1992 and 2001. Thirdly, census data are static and do not capture changes over time.

By contrast, the statistics of the SEF are frequently used to describe the foreign population. However, this source does not cover the entire foreign resident population. What the SEF database contains are data on all holders of residence permits, all applicants for residence permits and, since 2001, all holders of permits of stay.[5] Other forms of legal status, such as work or student visas, are not covered by this register. There is no published information on the characteristics of the holders of such visas, just on their volume and country of origin. Moreover, there is, by the very nature of the phenomenon, no continuous monitoring system that provides information on the illegal foreign population.

These shortcomings are particularly relevant in the Portuguese case because the overwhelming majority of the immigrants entered the country on tourist visas and overstayed. This means that our knowledge of the size and characteristics of the resident foreign population is incomplete, except for the years when the state granted general amnesties and information on the formerly illegal population was published.

11.2.2 *Main characteristics of the resident foreign population*

In 1960, the number of foreign residents in Portugal was insignificant. 29,428 foreign citizens were resident in the country at the time, which represented 0.3 per cent of the country's total resident population. Furthermore, of these 29,428 foreign residents, 67 per cent were from a Western European country, largely from neighbouring Spain.

This changed during the process of decolonisation in the aftermath of the 1974 Revolution. By 1980 the number of foreign residents had increased to 58,091 persons, representing approximately 0.6 per cent of the resident population; what is perhaps more important, of these 58,091 foreigners 47 per cent originated from an African country, mostly from a former Portuguese colony.

Table 11.1 presents the development of the resident foreign population or, to be more precise, of holders of residence permits from 1980 to 2005. As we can see in Table 11.1, the number of foreign residents increased continuously over the whole period, practically doubling every decade. The annual average growth rates by decade indicate that the inflow from Asia (mainly from China) grew faster than immigration from other countries, except during the 1990s when the fastest growing population was from Africa (mainly from Cape Verde).

At the same time, the composition of the resident foreign population did not change significantly between 1980 and 1999. During this period, the largest group of foreign residents was from Africa, accounting consistently for more than 40 per cent of the total foreign population (more than 95 per cent of these 40 per cent were from the PALOP, mainly from Cape Verde). This group was followed by residents from Western Europe and from Central and South America (in the latter case, overwhelmingly from Brazil). The other origins were of far less numerical significance.

However, over the last six years the composition of the resident foreign population has become more diversified, since the number of foreign residents from Europe, Asia and Central and South America has grown faster than that of foreign residents from Africa. While, up to 2000, the foreign resident population accounted for a meagre 2 per cent of the resident population, with the vast majority of these

Table 11.1 *Holders of residence permits in Portugal by region of origin, 1980-2005*

Year	*Total foreigners*	*Africa*[4]	*North America*	*Central & South America*	*Asia*	*Europe*[4]	*Other*
1980	58,091	27,748	4,821	6,403	1,153	17,706	260
1981	62,692	27,948	6,018	8,123	1,394	18,931	278
1982	68,153	28,903	6,855	10,481	1,663	19,924	327
1983	79,015	32,481	8,520	13,351	2,219	22,053	391
1984	89,625	37,128	9,887	15,394	2,860	23,896	460
1985	79,594	34,978	7,987	11,567	2,564	22,060	438
1986	86,982	37,829	9,047	12,629	2,958	24,040	479
1987	89,778	38,838	8,623	13,009	3,124	25,676	508
1988	94,453	40,253	8,338	14,645	3,413	27,280	524
1989	101,011	42,789	8,737	15,938	3,741	29,247	559
1990	107,767	45,255	8,993	17,376	4,154	31,410	579
1991	113,978	47,998	9,236	18,666	4,458	33,011	609
1992[1]	122,348	52,037	9,430	19,960	4,769	34,732	621
1993[1]	136,932	55,786	10,513	21,924	5,520	37,154	696
1994[2]	157,073	72,630	10,739	24,815	6,322	41,819	748
1995	168,316	79,231	10,853	25,867	6,730	44,867	768
1996	172,912	81,176	10,783	25,733	7,140	47,315	765
1997	175,263	81,717	10,573	25,274	7,192	49,747	760
1998	178,137	83,065	10,247	24,579	7,419	52,060	767
1999	191,143	89,797	10,169	25,767	7,935	56,689	786
2000[3]	208,198	99,107	10,259	27,638	8,734	61,635	807
2001[3]	223,976	107,273	10,187	28,856	9,721	67,121	818
2002[3]	238,746	114,193	10,195	30,592	10,815	72,121	830
2003[3]	250,231	118,012	10,119	32,458	11,584	77,216	842
2004[3]	265,361	123,093	10,129	35,032	12,410	83,859	838
2005[3]	276,460	127,001	10,138	37,420	12,841	88,217	843

[1] The values for 1992 and 1993 vary from table to table in the statistics due to the special regularisation process carried out in this period.
[2] The statistics for 1994 include those foreigners legalised in 1992 and 1993.
[3] Indicates provisional data.
[4] Over 95 per cent of the foreign residents from Africa are from the former Portuguese colonies, while 90 per cent of the European immigrants are from the EEC countries.
Sources: 1980-1999: INE, Demographic Statistics (Estatísticas Demográficas); SEF cited in Baganha 2001; 1999-2005: SEF statistical report for the given year

foreigners being from two very specific origins, either the EU or one of the Portuguese-speaking countries (Brazil and the former colonies in Africa), this changed drastically in 2001 when the number of legal residents rose markedly and the countries of origin became more diversified. Table 11.2, which summarises the numbers of valid residence permits and permits of stay between 2000 and 2005, shows that the number of legal foreign residents rose by 68 per cent from 208,198 to 350,877 between 2000 and 2001 (mainly due to a special

Table 11.2 *Foreign legally resident population in Portugal, 2000-2005*

Year	Residence permits	Permits of stay	Total stock
2000	208,198		208,198
2001	223,976	126,901	350,877
2002	238,746	47,657	413,304
2003	250,231	9,097	433,886
2004	265,361	178	449,194
2005	276,460		460,293

Source: See Table 1, SEF

regularisation process). Furthermore, the stock of the foreign resident population continued to grow, reaching 460,293 persons in 2005; this constitutes roughly 5 per cent of the total resident population in the country.

Table 11.3 illustrates the increased diversification of countries of origin of the foreign resident population in Portugal by comparing the ten most important third countries of origin of the foreign population in Portugal in 1999 and 2002.

Table 11.3 shows that the presence of nationals from countries with which Portugal had no historical or commercial links became predominant in 2002. This was essentially due to a wave of Eastern European migrants who entered the country in 2001 and 2002. Since then there

Table 11.3 *Third-country nationals legally residing in Portugal by countries of origin, 1999 and 2002*

Nationality	1999	2002
Ukraine		62,041
Cape Verde	43,797	60,368
Brazil	20,887	59,950
Angola	17,695	32,182
Guinea-Bissau	14,140	23,349
Moldavia		12,155
Romania		10,938
US	7,975	8,083
São Tomé & Principe	4,795	9,208
Mozambique	4,503	
Venezuela	3,412	
China	2,733	8,316
Canada	2,012	
Total from third countries	138,467	347,302*
Total from EU	52,429	66,602
Total foreign residents	190,896	238,746

* This total includes the permits of stay (see Note 5 at the end of this chapter) for 2001 and 2002.

Source: SEF, Statistics (*Estatísticas*) 1999, 2001, 2002

have been no noticeable changes in the stock of the foreign resident population.

11.2.3 General amnesties and special regularisations

As we have seen, some of the increases registered in the statistics of the foreign population residing legally in Portugal are not the result of new entries but of special legalisations of irregular immigrants already in the country. In order to understand the numerical impact of these processes on the evolution of the stock of the foreign legal population and to grasp the size of the irregular population living in the country at several points in time, we have to consider each of these processes in more detail.

The irregular foreign population residing in Portugal grew considerably over the 1980s when immigrants, particularly from the PALOP, took to entering the country on short-term visas and to overstaying the term of such visas.

Portugal's accession to the EEC in 1986 and the country's entry to the Schengen zone in the early 1990s implied a revision of the prevailing immigration law. Prior to this revision (Law 59/93 of 3 March 1993), the government launched a general amnesty for irregular immigrants already in the country to clear the migratory situation (Law 212/92 of 12 October 1992). At the time, 39,166 irregular immigrants, 72 per cent of whom were from the PALOP and 14 per cent from Brazil, applied for a residence permit. Nevertheless, a substantial number of illegal immigrants either failed to resolve their situation or to secure their legal status. That is why the government launched a second general amnesty in 1996 (Law 17/96 of 24 May 1996). This time, 35,082 illegal immigrants applied for regularisation of their status. Again, the overwhelming majority of these (73 per cent) were from a Portuguese-speaking country.

In 2001, under the pressure of several lobbies (e.g. construction and building, the tourism industry, pro-immigrant NGOs and the Catholic Church), the government introduced a special regularisation period (January to November 2001) for illegal immigrant workers who were either already in the country or entered during that period and who could prove that they held a legal work contract (Law 4/2001 of 10 January 2001). As a consequence of this selective regularisation 184,000 illegal immigrant workers received residence and work permits between 2001 and 2004.

In 2003, Portugal signed a bilateral agreement with Brazil, which included the regularisation of illegal immigrant workers from Brazil who entered Portugal prior to 11 July 2003. This special regularisation will be in force until 11 July 2008. By the end of October 2004, 29,622 illegal immigrant workers from Brazil had applied for regularisation of their status (SEF, unpublished data).

The most recent selective regularisation was launched on 26 April 2004. This time regularisation was open only to illegal immigrant workers who had entered Portugal before 12 March 2003 and who had paid their contributions to social security and the fiscal administration for at least 90 days (Law 6/2004, art. 71). Under the provisions of this new law, 53,196 illegal immigrant workers applied for regularisation of their status in the country (SEF, unpublished data).

In total, the Portuguese government carried out two general amnesties and three selective regularisations between 1992 and 2004. Since the most recent of these are still under review, it is unclear how many illegal immigrant workers will succeed in securing a permanent legal status in the country under these provisions. What we know is that the previous processes involved the regularisation of 257,903 immigrants, which means that at the end of 2003 close to 59 per cent of the foreign population legally residing in Portugal had entered and/or stayed in the country illegally (Baganha 2005: 38). Moreover, the two last regularisations that are still in effect indicate that 83,000 illegal immigrant workers currently reside in the country.

11.2.4 Demographic characteristics

There have traditionally been more men than women among the legally resident foreign population. In the early 1990s[6] men accounted for an average of 58 per cent of this group. However, between 1999 and 2005, the share of women grew continuously, increasing from 42 to 46 per cent, as shown in Table 11.4.

Table 11.4 *Holders of residence permits in Portugal by sex, 1999-2005*

Year	*Male*	*Male in %*	*Female*	*Total*
1999	109,965	58	80,931	190,896
2000	118,562	57	89,636	208,198
2001	125,941	56	98,035	223,976
2002	132,738	56	106,008	238,746
2003	137,695	55	112,536	250,231
2004	144,383	54	120,978	265,361
2005	149,203	54	127,257	276,460

Source: SEF, annual statistical report for the given year

The feminisation of the stock of the resident foreign population is linked to the origin of the migrants. Men still constitute the majority in most groups with a remarkable exception: the population from

South and Central America or, to be more precise, from Brazil. In 2004, this was made up of 13,815 males and 15,141 females.

Table 11.5 *Holders of residence permits in Portugal by sex and region of origin in 2004*

	Total	*Male*	*Female*	*Male (%)*
Total	265,361	144,383	120,978	54
Europe	83,859	44,016	39,843	52
Africa	123,093	70,259	52,834	57
North America	10,129	5,761	4,368	57
South and Central America	35,032	16,893	18,139	48
Asia	12,410	6,996	5,414	56
Other	838	458	380	55

Source: SEF, Annual Statistical Report 2004

The majority of the resident foreign population is of working age, with the largest group centred in the age range 25-44 years of age (46 per cent). On the other hand, the share of foreign residents under 14 (13 per cent) and over 65 (7 per cent) is very low. Hence, in general, the age structure is typical for economic migrants. However, the age structure differs significantly by region of origin.

Table 11.6 *Holders of residence permits in Portugal by region, sex and age cohorts in 2004*

	Total	*0-14*	*15-24*	*25-44*	*45-64*	*65 or over*
Europe	83,859	11.7	11.2	37.8	26.3	13.1
Africa	123,093	13.6	17.0	48.7	16.4	4.2
North America	10,129	16.6	24.0	31.2	15.2	13.0
South & Central America	35,032	10.4	16.4	57.5	12.6	3.0
Asia	12,410	12.7	11.3	53.4	17.8	4.8
Other	838	7.5	10.7	50.6	24.6	6.6
Total	265,361	12.7	15.1	45.9	19.1	7.2

Source: SEF, Annual Statistical Report 2004

On the one hand, Table 11.6 shows that the age structure of the resident foreign population from Europe and North America is biased towards the age cohort 65 or over (13.1 and 13 per cent, respectively), whereas the share of the working aged, particularly of those between 25 and 44 years of age (37.8 and 31.2 per cent, respectively), is significantly smaller than the average. This is due to the fact that several migrants from these regions are pensioners who move to Portugal after retirement or have a second home there where they spend several months each year.

On the other hand, the populations from South and Central America (particularly from Brazil) and from Asia (predominantly from China) have a higher concentration in the age cohort of 25-44 years of age, totalling 58 per cent and 53 per cent, respectively, while the average is 46 per cent. This is a clear indicator of the fact that migration from this area is driven by economic motives, i.e. earning money and escaping unemployment or relative deprivation in the home countries.

There is no information on the occupational structure of the resident foreign population after 1998. Up to that date, the occupational structure of the resident foreign population was extremely polarised. Table 11.7 presents the relative distribution by occupation of the resident foreign population between 1990 and 1998.

Table 11.7 *Holders of residence permits in Portugal by occupation, 1990-1998 (in per cent)*

Year	*Scientific and technical, executive and managerial occupations*	*Clerical workers*	*Sales workers and vendors*	*Safety, protection, personal and domestic services*	*Farmers, fishermen, hunters, etc.*	*Miners, industrial, construction and transport workers, etc.*
1990	31.3	5.0	7.9	3.5	1.8	50.5
1991	32.3	4.9	7.8	3.9	1.6	49.4
1992	32.2	4.8	8.0	4.4	1.6	49.1
1993	32.5	4.7	8.2	5.0	1.5	48.1
1994	29.8	4.2	8.0	6.9	1.3	49.9
1995	29.1	4.0	8.0	8.0	1.3	49.6
1996	29.4	4.0	8.2	8.3	1.3	48.9
1997	30.1	3.9	8.2	8.4	1.2	48.2
1998	30.3	3.9	8.4	8.5	1.2	47.7

Source: SEF, annual report for the given year

Between 1990 and 1998, an average of 31 per cent of the foreign population was concentrated at the top of the occupational structure and held professional or executive occupations. At the other extreme, an average of 49 per cent of the foreign population was concentrated at the bottom of the occupational structure, holding manual occupations.

11.3 Acquisition of nationality

The first statistics on acquisition of nationality by foreign residents were published by the National Statistical Bureau (Instituto Nacional de Estatística, INE) in 1994. The data published are difficult to analyse, since for some years they do not cover all forms of acquisition of nationality. Moreover, the Bureau does not explain what is subsumed under the heading 'other modes of acquisition'. Table 11.8 provides a synthesis of these data, which differ considerably from both the data published by the SEF (Foreign and Borders Bureau) on acquisition of nationality by naturalisation and the data provided by the Central Registry (Conservatória dos Registos Centrais).

According to Portuguese law, the acquisition of nationality only becomes effective after having been registered by the Central Registry. This means that the Central Registry is the only reliable source for acquisitions of Portuguese nationality by foreign residents. Unfortunately the information available only covers the years 1999 to 2003.

Table 11.8 *Acquisitions of Portuguese nationality after birth (including naturalisation and other modes) by previous nationality, 1994-2003*

	1994	*1995*	*1996*	*1997*	*1998*	*1999*	*2000*	*2001*	*2002*	*2003*
Angola	55	76	57	56	56	62	42	65	82	144
Cap Verde	129	169	80	93	159	117	69	228	271	370
Guinea Bissau	44	43	27	16	67	37	27	55	73	38
Mozambique	29	30	19	26	56	37	10	24	27	56
São Tomé & Principe	21	18	10	12	28	15	7	20	34	58
Total (ex-colonies in Africa)	278	336	193	203	366	268	155	392	487	666
EU	27	45	44	47	13	42	25	27	45	62
Other Europe	19	24	19	18	6	11	7	14	16	30
Canada	39	76	69	92	4	70	55	54	65	68
US	67	164	120	203	7	91	64	90	108	94
Brazil	176	235	241	296	46	186	175	283	345	343
Venezuela	266	431	411	431	0	219	186	162	221	311
Other/stateless	99	102	57	74	77	69	54	60	82	173
INE	971	1,413	1,154	1,364	519	946	721	1,082	1,369	1,747
SEF						584	1,142	955	1,136	2,043
Central Registry						602	629	1,198	968	1,075

Sources: National Statistical Bureau (INE); Foreign and Borders Bureau (SEF), annual report for the given year; Central Registry (Conservatória dos Registros Centrais), unpublished data

Table 11.8 illustrates that only very few foreign residents acquire Portuguese nationality. As a consequence, the rate of acquisition of nationality, whether by naturalisation, marriage to a Portuguese citizen or another mode of acquisition, is also very small and has been decreasing, particularly in the years 2002 and 2003, mostly due to the fact that the resident foreign population was growing at the time. Table 11.8 also reveals that most of the new Portuguese citizens were formerly citizens of Venezuela and Brazil. This might be due to the large number of citizens from these two countries who can claim Portuguese ancestry and, as such, are entitled to Portuguese nationality.

11.4 Flows

There is no published information on arrivals and departures, either for Portuguese nationals or for foreign citizens. The only data that provide information on migration flows in Portugal are visa statistics and statistics on foreigners who applied for residence permits.

11.4.1 *Residence and visa statistics*

Residence and visa statistics are frequently confused with inflows of immigrants and are treated as such, though, in reality, only a part of these data concern arrivals. In fact, this source registers the numbers of residence permits granted per year to the following categories of foreigners:

1. those who were residing in Portugal on a three-year visa to work and applied for a residence permit;
2. those who entered the country with a visa for purposes of residence and applied for a residence permit; and
3. those who, according to special regulations of the law, are exempt from providing the documentation usually needed to apply for a residence permit.[7]

Another source for inflows are data on entries by type of visa issued collected by the Ministry of Foreign Affairs. This database includes the number of visas for residence, work, study and temporary stay granted annually.[8] Table 11.9 provides a synthesis of the information available from this source.

Table 11.9 *Inflow of immigrants to Portugal by type of visa, 1999-2005*

	Entry for the purpose of				*Total**	*Short-term visas*
	*Work**	*Studies**	*Residence**	*Temporary stay**		
1999	1,931	3,487	1,890	1,281	8,589	99,664
2000	3,372	3,915	1,873	1,610	10,770	114,697
2001	3,024	4,392	1,547	2,896	11,859	108,761
2002	2,607	3,955	2,131	3,922	12,615	82,365
2003	2,762**	3,658	1,776	4,273	12,469	72,384
2004	2,770**	3,280	1,729	3,897	11,676	79,841
2005	3,742**	4,051	2,491	4,300	14,584	75,559

* visas granted for at least one year and that can be renewed

** Under the provisions of the 2003 Bilateral Agreement between Portugal and Brazil, 62 work visas were issued in 2003, 10,009 in 2004 and 3,995 in 2005. These visas were issued to illegal immigrants already in the country and as such were deducted from the total number of work visas issued in the respective year.

Source: Ministry of Foreign Affairs, unpublished data

The Table illustrates that the number of incoming permanent immigrants is relatively low, with an average of 11,795 permanent immigrants per year. The number of temporary immigrants, business people or visitors from countries that need entry visas is, however, quite remarkable. On average 90,467 of these enter the country each year. It is impossible to forecast what percentage of these short-term visa holders will overstay the term of their visas and thus stay in the country illegally. However, this is frequent practice among immigrants from the PALOP and Brazil, the two regions of origin of the overwhelming majority of holders of short-term visas. Finally, the above numbers also confirm what has been stated above; the remarkable increase of the stock of the resident foreign population in Portugal by 252,095 people between 2000 and 2005 (see Table 11.2) was due less to legal entries than to the special regularisation that took place in 2001. Through this process, 183,833 illegal immigrant workers were granted permits of stay, i.e. legal residence and permission to work.

11.4.2 *Asylum seekers*

In December 2004, 377 refugees recognised by the UNHCR were resident in Portugal. In the whole of Western and Southern Europe only Slovenia and Albania recognise fewer refugees than Portugal (see the statistics of the Portuguese Council for Refugees [Conselho Português para os Refugiados, CPR], that are available online).

The reason for this low figure is not the number of asylum applications. As Table 11.10 shows, the number of applications is comparatively low, yet very much higher than the number of recognised refu-

Table 11.10 *Asylum applications filed in Portugal, 1980-2004*

Year	*Applicants*	*Year*	*Applicants*
1980	1,638	1993	2,090
1981	600	1994	767
1982	1,115	1995	450
1983	609	1996	269
1984	378	1997	297
1985	70	1998	365
1986	275	1999	307
1987	442	2000	224
1988	326	2001	232
1989	156	2002	245
1990	75	2003	88
1991	255	2004	107
1992	690		

Source: UNHCR, Population Data Unit

gees. This is due to the rigidity of the process of evaluation of the applications. As a consequence, the overwhelming majority of applications are turned down. However, as a rule, Portugal does not expel unsuccessful applicants but either grants them residence permits on humanitarian grounds or allows them to stay and to apply for a residence permit or a permit of stay during one of the regularisation periods, which took place in 1992, 1996, 2001 and 2003.

11.5 Conclusion

In 1999, the number of immigrants residing in Portugal represented less than 2 per cent of the total resident population. Furthermore, these were overwhelmingly from a Portuguese-speaking country, either from Brazil or the PALOP. Brazilians and Western Europeans were concentrated at the top of the occupational ladder, mainly in professional and executive occupations, while immigrants from the former colonies in Africa were concentrated at the bottom, mainly in construction for males and domestic services for females.

This scenario changed drastically in 2001 with a sudden and intense migratory wave from Eastern Europe, particularly from Ukraine. Within a few years (2000-2005), the foreign resident population rose from 208,198 to 460,293 persons, representing approximately 5 per cent of total population in 2005. The same period saw a marked diversification in countries of origin and a significant feminisation of migration. In fact, the share of women in the stock of the foreign population increased from 43 per cent in 2000 to 46 per cent in 2005.

The evolution of the immigrant population in Portugal can be described from the 1980s to the present. Since that date, the SEF (Foreigners and Borders Bureau) has published yearly information on the main characteristics of residence permit holders – data usually treated as describing the stock of the resident foreign population. Although there are some gaps in this data set (e.g. information on the sex distribution and on the age structure is only available for some years and information on occupations and type of employment has not been published since 1998), this is, nevertheless, the most reliable and consistent source available with which to characterise the immigrant population in Portugal.

By contrast, there are no published data on flows. Outflows are unknown and information on inflows has only been collected over the last few years. Furthermore, the data on inflows are relatively poor, registering information only on two variables, inflows by type of visa and inflows by country of origin.

The data on refugees are extremely poor. The only information available from the UNHCR is the annual number of applications and the total number of refugees recognised.

Notes

1 The new countries were Cape Verde, Guinea-Bissau, Mozambique, Angola and São Tome and Principe.
2 There were many exceptions to this rule, particularly for African residents who could prove a special connection to Portugal and a clear desire to become Portuguese.
3 According to a national survey conducted in 2002, 57 per cent of the new immigrants arrived in 2001 (Baganha, Marques & Góis 2004: 32).
4 Work visas are valid for one year. After having held such a visa for three years, the holders can apply for a residence permit. The 23,000 work visas are the sum of the first visas issued between 2003 and 2005.
5 The permit of stay (*autorização de permanência*) was introduced during the regularisation process in 2001 and phased out in 2003. It was granted to immigrants who illegally resided and worked in Portugal in order to temporarily legalise their work and stay. In contrast to a residence permit, the permit of stay is only valid for one year, renewable up to a maximum of five years, and conditional upon a valid work contract.
6 Information is available only for 1992, 1994 and 1995.
7 Thus article 88 of Law 244/98 allows illegal immigrants to apply for a residence permit on humanitarian grounds.
8 Note that except for visas for short stays that are granted for periods of less than one year, all other visas are granted for at least one year and are renewable. For this reason (an expected stay of one year or more), the holders of these types of visa are considered permanent immigrants.

Statistical sources

Organisation	*Content*	*URL*
Central Registry	– acquisition of nationality by foreign residents.	
Portuguese Council for Refugees		www.cpr.pt
Foreigners and Borders Bureau (SEF)	– annual statistical reports (from 1999 onwards) – other relevant information connected to the foreign population in Portugal	www.sef.pt
Ministry of Foreign Affairs	– visa statistics	www.mne.gov.pt
National Statistical Bureau (INE)	– demographic statistics – statistics on acquisition of nationality after birth	www.ine.pt

Bibliography

High Commissariat for Immigration and Ethnic Minorities (ACIME), Foreigners and Borders Bureau (SEF) & General Labour Inspectorate (IGT) (2002), *Relatório sobre a evolução do fenómeno migratório*. Lisbon: ACIME, SEF, IGT.

Baganha, M. (2005), 'Política de Imigração: a Regulação dos Fluxos', *Revista Crítica de Ciências Sociais* 73: 29-44.

Baganha, M. (2007), 'The Migration Industry: a Case Study', in E. Berggren, B. Likic-Broboric, G. Toksöz & N. Trimikliniotis (eds.), *Irregular Migration, Informal Labour and Community: A Challenge for Europe*. Maastricht: Shaker.

Baganha, M. & J.C. Marques (2001), *Imigração e Política: o Caso Português*. Lisbon: FLAD.

Baganha, M., J. Ferrão & J.M. Malheiros (1998), 'Immigrants and the Labour Market: The Portuguese Case', in *Metropolis International Workshop, Proceedings*, 89-120. Lisbon: FLAD.

Baganha, M., J.C. Marques & P. Góis (2004), 'The Unforseen Wave: Migration from Eastern Europe to Portugal', in M. Baganha & L. Fonseca (eds), *New Waves: Migration from Eastern Europe to Southern Europe*, 23-39. Lisbon: FLAD.

Ministry of Social Security and Labour (*Ministério da Segurança Social e do Trabalho*) (2002), *Inquérito aos salários por profissões na Cosntrução Civil e Obras Públicas*. Lisbon: Ministry of Social Security and Labour.

Foreigners and Borders Bureau (*Serviço de Estrangeiros e Fronteiras*, SEF) (2000-2005), *Relatórios Estatísticos, 1999 to 2004*. Lisbon: SEF.

12 Turkey

Ahmet İçduygu

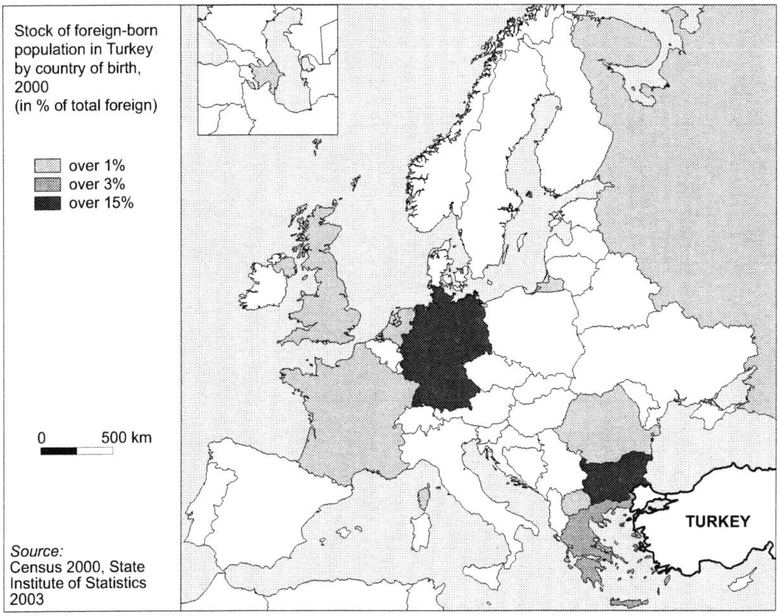

Cartography: Walter Lang, University of Vienna

12.1 Introduction

Turkey has only recently come to be recognised as a country of immigration and transit. In the past, Turkey was considered, and indeed regarded itself as, a country of emigration. Since the early 1960s it has experienced an exceptionally high level of emigration of its own citizens. It is estimated that in the last four decades more than four million people have left the country, of whom some two million left after 1980 (Ayhan, Ergöçmen, Hancıoğlu, İçduygu, Koç, Toros, Türkyılmaz, Ünalan, Üner & Yiğit 2000). More than four-fifths of the emigrants left for Europe; in particular, more than two-thirds went to Germany. The number of returnees amounted to more than half of the total number of emigrants since the early 1960s. Today more than 2.5 million Turkish citizens reside in Europe, with some 100,000 Turkish workers in the Arab countries, some 60,000 settlers in Australia and over 75,000 workers in the CIS countries. In addition, more than a quarter of a million Turkish migrants live in Canada and the United States. Thus, at any one point in the last four decades, some 6 per cent of the Turkish population was abroad (İçduygu 2004).

However, Turkish migration history was not exclusively characterised by emigration. Immigration was an important element of the nation-building process in Turkey in the early twentieth century. Naturally, these inflows were limited to people of Turkish and Muslim origin from the neighbouring regions. At the same time, and as part and parcel of the same process, Turkey also experienced the emigration of its non-Muslims citizens. Only in the 1960s did Turkey become a well-known country of emigration. Emigration slowed down but did not cease in the 1970s, while immigration of non-Turkish persons remained relatively insignificant. Turkey's change from being a country of emigration to one of immigration began in the 1980s and 1990s, but until a few years ago the phenomenon and its consequences remained a matter debated in relatively restricted circles. In the last few years, as the arrivals of foreigners in the country increased, immigration has also come onto the political agenda, in particular within the context of the country's application for EU membership.

There are four main factors that seem to be shaping the migratory movements to Turkey. Firstly, the long-established and ongoing political turmoil and clashes occurring in neighbouring areas have pushed people from their homelands in the hope of a better life, security and protection from persecution. Secondly, the collapse of communist regimes reactivated the mobility of millions of people in the neighbouring areas. As a consequence, Turkey has started receiving migrants from these countries. Thirdly, Turkey's geographical location between East and West and between South and North has made the country a preferable transit zone for those intending to reach western and northern countries. Fourthly, the policies and practices of 'Fortress Europe', with their application of very restrictive admission procedures and increasing immigration controls, have diverted immigration flows targeting Europe to peripheral zones around it, such as Turkey (İçduygu 2000).

Today there are four main types of migratory flows of foreign nationals to Turkey: 1) irregular transit migrants; 2) irregular labour migrants; 3) asylum seekers; and 4) regular migrants (for a detailed elaboration, see İçduygu 2005a). The first three types, which constitute the larger portion of immigration flows to the country, often overlap and fluctuate as migrants drift from one category to the other, depending on their circumstances and opportunities. Based on various official sources (BFBA of DGS of MoI, 2001a,b), the stock of foreign nationals in Turkey in the early 2000s was estimated at more than 200,000, of whom less than two-thirds (some 150,000) entered legally, while some 50,000 were irregular migrants. Asylum seekers only accounted for a small proportion (2 per cent) of the foreigners residing in Turkey.

12.2 Overview of stock and flow data

International migration statistics in Turkey are constrained by the scarcity and poor quality of the data. This becomes highly significant over time concerning both outflows and inflows. As a result, it is almost impossible to specify who immigrated or emigrated over the years, from or to which country and how they migrated. No precise data are available on the chronological course and directions of all relevant migration flows. Consequently, it is very difficult to obtain credible estimates of migratory flows from and/or to Turkey. In the 1960s, the fundamental official data sources on emigration were the records of the Turkish Employment Service (TES) and the Turkish Labour Ministry (TLM), which reported the annual number of workers sent through official state channels to various countries of destination. However, these data covered only the period before 1980, were incomplete and did not reflect the real volume of emigration from Turkey at the time. They did not even include all labour emigrants, let alone any other types of migratory flows.

Furthermore, there are no credible and reliable arrival and departure statistics that provide information on immigration and emigration flows to or from the country. While the available tourism statistics report on all departures and arrivals, they fall short of producing reasonable estimates of international migration, since they do not include any information on the purpose and length of stay.

Censuses, which have been carried out in Turkey every five years between 1935 and 1990 and every ten years since then, are theoretically and practically expected to collect some basic information on various characteristics of people entering and leaving the country. Indeed, all those censuses gathered information on the place of birth, residence and citizenship of people residing in the country,[1] which could normally be used (alone or in combination) to describe the countries of origin of the immigrants residing in Turkey. However, the responsible statistical institute, the State Institute of Statistics (SIS) renamed the Turkish Statistical Institute (TURKSTAT) in 2006, remained reluctant to furnish any statistics on migration-related data, apart from simple frequency tabulations of the total number of foreign-born persons living in the country. On the other hand, the last three censuses (1985, 1990 and 2000) included both a question on the number of household members who were abroad on the day of the census and a question on the number of household members who used to be abroad but had meanwhile come back permanently. Unfortunately, TURKSTAT has not disseminated any significant amount of this information. As a consequence, we lack basic figures of emigration from Turkey even for these years where data would be available. There are fairly similar problems within the context of immigration statistics. The main data source of immigration to Turkey is held by the Bureau for Foreigners, Borders and Asylum at the Directorate of General Security of the Ministry of Interior (BFBA of DGS of MoI). These data are also far from giving full and credible estimates of migratory flows to Turkey.

Data on legal immigration can be obtained from the Ministry of the Interior, which collects information on work, study and residence permit holders. But this information, which is based on a categorisation of foreigners according to their citizenship, is static and not processable. It only reflects some aggregate figures. Based on the new Law on Work Permits for Foreigners in 2003, the Ministry of Labour and Social Security, as the main responsible official department, is supposed to process all the work permits of foreigners and consequently is in charge of producing relevant statistics on the foreigners working in the country. However, until now this ministry has not made any attempt to compile such statistics.

Information on asylum seekers and refugees is compiled by the BFBA. Although the BFBA gathers very detailed personal background information from each applicant, it only publishes statistics on annual asylum applications broken down by nationality for security and confidentiality reasons. However, the figures they do publish are fairly reliable and comprehensive. In addition, the BFBA has compiled some statistics on apprehended irregular migrants. These include information on the nationality and the year of apprehension of those who were caught while crossing the borders illegally and those who were apprehended without a valid visa or were working on a visa which did not allow them to work.

Finally, the Bureau of Population and Citizenship of the Ministry of the Interior publishes naturalisation statistics which include aggregate figures on the previous citizenship of those who naturalised; unfortunately, these are neither comprehensive nor complete. In fact, this is due partly to the political sensitivity of the issue and partly to the lack of an administrative tradition of compiling statistics in this field.

Overall, immigration-related statistics in Turkey are inadequate, incomplete and often unreliable. However, in the period of the pre-EU accession process, various government departments, including three main agencies – the statistical institute, the State Planning Organisation (SPO), the Ministry of Interior (MoI) and the Ministry of Labour and Social Security (MoLaSS) – have made some independent attempts to improve the collection and compilation of data on international migration in Turkey. Conversely, there have also been discussions on the integration of international migration statistics into the recently established computer-based population registration system, the Central Population Management System (MERNIS). For a long time, these attempts have been insufficiently concrete to constitute any significant progress in gathering data on international migration. However, in 2007 the Turkish Statistical Institute was able to set up a new Address Based Population Registration System, which aims to improve existing administrative records based on addresses. If this attempt is successful, this new source will yield relatively good demographic data, including information on international migration.

12.3 Description of the stock of foreign population

There are two main data sources that provide us with some information on the stock of foreign population in Turkey: the first one is the census that categorises the people in the country according to their birthplace; the second is the database for residence permits, which categorises immigrants according to their nationality.

12.3.1 *Census*

Information about the foreign-born population is available from the 1990 and 2000 Censuses. The 1990 Census recorded 56.5 million people in Turkey. In the 2000 Census, the total population of the country amounted to 67.8 million. The population figure of 2000 represented a 1.8 per cent increase over the period since 1990, which is mainly due to the fact that the population still has a considerably high fertility rate. Although the foreign-born population grew from 1.1 million in 1990 to 1.3 million in 2000, its share in total population in Turkey slightly fell from 2 per cent to less than 1.9 per cent (see Table 12.1 and 12.2).

In 1990, Bulgaria was the largest source of foreign-born residents, with 462,767 people, or 41 per cent of the foreign-born, residing in the country at the time. With a total population of 183,499, people from former Yugoslavia constituted 16 per cent of the foreign-born in the country. Another 16 per cent (176,820) were German-born foreign residents, almost all of whom most probably were the children of Turkish migrants who had returned from Germany (see Table 12.1).

Nearly 70 per cent of the immigrants in Turkey were from one of the top five source countries in 2000. Various Balkan countries were

Table 12.1 *Turkish-born and foreign-born population in Turkey, 1990*

Place of birth	*Male*	*Female*	*Total*	*Per 1,000 of total population*	*Per 1,000 of foreign-born population*
Born in Turkey	28,044,415	27,291,456	55,335,871	(980)	
Born abroad	562,632	574,534	1,137,166	(20)	(1000)
Afghanistan	3,626	3,594	7,220	0.13	6.35
US	7,695	5,173	12,868	0.23	11.32
Australia	1,404	1,506	2,910	0.05	2.56
Austria	3,440	3,539	6,979	0.12	6.14
Germany	88,533	88,287	176,820	3.13	155.49
Belgium	2,287	2,416	4,703	0.08	4.14
Bulgaria	224,879	237,888	462,767	8.19	406.95
France	5,235	5,045	10,280	0.18	9.04
The Netherlands	4,899	5,017	9,916	0.18	8.72
Iraq	14,652	12,651	27,303	0.48	24.01
England	3,140	3,343	6,483	0.12	5.70
Iran	6,527	3,936	10,463	0.19	9.20
Switzerland	4,018	4,091	8,109	0.14	7.13
Italy	1,079	879	1,958	0.04	1.72
Japan	,512	460	,972	0.02	0.85
Cyprus	4,420	4,775	9,195	0.16	8.08
Egypt	1,314	1,004	2,318	0.04	2.03
Russian Federation	6,336	5,094	11,430	0.20	10.05
Syria	2,733	2,505	5,238	0.09	4.61
Saudi Arabia	1,762	1,582	3,344	0.06	2.94
Socialist Federal Republic of Yugoslavia	90,322	93,177	183,499	3.25	161.37
Greece	47,783	53,969	101,752	1.80	89.48
Others	33,712	32,913	66,625	1.18	58.59
Unknown	2,324	1,690	4,014	0.07	3.53
Total	28,607,047	27,865,988	56,473,035	20.00	1,000.00

Source: SIS 1995

the leading countries of origin of migrants to Turkey. The 480,817 Bulgarian-born migrants accounted for nearly 38 per cent of the foreign-born in the country. Greece, the Republic of Macedonia and Romania were the other Balkan countries that accounted for nearly 10 per cent of immigrants. In addition to these, approximately 21 per cent of immigrants in Turkey (273,535 people) were born in Germany. Other sizable foreign-born communities with a population of over 10,000 originated from Azerbaijan (16,787), Austria (14,335), France (16,787), Iran (12,957), the Netherlands (21,823), the Russian Federation (19,856), Switzerland (10,369), Cyprus (10,391), the UK (18,914) and the US (13,566). Again, those born in Austria, France, the Netherlands and Switzerland are most likely children of Turkish emigrants who returned home (see Table 12.2).

Table 12.2 *Turkish-born and foreign-born population in Turkey, 2000*

Place of birth	*Male*	*Female*	*Total*	*Per 1,000 of total population*	*Per 1,000 of foreign-born population*
Turkey	33,732,479	32,793,638	66,525,256	81.14	
Total outside Turkey	614,256	663,554	1,278,671	(18.86)	
Azerbaijan	8,661	8,126	16,787	0.25	13.13
Austria	7,114	7,221	14,335	0.21	11.21
Bulgaria	228,363	252,454	480,817	7.09	376.03
France	7,815	8,161	16,787	0.25	13.13
Germany	132,937	140,598	273,535	4.03	213.92
Greece	26,967	32,250	59,217	0.87	46.31
Iran	8,076	4,881	12,957	0.19	10.13
The Netherlands	10,769	11,054	21,823	0.32	17.07
Former Yugoslav Republic of Macedonia	16,625	14,890	31,515	0.46	24.65
Romania	8,330	12,356	20,736	0.31	16.22
Russian Federation	7,764	12,092	19,856	0.29	15.53
Switzerland	4,937	5,432	10,369	0.15	8.11
Cyprus	4,799	5,592	10,391	0.15	8.13
UK	8,807	10,107	18,914	0.27	14.79
US	7,457	6,109	13,566	0.20	10.61
Others	115,941	123,795	239,736	3.54	187.49
Unknown	8,894	8,436	17,330	0.26	13.55
Total	34,346,735	33,457,192	67,803,927	1,000.00	1,000.00

Source: SIS 2003

The female proportion of the foreign-born population was 51.5 per cent in 1990 compared with 51.9 per cent in 2000, although the sex ratio varies by origin. From 1990 to 2000, there was a slight trend towards feminisation in the foreign-born population in Turkey; 52.4 per cent were females from Bulgaria in 2000 compared with 51.4 per cent in 1990; similarly, 51.4 per cent were from Germany in 2000 compared with 50.0 per cent in 1990.

12.3.2 *Residence permit data*

The number of residence permits issued by the BFBA is an indirect measure of the stocks of regular migrants in Turkey. These permits are issued for durations of residence of more than three months. Turkey draws a significant number of immigrants from the Turkish-speaking populations of neighbouring countries; in 2005, the total number of residence permits was around 132,000, with over 50,000 of the permit holders coming from Bulgaria, 7,500 from Azerbaijan, 6,700 from Germany, another 5,000 from Iraq and 4,800 from the UK. According to this dataset, there were also other sizable communities of foreigners who have their residence in Turkey: Iranians (4,300), Russians (4,200), US citizens (3,700), former Yugoslavians (3,500), Greeks (3,400) and Afghans (2,800) (see Table 12.3).

Only 17 per cent of the residence permit holders in Turkey (over 22,000 persons) were people who work in the country and 19 per cent were students, while the remaining 64 per cent were their dependants.

Table 12.3 *Main migrant groups in Turkey with residence permits and by work status, 2005*

	With residence permit	%	*Working*	%	*Student*	%
Afghanistan	2,833	2.2	104	0.5	627	2.5
Azerbaijan	7,486	5.7	821	3.7	2,170	8.6
Bulgaria	49,727	37.8	450	2.0	3,521	14.0
UK	4,809	3.6	1,493	6.8	142	0.6
France	1,626	1.2	1,286	5.8	91	0.4
Germany	6,677	5.1	1,508	6.8	240	1.0
Greece	3,417	2.6	307	1.4	2,178	8.6
Iran	4,260	3.2	921	4.2	833	3.3
Iraq	4,970	3.8	648	2.9	515	2.0
Kazakhistan	2,613	2.0	168	0.8	1,115	4.4
Kyrgyzstan	1,458	1.1	128	0.6	1,439	5.7
Moldova	2,618	2.0	216	1.0	231	0.9
Russian Federation	4,212	3.2	1,308	5.9	924	3.7
Ukraine	2,299	1.8	715	3.2	408	1.6
US	3,726	2.8	2,062	9.3	331	1.3
Former Yugoslavia	3,467	2.6	286	1.3	766	3.0
Subtotal	106,198	(80.7)	12,421	(56.1)	15,531	(61.5)
Others	25,396	19.3	9,709	43.9	9,709	38.5
Total	131,594	100.0	22,130	100.0	25,240	100.0

Source: Bureau for Foreigners, Borders and Asylum of the Directorate of General Security of the Ministry of Interior

12.3.3 *Acquisition of citizenship*

Turkish citizenship can be acquired by birth, descent or naturalisation. While legally Turkish nationality is open to non-Turkish people who are willing to assimilate culturally and linguistically to Turkish culture,[2] the conditions and procedure for acquiring Turkish citizenship after birth, regulated by Law No. 403/1964 on Turkish Citizenship, favour the *ius sanguinus* principle. Thus, the law offers facilitated access to citizenship for those immigrants who can prove that they are of 'Turkish descent and culture', which is the vast majority of those who are granted Turkish citizenship after birth.

Most of these entered the country based on the 1934 Law of Settlement that differentiates between those settled by the state (*assisted/settled immigrants*) and those who settle themselves (*free immigrants*). In the period between 1995 and 2000, 56,449 free immigrants acquired Turkish citizenship. While 43 per cent of these acquisitions were based on marriages with Turkish citizens, the remaining 57 per cent were acquisitions by naturalisation. As to the previous nationality of the people who obtained Turkish citizenship, countries with the largest numbers were Bulgaria (23,634 or 42 per cent), Azerbaijan (3,876 or 7 per cent), Romania (2,894 or 5 per cent), the Russian Federation (2,193 or 4 per cent), Iraq (1,635 or 3 per cent), Iran (1,337 or 3 per cent) and Moldavia (1,292 or 2 per cent) (see Table 12.4).

Table 12.4 *Free immigrants who acquired Turkish citizenship, 1995-2001*

Previous nationality	*Naturalisation*	*Marriage*	*Total*	*%*
Bulgaria	19,998	3,636	23,634	
Iraq	1,384	251	1,635	
Iran	1,080	257	1,337	
Azerbaijan	-	3,876	3,876	
Romania	-	2,894	2,894	
Russia	-	2,193	2,193	
Moldovia	-	1,292	1,292	
Subtotal	22,462	14,399	36,861	65.3
Other countries	9,687	9,901	19,588	34.7
Total	32,149	24,300	56,449	100.0
Total in %	57.0	43.0	100.0	

Source: Ministry of the Interior, Bureau of Population and Citizenship

In addition, 900 immigrants settled by the state naturalised between 2001 and 2005. Various Balkan countries were the major source countries of these new Turkish citizens: Bulgaria (68), Macedonia (432), Serbia and Montenegro (285), Romania (3) and former Yugoslavia (52) (see Table 12.5).

Table 12.5 *Number of settled immigrants who naturalised in Turkey by country of origin, 2001-2005*

Previous nationality	*2001*	*2002*	*2003*	*2004*	*2005*	*Total*
Bulgaria	38	20	3	1	6	68
The former Yugoslav Republic of Macedonia	107	97	73	119	76	432
Serbia & Montenegro	-	-	126	107	72	285
Romania	1	-	1	-	1	3
Former Yugoslavia	23	29	-	-	-	52
Total	169	146	203	227	155	900

Source: Official Gazette of Turkey 2001-2005; author's calculation

12.4 Description of flows

As noted earlier, data on flows to and from Turkey are scarce and not very reliable. Nevertheless, the following sections will try to provide estimates of inflows and outflows of Turkish and foreign citizens.

12.4.1 Emigration and return migration of Turkish citizens

In recent decades there have been five main types of outflow of Turkish citizens (İçduygu 2005b): family-related emigration; asylum-seeking; irregular (undocumented or clandestine) labour emigration; contract-related (low-skilled) labour emigration; and international professional emigration.

Family-related migration is mainly due to the presence of sizable Turkish migrant communities in the migrant-receiving countries, in which networks keep the migratory flows continuously active. Long and short-term family related visits, family reunification and marriage-related migration where brides and grooms from Turkey join spouses living abroad, account for a significant part of Turkish emigration. These movements are primarily directed towards Western European countries and, to a certain extent, towards Australia and North America. From numbers of arrivals of Turkish citizens in several migrant-receiving countries, we can estimate that by the mid-1990s nearly 100,000 emigrants would leave Turkey annually, a vast majority of them directed to Europe and nearly half of them due to family ties with those already living abroad. These ranged from long-term visits for at least three months to long-term residence permits for a year as well as family reunification schemes. Overall, in the second half of the 1990s, there was a considerable decline in the family-related movement. It is estimated that the total number of Turkish emigrants to Europe fell to the level of 50,000 per year in the early 2000s and nearly one third of these are those who moved in the family-related flows.

Asylum-seeking contributed considerably to the overall level of emigration in the late 1990s and early 2000s. Data from the United Nations High Commissioner for Refugees (UNHCR) show that almost 39,000 people from Turkey filed asylum claims in 1996 (a large majority of these in Germany). This number fell to about 20,000 in 1999, increased again to almost 33,000 in 2001 and decreased continuously to about 12,000 in 2005. Claims filed in Germany have fallen from almost 32,000 in 1996 to only about 3,000 in 2005 (UNHCR 2007: 525).

It is extremely difficult to provide accurate estimates of the numbers of irregular labour migrants, due not only to the very nature of this form of migration but also to the diversity of groups included in this category, such as 'illegal entrants', 'overstayers' and 'rejected asylum seekers'. In addition, those who enter as family members or asylum seekers may at some stage also become 'overstayers' and 'rejected asylum seekers'. In a study conducted in the late 1990s in Turkey, nearly one-quarter of all the interviewed international migrants stated that they had tried to enter a country without the required papers (11 per cent) or attempted to overstay their visa or permit (11 per cent) (İçduygu & Ünalan 2002). Anecdotal evidence of irregular migration in Turkey and Europe indicates that although there were still ongoing flows of irregular migration, the trend was on the decline. For instance, while 2,350 Turkish citizens were apprehended in Central and Eastern Europe as irregular migrants in 2004, this figure dropped to 2,124 in 2005 (Futo & Jandl 2006).

In recent years contract-dependent labour migration has constituted a large part of Turkish emigration. In 2000, 13,645 workers obtained employment abroad through the Turkish Employment Office (TEO). This figure leapt to over 20,000 in 2001, to 27,000 in 2002, to 34,000 in 2003, to 40,000 in 2004 and to over 60,000 in 2005. These workers were hired for a period of three to 24 months by Turkish or foreign contracting firms operating mainly in the Commonwealth of Independent States (CIS) and in Arab countries. In 2005, the top three destination countries were the Russian Federation (32 per cent), Iraq (12 per cent) and Kazakhstan (9 per cent). This type of migration to EU countries was almost entirely directed to Germany, based on a bilateral agreement of 1991, which allowed German firms co-operating with Turkish partners to hire Turkish workers. 2,100 Turkish workers found employment in Germany in this framework in 2000, accounting for over 90 per cent of the total workers sent to Europe by the Turkish Employment Office (TEO). This figure was 82 per cent in 2001, 85 per cent in 2002, 78 per cent in 2003 and 71 per cent in 2004. In 2005, there were over 1,000 contract-based Turkish workers sent to Germany, accounting for 63 per cent of the workers sent by TEO to the EU countries in the context of the same migration scheme.

Although there are no adequate data on the outflow of university graduates and skilled workers, it is estimated that about 2,000 to 3,000 individuals, mostly specialising in the areas of computer sciences, finance and management, leave Turkey to work abroad annually. The main destinations are the traditional migrant-receiving countries, such as Australia, Canada, the US and some European countries.

In addition to these outflows, there is no doubt that there is a return migration of Turkish emigrants. However, the extent of our knowledge of this return migration is, for the most part, very limited. The reason for this is again the lack of data. The estimated annual number of returnees was around 100,000 in the 1980s; this stabilised at around 50,000 in the 1990s and currently lies below 50,000.

12.4.2 Immigration of foreign citizens to Turkey

The inflow of foreign nationals to Turkey has become increasingly significant in the last decade. Besides the flows of regular migrants that are mostly unknown due to the lack of adequate data (see Section 12.2), there are two main types of inflows: that of asylum seekers and of irregular migrants.

12.4.2.1 Asylum flows

Since the early 1980s, Turkey has become a major country of asylum. The change of the political regime in 1979 in Iran and then the Iran-Iraq War, the Gulf War of 1990/91 and recent political turmoil in Iraq contributed to the asylum flows from these two neighbouring countries to Turkey. Although *de iure* Turkey does not accept non-European refugees based on its 'geographical reservation' in the 1951 Geneva Convention, *de facto* almost all asylum applications in the country are filed by non-Europeans. From the late 1990s to the early 2000s, Turkey was receiving approximately 4,000-5,000 asylum applications a year. As a pragmatic solution, the Turkish authorities agreed to handle all applications in conjunction with the UNHCR Office in Ankara. Subsequently, the UNHCR would try to find a re-settlement country outside Turkey for the accepted non-European refugees. In the last decade, asylum applications in Turkey have come from over 30 different countries, mainly in the Middle East, Africa and Asia. Iran and Iraq are the two main source countries of asylum seekers. For instance, in 1997, 1,400 Iranians and 3,000 Iraqis sought asylum in Turkey. The respective figures in 2000 were 3,900 and 1,700. In 2005, 1,700 people from Iran and 1,000 from Iraq claimed asylum in Turkey (see Table 12.6).

Table 12.6 *Number of asylum applications and asylum seekers in Turkey, 1997-2005*

Year	*Iranians*		*Iraqis*		*Others*		*Total*	
	*Cases**	*Persons***	*Cases*	*Persons*	*Cases*	*Persons*	*Cases*	*Persons*
1997	746	1,392	1,275	2,939	83	117	2,104	4,448
1998	1,169	1,979	2,350	4,672	124	187	3,643	6,838
1999	2,069	3,843	1,148	2,472	184	290	3,401	6,605
2000	2,125	3,926	791	1,671	108	180	3,024	5,777
2001	1,841	3,485	497	998	372	709	2,710	5,177
2002	1,456	2,505	402	974	219	315	2,077	3,794
2003	1,715	3,092	159	342	373	514	2,247	3,948
2004	1,225	2,030	472	956	540	912	2,237	3,898
2005	1,021	1,716	490	1,047	753	1,151	2,264	3,914

* refers to number of applications filed

** indicates total number of asylum seekers, including applicants and their dependants

Source: UNHCR Office, Ankara; author's tabulation

12.4.2.2 *Flows of irregular migrants*

There are two main types of irregular migration flows into Turkey: from north to south – immigration of labourers from the Eastern European and former-Soviet Union countries – and from east to west – transit migration of people from various Middle Eastern, Asian and African countries.

The first group of irregular immigrants are *migrant workers* from countries such as Moldova, Romania, Ukraine and the Russian Federation, who are in search of employment in Turkey. Various sectors of the Turkish economy, in particular domestic work, sex and entertainment, textile, construction and some service sectors, absorb these as temporary workers. Many of them enter Turkey legally in accordance with Turkish visa requirements but overstay their visas and subsequently become illegal while in the country. The second form of irregular migration involves *transit migrants* who come to Turkey mainly from the Middle East (Iran and Iraq) and from Asia and Africa (Pakistan, Bangladesh, Sri Lanka, Nigeria, Somalia). These migrants intend to enter Turkey for a temporary stay and to find their way to the developed countries in the West and North. Most of these migrants are smuggled into Turkey, while some arrive legally with tourist visas, but often drift into illegality as they overstay their right of entry or try to enter a third country without proper travel documents.

There are no direct data on these irregular migration flows; however, some indicative figures are available. The BFBA reports that there were nearly 95,000 apprehended cases of irregular migrants in 2000, but this figure dropped to 56,000 in 2003 and to 43,000 in 2005. From 2001 to 2005, the first ten source countries were Iraq (19 per cent), Moldova (9 per cent), Pakistan (8 per cent), Afghanistan (6 per cent), Iran (4 per cent), Romania (4 per cent), the Russian Federation (3 per cent), Ukraine (3 per cent), Georgia (3 per cent) and Bangladesh (3 per cent). In the same period, 56 per cent of these migrants were caught when they were entering or departing illegally, while the remaining 44 were apprehended while they were overstaying the term of their visa (Table 12.7).

12.5 Conclusions

In the last two decades Turkey has fundamentally changed, from being an emigration country to a country attracting migrants of different kinds. Nevertheless, the country has failed to produce adequate statistics that provide a comprehensive and detailed picture of the migration flows into the country. It appears that the lack of a reliable body of information on immigration in Turkey is due partly to the absence of a

Table 12.7 *Irregular migration in Turkey, apprehended cases, 1995-2005*

Country of origin	*1995*	*1996*	*1997*	*1998*	*1999*	*2000*	*2001*	*2002*	*2003*	*2004*	*2005*	*Total*
Afghanistan	24	68	81	921	2,476	8,746	9,701	4,246	2,178	3,442	2,363	34,246
Albania		1		9	792	1,026	1,137	580	341	318	220	4,424
Algeria	27	25	69	207	102	430	305	542	378	397	375	2,857
Armenia	4	2		1	98	474	452	505	494	835	858	3,723
Azerbaijan	21	3	3	10	620	2,262	2,426	2,349	1,608	1,591	1,410	12,303
Bangladesh	113	322	301	2,408	1,193	3,228	1,497	1,810	1,722	3,271	1,524	17,389
Bulgaria	21	22	39	103	1,005	1,699	1,923	3,132	989	550	363	9,846
Egypt	4	12	99	29	94	382	184	182	222	257	137	1,602
Georgia	37	9	9	5	809	3,300	2,693	3,115	1,826	2,294	2,348	16,445
Germany		1	1		372	629	458	586	988	1,477	984	5,496
India	2	25	18	102	189	779	599	475	846	803	206	4,044
Iran	252	362	364	1,116	5,281	6,825	3,514	2,508	1,620	1,265	1,141	24,248
Iraq	2,128	3,319	5,689	14,237	11,546	17,280	18,846	20,926	3,757	6,393	3,591	107,712
The Former Yugoslav Republic of Macedonia	1				439	488	384	197	185	105	54	1,853
Moldavia	19		17	5	5,098	8,312	11,454	9,611	7,728	5,728	3,462	51,434
Morocco	28	53	93	295	369	1,401	849	603	361	402	171	4,625
Nigeria	1	20	30	84	137	450	301	733	117	142	34	2,049
Pakistan	708	435	307	1,798	2,650	5,027	4,829	4,813	6,258	9,396	11,001	47,222
PRC				1	115	545	264	674	787	788	339	3,513
Romania	68	12	107	36	3,395	4,500	4,883	2,674	2,785	1,785	1,274	21,519
Russian Federation	5	4	52	2	1,695	4,554	3,893	2,139	2,130	1,266	1,152	16,892
Sierra Leone				20	42	462	273	121	14	6	2	940
Stateless					61	322	235	0	0	0	0	618
Syria	78	86	144	476	776	1,399	782	462	623	1,097	983	6,906
Tunisia	3	48	81	44	76	255	216	191	274	301	300	1,789
Turkey					2,085	3,289	5,304	6,951	5,660	3,341	2,164	28,794
Ukraine	9	4	17	4	1,715	4,527	3,451	2,874	1,947	1,341	1,335	17,224
UK		2		4	233	643	423	451	510	563	662	3,491
Uzbekistan	1	1			142	587	535	533	584	714	652	3,749
Other	7,808	13,948	20,603	7,382	3,632	7,695	8,055	6,908	8,461	563	662	85,717
Unknown		20	315	127	292	2,998	2,499	1,934	826	716	4,074	13,801
Total	11,362	18,804	28,439	29,426	47,529	94,514	92,365	82,825	56,219	51,147	43,841	556,471

Source: Bureau for Foreigners, Borders and Asylum of the Directorate of General Security of the Ministry of the Interior (BFBA of DGS of MoI) fairly balanced and established system of collection and dissemination of data and partly to the irregular nature of the flows into the country.

It also appears that now that, while Turkey is in accession negotiations with the European Union, it does not only try to harmonise its migratory regime with the one in the EU, but also attempts to establish a statistical system compatible with that of the EU countries. Turkey's EU candidature certainly plays a key role in the country's state apparatus' concerns regarding harmonisation and subsequent efforts to improve and develop the data collection on the stocks of immigrants residing in the country and on the flows of people entering and leaving the country. Some of the initiatives focus directly on the improvement of the population registration system and the census, while others deal with the arrival and departure statistics. In fact, international migration statistics are central to the re-structuring of the national statistics in Turkey. Essential for this re-structuring is an adequate administrative and institutional capacity which can guarantee the efficient collection, processing and dissemination of international migration data.

Notes

1 No data are available on the length or the purpose of stay, which naturally limits any detailed structural analysis of international migrants and migration.

2 Those applying for naturalisation have to be adults (eighteen years or older) and they have to prove that they: a) have been residing in Turkey for at least five years, b) have decided to settle in Turkey, c) have good moral conduct, d) have no threatening illness, f) speak sufficient Turkish and g) have a job or income to support themselves and their dependants.

Statistical sources

Organisation	*Content*	*URL*
Bureau for Foreigners, Borders and Asylum of the Directorate of General Security of the Ministry of the Interior (BFBA of DGS of MoI)	– resident foreigners (based on permit data) – asylum applications – irregular migration	www.egm.gov.tr
Bureau of Population and Citizenship, Ministry of the Interior	– acquisition of nationality	www.nvi.gov.tr
Turkish Employment Service (TES)	– contract-based migration	www.iskur.gov.tr
Turkish Labour Ministry (TLM)	– Turkish workers and families living abroad	www.calisma.gov.tr
Turkish Statistical Institute (TURKSTAT)	– census	www.turkstat.gov.tr

Bibliography

Ayhan, H.Ö., B.A. Ergöçmen, A. Hancıoğlu, A. İçduygu, İ. Koç, A. Toros, A.S. Türkyılmaz, T. Ünalan, S. Üner & E. K. Yiğit (2000), *Push and Pull Factors of International Migration: Country Report-Turkey*. European Commission, Statistical Office of the European Communities. Luxembourg: Eurostat Press.

BFBA of DGS of MoI (Bureau for Foreigners, Borders and Asylum of the Directorate of General Security of the Ministry of the Interior) (2001a), *Documents and Views on Foreigners, Borders, and Asylum, 2000*. Ankara: Ministry of the Interior (in Turkish).

BFBA of DGS of MoI (Bureau for Foreigners, Borders and Asylum of the Directorate of General Security of the Ministry of the Interior) (2001b), *Illegal Migration around the World and in Turkey*. Ankara: Ministry of the Interior (in Turkish).

Futo, P. & M. Jandl (eds.) (2006), *2005 Year Book on Illegal Migration, Human Smuggling and Trafficking in Central and Eastern Europe*. Vienna: ICMPD.

İçduygu, A. (2000), 'The Politics of International Migratory Regimes: Transit Migration Flows in Turkey', *International Social Science Journal* 52 (165): 357-367.

İçduygu, A. (2004), 'Demographic Mobility over Turkey: Migration Experiences and Government Responses', *Mediterranean Quarterly* 15 (4): 88-99.

İçduygu, A. (2005a), 'Turkey: the demographic and economic dimension of migration', in P. Fargues (ed.), *Mediterranean Migration – 2005 Report*. Cooperation project on the social integration of immigrants, migration and the movement of persons, 327-337. Florence: EUI-RSCAS, CARIM Consortium. www.carim.org.

İçduygu, A. (2005b), *Turkey and International Migration, 2004*. Istanbul: SOPEMI Report for Turkey. www.mirekoc.com.

İçduygu, A. & T. Ünalan (2002), 'Tides between Mediterranean Shores: Undocumented Migration in the South of Europe', *HIPS Working Papers in Demography* 7: 1-24.

State Institute of Statistics (SIS) (1995), *1990 Census of Population: Social and Economic Characteristics of Population*. Ankara: SIS.

State Institute of Statistics (SIS) (2003), *2000 Census of Population: Social and Economic Characteristics of Population*. Ankara: SIS.

UNHCR (2007), *UNHCR Statistical Yearbook 2005: Trends in Displacements, Protections and Solutions*. www.unhcr.org.

Statistics and migration: Past, present and future

Ursula Reeger and Wiebke Sievers

In his book *The Politics of Large Numbers*, Alain Desrosières shows that the developments in statistical institutes were particularly dynamic when their surveys were closely linked to contemporary issues. To prove his point, Desrosières cites the Public Health Movement in 1840s England, Engel's *Verein der Socialpolitik* in 1860s Prussia, the economic crisis and the resulting unemployment in the United States of the 1930s and economic planning and growth in 1950s and 1960s France (see Desrosières 2005: 276 and chapters 5 and 6). The present publication shows that in many European countries statistical dynamism in recent decades has been closely linked to the topics of migration and integration. How to define and measure changing migration patterns and the integration of immigrants and their descendants and how to harmonise the gathered data have been topics discussed in many European countries.

That these issues are not easy to solve is also linked to the fact that the statistical tools used today were mainly invented to measure the growth of nation states in the nineteenth century, as will be explained in the first part of this summary, whereas the statistical measurement of migration is a more recent interest, as Heinz Fassmann shows in his introductory chapter to this book. After a short insight into the history of statistics that serves to put the following into perspective, we will summarise the findings of this volume.

1 Statistics and migration: A historical paradox?

The emergence of statistics, as we understand the concept today, is closely linked to the establishment of the nation state in the nineteenth century. Of course, some of the tools used in statistics today were introduced long before the nation state came into existence. It is well-known that ancient Babylonia, Palestine, China, Egypt and Rome conducted censuses. In addition, the Greek and Roman empires had birth registers and later also death registers. However, unlike their modern counterparts, these did not aim at providing a complete inventory of a specific society but at identifying those who were allowed to vote or could be taxed. Hence, the Roman censuses, for example, did not count all residents but only male citizens, thus excluding women, slaves and children (see Beloch 1979).

First attempts to understand states as a whole were made in Göttingen in the eighteenth century. These became known as statistics but are only vaguely related to statistics as we know them today, mainly because they did not draw on exact survey data (see Desrosières 2005: 22). At the same time, the gathering of such data was still very much driven by specific aims rather than by describing states as a whole. Thus the US census, which was to become the first regular census in the modern world, was designed to apportion both representation and taxation to the states based on their population and wealth. Hence, the 1790 Census was a full count of the population, albeit gathering only the basic information necessary for the apportionment. The inclusion of further details, such as occupation, was discussed yet dismissed by the Senate, on the grounds that it was 'a waste of trouble and supplying material for idle people to make a book' (James Madison in a letter to Thomas Jefferson, cited in Anderson 1988: 14).

Only in the course of the nineteenth century, when the population became the most important element for legitimising the existence of a state, did censuses become more exhaustive. They came to include more details not only on the population, but also on other topics, such as manufacturing, that would be relevant for the development of the people. As the growth of the population became equated with the growth of the nation, it became a source of pride both in the United States and in the evolving European nation states (see Anderson 1988: 21; Desrosières 2000: 125). Hence, the census, in particular, and statistics, more generally, became tools not only for measuring but also for securing national growth, for instance, by using such data to fight epidemics and child mortality (see Desrosières 2005: 93-98, 186-189). So, to put it in Foucauldian terms, in the course of the nineteenth century, statistics became a powerful mechanism for regulating and thereby increasing national populations, which in turn confirmed the importance of the respective nation state (see Foucault 1999).

This intricate relationship between statistics and the nation state has two major implications for the topic discussed in this volume, namely European migration statistics. Firstly, as the term implies, statistics were implemented on the state level. This was not at all an easy process as the natural link between statistics and states today might suggest. On the one hand, when statistics were introduced, states were only just becoming the 'common cognitive spaces', to use Desrosières' term, which they are today. In other words, the coherent grid that allows us to observe and describe them was only just emerging (Desrosières 2000: 125). This becomes immediately obvious when we look at the first national survey conducted in post-revolutionary France. While the results of this survey are useless for historians searching for exact and comparable data, they aptly illustrate how diverse the country was at the time and how little agreement there was on seemingly obvious definitions, such as categorisation of people by their property and income (see Desrosières 2005: 46-50). The reduction of this diversity within the states by way of introducing a common legal framework, for instance, automatically implied their differentiation from other states – which explains the incomparability of national statistics today. Another reason that the statistical tools that are, in principle, universal had to be reinterpreted was the existence of particular ideological traditions. Thus, the liberalist tradition in Britain made it very difficult to introduce a census, which explains why the first mathematical tools for population estimates were developed here (see Desrosières 2005: 28). This same tradition also explains why Britain, unlike most other European countries, has no population register, though uses a sample survey to measure immigration and emigration flows. Similarly, the late unification of German states into a federalist nation state explains why there are still differences between the measurements of migration in the individual *Länder*.

Secondly, the 'discovery of the population' and the goal of optimising the life of a specific people automatically implied a racist attitude to those not included, as Foucault rightly pointed out. This does not mean that racism did not exist before the nineteenth century. The novelty was that racism became an inherent element of state mechanisms, including statistics (Foucault 1999: 294-295). Again, this process of statistical inclusion and exclusion was handled differently in the different countries. Thus, from the start, American censuses made strict racial distinctions among whites, blacks/slaves and Indians, but did not clearly differentiate between original English settlers and the European newcomers, who were regarded as contributing to the growth and importance of the new state. Only when this ideological stance was questioned in the mid-nineteenth century did census takers include a question on place of birth in the census (see Thernstrom 1992: 83-86). The statistical exclusion of others was introduced at the same time in France, but in a different form. Firstly, differentiation by ethnicity has always been prohibited in France; secondly, French statistics did not exclude by origin but by citizenship, which was the decisive factor in French statistics between the 1850s and the 1990s, when the category 'immigrant' was introduced (see Simon 1999: 197-198). Citizenship is still the decisive factor for statistical differentiation in many European countries. However, as the following will show, this does not necessarily mean that the data are comparable, since nationality laws differ massively between the countries.

All of these differences between states are still of major importance. Nevertheless, as the following summary of our findings will show, similar migration regimes and histories have implied similar trends in the statistical description of immigration. Moreover, some findings are valid for almost all the countries in our sample:
1. data gathered in the individual countries are hardly comparable;
2. migration statistics in each country only ever reflect part of the truth, be it for historical and/or political reasons;
3. we have little or sometimes no knowledge about emigration, which also implies that the calculated migration balance tends to be too high in most countries;
4. we have little or no knowledge about illegal immigration, due to its very nature (exceptions to this rule can be found in countries that have carried out legalisation programmes, but the resulting data again only offer snapshots of a resident population and no information on flows).

The following sections not only provide a more detailed insight into recent debates on migration statistics per group of countries, but also point out the idiosyncrasies in each of these countries.

2 Statistics and migration: Current debates

2.1 *Post-colonial countries*

Belgium, France and the United Kingdom share long traditions of labour immigration, with a significant share of these immigrants originating from their (former) colonies, which implies that many of those who arrived were already citizens of the receiving country. In addition, all three countries have provided relatively broad access to their nationalities in order to facilitate the integration of their immigrants, a stance which has a long tradition in France and represents a more recent approach in Belgium (see Foblets & Loones 2006, Weil & Spire 2006 and Dummett 2006). Both of these factors imply that citizenship is not a sufficient indicator for measuring international migration in these three countries.

However, these similar points of departure do not mean that the countries have reached the same conclusions on who should be considered an immigrant, statistically speaking. While the UK describes all of its residents born abroad as immigrants (i.e. including British people born abroad, as well as naturalised citizens and aliens), France only includes those who were born abroad as foreigners and reside in France (i.e. excluding immigrants from French territories abroad such as Guadeloupe and Martinique), a decision which might be explained by its strong Republican tradition. Belgian statistics on immigration, on the other hand, simply count the number of foreign nationals residing in the country. Hence, they exclude all immigrants who have been naturalised since their arrival, who make up 45 per cent of the immigrants residing in the country, as a recent study has shown (see Eggerickx, Bahri & Perrin 2006). However, the demand for more detailed information on the foreign-born population residing in Belgium has grown among both researchers and policymakers. In response, researchers have tried to provide more detailed data on immigration to Belgium within the framework of the 'Charles Ullens Initiative', an inter-university survey, coordinated by the King Baudouin Foundation, which aims to provide comprehensive quantitative and qualitative data on immigration to Belgium. It remains to be seen whether this will also bring about a change in the conceptualisation of immigration in official Belgian statistics.

While this more recent demand for information on the foreign-born is a factor that Belgium shares with the other guestworker receiving countries in our sample (i.e. Austria, Germany and Switzerland), the Belgian interest in collecting detailed data on the ethnic minorities residing in the country (see Hanquinet, Vandezande, Jacobs & Swyngedouw 2006) justifies its classification in a group with Britain and France. As Kertzer and Arel (2002: 8-13) explain, data on ethnicity have been collected since the rise of cultural nationalism in the nineteenth century. At the time, Germany and Austria-Hungary gathered such data in order to justify their political and territorial demands based on cultural categorisations, whereas France, Britain and Belgium only distinguished between citizens and non-citizens in their territories, while gathering detailed information on imposed racial categorisations in their colonies. As racial categorisations were misused by the National Socialists, many countries abandoned gathering any data on such racial categories after the Second World War.

However, questions on race/ethnicity re-entered the census in Britain when the government prohibited discrimination based on 'colour, race, nationality (including citizenship) or ethnic or national origin' in 1976 and, for this purpose, needed detailed data on those targeted by such discrimination. The first attempt of the statistical institute to gather such data failed, due to strong objections against the suggested categorisations. Yet, since 1991 Britain has gathered data in the census on ethnic minorities based on racial categories, such as black, and on ethnic categories, such as Pakistani and Bangladeshi (see Kertzer & Arel 2002: 13-14). As a consequence, the debates on immigration focussed further on the black minority. This tension between the need for data that makes it possible to describe and subsequently fight existing discrimination and the fact that such data codifies these same discriminatory categories also characterised a fierce debate in France, which was triggered by a report in 1995 that pleaded for lifting the ban on the publication of data related to ethnicity (see Blum 2002). Here, the Republican position and the fear that such data would be abused by the extreme right prevailed. As of yet, official French statistics do not gather such data.[1]

Neither Britain nor France has a population register, which makes it difficult to gather data on migration flows. While Britain tries to make up for this lack by asking a sample of passengers entering and leaving the country by ship or plane for their intended stay abroad or in Britain, France only reports on inflows of foreigners based on residence permit data. France does not collect any data on the immigration of French citizens. Nor does it collate information on the emigration of either French or foreign citizens. The practice differs vastly in Belgium, which records inflows and outflows of both Belgian and foreign citizens in the National Register, which is divided into a population register for Belgians and those aliens who hold a settlement permit and an aliens register for all other foreigners staying in the country for an intended period exceeding three months, i.e. a shorter period than recommended by the UN. This is normal practice in many countries, since otherwise the published data would be outdated at the time of publication (see Fassmann in this publication).

2.2 *Guestworker receiving countries*

The concepts and tools used to measure immigration and emigration in Belgium bear close resemblances with those in the guestworker receiving countries of Austria, Germany and Switzerland, which share with Belgium a history of active labour recruitment in Southern Europe. Like Belgium, Austria, Germany and Switzerland currently identify their immigrant population by citizenship. However, this choice reflects less a Republican tradition, as in France, than a long history of not perceiving themselves as countries of immigration. All three based their recruitment on a rotation policy, which means that the workers received short-term contracts, after which they were expected to return to their countries of origin. As a consequence, the arriving workers were not perceived as immigrants, let alone as possible future citizens, but as foreigners who were therefore also registered in specific databases at the time. While Switzerland used to gather data on these workers in permit databases and Austria had a special guestworker register, Germany established an aliens register in 1953, i.e. before the foreign workers arrived, which is still the main source for information on the resident foreign population and has recently also been used to describe the inflows and outflows of foreigners. Switzerland later followed the German example. The German aliens register contains data on all foreigners legally residing in Germany for a minimum of three months. So, in this respect, the data are comparable to those gathered in Belgium. However, unlike in Belgium, the German and Swiss registers do not distinguish between the resident population (registered in the population register) and the other foreign population (registered in the aliens register) but still neatly distinguish between foreigners and citizens. Austria, by contrast, only recently introduced a population register that also includes data on all foreigners legally residing in the country for a minimum period of three months.

The long histories of exclusion in Austria, Germany and Switzerland are also inscribed in their respective citizenship legislations. All three countries regard the acquisition of their citizenships as the final step in the integration process rather than as an instrument facilitating this process, which means in practice that immigrants to Austria have to wait for at least ten years rather than three years, as in Belgium, before they can acquire the citizenship of their country of residence. Moreover, their long-established *ius sanguinis* traditions have even made and, in the case of Austria and Switzerland, still make it difficult for children born in these countries to foreign parents to acquire the nationality of their country of birth – in Germany this only changed in 2000 (Hailbronner 2006).[2] As a consequence of these different legislations, the number of foreign citizens residing in Austria, Germany and Switzerland is automatically higher than in Belgium. The effect of these differences should not be underestimated. About 16 per cent of the foreigners residing in Austria, 21 per cent of the foreigners residing in Germany and 23 per cent of the foreigners residing in Switzerland were born in these countries.

On the other hand, statistics based on citizenship exclude all immigrants who have naturalised since their arrival and whose success in education and the labour market might differ from those who have chosen not to acquire the citizenship of their country of residence. In Austria, these are 40.7 per cent of all those born abroad. More specifically, a definition of immigration by citizenship also excludes all those immigrants to Germany who are ethnic Germans and are counted as German citizens when they enter the country. Between 1991 and 2005, these were more than two million people usually not included in data on immigration to Germany. Consequently, the information available on immigration in Austria, Germany and Switzerland is biased. Not only are all naturalised immigrants excluded but the category 'foreigners' also includes two categories of people who differ in many respects: immigrants and foreigners born in these countries. As a consequence, the demand for data that include information on the place of birth of the resident population has grown both among researchers and policymakers in all three countries. Recent survey data gathered in Austria

(2001 Census), Germany (2005 Microcensus) and Switzerland (1990 and 2000 Censuses) include this variable; however, the next census to be held in Switzerland will not contain data on the place of birth. Moreover, the place of birth is not included in statistics produced on the basis of the population and aliens registers.[3]

2.3 *Post-communist countries*

In the three post-communist countries included in this volume – Hungary, Poland and Romania – both immigration and emigration were strictly controlled and therefore also limited in the communist period. Yet, recent studies in Poland show that the low figures can to some extent also be explained by the ways in which international migration was measured, since those who left the country were still counted as resident population, irrespective of their length of stay abroad. This was slightly different in Romania, where at least ethnic emigration was recorded meticulously, probably due to the fact that the Romanian government received a lump sum of money for each ethnic German and Jew who was allowed to leave. Despite these problems in measuring migration, there is no doubt that both emigration and immigration grew in importance in all three countries after the fall of the Iron Curtain. Large numbers of Poles and Romanians left for Western Europe but only a minority stayed, whereas the majority have become circular migrants, often working on an irregular basis. At the same time, all three countries also began to receive immigrants. While these were mostly short-term traders and irregular immigrants in the early 1990s, regular immigration has grown in significance since the beginning of the 21st century.

Unfortunately, the statistics in the three countries have not yet caught up with these new developments. To some extent this is due to the fact that these movements are, by nature, difficult to capture. This holds particularly true for any form of irregular migration that demands new forms of measuring migration, as described in the Hungarian chapter in this volume. However, measuring emigration, even if it is legal, is also a problem in many of the other countries described here. As explained above, France does not measure emigration at all but relies on estimates. Moreover, even if the countries have installed instruments to measure emigration, usually by deregistration from a population register, there are usually no incentives for deregistering, which means that emigration is underestimated and, in turn, that the migration balance is overestimated. Both the Polish and the Romanian chapters show how large the gap is between the numbers of emigrants registered in their countries and the numbers of immigrants from their countries registered abroad; in 2002 only 17.6 per cent of the Polish immigrants and 5.4 per cent of the Romanian immigrants registered in Germany had previously deregistered in Poland and Romania. However, this massive gap between the registration of emigration and immigration can also be explained by the conceptualisations underlying these two systems. While in Romania a person is counted as an emigrant if he or she goes to the police to permanently change the address in his or her passport, in Germany a person is counted as an immigrant if he or she stays for a period exceeding one to three months, depending on the federal state. Since many of the Romanian emigrants only go abroad for a limited period of time, they do not deregister in Romania but have to register in Germany, often more than once a year. Thus, neither the small numbers of emigrants from Romania and Poland nor the large numbers of immigrants from these countries registered in Germany depict reality, but, rather, reflect these operative conceptualisations.

This also holds true for the post-communist statistics on immigration. As in the guestworker receiving countries, these statistics are based on the concept of citizenship. However, since immigration is a more recent phenomenon in these countries, citizenship is still a relatively good indicator of immigration – with some exceptions. Thus, Hungarian statistics on the stocks of foreigners residing in the country include all dual citizens, although only slightly more than half of these were born abroad. And the Polish practice regarding this particular issue is even stranger; here it is only the Opolskie voivodship that counts all those who hold dual German and Polish citizenship as Germans, most probably for historical reasons. On the other hand, the country of birth of the resident population is often not a sufficient indicator of migration in these countries, due to the border changes in their recent histories. Moreover, like emigration, immigration is still conceived as a one-time event aimed at staying in the receiving society for good. This implies that Polish statistics on immigration only include those immigrants who hold a settlement permit for which they can apply after at least three years of residence in the country on the basis of a residence permit. This explains why even the statistics on immigration published in Poland only capture 3 per cent of the German immigrants recorded as having left Germany for Poland in the year in question. Furthermore, not only the Polish statistics but also those published in Hungary and Romania focus on nationals and co-ethnics. Both Poland and Hungary gather data on returnees. In addition, Hungary gathers elaborate statistics on the acquisition of Hungarian citizenship, access to which was facilitated for the Hungarian diaspora. Finally, Romanian statistics on immigration only contain data on those immigrants who were able to change their address in their passport at a Romanian police station; these were, in the majority, repatriates. Again, these figures only capture a tiny minority of the immigrants moving to and residing in these countries.

2.4 *New immigration countries*

Ethnic/postcolonial links also influence the respective statistics on international migration gathered and published in Greece, Turkey and Portugal. These three countries are major countries of origin of the foreign-born populations residing in Central, Western and Northern Europe. However, like many other countries, Greece, Portugal and Turkey did not properly count these emigrants. Hence, all figures cited are estimates. More recently, all three countries have also begun to receive immigrants. While this development goes back to the 1970s in Greece and Portugal, with significant increases since 1990 and 2000, respectively, immigration to Turkey began in the late 1980s. However, as in the Eastern European countries, the instruments used to measure the resident population in these countries have only slowly been catching up with these new developments and still only cover a part of the immigrant population, for various reasons.

Firstly, an unknown proportion of the immigrants who reside in the country have either entered or have been staying in the country illegally, which implies that they are usually not covered by any statistics. However, several legalisation programmes in both Greece and Portugal have not only served to improve the status of these immigrants in their countries of residence but have also yielded some data on those arriving or staying illegally. Sometimes these data are very limited, providing us only with the total numbers of those who have attained legal status; sometimes we also have figures on their nationalities and/or countries of origin. Moreover, prior to the 2001 Census, the Greek government made major efforts to convince immigrant populations to register, which has resulted in more reliable census data than those available in Portugal. However, as in Turkey, the data have not been made available to researchers or the general public.

Secondly, both Greece and Turkey facilitate immigration of their co-ethnics. As is the case in many other countries, these are not counted towards the immigrant population. However, in Greece matters are more complicated. While there are apparently no figures on those ethnic Greeks who arrived from the former Soviet Union, those arriving from Albania were regarded as illegal immigrants in the 1990s but have been issued special identity cards since 2000. Again, information on the number of cards issued was not published. Data on immigration and emigration flows to all three countries are similarly unreliable since there are no registers on emigration in these countries and only limited registration systems for measuring immigration flows.

The above discussion shows that the migration statistics of individual countries only ever reflect part of the truth, be that for historical and/or political reasons. This becomes particularly obvious when we look at the measurement of co-ethnic migration to many of the above countries. Usually, researchers are aware of such deficits in their respective data and may attempt to supplement these in surveys which supply them with the missing data. Other shortcomings, however, only become apparent in international comparison. This holds particularly true for concepts and definitions. While these are often accepted as natural in the individual countries, international comparison shows their contingency.

That data are dependent on their respective setting also becomes obvious in the second part of our joint exercise, which served to test the data in the respective countries by looking at two recently observed trends in international migration: the feminisation of migration and the diversification of the migrants' countries of origin. Before going into detail, we should mention that the results of this exercise are not comparable, since some authors based their observations on flow statistics whereas others looked at stocks, where such changes have less of an impact and appear later. Notwithstanding these differences, almost all authors observed varying patterns regarding the feminisation of migration for different countries of origin. Moreover, while the data in those countries with a long migration history confirmed a diversification of origins in recent years, they also showed that it did not have a significant quantitative impact, since the traditional sending countries still dominated the stocks.

2.5 *Feminisation of migration*

In 1998, Stephen Castles and Mark Miller claimed that one of the five main trends in recent international migration was that migration was becoming more female. True, more and more women migrate. However, female migration did not appear out of the blue. Women had always migrated, but this fact was not really acknowledged in statistics and research. Research on female participation in international migration only goes back some 30 years. Until then, migration had been perceived as a purely male domain. If women were included in the discussion at all, then they were usually regarded as dependent on their husbands. Statistics contributed to this perception, as they were often not broken down by gender. Moreover, if they were, they frequently underestimated the number of women, as these tended to work in the informal economy (see Oso Casas & Garson 2005: 2).

So what do the most recent statistics in the countries under discussion in this volume tell us with regard to this trend? Do our authors observe a feminisation of migration?

The three post-colonial countries (Belgium, France and the UK) based their observations on the stock of the foreign-born population. All authors found a (sometimes only slight) trend towards feminisation, varying according both to country of origin (namely, more females from Eastern Europe) and age, the latter for two reasons. On the one hand, the female population is younger than the male population, since they arrived more recently. On the other hand, women have a longer life expectancy, which also influences the sex ratio in stock statistics.

The results vary more in the guestworker receiving countries (Austria, Germany and Switzerland). What they have in common is that early immigration in the 1960s and 1970s was clearly dominated by men. This changed dramatically with family reunification, which was almost completed at the beginning of the new millennium, when the stocks of immigrants from the most important labour-sending countries was made up of more or less equal shares of men and women. Both the Austrian and the Swiss data confirm the trend towards the feminisation of migration. However, the Austrian results, which are based on the stocks of foreign nationals, also show clear differences between the countries of origin (more females than males from Germany, India or the Philippines). Unlike the Austrian data, the German and Swiss observations draw on flow statistics. As mentioned above, these confirm the trend towards feminisation in Switzerland, which the authors put down to the 'development of migration opportunities for more qualified women and to family reunification'. The German chapter, on the other hand, reports the opposite; less women than men immigrate to Germany per year, with the respective shares remaining stable.

The three post-communist countries (Hungary, Poland and Romania) have only just begun to receive immigrants. While the authors of the Hungarian chapter cannot observe a feminisation of immigration flows, they state that more and more women tend to leave the country. This also holds true for Poland and Romania. Yet, the Polish data also seem to show a growing inflow of women, taking over the domestic duties of Polish emigrant women, albeit only from the former Soviet Republics, while from all other continents immigration to Poland is predominantly male.

Finally, the data for the three new receiving countries – Greece, Portugal and Turkey – also show that feminisation is not a general but a country-specific trend, with Greece receiving more women from Eastern Europe, Portugal from Brazil and Turkey from Bulgaria and Germany. Moreover, Greece seems to be the only country in our sample where the gender imbalance has increased since 2001.

2.6 *Diversification of origins*

Over the past twenty years, international migration to and in Europe has changed enormously. The major event was the fall of the Iron Curtain and the ensuing freedom of movement for people from post-communist countries, although, contrary to expectations, this did not initiate mass migration movements. With the EU accession of many Eastern European countries, their inhabitants are now entitled to free movement within the European Union. Furthermore, globalised transport and communication offer cheaper and easier possibilities to move around. Supposedly, all of these changes have led to a diversification of migrants' origins in the countries under discussion in this volume. At the same time, many EU countries have imposed new restrictions on immigration from third countries, which might be expected to have the opposite effect.

The findings are similar for most of the countries in our sample; although there has been a diversification of origins, the great majority of all immigrants still come from the traditional countries of origin. Thus, the stock statistics in Belgium show that the pattern for the ten most important countries of origin has not changed over the past ten years, whereas the smaller groups from farther origins tend to diversify. Similar observations were made for Austria, Greece, the UK and France, mostly due to an increase of immigration from Africa and Asia. However, flow statistics in France seem to imply that the diversification of origins has come to a stop more recently.

Two countries report a more drastic change: Switzerland and Portugal. The data for Switzerland show not only a more rapid diversification of origins but also a clear decrease in immigrants from traditional countries of origin, namely Italy and Spain. While the decrease in Italians between 1970 and 1980 can mainly be traced back to the fact that following the oil crisis annual permits were not renewed, the decreasing number of Spanish nationals can be explained by growing return migration. When Switzerland recovered from the economic crisis, labour supply from the two traditional countries of origin was no longer available, so that workers were recruited in Portugal, Turkey and former Yugoslavia after 1980. At the same time, there has been an increase in asylum inflows, particularly from Sri Lanka and in students coming from China. Portugal has a completely different story to tell, with a drastic change in 2001 when an intense migratory wave from Eastern Europe was observed, resulting in a marked diversification of countries of origin.

Hungary is the only country in our sample where the data do not confirm the thesis of a diversification of origins. The majority of immigrants to Hungary still originate from Europe or, to be more precise, from the neighbouring countries with large Hungarian minorities.

Finally, the authors of the chapters on Poland, Romania and Turkey did not supply an answer to our question on the diversification of origins, as immigration is a rather new phenomenon and many of the newcomers are not included in migration statistics.

3 The future of European migration statistics?

The present publication clearly shows that concepts and measurements of migration in Europe still differ massively, in spite of all the time and money that has been invested in harmonising them. There is no agreement on either what should be counted or on how this should be technically achieved. In fact, recent decisions on these issues have to some extent increased diversity among the countries under discussion here. Thus, France decided to introduce a continuous annual census, which again makes comparison with other countries more difficult. Serious efforts are still necessary both on the state and on the EU level for the project of harmonising statistics to succeed.

However, the future of statistics on migration also raises more general issues, which have rarely been raised in recent discussions, either in the individual states or on the European level. Firstly, there has been a tendency towards further differentiation with regard to immigration. Thus, the UK introduced ethnic categorisations and France defined the new category of immigrant in the 1990s. Similar moves are currently being discussed and slowly being introduced in Austria, Belgium, Germany and Switzerland. This current interest in more and more data, not only on immigrants who have acquired the nationality of their country of residence but also on their children and grandchildren raises the question as to when differentiations (both of origin and of ethnicity) should be dropped. Or, to phrase it differently, when do these constructed boundaries become irrelevant?

Secondly, there has been a distinct trend towards harmonising the data gathered in the individual countries, but no discussion about the question as to whether the data should actually be gathered by the states. However, not only do states have their own specific agenda when gathering such data, as the previous discussion should have shown, but they also only gather data that are relevant from their perspective. This has resulted in a form of methodological nationalism in migration studies that posits the nation state as the natural unit of analysis and rarely looks at subnational, supranational or transnational aspects of migration (Wimmer & Glick-Schiller 2002: 306). Consequently, either states include these dimensions or other bodies will have to gather data that go beyond the state perspective.

Notes

1 Roxane Silberman (1992: 121) points out that such data was gathered on specific groups, such as Muslims of Algerian origin or on French immigrants from overseas territories in the 1954 census, which, according to her, shows that 'there exists a tradition of ethnic categories in France with a strong racist and colonial character'.

2 The most recent changes in the Austrian Citizenship Law that came into force in 2006 could be interpreted as a move towards *ius soli* as they entitle foreign citizens born in Austria to citizenship after six years. However, the children still have to fulfil the general naturalisation requirements that were increased by the same law (see Çınar & Waldrauch 2006: 53).

3 The Austrian population register includes data on the place of birth since 2006.

Bibliography

Anderson, M.J. (1988), *The American Census: A Social History*. New Haven and London: Yale University Press.

Beloch, J. (1979), *Die Bevölkerung der griechisch-römischen Welt*. New York: Arno Press.

Blum, A. (2002), 'Resistance to identity categorization in France', in D.I. Kertzer & D. Arel (eds.), *Census and Identity: The Politics of Race, Ethnicity and Language in National Censuses*, 121-147. Cambridge: Cambridge University Press.

Castles, S. & M.J. Miller (1998), *The Age of Migration: International Population Movements in the Modern World*. New York: The Guilford Press.

Çınar, D. & H. Waldrauch (2006), 'Austria', in R. Bauböck, E. Ersbøll, K. Groenendijk & H. Waldrauch (eds.), *Acquisition and Loss of Nationality. Policies and Trends in 15 European Countries. Vol. 2: Country Analyses*, 19-61. Amsterdam: Amsterdam University Press.

Desrosières, A. (2000), 'L'histoire de la statistique comme genre: style d'écriture et usages sociaux', *Genèses* 39: 121-137.

Desrosières, A. (2005), *Die Politik der großen Zahlen. Eine Geschichte der statistischen Denkweise*. Berlin: Springer.

Dummett, A. (2006), 'United Kingdom', in R. Bauböck, E. Ersbøll, K. Groenendijk & H. Waldrauch (eds.), *Acquisition and Loss of Nationality. Policies and Trends in 15 European Countries. Volume 2: Country Analyses*, 551-585. Amsterdam: Amsterdam University Press.

Eggerickx, T., A. Bahri & N. Perrin (2006), *Migrations internationales et populations d'origine étrangère'. Approches staistiques et démographiques*. www.kbs-frb.be.

Foblets, M.-C. & S. Loones (2006), 'Belgium', in R. Bauböck, E. Ersbøll, K. Groenendijk & H. Waldrauch (eds.), *Acquisition and Loss of Nationality. Policies and Trends in 15 European Countries. Volume 2: Country Analyses*, 63-104. Amsterdam: Amsterdam University Press.

Foucault, M. (1999), 'Vorlesung vom 17. März 1976', in *Verteidigung der Gesellschaft. Vorlesungen am Collège de France (1975-76)*, translated by Michaela Ott, 276-305. Frankfurt: Suhrkamp.

Hailbronner, K. (2006), 'Germany', in R. Bauböck, E. Ersbøll, K. Groenendijk & H. Waldrauch (eds.), *Acquisition and Loss of Nationality. Policies and Trends in 15 European Countries. Volume 2: Country Analyses*, 213-251. Amsterdam: Amsterdam University Press.

Hanquinet, L., V. Vandezande, D. Jacobs & M. Swyngedouw (2006), *Exploratory Comparative Study on the Notion of Ethnic (Immigrant Origin) Minorities and its Operationalisation*. www.kbs-frb.be.

Kertzer, D.I. & D. Arel (2002), 'Census and identity formation, and the struggle for political power', in D.I. Kertzer & D. Arel (eds.), *Census and Identity: The Politics of Race, Ethnicity and Language in National Censuses*, 1-42. Cambridge: Cambridge University Press.

Oso Casas, L. & J.-P. Garson (2005), 'The Feminisation of International Migration', Paper presented at the OECD and European Commission Seminar *Migrant Women and the Labour Market: Diversity and Challenges*, Brussels, 26-27 September.

Silberman, R. (1992), 'French immigration statistics', in D.L. Horowitz & G. Noiriel (eds.), *Immigrants in Two Democracies: French and American Experiences*, 112-123. New York: New York University Press.

Simon, P. (1999), 'Nationality and Origins in French Statistics: Ambiguous Categories', *Population: An English Selection* 11: 193-220.

Thernstrom, S. (1992), 'American Ethnic Statistics', in D.L. Horowitz & G. Noiriel (eds.), *Immigrants in Two Democracies: French and American Experiences*, 80-110. New York: New York University Press.

Weil, P. & A. Spire (2006), 'France', in R. Bauböck, E. Ersbøll, K. Groenendijk & H. Waldrauch (eds.), *Acquisition and Loss of Nationality. Policies and Trends in 15 European Countries. Volume 2: Country Analyses*, 187-211. Amsterdam: Amsterdam University Press.

Wimmer, A. & N. Glick-Schiller (2002), 'Methodological nationalism and beyond: nation-state building, migration and the social sciences', *Global Networks* 2 (4): 301-334.

List of contributors

Katerina Apostolatou, Freelance researcher, Munich and Athens
apostolatoukate@freenet.de

Martin Baldwin-Edwards, Mediterranean Migration Observatory, Athens
baldwin-edwards@migrationresearch.info

Maria I. Baganha, Centre for Social Studies (CES), University of Coimbra
mbaganha@fe.uc.pt

Jakub Bijak, Division of Social Statistics, School of Social Sciences, University of Southampton
j.bijak@soton.ac.uk

Denise Efionayi, Swiss Forum for Migration and Population Studies (SFM/FSM), University of Neuchâtel
denise.efionayi@unine.ch

Heinz Fassmann, Institute for Urban and Regional Research (ISR), Austrian Academy of Sciences, Vienna
heinz.fassmann@oeaw.ac.at

Rosita Fibbi, Swiss Forum for Migration and Population Studies (SFM/FSM), University of Neuchâtel
rosita.fibbi@unine.at

François Gemenne, Center for Ethnic and Migration Studies (CEDEM), University of Liège
f.a.gemenne@lse.ac.uk

Ágnes Hárs, TÁRKI, Budapest
h8129har@ella.hu

Ahmet İçduygu, Migration Research Program (MiReKoc), Koç University, Istanbul
aicduygu@ku.edu.tr

Izabela Koryś, Central European Forum for Migration Research (CEFMR), Warsaw
korys@twarda.pan.pl

Sebastian Năstuţă, Petre Andrei University, Iasi
sebastian.nastuta@gmail.com

Ursula Reeger, Institute for Urban and Regional Research (ISR), Austrian Academy of Sciences, Vienna
ursula.reeger@oeaw.ac.at

Stefan Rühl, European Forum for Migration Studies (efms), University of Bamberg
stefan.ruehl@sowi.uni-bamberg.de

Wiebke Sievers, Commission for Migration and Integration Research (KMI), Austrian Academy of Sciences, Vienna
wiebke.sievers@oeaw.ac.at

Endre Sik, TÁRKI, Budapest
sik@tarki.hu

Xavier Thierry, National Institute for Demographic Studies (INED), Paris
thierry@ined.fr

Ancuţa Daniela Tompea, Petre Andrei University, Iasi
atompea@yahoo.com

Philippe Wanner, Swiss Forum for Migration and Population Studies (SFM/FSM), University of Neuchâtel
philippe.wanner@ses.unige.ch

Other IMISCOE titles

IMISCOE Research

Rinus Penninx, Maria Berger, Karen Kraal, Eds.
The Dynamics of International Migration and Settlement in Europe: A State of the Art
2006 (ISBN 978 90 5356 866 8)
(originally appearing in IMISCOE Joint Studies)

Leo Lucassen, David Feldman, Jochen Oltmer, Eds.
Paths of Integration: Migrants in Western Europe (1880-2004)
2006 (ISBN 978 90 5356 883 5)

Rainer Bauböck, Eva Ersbøll, Kees Groenendijk, Harald Waldrauch, Eds.
Acquisition and Loss of Nationality: Policies and Trends in 15 European Countries, Volume 1: Comparative Analyses
2006 (ISBN 978 90 5356 920 7)

Rainer Bauböck, Eva Ersbøll, Kees Groenendijk, Harald Waldrauch, Eds.
Acquisition and Loss of Nationality: Policies and Trends in 15 European Countries, Volume 2: Country Analyses
2006 (ISBN 978 90 5356 921 4)

Rainer Bauböck, Bernhard Perchinig, Wiebke Sievers, Eds.
Citizenship Policies in the New Europe
2007 (ISBN 978 90 5356 922 1)

Veit Bader
Secularism or Democracy? Associational Governance of Religious Diversity
2007 (ISBN 978 90 5356 999 3)

Holger Kolb & Henrik Egbert, Eds.
Migrants and Markets: Perspectives from Economics and the Other Social Sciences
2008 (ISBN 978 90 5356 684 8)

Ralph Grillo, Ed.
The Family in Question: Immigrant and Ethnic Minorities in Multicultural Europe
2008 (ISBN 978 90 5356 869 9)

Corrado Bonifazi, Marek Okólski, Jeannette Schoorl, Patrick Simon, Eds.
International Migration in Europe: New Trends and New Methods of Analysis
2008 (ISBN 978 90 5356 894 1)

Maurice Crul, Liesbeth Heering, Eds.
The Position of the Turkish and Moroccan Second Generation in Amsterdam and Rotterdam: The TIES Study in the Netherlands
2008 (ISBN 978 90 8964 061 1)

Marlou Schrover, Joanne van der Leun, Leo Lucassen, Chris Quispel, Eds.
Illegal Migration and Gender in a Global and Historical Perspective
2008 (ISBN 978 90 8964 047 5)

Gianluca P. Parolin
Citizenship in the Arab World: Kin, Religion and Nation-State
2009 (ISBN 978 90 8964 045 1)

Rainer Bauböck, Bernhard Perchinig, Wiebke Sievers, Eds.
Citizenship Policies in the New Europe: Expanded and Updated Edition
2009 (ISBN 978 90 8964 108 3)

IMISCOE Reports

Rainer Bauböck, Ed.
Migration and Citizenship: Legal Status, Rights and Political Participation
2006 (ISBN 978 90 5356 888 0)

Michael Jandl, Ed.
Innovative Concepts for Alternative Migration Policies: Ten Innovative Approaches to the Challenges of Migration in the 21st Century
2007 (ISBN 978 90 5356 990 0)

Jeroen Doomernik, Michael Jandl, Eds.
Modes of Migration Regulation and Control in Europe
2008 (ISBN 978 90 5356 689 3)

Michael Jandl, Christina Hollomey, Sandra Gendera, Anna Stepien, Veronika Bilger
Migration and Irregular Work in Austria. A Case Study of the Structure and Dynamics of Irregular Foreign Employment in Europe at the Beginning of the 21st Century
2008 (ISBN 978 90 8964 053 6)

IMISCOE Dissertations

Panos Arion Hatziprokopiou
Globalisation, Migration and Socio-Economic Change in Contemporary Greece: Processes of Social Incorporation of Balkan Immigrants in Thessaloniki
2006 (ISBN 978 90 5356 873 6)

Floris Vermeulen
The Immigrant Organising Process: Turkish Organisations in Amsterdam and Berlin and Surinamese Organisations in Amsterdam, 1960-2000
2006 (ISBN 978 90 5356 875 0)

Anastasia Christou
Narratives of Place, Culture and Identity: Second-Generation Greek-Americans Return 'Home'
2006 (ISBN 978 90 5356 878 1)

Katja Rušinović
Dynamic Entrepreneurship: First and Second-Generation Immigrant Entrepreneurs in Dutch Cities
2006 (ISBN 978 90 5356 972 6)

Ilse van Liempt
Navigating Borders: Inside Perspectives on the Process of Human Smuggling into the Netherlands
2007 (ISBN 978 90 5356 930 6)

Myriam Cherti
Paradoxes of Social Capital: A Multi-Generational Study of Moroccans in London
2008 (ISBN 978 90 5356 032 7)

Marc Helbling
Practising Citizenship and Heterogeneous Nationhood: Naturalisations in Swiss Municipalities
2008 (ISBN 978 90 8964 034 5)

Inge Van Nieuwenhuyze
Getting by in Europe's Urban Labour Markets. Senegambian Migrants' Strategies for Survival, Documentation and Mobility
2009 (ISBN 978 90 8964 050 5)

Nayla Moukarbel
Sri Lankan Housemaids in Lebanon. A Case of 'Symbolic Violence' and 'Everyday Forms of Resistance'
2009 (ISBN 978 90 8964 051 2)

Jérôme Jamin
L'Imaginaire du Complot: Discours d'Extrême Droite en France et aux Etats-Unis
2009 (ISBN 978 90 8964 048 2)

John Davies
'My Name Is Not Natasha': How Albanian Women in France Use Trafficking to Overcome Social Exclusion (1998-2001)
2009 (ISBN 978 90 5356 707 4)